BOOTLEGGER'S
BOY

BOOTLEGGER'S BOY

Barry Switzer
with
Bud Shrake

WILLIAM MORROW AND COMPANY, INC.
NEW YORK

Library of Congress Cataloging-in-Publication Data

Switzer, Barry.
    Bootlegger's boy / Barry Switzer with Bud Shrake.
        p.   cm.
    ISBN 0-688-09384-1
    1. Switzer, Barry. 2. Football—United States—Coaches—
Biography. 3. University of Oklahoma—Football—History.
I. Shrake, Edwin. II. Title.
GV939.S93A3 1990
796.332′092—dc20
    [B]   90-40674
                                                                                                 CIP

Printed in the United States of America

        5   6   7   8   9   10

My mother told me long ago that only when I had children of my own would I know the true meaning of the word *love*—only then, Greg, Kathy, and Doug, will you know how much I love you.

FOREWORD

You might wonder why I am writing a foreword to a book written by Barry Switzer because you might believe that Barry and I have different, contrary perceptions as to what college football should be, what position it should occupy in university life and in the education of the people who play at Division IA schools. To a degree, the query is germane. I do disagree with Barry about many things. Our life-styles and values are dramatically different, which will become understandable after you learn of his experiences growing up as a bootlegger's son.

So why am I doing this for Barry Switzer? Because Barry has many qualities I admire: loyalty, a lack of hypocrisy, a warmth for young people and friends, a deep and honest concern for poor black athletes, a zest for life, and, most of all, a devotion to his children and unswerving appreciation and respect for their mother. As a coach, I admire his competence, hard work, and his competitive fire. Basically, above all, I'm doing this because Barry is a friend.

Barry has a story to tell—a fascinating saga of his childhood, youth, his college days, and his life as a beginning coach. His days as head coach at Oklahoma are exciting if sometimes disturbing, and the sordid tale leading up to his resignation is shocking. It is the story of a tough man determined to overcome all odds and who at times gives way to self-serving rationalization to support the rightness of many of his actions. It is the story of excesses, of the clash of proud people, of strong-willed individuals caught up in the exhilaration that surrounds great athletes, great teams, and being number 1, and it is unwittingly an indictment of big-time intercollegiate athletics. It brings into sharp focus this society's obsession with winning and with its fickle and fragile adulation of winners, which can turn so quickly into scorn.

This is an important book because it shows a side of big-time college football that, to be frank with you, I naively didn't really believe existed. Barry Switzer is remarkably candid and honest even to the point where, in this reader's opinion, he doesn't do himself any good and certainly will give many people who hold to the philosophy of institutional control and a diminished position for the coach and alumni further impetus to get on with reforms.

I hope you will read this book with an open mind and heart. I hope that you will get a feel for the force of this man's personality, his generous spirit, the joy he had in coaching and winning, and the bitterness that comes through when the system beats him—fairly or unfairly. I will let you make that decision.

—Joe Paterno
Head Football Coach,
Pennsylvania State University, 1990

ACKNOWLEDGMENTS

For quite a few years I have figured that eventually I would write a book about my career; but I was in no hurry to do it. As the incredible events of 1989 unfolded, however, and especially after those events left me with no option but to resign, it became dramatically obvious that my story was a story that had to be told . . . and told now. I had to rely upon a number of special people to get it done, and without their help it could not have been accomplished. My acknowledgments, and my thanks, go:

- To Dan Jenkins, a good friend who counseled me early on and urged me to write the story;
- To Bud Shrake, whose professionalism and ability to reflect the events that happened with a vivid sense of tragedy, or humor, as appropriate, made the story much more interesting and readable than it would otherwise have been;
- To Donnie Duncan, the best athletic director and wisest counselor a coach could ever have;
- To Fred Gipson, whose confidence in me, friendship, and loyalty never waivered during the flood of events that swept over both of us in 1989;
- To Dan Gibbens, who as our faculty representative for athletics helped me for many years with his advice and stood by me during the toughest of times;
- To Joe Paterno, head football coach of Penn State and my "Nike Family" buddy, who has shown me what a friend can really be;

- To Bill Connors, sports editor of the *Tulsa World,* who always wrote it the way it really was;
- To George and Cleo Cross, my favorite president and his wife, who not only contributed an indispensable chapter to the story, but who also know me and the way it has been in Norman, Oklahoma, all these years better than anyone else; *and*
- To Donnie Switzer, my brother, whose unique talents, abilities, and hard work, ultimately, are what put this book together—with his writing of much of it and with his editorial and organizational skills; and, too, who stuck with me through the darkest days.

CONTENTS

PART ONE

THE
CHRONOLOGY

1

THE NIGHTMARE WORSENS

I was traveling through the place that has no day or night when I received a message that would abruptly change my life.

This was June 12, 1989, in Las Vegas, at the front desk of Caesars Palace. The slip of paper the clerk handed me read, "Call David Swank as soon as possible."

The first thing that entered my mind was: I wonder who the hell has shot who now?

In a casino the light is always the same, with no shadows and no clocks. I checked my watch and saw it was the middle of the afternoon Vegas time. They would be getting ready to go home from work in Norman, Oklahoma, where University of Oklahoma interim president David Swank was waiting.

As the head football coach at the University of Oklahoma, I had been living a *Twilight Zone* nightmare for the last six months. We'd had a rape and a shooting in Bud Wilkinson House, our football dorm. My quarterback, Charles Thompson, had been arrested for selling cocaine to an undercover cop. The NCAA had charged our football program with sixteen rules violations and had put us on three years' probation.

I was still limping from a knee operation because of a freak skiing accident, which had occurred in March, when I was on spring break with my daughter, Kathy.

And as a weird kind of topper to this insanity, my quarterback, Charles Thompson, would soon help his dope-dealer pal break into my home and steal my trophy case with twenty-five conference, bowl, and national-championship rings in it.

15

The fact is, it was four players who were accused and charged with the raping, shooting, and doping. But because we are the Oklahoma football team and these things occurred in such a short period of time, the media made it seem as if our entire squad of about a hundred was running around like a blood-crazed horde plundering the countryside, and as if I had no rules of conduct for the team. *Sports Illustrated* even used a photo of Charles Thompson in handcuffs and orange prison coveralls on its cover, with the idiotic headline: "HOW BARRY SWITZER'S SOONERS TERRORIZED THEIR CAMPUS."

I never thought I needed to post rules against committing felonies. These were crimes, violations of the very rules of our society, not just athletic or academic infractions. No university has ever been totally safe, ivory tower or not. For example, back in 1974 coach Ara Parseghian of Notre Dame—the most sacred cow in the NCAA—kicked seven players off his team for raping a professor's daughter on campus. Do you think Ara should have had a sign in the locker room at South Bend that said RAPING IS NOT ALLOWED?

Strange as this sounds, when I look back on everything that was happening, I still believed, prior to receiving David Swank's message, that I would not only survive as head coach at Oklahoma, I would eventually triumph.

I would do what I had done in 1983, when there was a conspiracy to get me fired. The way I crushed that movement for a while was by winning four consecutive Big Eight Championships, winning the national championship in 1985, and by almost finishing number one again in 1986 and 1987.

The "crime" that had given my opponents strength against me in the early eighties was having three "losing" seasons in a row.

You need to understand that at the University of Oklahoma, an 8–4 record is considered a losing season. In my three "losing" seasons (7–4–1, 8–4, 8–4), eight of the twelve losses were to USC, Texas, Nebraska, and Ohio State. That didn't make me or the program a failure in my eyes, but it wasn't good enough for the group of Oilys we were embarrassing at that time.

During that short period when we made these Oilys uneasy by only going to the Sun Bowl and Fiesta Bowl instead of the three expected Orange Bowls, the president of the university, Bill Banowsky, gave me the bottom line on my situation. It pointed out very clearly the hypocrisy of big-time college athletics.

Banowsky had summoned me and Wade Walker, our athletic director at the time, to the president's house for a "state of our union" address. Gerald Turner, liaison between the president's office and the athletic department, was there. Bill Saxon, a Sooner Oily who is major-league rich and lives in Texas and Palm Springs, shook hands and left when Wade and I arrived. Banowsky is a Church of Christ preacher and a real charmer. He was courting Saxon for contributions to the university, and Banowsky's top priority at OU always was raising money.

Banowsky said, "Barry, if you will start going to church every Sunday morning and Sunday night and Wednesday night and marry that little girl you're dating, you could lose four games again next season and still be my coach as long as I'm here, but I can't guarantee how the board of regents will feel.

"However, if you go ten-two next season and beat Texas and Nebraska, you don't have to attend church or get married and we won't fire you."

While he was talking I was thinking, This is the damnedest thing I've ever heard; this guy doesn't know anything about football. It's no disgrace to lose to great teams like Texas and Nebraska. If I go 10–2 and lose to Kansas State and Iowa State, that's when you ought to fire me.

Banowsky continued. "But, Barry, if you win the national championship, the regents won't fire you even if we catch you smoking dope."

When Wade and I walked out of the president's house that day, I said, "Wade, what the hell kind of a profession is this?"

Wade responded with a statement I could never forget. "Banowsky's little speech has just emphasized what we've known all along, Barry. They expect us to pay lip service to all the high-sounding goals, but what it really all comes down to is money and winning, and those two things really control everything. It's institutional hypocrisy."

Wade wasn't far from retirement, and I think he was looking forward to escaping from the Oklahoma Football Monster, which he had served off and on since he was an all-American lineman for the Sooners in 1949.

I didn't create the Oklahoma Football Monster. It was born after World War II, when Bud Wilkinson won a national championship in 1950. It grew bigger from winning back-to-back national championships in 1955 and 1956, which included two separate streaks of thirty-one and forty-seven games without being beaten and of never losing a conference game for twelve consecutive seasons.

The Oklahoma Football Monster is real, it is huge and hungry, and it was my job to feed it. The ironic thing is, I may have fed it too well. I shoved 157 victories, three national championships, and twelve Big Eight titles down its throat, but it kept roaring for more. It gets fatter and fatter, and it never has enough to eat.

Also, I might point out here that I didn't create the national college football system or do anything worse to it than Knute Rockne did. I was just one of those who contributed to it.

College football was big-time at Yale and Harvard long before anybody heard of Norman, Oklahoma. What, for example, was Harvard doing building the first pure football stadium in 1903 (57,000 seats)—which also happens to be the first reinforced-steel structure in the world—if football, money, and academics weren't all tied together?

But there I was in Las Vegas on June 12, 1989. I stuck the message from the desk clerk in my pocket and went up to my room to phone David Swank, who had been dean of the Oklahoma law school prior to his appointment as interim president of the university. He had clearly wanted to become the full-time president but was felt by some to not be an effective enough administrator. And after he did a really terrible job on ABC's *Nightline* and did the same in a speech in, of all places, Austin, Texas, a lot of people in the athletic department began referring to him as King Nerd.

Earlier in his career, Swank had been removed as our faculty athletic representative to the Big Eight Conference for two reasons, one of them a really terrible one. Swank was a graduate of Oklahoma State, and for that reason alone several regents didn't like him or trust him and wanted to get rid of him. But more important, there was a consensus among the regents that Swank was a total political animal and was much more interested in serving the interests of the NCAA and his own career than in furthering the well-being of Oklahoma University's athletic interests—which was his job.

When I reached him on the telephone, Swank said he wanted me to be at a meeting in his office at noon the next day, June 13.

I said, "David, there's no way I can be back by then. I'm here to see the Leonard-Hearns fight tonight. The fight doesn't start until late. My plane doesn't leave until nearly noon. With the time difference, I can be in Norman by about five-thirty in the afternoon."

"Very well. I'll set up the meeting in the president's office for six P.M.," David said.

I hung up from David and wondered what this urgent meeting could be about. If there had been any new assaults or arrests, I would be getting calls from persons other than David Swank. *No, this meeting figured to be about me.*

I tried to push my concern away for the rest of the night and enjoy the fight. I'm a big-time fight fan. I'd met Sugar Ray Leonard, Hagler, and Ali, shook their hands, been around them a little. One of the best fights I had ever seen was the first Hearns-Leonard fight in Las Vegas in September 1981.

After the fight, I did what you do in Las Vegas. You gamble. I don't shoot craps. My favorite casino game is blackjack. I played cards until pretty late, but I woke up early and grabbed the phone.

I called Fred Gipson, general counsel for the university. I think of Fred as a friend, and I wanted to find out what to expect at this urgent meeting. But I couldn't reach Fred and I couldn't reach Donnie Duncan, our athletic director. I discovered later that David Swank had told Fred and Donnie not to talk to me, but Fred had tried to call me anyhow. I heard his message on my answering machine at home, but not until after the meeting.

My flight was forty-five minutes late. I drove straight from the airport to Norman and turned onto the campus. I love Norman and I love the Oklahoma campus. This has been my home for twenty-four years. My three children were born here. Norman is a small town, but that's one reason I love it. I have been described as a rogue who lives on the edge, like my daddy did, but I am a small-town boy at heart. Give me a plate of cream gravy, biscuits, and country sausage for breakfast and let me go fishing or quail hunting, and you've made me happy.

The lights were coming on in the houses along Fraternity Row. I went past the building that has always dominated the campus—Owen Field, with its red-brick walls and its 75,000 seats and its enormous national-championship scoreboard. A few years ago, a university program erected a ten-story building called the Energy Center, and it was announced that no longer was Owen Field the tallest thing on campus. Swank always mentioned that in his speeches, but he didn't fool anybody. Owen Field still dominated the campus.

When I drove up to the entrance of Evans Hall, I was kind of surprised to see Ron White, president of the board of regents, coming out the door and walking toward his car.

Ron White is a wealthy cardiologist who was appointed to the board for fourteen straight years by two different governors he had supported heavily with his checkbook.

Ron is one of those guys who really enjoys being called regent and to whom being a regent is really important. I'll never understand why, but being a regent is one of the most prestigious appointments an Oklahoma governor can make.

"Hey, Ron," I yelled. "Are you here for the meeting?"

"Yeah," he said.

He had been leaving because I was late. I never really knew where I stood with him. Some regents had changed allegiances whenever the wind shifted, which, of course, is the nature of politics. Ron White turned around and the two of us walked into Evans Hall and on into the president's office.

Sitting at the head of the conference table was David Swank. To his left was Andy Coats, the lawyer the university uses as its outside legal counsel. Andy had been the mayor of Oklahoma City and had run for the U.S. Senate. He represented us when we joined with the University of Georgia to sue the NCAA and win our television rights. I had always considered Andy a friend and a real gentleman, but I've learned over the years in the public eye that it is really difficult to know who your true friends are.

Ron White took a chair across from Andy, beside Fred Gipson. At the near end of the table, about three empty chairs away from the others, sat our athletic director, Donnie Duncan. I had hired Donnie as an assistant coach in 1973 and fully endorsed and supported him for the job of athletic director when Wade Walker resigned. I admire Donnie and trust him. I couldn't believe he would be involved in an attempt to lynch me, so I relaxed a bit.

They started asking me what I thought of the Leonard-Hearns fight and how were things going with me in general, nothing but meaningless chitchat.

Finally, I looked at Donnie and said, "What the hell is this all about?"

Donnie said, "President Swank will tell you."

Swank took a deep breath and scrunched up his face and squinted through his glasses and started into a speech that I figured would be twenty minutes of gas. Instead, his words eventually made my mouth drop open.

"Barry," he said. "We have some things to discuss with you that concern us and the university. We'll just tell you that we have information in regard to the FBI investigation into the Charles Thompson affair and the conduct of Scott Hill . . ."

Scott Hill was a former assistant coach who had been a good player on our national-championship team of 1975. He's the man who knocked out Tony Dorsett in a famous head-on collision in our Pitt game. Scott was in charge of our recruiting and the sort of guy most people liked.

Swank, as interim president, had forced us to fire Scott and also wanted us to fire assistant coach Mike Jones as well, because of their involvement in the NCAA problems, but Mike had been able to survive because he was able to battle Swank with some of the regents he knew personally. Since Scott's dismissal from the university, his name had come up in an FBI investigation on drugs.

Swank cleared his throat and said, "There are some alle-

gations that you and Scott Hill were in a suite at the Las Vegas
Dunes in 1983 with some people from Oklahoma and that cocaine was present.

"The FBI doesn't have you involved with their Scott Hill
investigation. But we have found out through the United
States Attorney's office in Oklahoma City that they have you
on something much worse, more embarrassing to the university than what Scott Hill may be involved in . . ."

I interrupted Swank.

"What the hell are you talking about?" I said. "Who is
saying these things?"

"This comes from assistant United States attorney Blair
Watson's office. Our information is that they have you on wire
transfer of funds across interstate lines for gambling on Oklahoma and other college football games. And there are charges
you manipulated drug testing of your athletes to allow them to
play."

I looked at my friend Donnie and said, "This sounds like
some kind of rap sheet. It's total bullshit! You people are trying to railroad me. This is science fiction. Donnie, do you believe this crap?"

"I already told them I know it's not true," Donnie said.

"You're damn right it's not," I said. "Who is saying these
things?"

Swank gestured to Andy Coats. Andy got up from his
chair and said, "Barry, the FBI has a bookie in Las Vegas that
they have interrogated, and he brought forth your name as
someone he is involved with."

"This is a fantasy," I said. "I gamble at the tables, not with
bookies."

"They have you cold," Andy said.

Andy walked around the room with his hands in his
pockets, repeating the story that supposedly came from Blair
Watson. He wouldn't look at me. I was starting to feel like I
wouldn't have a cut dog's chance in this room.

Ron White said, "Well, I've got to inform the regents. *This
week is time to renew the coaches' contracts. The board of regents must
be informed of this.*" It is interesting to note that all OU coaches'
contracts are renewed in July of every year. The timing of all
this crap was really fascinating.

I looked at each face in the room as I stood up.

"There's no need to continue this meeting," I said. "I want you to know there's not a damn bit of truth in any of this. I'll be in contact with my lawyers, and I'll get back to you."

At the door, I glanced back and said, "I'll call you later, Donnie."

After sixteen years as the head football coach at Oklahoma, I thought I was shockproof. But this meeting stunned me. I was wondering, Who in the hell is Blair Watson? I know many people in Oklahoma, but I'd never heard of Blair Watson. Even if I had gambled on college football games, did they think I would be dumb enough to put my own name on an interstate wire transfer to a bookie? I never tried to hide the fact that I occasionally go to Las Vegas and visit the race track at Remington Park, but I haven't bet on a college football game since I was a player at the University of Arkansas and bought one of those yellow pick-three-of-five cards and lost a dollar.

There might be some college coaches who bet on college football games, but I think it's wrong for a coach to bet on football. Besides that, college football is a hard game to bet. I pay attention to the gambling line. Those odds makers amaze me. I'd be a loser if I were a bettor.

How did anybody think I could manipulate drug tests? I demanded that our trainer, Dan Pickett, personally put an eyeball on every one of our football players' penises as they peed into a bottle two or three times each week. It was a demeaning chore that made Dan feel kind of psycho, looking at all those penises every day, even Sunday morning. But we had the toughest drug-testing program in the NCAA, whether you believe it or not, regent Sam Noble.

And the charge that years ago I had been seen in a hotel suite in Las Vegas when cocaine was present?

Well, that may have been true. I don't know. You could walk into any restaurant or saloon or board room at any time, especially seven or eight years ago, and cocaine might be present. What was I supposed to do, shout, "Here comes Barry Switzer! Hide your dope!" every place I went?

I was growing angrier by the minute.

Things that had happened in my youth had created my mental toughness. I am a fighter, a competitor. I am tenacious. I am a winner.

But now I didn't understand exactly what I was fighting. The angrier I became, the more frustrated I became. Then the old paranoia set in. It was a conspiracy. I was surrounded by enemies.

I needed to talk to the one person I know who is unquestionably intelligent, educated, and experienced and who loves me and has my best interest at heart.

That would be my brother, Donnie Switzer, six years younger than me. Donnie left Daddy's shotgun house in the Arkansas pines on a scholastic scholarship to Dartmouth College. He rode the Penn Central Railroad all the way to Hanover, New Hampshire, all alone, and graduated with his B.A. in 1965. Donnie was an exchange student in Spain, later earned his law degree at Vanderbilt, and became vice-president and general counsel of the American General Life Insurance Companies in Houston before deciding to go into private practice in a small Oklahoma town.

Donnie would know what I should do next.

2

IN THE JAWS OF THE MONSTER

I believe that most of you, even those who don't follow sports closely, heard of the incredible series of criminal incidents that struck the Oklahoma football program in early 1989. Hell, it was on the front page of most papers coast to coast, not just the sports pages, so you would almost have to be blind not to have seen the stories.

But let's briefly review the events so we will all feel the situation as I was feeling it then. Nineteen eight-nine was pure hell. And it really began on November 19, 1988, in our last game of the 1988 season, when Nebraska beat us 7–3 for the Big Eight Championship in Norman.

Then, on December 19, 1988, the NCAA put Oklahoma on probation for the first time since just before I had become head coach in 1973. And I had to admit to the truth of a *few* of the sixteen allegations the NCAA made against us.

Two weeks later, January 2—officially into 1989, now—Jamelle Holieway had to play quarterback against Clemson in the Citrus Bowl, since Charles Thompson had broken his leg in the Nebraska game. Jamelle had to play the game essentially on one leg, since his knee, crippled a year earlier, was bound in a heavy brace. We had the ball on their 1-yard line early in the game, but Jamelle somehow lost 16 yards on the Wishbone option. Clemson beat our 9–2 Sooners by 13–6.

When we returned to Norman, a little cornerback who roomed with Charles Thompson lost his head and shot and wounded his high school friend, a big offensive lineman, with

25

a .22 revolver during an argument over a haircut and a rap tape! Eight days later, three football players were accused of raping a twenty-year-old Oklahoma City woman in Bud Wilkinson House.

Shortly after the rape, the FBI charged Charles Thompson with selling 17 grams of cocaine to an undercover agent for $4,000. Charles Thompson had tested positive for cocaine once after the spring game in 1988 and again in the summer of that year.

Thompson had gone to a rehabilitation center during the summer prior to the 1988 season, at his family's expense. During the 1988 season, Charles passed all sixteen drug tests while Dan Pickett stood there and watched him pee into a bottle. But Charles, who still had a cast on his leg, drove in his black sports car—it had smoked-glass windows and KINGEORGE V vanity plates, but it was seven years old—with his buddy Otha Armstrong III, a convicted burglar, to a shopping center parking lot and sold cocaine to a policeman.

It devastated me and our coaches that he would do something like this.

In July before he went to prison, Charles Thompson drove Otha Armstrong III to my home, found my door key where Charles knew I once kept it, and told Otha to steal my case of rings and other valuables and meet him in the parking lot down the street.

Along with my rings, Armstrong stole my bowl-game watches, my shotgun, and my camera. What Charles didn't know is that Armstrong was also a paid informant who had set up Charles to get busted for selling cocaine in the first place.

That's what I mean about 1989.

During this time when bad things were happening so fast, David Swank came up with a standard reply or answer whenever anything new would be thrown at him. He'd say, "We're going to *stress academics* at Oklahoma." Taking his cue from Swank, when some joker called athletic director Donnie Duncan and reported Jack the Ripper and the Werewolf were loose in the football dorm, Donnie said, "Give them each two academic stress tablets and lock them in the library."

You sports fans, and all you people who deplore college football, deserve to know what really happened. I'm going to tell you some crazy things that happened, things you never heard of, things that kept happening right up until a few months ago, when I had to stop writing because of my deadline. I promise you will be surprised.

Before I reach 1989 again, I will discuss with fondness our glory years and great teams and great players like the Selmon brothers and Joe Washington and Billy Sims and Keith Jackson and Brian Bosworth, to name just a few. I'll discuss recruiting, our big money and hot blood rivalries with Texas and Nebraska, and my view of Darrell Royal, who more than anyone else saw to it that I was branded a cheater so slick that I could get away with anything. When they throw dirt on Darrell's box, he'll still believe it, I guess. It's a pity, because I respect Darrell Royal.

But first, let me get back to the week of June 12–19, 1989.

It was now Wednesday night, June 13. I had left the meeting at Swank's office and was seeking guidance from my brother, Donnie.

I phoned my brother at his home in Vinita, Oklahoma, where he now practices law. He listened to my story and said, "I'll meet you in the morning at the Quarter Horse Inn. I'll bring O. B. Johnston with me."

Johnston had been the assistant United States attorney in Oklahoma City who, along with United States attorney Bill Burkett, had prosecuted former Oklahoma governor David Hall and convicted him of extorting a bribe while in public office. O. B. now was a partner in Donnie's firm.

This sounded like a good start, but I was feeling very agitated and curious. It appeared to me that Swank and some others were out to bring me down. Where did they come up with these charges? And who in the hell was Blair Watson?

I drove over to Donnie Duncan's house. Donnie is a solid person. He had been an assistant for me at Oklahoma and a good head football coach at Iowa State for four years. He had been executive director of both the Sun Bowl and the Gator Bowl. Donnie has been around the block in college football.

Donnie said, "All this started happening before you left for the fight. They are obviously going to pursue it because they're hearing it from sources they believe. All of the coaches' contracts are on hold—the basketball coach and the baseball coach and yours. This is so it won't be clear that you're the one they're after. And Swank is refusing to sign the NCAA compliance certification letter as long as you are the head football coach. He's wrong, but he feels that some of the things we uncovered in our own subsequent internal investigation weren't made known to the NCAA and that it constitutes a new violation."

"I'm going to go visit each regent individually in person," I said.

"Not tonight, Barry. All of them haven't even been informed yet. They're going to be in shock when they hear it from Swank and Ron White."

In the morning I drove to Stroud, on the Turner Turnpike about halfway between Norman and Vinita. My brother, O. B., and I talked for a couple of hours in a motel room at the Quarter Horse Inn, now renamed the Stroud Motor Inn. During the conversation I mentioned that I had just received a demand for a three-year audit by the IRS, my first audit in ten or twelve years.

"If the FBI is doing an investigation, it's not unusual for there to be a simultaneous audit," O. B. said. "If they think you're involved in interstate gambling, they'd want to establish a basis for all your accounts and income."

This gave my paranoia a jolt.

But O. B. was skeptical about the Blair Watson connection. He didn't believe an assistant U.S. attorney would reveal sensitive information concerning an investigation to David Swank or anyone else. See him? Sure. Tell him any secrets? No.

Both O. B. and Donnie told me to "slow-play" the situation because we did not yet know what was going to happen with Scott Hill's situation, and there still might be some way to handle Swank's problem with the NCAA compliance certification letter, since Swank was only an interim president.

My brother walked me out to my car. He said, "Barry, I am really concerned that you may not be the coach at Oklahoma next year."

That hurt. I glared at Donnie like I used to when we were kids and he made me mad.

But Donnie went on telling me the truth as he saw it.

"Regardless of whether the regents want to believe that these allegations are true, with all of the things that have gone on in your program this year, all of the bad publicity, I am really afraid that when David Swank and Ron White communicate these new allegations to the regents, the pressure will simply be too much on them . . . no matter how hard you fight them and no matter how untrue the charges are. There are an enormous number of people calling for your scalp, because you never had a pure-as-the-driven-snow image and you have been the coach when all of those unspeakable things occurred. There are powerful forces allied against you, and they may well be willing to do anything to make certain that you leave, even fabricate stories like these."

I stood there, still glaring at Donnie. I kept thinking to myself that I hadn't done any of the things these bastards were accusing me of. How could this be the end? How could things have gotten this bad?

For the first time I was becoming frightened, but even then I never would have dreamed that within a week these lies would have forced me to resign one of the best head-coaching jobs in the country.

It had been a long and wonderful ride. All the way from the Arkansas swamp bottoms and running whiskey with Daddy to the pinnacle of college football. But was it now all going to come to an end?

What could possibly have led to all of this?

3

THE LIGHT ON DAISY'S DOCK . . .

At a party in Miami before one of our Orange Bowl games, the elegant wife of a Sooner Oily walked over to me at the table where I was picking at the shrimp and smiling and being charming, killing everyone with kindness. From the way she was staring at me, I knew she had packed away enough cocktails that she was determined to tell me something that had been on her mind.

"Barry, I've finally figured out who it is you remind me of," she said.

"Really?" I said. "Who?"

"You remind me of Jay Gatsby."

People had told me before that I reminded them of Roy Rogers. One night at a private party in Las Vegas, Muhammad Ali told me I reminded him of John Wayne. I said I had been told that before, too, but more people said I looked like Roy Rogers and I always said, "That's better than looking like Trigger." Ali leaned over and squinted into my face and said, "Did you call me a nigger?" I ducked and said, "Trigger! Trigger!" The champ then started laughing . . . thank God!

But Jay Gatsby? The name was familiar. I was trying to remember where he had played football. Sounded like an Ivy League tailback.

I grinned at the Oily wife and said, "Hell of a guy, old Jay."

Later at the party I got my brother, Donnie, the Dartmouth grad, off in a corner and asked him who was Jay Gatsby.

"He's the main character in a novel called *The Great Gatsby*," Donnie said. "He's a good-looking, very successful fellow, a fancy dresser, very smooth. Lives in a big house and gives extravagant parties. Robert Redford played the role in the movie."

Oh yeah, now I remembered. The book had been on my reading list in an English class at the University of Arkansas. Yeah, this Gatsby was a famous character.

"But no matter how successful he is, the social elite never really accept him," Donnie said.

"Why not?"

"He comes from a rough background and is in a business they don't understand. They want him to entertain them but not to cross the line. Symbolically, he can't come closer to them than the light on the dock at the house of the rich girl he loves. Her name is Daisy. She looks like Mia Farrow."

"He's a bootlegger's boy, huh?" I said.

Donnie nodded. "In fact, he's a bootlegger himself. What do you want to know for?"

I gestured toward the Oily wife across the room. She was knocking down another vodka and chatting with some of her country-club pals.

"That woman says I remind her of Jay Gatsby," I said.

"I didn't realize she could read," Donnie said.

I never did read the novel, either, and probably never will, but I did understand the Oily wife wasn't telling me I reminded her of Robert Redford in the movie version of it.

She was telling me that no matter how many national championships my teams win, to her I would always be a bootlegger's boy.

I've known people like her all my life.

This was the kind of woman who wouldn't have let me date her daughter when I was in high school.

Nice girls weren't supposed to go out with the bootlegger's boy. But they did. Hey, I had the use of my buddy's car and five bucks in my pocket and wore my all-state letter jacket. Nice girls liked me.

They had no idea how insecure I felt.

Let me tell you what people will do to you in the name of good when you're the bootlegger's boy.

Daddy wouldn't let us go to church. We had a Baptist

church and a Methodist church in Crossett, Arkansas. Besides
the pool hall, church was about the only social activity in town.
Some of the church members would send their black ser-
vants—in those days, everything in Crossett was segregated
except my daddy's house—to buy a pint of whiskey from "Mr.
Frank," but in public they deplored him.

Daddy said the churches were full of pious hypocrites and
bigots who preached and supposedly followed the teachings of
Jesus but wouldn't even sit next to a black person on a bench.

He blamed a hell-fire preacher for the death of one of his
friends, Robert Rainwater. The preacher visited Rainwater in
the hospital after an accident that killed a boy and laid so
much heavy guilt and fire and brimstone on him that Rainwater had a really bad time. He even asked our good black
friend Irma Reynolds for a rope from the dumbwaiter to
hang himself with. He died shortly thereafter from a heart
attack.

If Daddy had known I was going to church that night, he
wouldn't have let me leave the house.

I was in the ninth grade and had a date with a real nice
girl who wanted me to take her to Brother Burkhead's big
revival meeting at the Baptist church.

Usually, I had to ask a friend to go up to my date's front
door to pick her up so her folks wouldn't know it was me she
was going out with. But this night my date came right on out
because we were going to the Baptist church.

The girl and I entered church during the service and sat
in the back. All of a sudden the word started spreading that I
was there. The bootlegger's boy. In the Baptist church. People
were singing hymns and glancing around at me. I felt like a
freak and was scared to death.

Brother Burkhead sent a message that he wanted to talk
to me in his office right after the service.

My date went with me down the aisle in front of everybody and into Brother Burkhead's office. People started following us.

Those who couldn't get in crowded around the door.
Brother Burkhead was worked up into a high preaching
fever. He said, "Barry, wouldn't you like to have your soul
saved? Wouldn't you like to become a Christian? Wouldn't you
like to join our church?"

People were praying, and before I knew it Brother Burkhead had me down on my knees. He put his arms around me
and prayed real loud, "Oh, Jesus, save this poor boy."

I'm sure he said more, but I didn't hear it. My mind was
racing. All I was thinking was that I wanted to run, but I
didn't have enough guts to get up off my knees and sprint out
of the room.

Brother Burkhead was rejoicing, and people flowed all
over me, hugging me and crying. They had done it—they had
brought the black sheep into the fold, they had saved the
bootlegger's boy! They had him on his knees in front of them!

I said to myself, If this is what religion is and what I'm
feeling now is supposed to be a religious experience and my
soul is supposed to be saved by these whooping and hollering
idiots, then let me get out of here.

I had never been so embarrassed and frightened in my
life. It was a terrible experience. All of those people, some of
them hypocrites, were saving my soul, and I felt horrible. I
didn't want to be one of them. I looked at my date and
couldn't tell whether she was sort of proud at having delivered
the heathen to church or if she was maybe a little sorry about
what was happening to me, with all the weeping and carrying
on, like, *We got him, Lord! We got the bootlegger's boy!*

To me this did not seem like the way Jesus would have
done it.

I jumped up and tore away from Brother Burkhead and
broke through the crowd and ran off into the night by myself.

I was still thoroughly shaken and bewildered a couple of
hours later when a Ford coupe pulled up at the house and I
heard a black man call out, "Mr. Frank, I need two half pints
and one pint."

I recognized the voice of the yard man of one of our leading Baptists. I prayed he wouldn't tell Daddy what had happened, especially not joke about it. Daddy had a hot temper
and always carried a gun. Not that he would have shot the
messenger, of course. But he would have blasted a few rounds
into the sky to let the Crossett Baptists know that he, Frank
Switzer the bootlegger, was still doing business in his shotgun
house out here on the edge of Colored Town—and leave his
boy alone!

It was like those people wanted my scalp.

*   *   *

My first home was in a houseboat on the Ouachita River, about nine miles out of Crossett on Highway 82.

Actually, the houseboat was a forty-foot cabin cruiser—they called it the yacht—that Daddy had acquired somehow, but it was home.

I was born October 5, 1937, at the height of the Great Depression. Mary Louise Wood Switzer, my mother, had been valedictorian of her class at Crossett High School. My daddy, Frank Mays Switzer, had three brothers, two of whom studied law. One of them, Uncle Billy, is a tough old municipal court judge in Crossett today. The other lawyer brother, Uncle Ovid, is eighty-five years old and still practices law every day.

My grandfather, F. H. Switzer, owned thousands of acres of cotton and pine forest outside of Crossett and served twice as a state representative before he became ill and lost it all. My grandfather on my mother's side was a housepainter who painted nearly every house in town. It was a paper-mill town that was owned by the Crossett Company. There's still a color of paint called Crossett Gray.

Mother was the smartest, prettiest girl in Crossett. Daddy was a handsome man with a powerful physique—he used to chop logs and climb ropes and run long distances just for the fun of it. He had attended the University of Arkansas in 1925, and he was the first eligible bachelor in Ashley County to own a two-door Model A Ford roadster. So it was kind of natural that they would get together.

I have claimed (joking, of course) that I was the best football player born in the Crossett Hospital. A few years ago, however, when I was coaching the Hula Bowl in Honolulu, I was visiting with O. J. Simpson and found that his family was originally from Parkdale, Arkansas, in the southern part of the state, and that his daddy had been born in the Crossett Hospital. When he told me this, I told O. J., "It's fortunate for you that your family moved, because you would have been the second best player to come out of Crossett."

They took me home to the houseboat, where we lived while Daddy ran the toll bridge over the Ouachita River. The toll bridge was a new WPA project. Until then, you had to take a ferry to go from Crossett to El Dorado or go the long way around through Louisiana, an extra fifty miles or so. Jobs were hard to find. My mother's folks moved to El Dorado, forty miles away, and we lived back and forth until Daddy decided to join the great exodus.

I was too little to know it, but this was the *Grapes of Wrath* period that John Steinbeck wrote about. People in Arkansas and Texas and Oklahoma were packing their belongings on top of their old cars and wagons and heading west, hoping to find jobs in California.

When the Japanese bombed Pearl Harbor on December 7, 1941, and the United States got into World War II, my daddy took off for California and left us behind. He got work as a paint chipper in a shipyard at Terminal Island in San Pedro for $1.07 an hour, which must have seemed like a fortune.

Mother and I joined him and moved into a three-room house at 257 Loma Avenue in Long Beach. The house was five blocks from the ocean, a really neat place to grow up, with the beach close by. Much of our family moved out there. Mother's mother, Mrs. Lillie Wood, worked at Douglas Aircraft in Long Beach, and she and my Uncle Vernon and Aunt Alene lived just down the street, at 264 Loma Avenue.

I started kindergarten in Long Beach. Mother and a friend from Arkansas opened a cafe called Arkies'. They served chicken-fried steak and biscuits and gravy, the sort of food they'd known back home. I remember a song on the jukebox at the cafe. The song went, "Dear old Okie, if you see Arkie, tell him Tex is out in California picking prunes and squeezing orange juice out of olives . . ."

My brother, Donnie, was born at Harriman Jones Clinic in Long Beach in 1943. The first thing I did when I came home from school every day was go to the crib and look at the baby. I called him Strawberry, because it was the best thing I could think of at that age. It was a great life for me and my buddies, who didn't even realize there was a war going on. One day we were crossing Broadway, coming back from the beach, and all of a sudden horns started blaring and sirens were going off and the ships in the harbor were blowing their whistles. I stopped a grown-up and asked where was the fire.

"The war is over, kid!" he yelled.

"What war?" we said.

Our lives changed quickly. The shipyards and aircraft plants started shutting down, and people were laid off. Now there was this tide of people turning around and going back to Arkansas, Texas, and Oklahoma.

Mother, Donnie, and I stayed in Long Beach so I could finish the third grade, but Daddy hooked it on home to Crossett to go into business for himself.

He got involved in a dry cleaners, a furniture store, a department store, a bakery, a fishing camp, and a used-car lot, but he never made a dime out of any of them.

But he did discover a way to make a living for his family.

Ashley County was Bible-belt country, voted dry by local option. In a scheme to earn some money, Daddy made a trip down to Louisiana and brought back a few cases of whiskey. He sold the liquor by the pint and made a good profit.

That's how Daddy got into the occupation that lasted the rest of his life.

He became a bootlegger.

4

LEARNING ABOUT THE BUSINESS

We lived in a gray shotgun house about four miles west of Crossett, on a gravel road near a swamp bottom down toward the Louisiana line.

The main street, a state highway, runs right through the middle of Crossett and divides the town. The east side of the town was white, and the west side of town was black.

Crossett was a company town with a big labor force of blacks. Daddy hadn't been bootlegging long before he had five or six black guys selling whiskey for him.

When Mother, Donnie, and I returned from California, we moved in with Daddy and Granddaddy Switzer in the old house. Mother was not comfortable with Daddy being a bootlegger, but there really wasn't any other choice for her. After all, that was 1945 or 1946. Donnie and I weren't uncomfortable with or concerned about Daddy's bootlegging. I was in the fourth grade and Donnie was just a toddler. What did we know about bootlegging?

The shotgun house was built on stump logs. I always thought the house was built up off the ground so the chickens, dogs, and hogs would have a place to live. We had no electricity, no running water, no telephone (I was a senior in college before we got a telephone at home in Crossett). There was a three-holer outhouse with a Sears, Roebuck catalog that wasn't for reading, and a sack of lime in the corner. Dirt dobbers built their nests in the privy in the spring, and bumblebees bored their holes in the summer.

When I got a little older I would escort Mother to the outhouse at night with a flashlight and a pistol to shoot copperheads because a nest of dozens of them had been found there and Mother was scared to death.

Lying in bed late at night, Donnie and I could hear music blaring from Sam Lawson's Cafe and the blacks partying and making runs back and forth to Daddy to get their whiskey. Lawson's Cafe was in a rural black community about three hundred yards from us if you went through the woods and maybe a quarter of a mile if you took the road. This particular black settlement was a dozen or more shanty houses. The people who lived there raised cotton and sugarcane and had an old sorghum mill, and an old black mechanic named Sam Patton had a garage of sorts. In the fourth grade I used to pick cotton for a black man, and I'd go swim in the creek with the black kids. They had a barrel stay that we used for a basketball hoop.

Other than my big collie dog, Major, black kids were my best friends.

Daddy was a rounder and a womanizer and was doing well in the bootlegging business. He knew the sheriff and had no trouble with the local law. Pretty soon he started lending money at 20 percent interest. A black woman named Irma Reynolds moved in to help Daddy with his business. Irma was fifteen years older than Daddy and had helped raise him when he was a child.

At the end of my fifth-grade year, Mother had had enough of Daddy and the bootlegging. She left Daddy and took Donnie and me to live in El Dorado. The three of us shared a little trailer next to my Aunt Newell's house, who also lived in the country. Donnie was so young he didn't realize Mother and Daddy had separated. He had not started school yet and only started school the next year, when I was in the seventh grade. Daddy would come see us on weekends and then drive forty miles back to Crossett. Mother wanted to do something, so he bought her a cafe called the Coffee Cup on Northwest Ave. in El Dorado. It was a hole-in-the-wall with a counter and a row of stools, no booths, and people would come in to eat breakfast and lunch. Mother and Donnie and I lived upstairs.

I started my football career in the sixth grade at Reta Brown Grade School and played my seventh-grade year at the Yoakum Grade School in El Dorado. This is where I first met kids like Jim Mooty and Wayne Harris, who would become great players and all-Americans at the University of Arkansas. Down the road in Fordyce—hometown of Bear Bryant—was a brash little kid named Larry Lacewell, who eventually became my assistant head coach at Oklahoma.

They picked an all-star team from the grade school to play the Catholics in the high school stadium, and I was a starter. I had found a game I really loved. I was looking forward to starting the eighth grade and having a big year. There were at least ninety kids who showed up for fall practice. I had my new locker and a lot of new friends and was beginning to get the attention of the coaches.

Mother came to fall practice the third day and called me off to the side.

"Barry, we're moving back to Crossett," she said.

This was a horrible blow to me. I'd been in El Dorado two years.

"Please, Mother, I want to stay here," I said.

But she had decided to move in with Daddy again.

School had already started in Crossett. I enrolled late and went out for football. The yellow-dog school bus wouldn't wait until the end of practice, so I would walk five miles home at night down a long straight gravel road that passed through Colored Town. The black kids had their own segregated school, T. W. Daniels School, but I still knew many of them from before, and all their folks knew me—I was "Mr. Frank's boy."

It didn't take long for me to get tired of walking home. I wouldn't get home until after dark, and I would still have chores to do. I quit the football team. But thank heaven there was a physical-education teacher at Crossett named Lynn Yarborough, who had retired as football coach and was then the athletic director. Mr. Yarborough came to me in P.E. class and told me I had a chance to be a really good player. He brought coach Harry Denson to appeal to me to come back and help the team.

When I told them the reason I had quit, those two gentlemen promised to take turns driving me home after practice or make other arrangements for me. This would be against the NCAA rules in college today, I'm sure, but if Mr. Yarborough and Coach Denson hadn't taken such an interest in me in the eighth grade, I doubt I'd be telling you my story.

Now I was beginning to learn what Daddy's business was and what it meant to be the bootlegger's boy. I would ask the good-looking white girls from the east side of town to go out with me, and many of their parents wouldn't allow it. I started realizing the social stigma I had to live with. I had to deal with emotions of inferiority and insecurity. It was no fun to hide in the backseat of the car while a friend went to the front door to pick up my date. The worst part of this situation was that my friend got to walk my girl back to the front door at the end of the evening.

Mostly, I would hang out with black kids. I considered myself a pretty good athlete, but when I got into basketball games with my black buddies, I found out at a young age that there was a basic difference between me and most of them—they could run faster and jump higher and stay in the air longer than most of the white kids.

I would go down to the creeks with the black kids. The girls would undress on one side of the creek and get in the water and the boys would undress on the other side, and we'd all swim together.

I was becoming a star in all sports at the white school, but I knew I wouldn't be such a star if I had to play against my black friends.

In the ninth grade, Daddy took me on a business trip for the first time. We pulled the backseat out of an old green Rocket 88 Oldsmobile and drove down to Vicksburg, Mississippi. Daddy bought twenty-two cases of whiskey in pints and half pints. With the backseat out of the Olds, we could stack whiskey all the way into the trunk and cover it with a couple of quilts. The first time I ever crossed the Mississippi River was on a bootlegging expedition.

Daddy began having trouble with the state liquor people. The local law would tip him off that a raid was coming and he wasn't getting caught yet, but the raids were scary, anyhow. Daddy buried his money in the woods and near the smokehouse, where we cured meat. He would hide his whiskey inside the walls of the house. You could pull aside a baseboard and reach in and get a pint of Early Times. The other bottles would slide down, just like in a vending machine.

A customer would come up to a big oak tree beside the house and signal how much he wanted. Daddy or Irma would take the whiskey out to the customer and collect the money. They wouldn't sell to anybody they didn't know.

Obviously, this was a tough situation for Mother.

Mother didn't ever get to go anywhere. She had few friends. She read all the time, lived in a world of fiction. I didn't know it, but she had started taking barbiturates by prescription, and she was drinking. She would kind of glide through the day with a glaze around her.

There wasn't another damn thing for her to do for entertainment. We had no television, of course. Mother would read, and Donnie and I would do our homework by the light from coal oil lamps. We had a battery radio that we'd use to listen to "The Grand Ole Opry" on Saturday nights. Sometimes someone from the groundhog sawmill that was a mile further down the road would take a pickup load of kids to the movie to see Wild Bill Elliott or Lash Larue or whatever Western was showing.

I remember in the ninth grade one of our teachers, Mr. Grider, came to the house taking a survey for Arkansas Power and Light, which was thinking about running electric lines out in our direction. Mr. Grider asked if we would like to have electricity. After he left, Daddy turned to me and said, "What a stupid question. I hope you aren't taking classes from that fellow."

It gets very cold in south Arkansas. We had no heat in the house—just a fireplace in the front room and a wood stove for cooking in the kitchen and a large potbellied stove for heating. They were called shotgun houses because there was a hallway down the middle, with the rooms on either side, and you could shoot a shotgun down the hall and out the back porch without hitting anything unless someone happened to walk across when you fired. In the winter Donnie would go to bed early. I would wait until he got the bed warm and then go in and roll him over and take the warm spot. Daddy would get up at six every morning—after drinking a fifth of whiskey the night before—and build a fire in the potbellied stove to heat the kitchen and the coffee. I would leap out of bed and sprint down that shotgun hallway and go out to the back porch and break the layer of ice so I could dip myself a drink of water with a gourd.

We would use barrels to catch rainwater that ran off the eaves of the house and use it to take baths in a number-three washtub.

Larry Lacewell likes to tell people, "I thought I was poor until I went to see Barry."

But, hell, we weren't poor. It was just the times . . . and Daddy's business.

When he wasn't out carousing, Daddy would sit at the kitchen table and drink a bottle of whiskey and visit with his friends. Like as not, before bedtime Daddy would pull out his pistol and shoot it. Our walls and ceilings were full of holes that the wind and rain poured through. One night Daddy and a drinking buddy were sitting in the kitchen shooting at the naked light bulb on the cord that hung from the ceiling on the back porch, but they were too drunk to hit it. So they handed a pistol to Donnie, who was just a little kid, and he hit it first shot. I wasn't there, so he might have been bragging, since that took place after I was already in college and Daddy had electricity.

Donnie says he was raised on chicken pot pies and rice burgers. Daddy kept so much rice in the salt shakers to absorb moisture that when he'd try to salt a hamburger patty, he'd cover it with hard rice that would swell when the hamburger was cooked.

Cold as it was in the winter, it was just as hot in the summer. Swamp-bottom mosquitoes would swarm through the cracks in the wall and holes in the screens, and we'd fog the bedroom with Real Kill so we could sleep.

If I wasn't working on a bull gang at the mill or out bass fishing—Daddy ran a fishing camp for a while, and fishing is still one of my favorite pastimes—or shooting pool or playing dominoes, I was playing football or competing in free-style swimming or putting the shot or throwing the discus. I held our school shotput record for a year or two. Later my brother,

Donnie, broke it and set a state AA record in the 1961 Meet of Champions.

While I was in high school, Daddy's troubles with the law became more and more serious.

One afternoon in my senior year, the Alcoholic Beverage Control Commission boys came to the house and arrested Daddy. Mind you, Daddy was a big, broad-shouldered man with a powerful body and a set of the finest, whitest teeth that you ever saw. Well, the ABCC bastards handcuffed his arms behind his back and then one of them smashed him in the mouth with a gun butt.

"You sons of bitches, you broke my teeth," he said.

A couple of times before, Daddy had been picked up and had spent a day or two in the county jail over in Hamburg. But that was among friends. The sheriff would let Mother and Donnie and me come see him, and then the prosecutor would dismiss the case for lack of evidence.

It was a different matter with the ABCC.

They sent Daddy to the Arkansas State Penitentiary. Remember that movie *Brubaker*, where Robert Redford played a warden? That's what this prison farm was like. It's in the town of Varner, on the delta by the Arkansas River.

Every other Sunday, Mother and Donnie and I would drive up to see him. The prison is backed up against the levee, and out in front were thousands of acres of waist-high cotton. I have a vivid memory of seeing all these chain gangs of convicts in black-and-white-striped uniforms picking cotton and throwing their sacks on these flatbed trailers while guards sat on horses with 30-30 rifles across their laps.

We would drive three miles down this dusty road through the cotton fields. At the gate, the guards would check our car and inspect the lunches we had brought. Then we'd go to the dining hall to meet Daddy and on over to the barracks where he bunked. We had hired the top attorneys in Little Rock to try to get him out, and it cost a hell of a lot of money.

Of course, my brother and I were embarrassed to go see Daddy in the pen. Occasionally, we'd see some other kids we knew who had relatives behind bars and we'd all kind of act like we hadn't seen each other.

But I loved Daddy and I know he loved us, even though I

can't remember that he ever told Donnie or me that he did. Daddy never kissed me or Donnie or hugged either one of us. I guess it just didn't occur to him. And Mother loved him dearly despite all the crap he had put her through.

Every time we visited him in prison, he was laughing and in good humor.

He said, "Barry, I've got a tip for you. If you ever get put in prison, try to get a job like I've got. It's the best job in any prison."

"What is it?" I said.

"Raising rabbits," he said.

The basic diet of a prison farm back in the fifties was rabbits and chicken—the cheapest form of protein.

"Raising rabbits sure beats the hell out of picking cotton," Daddy said.

Psychologists have since told me that Donnie and I were raised in a "totally dysfunctional environment" because both of our parents were alcoholic or drug dependent and we didn't know the meaning of stability.

How deeply I was affected by all of this, you can judge for yourself.

One thing I do remember is that in my senior year of high school I was selected the outstanding lineman in the state.

And Daddy didn't see me play a single game that year. He was in prison, raising rabbits.

5

ALL I NEED TO KNOW ABOUT PHYSIOLOGY I LEARNED IN THE EIGHTH GRADE

I always said the key to my success as a college football player was that there were no films of me playing high school ball in Crossett. Therefore, the college coaches hadn't seen me and had nothing to go on but my reputation.

When I was head coach at Oklahoma, if one of my assistants had come to me and said, "I've found this 6-foot-1, 185-pound blond-haired guard and linebacker at a little town in Arkansas who's not especially fast, but I want to give him a scholarship," I would have told that assistant to go home and sleep it off, or maybe I would even have fired him.

There is no way I could have played football for me at Oklahoma.

In fact, I have to chuckle now when I look at a picture of our 1959 University of Arkansas team, which finished in a three-way tie for the Southwest Conference championship and beat Georgia Tech in the Gator Bowl with me as tri-captain.

On that whole team there were three, maybe four, guys who could have played at Oklahoma in the 1970s and 1980s. Halfbacks Jim Mooty and Lance Alworth, a couple of 9.7 sprinters, would have made it. I would have found a spot for Wayne Harris, a center-linebacker who only weighed about 190 but was smart and a vicious tackler. And probably we

45

could have used 170-pound halfback Billy Kyser somewhere because of his great speed and athletic ability.

But the rest of us? Forget it.

T.C.U. coach Abe Martin claimed our 1959 team was bigger than listed in our program. So our coach, Frank Broyles, put everybody on the scales in public. Other than 212-pound tackle Jim Hollander, the biggest guy we had was Frank Broyles himself, at 208 (assistant coach Dixie White refused to be weighed).

These days if your coach is the second biggest guy on your team, you had better be coached by Art Shell.

The main reason for the difference between then and now is that blacks weren't playing then.

In 1959 black was just the color of your shoes if you played in the Big Eight Conference or the Southwest Conference or the Southeastern Conference.

Oh, there were a few black players. Prentice Gautt, for example, enrolled at Oklahoma in 1956 and became the first black Sooner. But mostly, the high schools and colleges in our part of the country were still segregated.

Mississippi hasn't gotten over it yet. Ole Miss had a powerful football program until the people fighting integration destroyed high school football in Mississippi by starting so many private academies where blacks weren't allowed.

The emergence of the black athlete has totally changed the game since I got my business degree at Arkansas in the spring of 1960.

I'm not a licensed physiologist, but for more than forty years I have played and coached football, lived with athletes every day, competed with them, competed against them, watched them in action, seen them get beat up, exhorted them, inspired them, made them angry, seen them perform under extreme pressure.

But all I needed to know about physiology I learned in the eighth grade.

I'm going to anticipate something here since unless I precede what I am about to say with the point that I am one of the country's foremost "experts" on the subject, I believe there are a lot of "knee-jerk" liberal types out there who are going to try to label me a racist. I am, in fact, the world's leading nonracist. Ask any of my black friends or players. And also recognize that I have been in the business of coaching superior athletes of all colors for over thirty years. I have seen all of them perform, and my recognition that, *in general,* blacks were better athletes than whites, particularly in certain areas, led me to be one of the leaders of integration in intercollegiate athletics. I believe, then, that what I say in this area is indisputable, and those who would dispute me simply haven't been looking at athletics for the last thirty years or so.

In general there is no question but that the black athlete has superior physical skills in all games that involve running and jumping and catching. In fact, I personally believe that it was probably the black athlete who drove the whites into inventing the weight room and also into taking steroids. I think the first weight program was started at L.S.U. when that school was all white, because of the influence of Alvin Roy, a Baton Rouge resident who was one of the first devotees of weight lifting.

Not that Alvin had anything to do with it, but it really is clear that at least in the sport of football, steroids are a white man's drug. Clearly, some blacks have been revealed as using steroids (black Canadian sprinter Ben Johnson quickly comes to mind), but they normally don't use them in sports other than track, as very few blacks have any use for them. The black athlete is usually a much more efficient machine physiologically than his white competition.

Some of you may be shocked to hear it, but it is a fact that today one of the common jokes that is used totally in fun by athletes, both black and white, is a comical reference to "white boy's disease." If a white *or* black kid is made to look silly by some of the better black *or* white athletes, the comment is often that that athlete suffers from white boy's disease—which simply recognizes that white boys (*generally*) can't do it the way black boys can. And our black kids would use that phrase as a jab to their other black friends whom they may have blasted on a particular play. "Hey, man! You've got white boy's disease!" Just think about it. How many *great* college or pro running backs and receivers in the last twenty-five years or so have been white? A few. But just a very few. And we've only been talking about football! We haven't even gotten into the sport of basketball! Enough said.

But back in the all-white game of 1955, an offensive guard and linebacker like me (who could grow to 200 or 210 pounds eating at the training table) was a fairly good size. I was pursued hotly by L.S.U. Assistant coaches Charlie McClendon and George Terry were recruiting the state of Arkansas for L.S.U.'s head coach Paul Dietzel, and they offered me a scholarship to come play on a team with Billy Cannon, Johnny Robinson, Warren Rabb, Max Fugler, and a lot of other stars who went on to win a national championship.

I received a congressional appointment to the naval academy, but I would have had to first attend Columbia Prep School in Washington, D.C., to bring up my grades in math. I was too introverted and had too many complexes to believe I could cope with the naval academy. I knew that I wasn't prepared academically for that type of competition. There were other schools interested in me, too, but I was an Arkansas boy, and nearly every Arkansas boy deep in his heart wanted to play for the Razorbacks.

Coach Bowden Wyatt, who recruited me for Arkansas, had come over from Wyoming to replace Otis Douglas. Wyatt had two great years at Arkansas, won the Southwest Conference title in 1954 with an 8–2 record, and played Georgia Tech in the Cotton Bowl. Then Bowden abruptly quit and went to Tennessee. He had come from Wyoming in a ratty old pickup truck and left for Knoxville in a new Cadillac.

I hadn't signed with Arkansas when Bowden left, so I didn't know if I really had a scholarship. But Jack Mitchell, a flamboyant kind of guy, took Bowden's place and sent George Cole down to Crossett to see me.

George, a great player and assistant coach who later became athletic director at Arkansas, took me out to the Wagon Wheel Cafe. After we ate our chicken-fried steak, he gave me his recruiting speech: "I'll tell you what, son. I'm going to give you a bed to sleep in and a plate to eat off of, and as long as you make your bed and behave yourself, I won't break your plate."

I thought that sounded really good. Recruiting is a hell of a lot different today.

Our Little Rock lawyers had just proved a legal error in Daddy's bootlegging sentence and got him released from the pen in time to see me take off for Fayetteville in the fall of 1955.

My scholarship was room, board, books, tuition, and fees, same as it is today. But in those days a player also was given $15 per month for laundry money—which is now forbidden—and with the free room and board, you could damn near live on $15 per month.

I packed my blue jeans and T-shirts in a cardboard Early Times whiskey box and headed for college.

They showed me my room at old Gregson Hall and pointed out a locker and said, "This is for your books."

I took that instruction literally in my freshman year. My books stayed in the locker. I was lonesome, homesick, and sort of confused.

Recently, I came across a tear-stained letter I wrote home soon after I arrived in Fayetteville:

> Hello Mom & Dad
>
> How is everything? I sure wish I was there. I didn't think I could get homesick, but I sure am. You ought to see me now. I haven't got a hair on my head. Boy! Is it miserable! I wish I had a picture I could send you. Daddy would get a kick out of it.
>
> When I got up here Sunday they stuck me $10 for a room. It's for breakage, but I'll get it back at the end of the year. That left me with $8, but it will last me a while.
>
> I hate football practice. There sure is a lot of good boys up here. I am playing behind an ex-Marine. I believe I could make first team at left guard, but I am playing right guard on the second team, but I hope to make the first team by our first game. That would be Oct. 6 at Texarkana with S.M.U. Excuse my writing, I know it's a mess.
>
> I'm scared to death up here. I feel just like Donnie does. There sure are some big boys up here. I don't know what I would do if Freddy and Chambers

weren't here. They say you will get used to it after a while. I hope so.

My room mate is from De Witt. He plays end. He's an old homesick country boy. We just started school yesterday and I'm already tired of it. You just don't know how I feel. I didn't think I would ever be like this.

There's a fullback from Oklahoma who might have to quit school and get married. Boy! Is he in a fix. He let me read the letter he got from the girl. He's a Dead Duck.

I was down in the dressing room yesterday when this guy asked me if I was Switzer. I told him yes, and he said he wanted me out for track after football season. He said he could have me putting the 16-pound shot 50 feet by the end of the season. Boy!

This getting up at 7 o'clock is ruff. I will be glad when I get to know everybody. I've got an English class about 20 minutes from now. I hope this is not too much paper to use for just one letter.

I guess I have to go now. I love you all a lot.

Barry Switzer
Box 224, Gregson Hall

The next year the football players moved out of Gregson Hall and down the hill to Wilson Sharpe House, a new athletic dorm that overlooked the stadium. Freshmen weren't eligible for varsity play in those days, and I was redshirted my sophomore year. By now I was beginning to understand I was in college to get an education. Kids will choose a college for all sorts of reasons, often the wrong ones. If you have a choice, there's really only reason to decide where you want to go to college—where do you want to get your education? Where do you want to live and make your home?

I was learning the University of Arkansas offered me a lot more than just football. I started hitting the books and eventually made the dean's list in the business department. But the university offered more than just books, too. I learned to express myself well in public, for one thing. I learned to be a leader and get along with people at the same time. I was elected president of Wilson Sharpe House (future University of Texas head coach Fred Akers, a gritty little halfback, was social chairman). I began to feel more secure and confident. All these things make up what I call an education. So much is learned that is not in the classrooms or in the books. My social experiences and maturing meant as much to me as my degree.

All you college players out there, listen to the old ex-coach. You need to get that degree, son. Somewhere down the road, they're going to let the air out of your ball . . .

Nobody owes you a degree. An athletic scholarship puts you in the position to get one, but you have to earn it for yourself.

It really makes me furious to read about the exploitation of the college athlete. In the academic sense, I mean.

It's true that college football players are exploited for financial gain, and I believe they should be paid by the university for their contribution. This is a complicated issue that is discussed later.

But every decent university wants its athletes to graduate and go on to a successful life. Like Prentice Gautt, the black fullback of 1956–1959, who got his doctorate and is now assistant commissioner of the Big Eight.

Football made it possible, but Prentice had to take advantage of it for himself.

I read all the time where some athlete played basketball or football and didn't get his degree and then didn't make it as a pro—and then some of the athletes, and sportswriters, bitch and gripe that the athlete was exploited because he wasn't given the degree he was promised when he went off to college.

Who the hell can promise you a degree?

I saw kids come to Oklahoma with low scores on their ACT tests and go on to get their degrees because they were motivated personally to do it. Billy Sims and Greg Pruitt are two who come to mind.

I saw other kids come to Oklahoma with no motivation other than to scrape through school for four years so they could turn pro.

But even those kids—black or white, from the ghetto, the

farm, or the country club—couldn't help but grow and benefit from the social and academic exposure.

Many people, including sportswriters, looked at me with the view that all I cared about was winning, that I ran a loose ship, that I didn't care about the kids who played for me. What a bunch of bullshit! Any coach who is worth a damn has compassion and love for his players and wants nothing but success for them. We have in our care the most important possessions a parent will ever have—their children. Why do we care? Because we all have children of our own and want nothing but the best for them wherever they may be.

But I learned at the University of Arkansas that if I wanted to go to the well, I had to carry my own bucket. Daddy had never carried it for me, and no football coach was going to, either; and by the 1957 season I was on my way to making the dean's list.

One of the most exciting days of my life came when I was playing as a redshirt sophomore in our game in Fayetteville against Bear Bryant's number-one-ranked Texas A&M.

Coach Bryant was already a legend in coaching. To us Arkansas kids, knowing he came from Fordyce and had once been just like us, it was awesome to see him leaning on the goalpost with his hat down over his eyes and a piece of grass in his mouth, watching his players, like John David Crow, warming up to kick our ass.

Like most of the players, I read the sports pages. I knew the mystique that built up around a big game like this.

We led them early and had them 6–0 with a missed extra point. I was in the ball game at linebacker and looked across the line at their Heisman Trophy winner, John David Crow. John David was 220 pounds, faster than most halfbacks, and I'm sure that tackling John David was a great deal like my players tackling Texas University's Earl Campbell.

From our 12-yard line John David ran a sweep around my side. Several of us hit him, but he knocked our butts down and stomped into the end zone. They went up 7–6 at the half.

We took the ball back to their 11-yard line but could go no further. Jack Mitchell decided to send in little Freddy Akers to make the kick. Freddy missed. Sorry to bring that up again, Freddy, but I'll make it up to you when we get to the 1959 T.C.U. game.

Late in the fourth quarter against the Aggies, something happened that became a famous story on the banquet circuit. You've no doubt heard it, but since I was on the field at the time, I'm going to tell it again.

They had the ball at midfield, leading 7–6, about to go into the four-down zone against us. I'm at linebacker, waiting for John David Crow to head my way again. But all of a sudden Roddy Osborne, their quarterback, sprints out to his left and throws a pass into the flat, a play I'm sure Coach Bryant didn't call.

Our cornerback, Donald Horton, intercepts the ball. Horton is running down the sideline right in front of our bench. The only one who's got an angle to catch him is Roddy Osborne, but Roddy is slow and Donald is fast. We are about to go in for the winning touchdown over the number-one team in the nation!

With some kind of superhuman effort, Roddy chases down Donald and knocks him out of bounds and we don't score. John David Crow, playing both ways, intercepted a pass in the end zone and prevented a fourth-down field-goal attempt from the 7-yard line.

After the game, sportswriters asked Roddy how he did it. How could a slow quarterback like him catch one of those fast Arkansas backs?

Roddy said, "He was just running for a touchdown. I was running for my life."

6

A FIELD OF DREAMS

It was a turning point in my life when Frank Broyles became head coach at Arkansas in 1958. Jack Mitchell quit and went to Kansas, and Frank left Missouri for his new home in Fayetteville. Thirty-one years later, Frank is still at Arkansas as athletic director and runs what I think is the best all-around athletic program in the country.

We lost our first six games in 1958. Frank was trying to run the Delaware Wing T, but we just couldn't execute it. Finally, we went back to the straight Wing T and Split T and gave the ball to Jim Mooty and ran north and south on people. We won our last four games.

So I was really looking forward to 1959, my senior season. I had played behind all-conference center Jay Donathan as a soph, and I started as a junior until I injured my shoulder in the fifth game. The substitution rules in those days were too complicated to bother to explain all these years later. They called for you to use two teams, each of which played both offense and defense when they were in the game. The second teams played about as much as the first. At L.S.U. they called their second unit the Chinese Bandits. At Arkansas we were the Wild Hogs.

As leader of the Wild Hogs in 1959, I was elected tri-captain with first-teamers' guard Billy Luplow and quarterback James Monroe.

Coach Broyles had figured out a substitution scheme using the "wild card," which would mean I would be playing nearly all the offense at center, and Wayne Harris, who became a two-time all-American, would play nearly all the defense at linebacker.

I spent the summer of 1959 before the season working during the day at the paper mill and spending most of the nights at the pool hall, playing dominoes or pool with Billy Joe Holder, my best friend. On weekends Billy Joe and I would most likely be found at Mud Lake or at Fish Trap Slough on the Ouachita River. But I was anxious for fall to arrive. Where once I had hated practice, now I was the first guy on the field. I couldn't wait for the start of two-a-days.

Things hadn't gotten any better around the house while I was off at college. We had electricity now and an electric pump that brought up water from the well. They had put in our first telephone. But with Mother and Daddy it was the same old story, only worse.

There was a bullet hole right in the heart of our Nu Grape clock, an advertising sign like you see in a cafe, but the clock was still keeping time. While Daddy and one of his best drinking pals, Pete Mizell, were sitting in Pete's new pickup, Daddy shot a hole through the windshield. They both thought it was funny.

Daddy's bootlegging and money lending businesses were doing well. He had been sending me $20 every week or two so I'd have some cash in my pocket. He'd go out in the yard and throw the 12-pound shot for the joy of it. He'd gotten his teeth fixed. He was a fine-looking man, very popular in the black community, where he strolled about giving dimes to little kids. But his life still revolved around drinking, gambling, and women. He was out every night doing whatever it was he did.

I don't know why Mother stayed with him. I really don't. They were two fine, handsome people, but together they were an absolute disaster.

Mother was a very beautiful, intelligent, demonstrative, loving person. She grew up in a strongly religious family. She loved her mother and her sisters and always kept in close contact with them.

Life with Daddy had to be a pure living hell for her.

One example of her hell, and all of our hells, really, came when I was a freshman at Arkansas in 1955. Mother and Daddy had just gotten a telephone, and one night (while Daddy was gone) Mother received a telephone call from a "friend" who told her where Daddy was with his girlfriend.

Mother, who was very intoxicated at the time, lost control, grabbed a .38 caliber Smith & Wesson revolver, and jumped into the only vehicle she had to drive, an old Jeep, and raced off to kill Daddy and his girlfriend.

Donnie was eleven at the time and in his own traumatic despair of the moment, not knowing who to call or what to do, found the only Bible in the house, dropped to his knees, and through his tears prayed that something would happen and Mother wouldn't get there. She didn't. The old Jeep broke down on the way to town.

But from that day forward, if Daddy was ever in the house, he never let Mother talk on the telephone without knowing who was on the other end of the line.

She went always deeper into the world of fiction, reading one novel after the other. She would fall into periods of heavy depression. To come out of it, she would get her barbiturate prescriptions refilled and have a few drinks. Pretty soon this glaze would come over her eyes and she would have this sort of gentle, confused smile on her face and her tongue would get a little thick. She'd sit in her favorite chair and read her novels, never leaving the house but lost somewhere in her imagination, the pills and the booze inside working on her, and she'd smile as though she wasn't really living this horrible life.

It tore me up to see her that way.

Donnie was fifteen that summer, just starting into his football and track career at Crossett High. He could go hand over hand up a 25-foot rope hanging from a big oak tree faster than Daddy could. Donnie didn't really like football, but he had to play because he was my little brother, and he made all-district playing fullback and inside linebacker before he eventually gave up Crossett and went off to Dartmouth.

So Donnie was still living at home. He saw Mother and Daddy as they daily grew farther apart. He told me that summer he couldn't understand how two people so different had ever come to get married.

On August 26, 1959, Mother was in El Dorado with her sister, Newell Hammond. Mother asked my friend Jim Mooty to drive her to the drugstore, and then she came home to Crossett with Mamma and two of my little cousins. I didn't realize this until later, but as it turned out she had gathered those she loved the most around her—her mother, Lillie Wood (our Mamma), our cousins Jamie and Gary Hammond. Donnie and me. As usual, Daddy was gone someplace.

That night I went to bed in the front bedroom and was lying there with the electric fan blowing the mosquitoes off me. I hadn't turned out the light yet. Mother came in and sat on the bed. I didn't totally understand the hell she was living through. I was too young to know how really desperate her everyday life was. Like her, I had my own world. She loved me and she needed my love so much, but as I looked at her sitting there on the bed kind of glassy and smiling, loaded on prescription drugs and booze, something broke inside me and I said things to her I will always regret.

I said, "Mother, I would rather not ever see you again, and know you are safe and well taken care of, than to see you like this all the time."

She leaned over to kiss me.

I turned my head away.

She looked at me and got up and went to the closet and took out a pistol. I don't know why I didn't jump up and take the gun from her. She walked out of my room and started toward the back porch. I don't know why I didn't call out for her to come back.

I heard the shot.

I leaped out of bed and ran down the hall and saw her body on the back porch. I picked her up and carried her into the house and laid her in her bed. I didn't know what to do, so I phoned Uncle Billy Switzer and told him what had happened. He called the sheriff and the coroner and got to the house a few minutes before the ambulance.

I was in total shock. I felt like I was the one who had caused her to pull the trigger. All she wanted was my love, and I had turned my face away. I have carried this guilt with me the rest of my life. Professional people, psychiatrists, have told me I was not to blame, that she had made up her mind to do it and the right time had presented itself, but still I've never been able to forget turning my face away.

But finally, after over twenty years, Donnie and I found the ability to talk to one another about what had happened that night. I found out he had been living with the same sort of guilt as I had, because mother had also been to see him that night, and he had reacted to her drunkenness in much the same way that I had. I also found out that she had left a suicide note.

Several weeks after she died, Donnie opened the little case she kept her hair curlers in. For some reason he reached into the back pocket inside the case and pulled out a piece of paper that in effect stayed a secret between Daddy and Donnie for a long time. Mother's suicide had hurt Donnie and me terribly, and it was just something that he and I had a hard time talking about.

Mother had written, "Dear Frank . . . You can't imagine how hard it is, and how much courage it takes to do this. My one request is please don't let Jewel see me."

Jewel was Daddy's girlfriend.

We buried Mother two days later in El Dorado. She had wanted to be buried beside her father, but there was only one lot left and that was for her mother, Mamma Lillie. So we put Mother as close as we could, across the little road in the peaceful cemetery at El Dorado. There she found a place to rest at last.

7

HELLO, ROMANCE

A few weeks later, Jim Mooty and I were walking across the campus in Fayetteville when a really cute young girl stopped us and asked if we knew the way to the law library.

Before Mooty could answer, I took her arm and said, "Sure I do, little girl. Come with me. I'll show you."

Jim was a handsome guy who was following his destiny by having an all-American season at halfback. He was my pal. But I wasn't about to let him have first shot at this girl, even if he was married. There was something about her that shined like a light, something electric in her personality. Walking to the law library, I introduced myself. The name meant nothing to her. She smiled and said she was Kay McCollum, a freshman from Stuttgart, Arkansas. She was going to major in math. It didn't sound likely that I would have much to talk about with a math major, but I invited her to go out for a Coca-Cola sometime.

The next time I saw her was in the auditorium when they were selecting the homecoming queen and her court. As a freshman, Kay wasn't eligible for queen, but she was eligible to be a maid in the queen's court, and I told the guys on the football team to vote for number 7. Kay would have won without me, I'm sure—she went on to become the feature twirler for the Razorback band—but I climbed on stage right after the election and told her it was the moment to go get that Coke now. We started dating.

On October 3, our ball club was unbeaten and Texas Christian came to Fayetteville on a cold, rainy, miserable Saturday. T.C.U. was defending conference champion. The

Frogs had strong teams in that period under Coach Abe Martin. I remember watching them warm up and wondering
where they found these monsters. Their fullback, Jack Spikes,
was bigger than any of our linemen. They had two future
pro stars—Bob Lilly (246 pounds) and Don Floyd (220)—at
tackles.

Our strengths were our speed and quickness, and the
field was turning into slop.

In the second quarter we recovered a fumble at their 40
and drove it down to their 10, where they held us. On fourth
down in a steadily pouring rain, into the game came little
Freddy Akers. I snapped the ball to the kneeling Jim Monroe
at the 18, he placed it nose down in the mud, and Fred kicked
a 28-yard field goal to put us ahead 3–0.

Not only was Fred's kick the only score of the day, it eventually put us into a three-way tie with Texas and T.C.U. for
the Southwest Conference championship.

Coached by Darrell Royal and ranked third in the nation,
Texas beat us 13–12 at War Memorial Stadium in Little Rock
before a crowd of 40,000, the most people that had ever seen
a game in Arkansas. I remember the Texas quarterback,
Bobby Lackey, had a hell of a day and kicked the winning
extra point, but it was a dinky little pitchout pass from Bart
Shirley three yards into the end zone to Jack Collins for the
touchdown that put them ahead to stay. Then T.C.U. beat
Texas, to cause the SWC tie. Texas went to the Cotton Bowl,
T.C.U. to the Bluebonnet Bowl, and we went to the Gator
Bowl, where we gave Georgia Tech its first bowl defeat in
seven trips under Coach Bobby Dodd—a very big win for
Coach Broyles, who had played quarterback at Georgia Tech
for Dodd.

The town of Crossett threw me a Barry Switzer Appreciation Banquet at the Rose Inn on January 26. Two hundred
people paid $1.75 per ticket to show up for speeches by Coach
Broyles and the dean of Arkansas sportswriters, Orville
Henry, of *The Gazette.* Billy Jack Edwards, a friend and the
best pool player in Crossett, presented me a personalized engraved case with a $1,000 U.S. savings bond inside. From the
dais I looked out and saw Daddy in the audience and knew
how proud he was of me. The bootlegger's boy was doing all

right. (Thirty years later, Otha Armstrong III told the Norman police that he had thrown that case into the Canadian River.)

In my acceptance speech I said I hoped to follow Coach Broyles's example and go into coaching.

But I didn't really know if I would ever have the opportunity. I was going to get my business degree in the spring and had started thinking I might go on to law school or move to Little Rock and get into business of some kind.

In the fall of 1960 I was still hanging around the campus, dating Kay and helping coach the freshman football team while I waited for my call into military service. There were all sorts of ways you could join the military reserves in those days to get out of the draft, but you always had to go on active duty sooner or later.

Kay's dad, Slick McCollum, was a farmer who owned a hunting club at Stuttgart. It was two thousand acres of pin oak flats and the best duck hunting in the world. People like Ted Williams went there to hunt. Kay was the oldest of three daughters. Her mother had died, and she had more or less grown up as the mistress of the place. The first time I went to Stuttgart, I found her driving a Minneapolis Molene tractor. Kay was a tomboy and a hell of an athlete. If you don't think it requires superior athletic skill to toss a twirling baton thirty feet in the air and catch it while you're tumbling and doing a split, just try it sometime. To this day, Kay can make music on a duck caller that brings wild ducks diving out of the clouds like they're zooming in for a duck mating party. She should be good—Slick, her dad, was the 1939 world champion duck caller. This is a contest they still have every year in Stuttgart.

After the Razorbacks had again won the championship in 1960, I was summoned to active duty at Fort Leonard Wood, Missouri, for basic training and then sent to Aberdeen, Maryland, supposedly for six months.

That summer I was in my barracks when I heard the loudspeakers saying, "Private Switzer, report to company headquarters."

It was Dixie White on the phone. "Hey, Barry," he said. "Coach Broyles has just had a staff meeting and wants to know if you'll come back here and join us as a full-time assistant."

The minute I hung up, I started writing letters to Congressman Wilbur Mills and all of Uncle Billy's associates and everybody else I could think of who might be able to pull some strings.

Sure enough, I got released from service just in time to join the Razorbacks for two-a-days in 1961. I was now officially a football coach, living in Wilson Sharpe House again. In fact, I lived in the athletic dorm at Arkansas for nine years.

Kay and I had become a steady romance. I'd go by to pick her up after class and she'd be in a room with eighteen guys studying calculus. On Saturdays, she was the star of halftime with her incredible feats with the baton. It turned out we found plenty to talk about besides math. After she received her degree in 1963, we got married and set up house and started playing grownup, as much as a football coach and his wife ever can.

I was lucky to start into coaching surrounded by some of the finest minds in the game.

See, Arkansas has long had a Tennessee connection that began when John Barnhill left General Bob Neyland's staff in Knoxville and coached the Razorbacks to a SWC title. Barnhill then became athletic director and started hiring a procession of great coaches—Bowden Wyatt, Jack Mitchell, and the master, Frank Broyles.

Barnhill laid out to every coach General Neyland's Four Maxims of Football:

1. If you throw a forward pass three things can happen, and two of them are bad.
2. Defense wins championships.
3. The kicking game and field position are vital.
4. Better you die a baby than fumble that football.

On our staff we had Broyles, Jim MacKenzie, Doug Dickey, Johnny Majors, Wilson Matthews, Bill Pace, Dixie White, Merv Johnson, Hayden Fry, and Merrill Green. These were my teachers as a young coach. At first I kind of had an inferiority complex. I felt like, Well, I'm not as smart as these other coaches—but I'm learning. Before long, I would go to coaching clinics around the country and my eyes would pop open when I heard other coaches speak. After a while, I began to think, Hell, I know as much about football as this guy at the microphone. If he can be a head coach, I can be, too.

I started thinking about becoming a head coach and preparing myself for the responsibilities you must assume as the focal point of an institution. But I knew I had to wait for the right job to come along. I didn't want to be a head coach just to be a head coach. Some guys have such egos that they think they can go to a perennial loser and turn it into a winner just by their brains and charm and hard work. I never had that delusion. I knew it wasn't my X's and O's on the blackboard that would win championships as much as it was the players represented by those X's and O's. I wanted to go to someplace where I would have a chance to win when I became head coach. And those jobs didn't open very often, so I wasn't in a hurry.

Meanwhile, we had a winning tradition right there in Fayetteville.

I didn't hurt it any in 1963 when I started recruiting West Texas. Arkansas had never recruited in West Texas before, and that year I signed three blue-chippers from the area, kids who probably would have gone to Texas or Oklahoma.

Let me mention here that I lost one of the first recruits I went after. He made the all-district team playing fullback, guard, and linebacker and was state shotput and discus champion from Crossett, and since he was my brother, everybody expected me to sign him. Instead, Daddy and I wound up putting Donnie on a train to Hanover, New Hampshire, with his belongings packed in an Early Times whiskey box like the one I had gone off to school with.

In 1964 and 1965, Arkansas won twenty-two games in a row and two Southwest Conference championships. Our 1964 team beat defending national champion Texas in a 14–13 classic, defeated Nebraska in the Cotton Bowl, and won the Mac-Arthur Bowl Trophy with an 11–0 record as the best team in the country—the only national title in Arkansas football history.

We had three players on that 1964 team that you read a lot about today. One was a little halfback named Ken Hatfield, who did coach at Arkansas, but is now the head coach at

Clemson. Another was a 200-pound guard named Jerry Jones, who got rich and bought the Dallas Cowboys. The third was Jimmy Johnson, who now coaches the Cowboys with the security of a ten-year contract bestowed by his old teammate and roomie. After this happened, I called my old college roomie from Blytheville, Arkansas, Billy Gilbow, and asked him why he wasn't rich enough to buy me a pro team. His retort was, "What the hell makes you think I'd consider you anyway?"

Maybe if I'd known then what grief Jimmy Johnson was going to cause me, I would have run him off the squad and seen to it that he become a railroad engineer or a landscape artist—anything but a football coach. But I had no way to know Jimmy would be head coach of the Miami Hurricanes during the 1985–87 period, when Oklahoma was 30–0 against the rest of the world but 0–3 against Miami. By the way, these were the three years Banowsky wanted to buy up.

It's amazing how "smart" Jimmy got when he went to Miami. He was 0–5 against me when he was head coach at Oklahoma State. But maybe he really didn't get any smarter; maybe he just had more players who were better, which is what it's all about anyway.

Jerry Jones, by the way, owes me an automobile.

Wilson Sharpe House sits up high above the stadium. The parking lot had some little logs that helped keep cars from rolling down the hill. One night I parked my old 1955 turquoise-blue Ford Fairlane in the lot with my standard-shift gear in reverse and the emergency brake pulled. The next morning people came into my room and said, "Barry, you had better come see your car."

There was my Ford about fifty yards down the hill, centered dead smack against a tree. If it hadn't hit that tree, my car would have been in the middle of the stadium.

I thought someone had done it on purpose. It was a very unfunny joke. If I could have found out who did it, I would have strangled him.

Years later Jerry Jones confessed it was him but that it wasn't meant as a joke. Jerry had come out of the dorm that night to borrow someone else's car that looked similar to mine. He got into my car by mistake, put it into gear, released the emergency brake—and discovered the key wouldn't fit the ignition. Jerry got out of my car to look around. The damn car started rolling, gained speed, jumped the log, and headed downhill fast, straight into the only tree it could have hit before it reached the end zone.

Jerry was scared to tell me at the time, and I don't blame him.

But, Jerry, when you finally do save up enough money to replace my car, don't bust yourself on something fancy. An old 1955 Ford will do nicely, as long as it's a mint-condition Thunderbird.

Of all the assistant coaches at Arkansas, I felt the closest to Jim MacKenzie. Jim was in charge of defense and was assistant head coach for Frank Broyles. He had played tackle for Bear Bryant's Kentucky team that beat Oklahoma's 1950 national champions in the Sugar Bowl. He used to tell me stories about playing in the years immediately following World War II, when there were hardly any eligibility rules. Players would travel coast to coast the year round, working out with different schools. You'd look around, Jim said, and see two hundred tackles on the field competing for your spot. In the dorm you'd hear these wise old war veterans saying, "This place ain't so hot, they treat you a lot better over at such and such school. I'm going to transfer." But the veteran didn't really intend to transfer, he was just trying to talk the other guys into leaving.

I was offered an assistant coaching job at Tennessee when Doug Dickey was hired there, but Coach Broyles gave me a raise and a promotion to stay. I wasn't serious about leaving Arkansas then, anyhow. I knew it wouldn't be long before Jim MacKenzie was offered a head job someplace and I had decided to follow Jim wherever he went.

In 1965 Arkansas went undefeated until we were upset by L.S.U. in the Cotton Bowl. Oklahoma fell to a 3–7 record that year, which meant Gomer Jones was out as head coach. Oklahoma offered the job first to the former Sooner all-American Darrell Royal, who had won a national championship in 1963 at Texas. Darrell turned them down, and then Vince Dooley and Doug Dickey, who had been mentioned in the press as being candidates, said they weren't interested.

Our Arkansas team was in San Antonio preparing for the Cotton Bowl when Jim got a call to come to Oklahoma and be interviewed by the president, Dr. George Cross, and the regents.

Jim crawled on board one of those old DC-3 puddle jumpers to fly to Oklahoma City. He fell asleep and snored right through the stop in Oklahoma City. He woke up hearing the stewardess announce they were landing in Denver. Jim ran off the plane thinking, Oh my God, I've blown the job. He phoned Dr. Cross and the regents, who were waiting for him in Norman. Instead of telling him they'd drawn a line through his name, they laughed at his mishap and told him to come on to Norman. Jim did a great interview. He was offered the Oklahoma job the day before Christmas.

We were back in Fayetteville by then, planning to go down to Dallas and the Cotton Bowl after the holiday. Christmas afternoon, Jim came over to the house and talked to Kay and me for hours. He wanted us to go to Norman with him. I went to Coach Broyles to let him know I had decided to leave. He gave me his blessing and assured me it was the right career decision.

On January 3, 1966, I flew on a DC-3 to Oklahoma City, and Jim met me at the old Will Rogers Airport.

I became a Sooner for the next twenty-three years.

8

THE FOUNDATION IS LAID

In Jim MacKenzie's first and only season at Oklahoma, we beat Texas for the first time in ten years and knocked off Nebraska in a major upset, on national television, in Norman.

We finished with a 6–4 record. Three of our losses were by a total of seven points. Notre Dame was the only team that kicked us around, and that was a case of men against boys. Notre Dame put a team of future pro stars like Alan Page and Jim Lynch on the field and just totally snuffed us out, 38–0.

But what we really accomplished in the fall of 1966 and the spring of 1967 was laying the foundation to make Oklahoma football a national power again.

We did this in two ways:

1. We started aggressively recruiting blacks at every position.

2. We launched an all-out recruiting war in Texas.

Further along in this book I will guide you into the alleys and gutters of the recruiting "jungle."

But for now, let me remind you that many black athletes from Texas had a great deal to do with our success for the next twenty years. I could name at least a hundred right now without straining, but how about Greg Pruitt, Joe Washington, and Billy Sims for starters?

Of course, we got our share of great *white* athletes from south of the Red River, too. Foremost would have to be Jack Mildren, the quarterback I recruited from Abilene. Jack would become known as the father of the Oklahoma Wishbone—and we would produce what was unquestionably the most explosive offense in the history of college football. We had track meets on people. We would say, Okay, guys, let's go hang half a hundred on them today—meaning fifty points or more—and we did it thirty-two times while I was at Oklahoma.

We also had twenty all-Americans, black and white, from the state of Texas.

One Hang 50 that might have been a mistake for me personally was when we ran up and down the field like a fast-break basketball team against Texas in 1973 and pounded the Longhorns 52–13 using the Wishbone offense, which Darrell Royal and his staff invented.

But that wasn't me out there running with the football for Oklahoma. It was a backfield of former Texas high school all-stars.

On April 26, 1967, in the middle of spring practice, Jim MacKenzie stopped by my office. I had been offensive-line coach in 1966, but I had wanted to move to defense. Jim had promised that I could move to defense after one year. Having played and been trained as a lineman, with no experience as a backfield coach or quarterback coach, defense was the right place for me to go at the time. To have a chance to be a head coach, I needed to be put in charge of some phase of the game—to put my mark on it. Defense appeared to be the best shot. Jim understood that.

"I'm leaving for the airport in a few minutes," he said. "I'm going to get us a quarterback. Don't run anyone off while I'm gone."

Of course at the time I didn't know those would be the last words he would ever speak to me.

Jim was flying to Amarillo to recruit a quarterback from Tascosa High named Monty Johnson. This was in the days when there was no national letter of intent, and recruiting went on all spring.

About two o'clock the next morning, the phone rang at our home. From the look on Kay's face and the tone of her voice, I knew something terrible had happened. The first thought that flashed through my mind was, Daddy is dead.

Then I heard Kay mention Jim, and I thought of a plane crash.

She handed me the phone. It was Ken Rawlinson, who had been the Oklahoma trainer for more than twenty years.

Jim had come back to Norman about midnight. He went home and sat in the living room talking to his wife, Sue. Jim told her he was tired and not feeling well. He got up and walked into the bathroom. After he was gone a while, their daughter went to see if anything was wrong. Jim was sprawled on the bathroom floor.

Sue sent Kathy, their daughter, across the street to wake up Galen Hall, our receiver coach. They phoned an ambulance, and Galen gave mouth-to-mouth to Jim until the medics arrived. Jim was already blue and cool, and Galen knew he was gone, but he couldn't quit because Sue and their daughter, Kathy, and son, Alex, were watching and praying for Jim to be all right.

Pat James came by to pick me up, and we picked up Chuck Fairbanks, and the three of us drove to the hospital, not knowing Jim's condition yet.

The hospital looked deserted. An attendant recognized us and said we were too late. Jim's body had been removed to the mortuary. He was dead of a massive coronary.

The next day we flew in a private airplane with Jim's body to his hometown, Gary, Indiana. We coaches were his pall-bearers.

The night before the funeral, we were at the motel in Gary when Chuck Fairbanks got a call from Dr. George Cross, Oklahoma president.

Jim's death had obviously been a tremendous jolt to the Oklahoma football program and everyone connected with it. We weren't thinking football that night, but there's no denying it was on everybody's mind when Dr. Cross phoned.

Dr. Cross told Chuck that he would be named head coach in a few days, nobody's position was in jeopardy, and we should continue our program as is.

I'm sure Pat James was disappointed. He had been assistant head coach, was a very close friend and old teammate of Jim's, and everyone liked and respected him. Chuck was our defensive backfield coach and highly respected. It was a close call between them.

I heard some regents had wanted to offer the job to Darrell Royal again—and maybe they did sound him out, I don't know—but he had just turned them down a year ago, and besides, we had such a solid program started that even the regents could feel it.

After we returned to Norman from the funeral, Chuck called me in and told me he wanted me back on offense, coaching the backs.

In the 1967 season we set the proof on the table that Oklahoma had returned to the game big-time.

We had several of the type of players I call difference makers.

Granville Liggins, our nose guard from Tulsa, was on his way to his second all-America team. Wingback Eddie Hinton didn't make all-America, but he was the number-one draft choice of the world-champion Baltimore Colts.

And that was the first varsity season for Steve Owens, from Miami, Oklahoma. Talk about a difference maker. The I formation was invented for big backs like Steve. He led the conference in rushing and scoring for three straight years and won the Heisman Trophy as a senior.

I'll always remember Steve's last game for us. It was against Oklahoma State, a very big game for in-state recruiting influence. We were playing in Stillwater. Late in the fourth quarter, Oklahoma State was up by a touchdown and took the ball down to our goal line before we held. Now we had to drive the length of the field to win the game.

We ran Steve Owens off tackle seven times in a row and moved out to midfield. All of a sudden, Jack Mildren stepped out of our huddle, called time-out, and walked to the sidelines.

As offensive coach, I was up in the press box. I didn't want to stop the clock. Their defense was dead tired. I yelled for them to put Jack on the headset.

"Jack, why the hell did you call time out?" I asked.

"I didn't, coach. Steve told me to call time-out. He says he needs a rest to get his breath, because he knows he's going to carry the ball the next seven plays, too."

I said, "Well, I'll tell you what. You go inform that big stud he ain't supposed to get tired. Tell him to saddle up because he *is* going to run the ball the next seven plays, and we're not going to a bowl, so he can rest all spring."

Steve carried it six more times, crashed into the end zone,

and we won 28–27. Steve carried the ball fifty-five times that day. It's still an Oklahoma record.

But back to 1967. The only game we lost was 9–7 to Texas. We won the Big Eight, beat Tennessee in the Orange Bowl, and finished 10–1 and second in both polls.

Oklahoma had returned.

We fell off to "losing" seasons of 7–4 and 6–4 the next two years. It was an incredible mixture of elation and despair on the field. But we were stocking our pantry with quality recruits, and it was only a matter of time until the Sooners would be on top as a regular thing—the question was, Would our regents give us the time?

When Steve Owens graduated in 1970, Chuck Fairbanks scrapped the I formation and changed our offense to the Veer that Bill Yeoman was running down in Houston.

The Houston Veer was a good rushing offense. But it was a two back offense that relied on the quarterback being able to throw the ball to the tight end if it was going to be successful against good teams. The Veer was a triple-option offense, but—unlike the Wishbone—it wouldn't work consistently without the threat of the pass.

We beat S.M.U. and Wisconsin to open the 1970 season. But then—what a disaster—we lost to Oregon State. Oklahoma fans took this as a major embarrassment. You could almost hear our Oilys howling to load the entire coaching staff on the first boxcar heading to the Yukon.

We had a week off before our next game, which would be against Texas.

I had watched people try to stop Darrell's Wishbone for the last couple of years. Nobody could do it. In 1968 Texas was 9–1–1, won the SWC, and beat Tennessee in the Cotton Bowl. In 1969 Texas went 11–0 and beat Notre Dame in the Cotton Bowl to become national champions. So far in 1970, Texas had won three straight and scored 116 points.

It seemed to me that we should be running the Wishbone, too.

Just like Bud Wilkinson's teams had dominated football with the Split T in the 1950s, I believed we could do the same thing with the Wishbone in the 1970s.

In the Wishbone, the fullback lines up a step behind the

quarterback. The halfbacks are another step back on either side of the fullback, giving it the look of a chicken's wishbone. I've heard that a junior-high coach in Fort Worth, Spud Cason, invented the formation in an effort to get a slow fullback into the play quicker. But it was Emory Bellard as offensive coach for Darrell Royal who took the alignment and added the triple option that made it almost unstoppable . . . if you had the right people to run it.

Quarterback was the key. The quarterback took the snap and either handed the ball to the fullback immediately or else took off down the line and kept it or pitched it to a halfback, depending on the reaction of the defense and how he read it. Texas had the quick, heady James Street to run their Wishbone.

And we had Jack Mildren, who was sort of lost in the Veer but was born to run the Wishbone. Plus, we had the speed at halfback in two more Texans—Greg Pruitt and also Joe Wylie, a white kid from Henderson, Texas, who was split high and ran a 9.5 hundred.

During our week off before the Texas game, Pat James and I studied Texas running the Wishbone on films. People didn't even know how to line up against them. I said, "Pat, this is what we ought to be doing."

I met with the other assistant coaches on both offense and defense and asked what they thought about us changing to the Wishbone.

I didn't mean next season.

I meant today.

The other coaches said it would be an interesting experiment, all right, and it might even work. But didn't I think I better ask Chuck Fairbanks about it first? "Yes, of course. But I first wanted to make sure I had your support."

Chuck was kind of depressed. CHUCK CHUCK bumper stickers were beginning to appear around the state. He was about ready to listen to any damn fool thing—including changing our whole offense in the few days before playing one of the two teams any Oklahoma head coach had rather beat. Chuck was reluctant to copy anything from Darrell, but he promised to sleep on it.

The next day Chuck gathered the staff and said, Well,

hell, let's give it a shot. Nothing much depended on it except our futures.

I would like to report here that we went into Dallas and dazzled Texas with our new Oklahoma Wishbone and every Sooner in the land greeted us with joy and celebration.

But the fact is, our Wishbone didn't impress Texas a bit. Their defense played against a much better Wishbone in practice every day than we showed them in Dallas.

They whipped us 41–9 on their way to their second national championship in a row.

Instead of greeting us with joy and celebration, our fans organized CHUCK CHUCK parties in their homes.

The newspapers practically demanded that we commit suicide.

Our wealthy Oilys—especially the many who'd taken their Oklahoma geology and petroleum-engineering degrees into the Texas oil fields to get rich—were ashamed to go into the men's grill at their country clubs.

The funny thing about it is, I felt good. We had moved the ball against a great Texas defense in our first try at the Wishbone. If we only had a few more weeks, we could really put some speed into this machine.

But with Colorado coming up Saturday, we all figured we were going to get fired.

Since there were CHUCK CHUCK parties around town already, we decided to have a party of our own and name it the BEAT COLORADO party.

Jimmy Johnson had been hired out of Clemson as our defensive line coach. My old Arkansas buddy Larry Lacewell had joined our staff as a defensive assistant. Larry is a hell of a defensive coach and recruiter, and he has a wild streak in him that is liable to burst out after a few cocktails. He is as entertaining a person as you'll ever meet.

Larry and Jimmy and Gene Hochevar came over to my house, and we were going to have a BEAT COLORADO party, and we didn't give a damn.

We sloshed back a number of social beverages and then summoned our wives to go open the closets.

We had decided to play costumes. The men would dress up in their wives' clothes and the women would dress up in their husbands' clothes, and then all four couples would go around to each coach's house and demand that at least one spouse get dressed in drag and accompany us to the next house.

It sounded like a hell of an idea at the time—which was Thursday night, about forty-eight hours before we figured to get fired.

I mean we put the bras on and the panties and hose and high heels and wigs. And dresses, of course. You should have seen Jimmy Johnson. He wore the biggest set of boobies this side of Las Vegas. Jimmy, I've still got the pictures.

At every house we went to, we were invited in for drinks. Every coach and every wife decided to dress up and join us.

Pretty late at night there were about twenty of us in three or four cars on the road to Chuck's house. Norman's not that big a town, but I guess nobody recognized us—or if they did, they thought they'd lost their minds.

Chuck was asleep when we knocked on the door.

You will have to imagine the expression on his face when we barged in shouting, "BEAT COLORADO!"

But what the hell, Chuck got up and put on a bra and a wig and a dress and joined right in. We took Polaroid pictures and laughed our asses off. Word was going around, and some friends of our program began showing up in drag; not many people, but the few who still believed in us.

The press has always portrayed me as a party animal, and I admit that I did go through a period when every weekend all of the coaches and friends would gather at my house for a party. But even though those days are long gone, I do still claim to have impeccable judgment on parties of the past.

That BEAT COLORADO party set every known NCAA record for coaches and their wives in drag.

Jimmy Johnson and Gene Hochevar, without their wives, drove home together about dawn, with their wigs on, all dressed up.

They halted at a stop light on Lindsey Street. Two rednecks wearing baseball caps pulled up beside them in a pickup truck. The old redneck rolled down his window and said, "Hey, babies. Where you all headed?"

Johnson had his window up and wasn't paying attention.

The old redneck yelled louder and honked. "Hey, honey! Hey, baby! You all looking to have a little fun?"

Jimmy opened his window and leaned out and glared at the rednecks and said, "Go fuck yourself."

Scared the hell out of the rednecks. They laid rubber half a mile down the street. Johnson was laughing.

"You know, this ain't too damn funny," Gene said. "What if that had been a police car? You like to see tomorrow's headlines say OKLAHOMA COACHES DRAG QUEENS?"

We flew up to Boulder that afternoon, and on Saturday we beat Colorado 23–15. We were still pretty rough at handling the Wishbone, but we looked like a damn good football team.

Next thing you know, we had won three more conference games and were playing Nebraska in Lincoln for the Big Eight title. They beat us 28–21 in the fourth quarter and were named national champs in one poll.

We were invited to play Alabama in the Bluebonnet Bowl. Our Wishbone brought us back and tied the game 24–24. Coach Bryant had been running a split back offense, pro sets, throwing the ball. But he had been watching his friend Darrell Royal roll over everybody with the Wishbone, and now he saw our Wishbone move the ball against his defense.

For the next season, 1971, Bryant changed to the Wishbone. Before long there were three football teams in the country running track meets on everybody—Texas, Oklahoma, and Alabama.

That was the season, 1971, when Oklahoma was statistically the best offensive team in the history of the game. Oklahoma and Alabama would be the only two teams to win over a hundred games during the decade of the seventies.

9

THE TRACK MEETS BEGIN

Having spent our whole lives in the pine forests, marshes, and mountains of Arkansas, it was quite an adjustment for Kay and me to move to the plains of Norman.

Luckily for me, I was drinking coffee in a cafe one day and heard a fellow talking about hunting and fishing. The longer I listened, the more I realized he had a lot to teach me. I introduced myself to him and appointed him the official Oklahoma hunting and fishing coach, promised him a regular coaching outfit with a cap and a whistle.

Bobby Bell immediately took me fishing, and we've been friends and frequent companions ever since.

In the spring and summer of 1971, if I wasn't gone recruiting or working at spring practice or sitting at a projector studying Wishbone films, I was somewhere fishing with Bobby. This made it kind of tough on Kay, who had to stay home with the babies, but she tolerated me pretty well.

I turned down golf games that summer. The Wishbone had me obsessed.

I really believe that back in the 1950s, and maybe the early 1960s, there were coaches who could consistently out-coach other coaches and win ball games by their superior knowledge. Bud Wilkinson and Bear Bryant were probably the last two who could do it.

By the 1970s there were so many good coaches who were products of winning systems and had sound philosophies, who knew what it takes to win, that no coach could really ever out-smart everybody.

The magic was in the players.

All summer I worked on our offense, getting it refined and coordinated so I could teach our rules of execution to our players.

The Wishbone is easy to teach. You can spend all your time on the running game and very little on passing. Your linemen did not have to be the superior talent that it took, say, to hold a block an extra second for an I formation tailback to reach the hole from 7 or 8 yards deep. Your Wishbone fullback being so close and quick-hitting, things happened fast. The blocking took finesse, but it was done in an instant.

Most big plays in football basically come on the corners of defenses. With the fullback hitting the middle every down to keep the defense honest, it comes to the ability of your triple-option quarterback to attack the corners with one of the most dangerous plays of all time—the pitchout to a halfback with startling speed with a lead blocker, or the quarterback keeping with a lead blocker.

So we had the offensive philosophy, and we had the players to fit it.

We beat S.M.U. by 30, Hung 50 on Pitt, and put 33 on the board against USC to win our first three games. Southern Cal was ranked fifth in the nation, and we set an all-opponent record against them—516 yards rushing and zero yards passing.

That brought us to the Wishbone rematch against Texas.

The Longhorns were ranked third in the nation. We lined up a backfield of Jack Mildren from Abilene, long hair hanging down his neck; tough fullback Leon Crosswhite from Hennessey, Oklahoma; Joe Wylie, a top blue-chipper from Henderson, Texas, at one halfback, and at the other halfback, Greg Pruitt from Houston, a little black kid Texas didn't even try to recruit. And really, they didn't even know about him, because in those days Texas recruiters wouldn't even walk into an all-black high school.

I don't remember Texas having a black player on the field that day.

Greg Pruitt carried the ball twenty times for 216 yards and three touchdowns, we rushed for 435, and beat Texas 48–27. It was only the *second time Oklahoma had beaten Texas in fifteen years.* Darrell remarked after the game, "Oklahoma looked like they were running downhill all day."

We couldn't stop their Wishbone, but they sure as hell couldn't stop ours. Looking at the talent on the field that day, it was clear to me that we had become the better team in one year. In fact beginning with that game in 1971, we didn't lose to Texas for six straight years.

The Oilys who had wanted to CHUCK CHUCK after the 1970 Texas game now wanted him to come to the club for dinner.

Most of our games that season were over by the second series of downs.

We didn't know how people would line up against us until our first series. They would try trick defenses to halt our Wishbone, and the tricks wouldn't work. Then they'd go to their basic defenses and we'd look at how they were lined up, and we'd know, well, we're going to get half a hundred today. Out at the corners we would have them outmanned, attacking with a ratio of three on two and two on one and one on none, always in our favor.

I know you keep hearing the TV commentators putting the knock on the Wishbone by saying it is not a good catch-up offense because you're not out there to throw long passes all day.

But the Wishbone is the greatest passing offense there is if the offense is strong enough to control the down and distance. If it is first and ten, second and five, or third and two, the offense is in control. Just don't let the defense put you into long yardage situations where you have to get into foreign formations, and the Wishbone is capable of catching you up fast with play action passes and breakaways up the middle. We came from behind to beat good teams like Nebraska several times—and Nebraska is as strong a test as you can find year in and year out.

When we met Nebraska in 1971, the media was calling it the Game of the Century.

It was Thanksgiving Day, on national TV. Nebraska was number one in the nation, and we were ranked second. Johnny Rodgers, future Heisman Trophy winner, scored on a 72-yard punt return and they led us 14–3. But Jack Mildren passed us to a 17–14 lead at the half. Nebraska went up 28–17. We came back and scored with five minutes left and led 31–28. With everybody going crazy and 38 seconds to play, Nebraska scored and beat us 35–31—and laid claim to their second straight national championship.

But Nebraska still had to play unbeaten Alabama in the Orange Bowl. We faced Auburn, ranked fourth in the nation, with their quarterback Pat Sullivan, who won the Heisman Trophy that year, in the Sugar Bowl at old Tulane Stadium.

The Sugar Bowl was in the afternoon. At the half we led Auburn 31–0 and knew we could Hang 50 on them if we wanted. We played our reserves the second half, won 40–22.

To win a national championship, you always have to have help. Somebody's got to knock off somebody. There was nobody left to knock off that would help us. Nebraska dominated Alabama and finished first in the nation, with us second.

Jack Mildren rushed for 1,140 yards, passed for 878 more, and accounted for 27 touchdowns in 1971. Greg Pruitt ran for 1,665 yards, with an average gain of 9.4 yards per carry. Our whole team rushed for an average of 472 yards per game—an NCAA record that will probably not be broken. Think of it—472 yards per game *average* for eleven games that included Southern Cal, Texas, Colorado, Nebraska, and Auburn.

People were always asking Greg Pruitt—about 5-foot-9 and 175 pounds—how a little short guy like him could lead the nation in rushing.

"We've got it figured out," he would say. "At Oklahoma, we open our holes from side to side, not from down to up."

If our defense had been as good as our offense that year, it just wouldn't have been fair. But we were building strong defensive teams for years to come and were already playing a sophomore defensive tackle from Eufaula, Oklahoma, named Lucious Selmon, an all-American who could lift our defense to the elite class just by bringing his two brothers to us.

Lucious had played fullback in high school at Eufaula. Everybody in town said he was going to be the next Jim Brown. He weighed 220 and ran a 10-flat hundred and just flattened those high school kids. But Lucious's defensive potential was what excited us.

Eddie Crowder from Colorado was our top competition for Lucious. Eddie promised him he could play fullback. We were thinking of him as a nose guard. Larry Lacewell, who was recruiting Lucious, brought him to the chow hall one day on an official visit. I looked up and saw Lucious, and then I saw these two massive friends he had brought with him. They were piling food a foot high on their cafeteria trays.

"Who's that?" I asked.

Larry smiled. "Those are Lucious's two little brothers, only sophomores."

They both weighed 240–250 and were also backs at Eufaula, with another two years to go. Dewey was the fullback who had replaced Lucious, and Lee Roy, the biggest, was the tailback. Nobody in high school could tackle them. But they were even better on defense. Obviously, Eufaula was going to win the state championship. Which they did.

Even if Lucious had been on crutches with a wooden leg, we would have wanted him because of his brothers. Lu, you know I still love you.

Mama Selmon didn't want Lucious to go far from home. Lucious had four older brothers who were bigger and better athletes than anybody in the family, but they never had the opportunity to show it because of segregation. Eufaula High was integrated in the late '60s. Therefore, Lucious and the two younger brothers and the two sisters got to go to Eufaula High School.

Lee Roy and Dewey were in the same class, but they were eleven months apart in age. Lucious told us how it happened. The day the old yellow-dog school bus picked up Dewey eight miles out in the country to take him to first grade, Lee Roy was the only boy left home. He cried and cried and pulled Mrs. Selmon's skirts so she couldn't get her chores done. The next day when the school bus came by, Mrs. Selmon put Lee Roy on it with his brothers and told him to start the first grade.

Lucious made all-America at nose tackle in 1973. In 1973 Dewey moved in at right tackle and Lee Roy at left tackle, and all three brothers made all-America—the only time that has happened in NCAA history—and our defense became first-class. Lee Roy, probably the greatest player ever to play for me, won the Outland and Lombardi trophies in his senior year and was the first player chosen in the pro draft . . . by

Tampa Bay in their first year as an expansion team. So Lee Roy was truly the original Bucaneer.

We had signed some great white defensive players from Oklahoma, too, like safety Randy Hughes—who was a two-time all-American.

In 1972 we had an all-American defensive tackle named Derland Moore from Poplar Bluff, Missouri. Derland was a shot-putter on the track team and decided to try out for football as a walk-on. His first day he got into a toe-to-toe fistfight with Steve Zabel, our big all-American tight end of 1967–69. Derland never backed down from anybody.

Derland would be back in 1972 to join the Selmon brothers, Shoate, Hughes, and half a dozen other studs.

So we knew our defense would be vastly better in 1972, and we had seven starters returning off our fantastic offense of 1971.

The only problem we foresaw was at quarterback. Jack Mildren was graduating.

His replacement was going to be Dave Robertson, from Garden Grove, California. Dave was a fifth-year senior, more of a passer than an option runner, but he didn't make mistakes. With his surrounding cast, Dave should do well.

We were sitting in a meeting during recruiting in early spring when assistant coach Wendell Mosley brought up a problem we didn't know we had.

Everybody got a kick out of Wendell. We called him Dead Set because he liked to wear earphones on the sidelines—even though they weren't plugged in—so his girlfriends in the stands would think he was directing the game.

But Wendell was a tremendous recruiter, with a sharp eye for talent. He scouted the Houston-Beaumont-Port Arthur area of south Texas and had sent us Greg Pruitt back when he was still a high school coach.

"You guys think quarterback is our problem?" Wendell said in the meeting. "Naw, our real problem is—where are we going to play Greg Pruitt?"

"What are you talking about, Wendell?"

"I'm about to sign a kid from Port Arthur who is better than Greg."

"Impossible."

"Well, you remember what I'm saying. He is the best high school player in Texas this season. The kid's name is Joe Washington."

We had two hundred players at practice in the fall of 1972. That was the first year the NCAA had put a limit of thirty scholarships on everybody and made freshman players eligible again. Joe Washington was one of our thirty, but we had built up big numbers of players before the rule went into effect.

The first scrimmage we had at Owen Field before the 1972 season was a three-hour session under the lights. We scrimmaged the first team, the second team, the third team.

Finally we called for Joe Washington, and here came this kid wearing silver shoes—football shoes painted silver, I should say. He was about an inch shorter than Greg Pruitt and certainly no heavier.

We had our first defense on the field. We brought Joe Washington into the huddle to see what he could do at left halfback against the big boys.

We had the ball on the 20-yard line going north to south. I sent word to the huddle to call a counter play. Everybody in the stadium—coaches, players, and spectators—had heard about Joe Washington by now. He looked so small and kind of cute in those silver shoes.

But this kid was going to make us move Greg Pruitt? Show us something, Joe.

Our quarterback spun and handed the ball to Joe on the counter play and—zip, zag, zip, zag, zip—Joe went north, east, south, and west, all at the same time, and you broke your knees and ankles reaching for him. He put skid marks and turf burns on our all-Americans. He ran 80 yards right through our entire first-team defense and nobody laid a hand on him. I mean, nobody touched him. I looked at Chuck, who stood ten yards away. We didn't say a word. We just stared at each other. We both knew what we had just seen.

So maybe we really did have a problem at left halfback, but it was one we looked forward to facing.

We had another problem that had happened in the spring, with a player from Texas named Kerry Jackson, but we wouldn't discover that one until after the 1972 season.

And when we did, it would be devastating.

But that September you could find nothing but smiles as we waded into our schedule.

We won our first four games by a combined score of 176–6. We shut out the Texas Wishbone 27–0. Colorado beat us 20–14 in the rain in Boulder. Then we bounced back and won our next three.

We were 7–1 and preparing for Kansas.

All I was thinking was football. I was completely absorbed in it. I had forgotten the rest of the world. If it didn't wear a Kansas uniform, I wasn't interested in it this week.

That's when the call that I had always subconsciously feared came and shook me out of my nest.

Assistant coach Billy Michaels, my old Arkansas team-mate, entered an offensive-staff meeting while I was talking and signaled for me to follow him into the hall.

"Barry, I need to take you home," he said.

I was still wrapped up in thinking about Kansas, and I thought he meant we were going to Billy's house. Something he wanted me to help him with.

"What is it, Billy? What can I do for you?"

"It's not me," he said.

We drove to my house, where Kay was waiting for me with the news.

Daddy had been murdered.

10

THE LAST RIDE HOME

Three years after Mother's death, Daddy had built himself a new white brick home on the site of our old shotgun house and had added a new pumphouse with an electric pump near the old smokehouse, which reeked of hog fat.

The pumphouse was another place for him to bury his Mason jars crammed with money.

In the summer of 1972, Kay, Greg, Kathy, and I had gone to Crossett for a visit, and Daddy had taken me out and showed me all the different spots where his money was hidden.

I was worried about him. On the ledger he let me look at, he had $80,000 in outstanding loans owed to him by black people around town. That was a lot of money in those days.

Daddy lived alone, and everybody knew he had cash.

Well, he didn't live entirely alone. In the daytime his black girlfriend, Lula Mae Dawkins, came to the house and took care of things for him, and sometimes she spent the night.

Also, he had a big German shepherd and a collie that slept at night on his bedroom floor. He kept a pistol on him all the time, put it under his pillow when he went to bed.

Irma Reynolds, who had looked after him most of his life, was eighty years old now and sick. Daddy kept her on his payroll, but she had gone to live in a house in town that Daddy bought for her, where she could get the attention she needed from all of her friends.

It didn't seem possible for time to have gone so fast and you couldn't tell it by looking at him, but I realized on that summer visit that Daddy had turned sixty-four.

Now that I reflect on it, death must have been on our minds pretty strongly on that last visit.

I remembered I was out deer hunting one day during high school, following an old cow trail through the woods, and I came upon an old wrought-iron fence grown over with weeds. Dead trees had fallen and knocked down pieces of the fence. It was way down in the middle of a swamp bottom with nothing around for miles, so peaceful and quiet, with no sound but the breeze in the pines and a mockingbird up there somewhere singing.

I climbed over the fence and pushed aside the weeds and found a bunch of headstones. Crouching down to read them, I saw the name Switzer. All around me were the old graves of a bunch of Switzers, with dates in the 1840s on the headstones.

At home that night I asked Daddy about it.

"That's the old Macedonia Cemetery," he said. "That's where your great-granddaddy and great-grandmother are buried, and their folks before them. Used to be a community there called Petersburg, but it died out long ago."

In the summer of 1972, Daddy and I went to the Macedonia Cemetery to visit the graves of our ancestors. Daddy and his nephew Bruce and others had cleaned the place up to make it pretty again so they could bury Bruce's infant son, Doug.

Daddy pointed out a piece of earth among the Switzer headstones and said, "This is where I want you to put me when my time comes."

"Aw, that's a long way off. You look younger than I do," I said.

But we both knew that a man who lived Daddy's kind of life could be robbed and shot at any moment. Daddy was loved by the black community, but I was afraid that some militant or stranger would ambush him and steal his money.

But it was his love life that did him in.

Uncle Billy Switzer picked up Kay and me at the airport, where we landed in a private plane that night of November 16, 1972.

From what Uncle Billy, a judge, told us and what my brother, Donnie, and I later put together from the sheriff and a witness, this is how Daddy died:

Late that afternoon, Daddy walked Lula Mae out to her car and told her to go on home and not come back that night. Probably, he said he had a poker game someplace.

As soon as Lula Mae drove away down the gravel road, another car appeared and approached the house. In it was Daddy's new black lady friend. It's not her name, but let's call her Ruby.

Lula Mae didn't know about Ruby. But Daddy's behavior lately had made her suspicious. Lula Mae sat and thought about it for a while, and then she got back into her car and returned to Daddy's house.

First thing Lula Mae saw, of course, was Ruby's car behind the house, but still in view from the drive near the house.

Daddy walked out into the carport. I can hear him now, yelling down at Lula Mae, "What the hell are you doing here? I told you not to come back tonight."

"Whose car is that?"

"Nobody. Just a customer."

"You're lying, Frank. Who is in there with you?"

"It's my personal business, I said. You go on home and come back in the morning."

"You got a bitch in there. I'm coming in and whipping her ass," Lula Mae said.

She took her .38 pistol out from under the seat.

"You stay in that damn car," he said.

Lula Mae opened the door and got out.

"Stand aside from that door, Frank."

I can hear Daddy yelling, "Damn you, Lula Mae, you're not coming in this house. Get your butt on away from here before you make me mad."

Lula Mae lost her head and shot him in the chest.

From the blood in the carport and the bloody handprints on the door, we know Daddy pulled himself up and staggered into the house.

He tracked blood across the kitchen floor, and there was a pool of blood on the floor underneath the wall phone. Ruby was terrified. She locked herself in the bedroom.

Daddy tried to call the hospital, but he couldn't get through. He had a party line. It could have been busy and the people wouldn't get off the line no matter what he told them— people could be unbelievably rude on party lines. Could have been that somebody had just left a phone off the hook.

Daddy staggered back outside. Lula Mae was still standing beside her car, probably thinking, My God, what have I done?

"Get me to the hospital, Lula Mae," he said.

She helped him into the backseat of her car. With Ruby peeking out the bedroom window, Lula Mae sped off down the gravel road toward Crossett.

I can imagine Daddy slumped over bleeding and Lula Mae frightened and sorry and in a blind rush to make it to the hospital and save his life. She loved him, after all.

Just before one of the three little bridges you have to cross over the creeks on the way to Crossett, the loose gravel road makes a sharp curve.

It was getting dark by now, and I can imagine Lula Mae crying and frantic and Daddy urging her to hurry while he pressed his shirt against the wound.

Lula Mae was going too fast for the curve, the car left the road, hit a power pole, and exploded into flames.

Daddy and Lula Mae were both burned to death.

And when the light pole fell, all the lights went out in Crossett . . . for a few moments.

The autopsy showed he could have lived if Lula Mae had reached the hospital. That was the opinion of the state medical examiner. He had a bullet in his left lung and had lost a lot of blood, but he was in such powerful health that he could have survived it.

I drove by myself in Uncle Billy's car out to Daddy's house, past the downed power pole. I parked up at the gravel road that I've walked a thousand times to town and walked the last 150 yards on the dirt path to his house. I guess the reason I did this was to prepare myself for what I knew I was about to experience. I retraced his bloody path, trying to imagine what he had experienced.

I then walked out to the smokehouse. The ground was dug up where Daddy had buried his money. It was the same thing at the pumphouse.

All his money had been stolen.

During a family meeting the next day in Uncle Billy's den, I asked what preacher we should get to conduct the funeral.

"I don't think Daddy would want a preacher," Donnie said. Donnie was now a lawyer working in Nashville. "Daddy was always repulsed by preachers. I think he'd rather have one of his old friends deliver a eulogy."

Uncle Billy suggested Mickey Smart, who ran a convenience store on Highway 82 at the edge of the black section of town.

The chapel was packed for the funeral. Dozens of people couldn't squeeze in and had to stand outside. There were more blacks than whites listening to Mickey Smart, who told stories about Daddy for an hour. Mickey is the man who started a collection box in the black section a few years earlier to buy Daddy a set of Samsonite luggage that he used when he came to see my games in Fayetteville and later in Norman. That luggage was bought with pennies, nickels, dimes, and quarters. Daddy was proud of it.

We buried him in the old Macedonia Cemetery in the pines, with generations of Switzers.

11

THE CHANGE OF COMMAND

Remember that Kansas game that I was preparing for as if it were the most important thing on earth before my daddy was killed?

On Saturday, November 18, 1972, the day my daddy was buried, the Sooners beat Kansas 31–14. On the scoreboard, I mean. If you look in the record book for 1972, you will note an asterisk that means we lost the game by forfeit to Kansas, and lost also to Missouri and Oklahoma State.

But we didn't know anything about that yet when we used our Sooner Magic to slip past Nebraska, 17–14, in the game for the Big Eight title. Split end Tinker Owens, younger brother of Steve, emerged as a star that day, with five catches for 108 yards. It was billed as a match between Johnny Rodgers and Greg Pruitt, but Greg was hurt and didn't even play. Little Joe Washington, a freshman, started in Greg's place and juked Nebraska out of their jocks on a touchdown run in the fourth quarter.

We didn't have to forfeit the victory over Nebraska because Kerry Jackson didn't play in it. But I'm getting ahead of the story . . .

Everyone realized it would be the great Bob Devaney's last game against us as head coach of Nebraska, since he had announced his coming retirement at the beginning of the 1972 season.

I consider Bob to have been one of the greatest coaches of young men ever, and a personal friend of mine.

But if you go back to Bob's last Oklahoma-Nebraska game, no one knew—and you could have gotten huge odds

89

against it—but it would also be Chuck Fairbanks's last OU-Nebraska game and last season as OU's head coach.

We thought we had a 10–1 record—losing only that rainy day in Colorado. We were Big Eight champions and ranked second in the nation when we rolled into New Orleans for the Sugar Bowl game against Penn State. That was during a brief period when the Big Eight did not have a deal to send its champion to the Orange Bowl. Ironically, Nebraska played in the Orange Bowl at the end of the 1972 season, but not as the Big Eight champion.

In fact, this was the second Sugar Bowl game for us in 1972. On January 1, we had opened the year by beating Auburn and their Heisman Trophy winner Pat Sullivan 44–24 in the Sugar Bowl.

Now we were closing out the 1972 season on December 31 by playing still another Sugar Bowl game, this one against Penn State. We had become a really dominant college football team in the last two years, going 11–1 and being ranked second in the nation both seasons.

We beat Penn State 14–0 in the Sugar Bowl, but we were much more impressive than that score may sound. We lost five fumbles, three of them inside Penn State's 5-yard line. But we ran up and down the field against them, and our defense just flat knocked them backward. In nine of our games that year, we gave up a touchdown or less. Four were shutouts.

We had hoped to get some help at the end of the season from Ohio State when the Buckeyes played the number-one-ranked University of Southern California in the Rose Bowl.

But USC won the Rose Bowl and the national championship—which set up a tremendous beginning for the 1973 season.

USC was the second game on our schedule in 1973, following Baylor. I felt confident we would beat Baylor. Our USC game could very well be for the national championship, because they were going to be strong again and we had become a seriously powerful outfit.

Chuck had survived the CHUCK CHUCK days in grand style. We had established a great wealth of talent. We were doing the right things and believing the right things. Our recruiting nets were spread wide, and we were going to have another outstanding haul.

On January 20, one day shy of three weeks since the Sugar Bowl, we were in the middle of recruiting and I was in my office picking up some things to take on a trip to see a prospect in Texas.

Chuck stepped into the hall and asked if he could see me for a minute.

I sat down in a chair in front of his desk and wondered what was up. Probably some routine matter, I guessed. Chuck certainly wasn't in any trouble that I knew about. Maybe he just wanted to talk about golf, for all I knew. Whatever it was, we would get right to it. Chuck was never one for beating about the bush.

"Barry, I'm going to take a pro job," said Chuck.

I was stunned.

"You're going to what?"

"I'm going to take a job with a professional football team. I don't want you to tell anyone. My wife, Puddy, is the only person around here who knows. I have had several meetings with Billy Sullivan at the Love Field Airport in Dallas, and I have decided to take the job as head coach of the New England Patriots."

I was so dumbfounded I could hardly move my lips. We were all a really close group, but none of us had picked up even the slightest hint that anything like this was in the air.

"Well, Chuck, I'm sure you know what you're doing," I managed to say. "I don't know what will happen here with the staff when you leave, but obviously I would like to have the head job."

Chuck had already promoted me to assistant head coach, which is basically a cosmetic title that doesn't pay extra but seems to elevate you slightly. Frank Broyles was the first head coach I knew of to use that move when he promoted Jim Mac-Kenzie to assistant head coach in an effort to keep him from leaving.

"I'm going to support you for the job," Chuck said. "I'll talk to all the regents and the president on your behalf."

"I'd appreciate that," I said.

I had never dreamed Chuck would leave so soon and

walk away from such richness of talent that we had around us. I had turned down a couple of head-coaching jobs, including the Iowa State job before Johnny Majors got it, because I never wanted to go coach anywhere that there was no possibility of consistent winning. I was accustomed to Arkansas and Oklahoma, where winning was a tradition. You go off to a place like Iowa State, you have no real chance to win the Big Eight.

I'd had three other job interviews. One that had sounded more promising was at Michigan State. The other two were at S.M.U. and Rice.

Michigan State athletic director Burt Smith took me to a meeting in East Lansing with MSU president Clifton Wharton, vice-president Jack Breslin, and assistant athletic director Clarence Underwood. It was Burt who brought me into the room, but then he had the least to say, which bothered me. I think I came on too strong for them. They asked me how I felt about a lot of things, and I told them, but evidently not what they wanted to hear. I thought Michigan State would be a good place to work. I felt I could win there. They have a tradition, and there's enough population in that part of the country to draw players from.

But I guess our philosophies didn't mesh. They were from the north and I was an Oklahoma boy—Arkansas, really—and we didn't see eye to eye. Breslin was the stern one. He sat there with a notebook and kept flipping through the pages and looking tough.

Later Burt took me aside and said, "Barry, you were too candid with them."

The job interview with S.M.U. was something else entirely. They had about twenty-six people in the room, and we met at the First National Bank of Dallas. They had everybody there, including three of their players, some cheerleaders, and several alumni. It was a circus. I was genuinely surprised that the S.M.U. band didn't parade through. I left there feeling that there was real trouble lying ahead for S.M.U., and I immediately withdrew my name from consideration at S.M.U. and at Rice. I would clearly have taken the Michigan State job if it had been offered to me. But all in all, I felt the interviewing experience had been good for me. I was glad that I had done it.

Now my big chance had come at Oklahoma. It was here and this was the moment.

I knew this Oklahoma football team had some great years coming up, and I felt in my heart that I must be part of it.

"If you don't get the head job here, I'll bring you to New England as my backfield coach," Chuck said. "Don't worry, you'll have a good job no matter what happens. But I hope you get to stay here."

Man, so did I.

On January 26, Chuck announced his resignation and shocked the hell out of everybody.

Two days went by with no word to me from the president and the regents. It seemed like an eternity. I knew some of the regents might go after Darrell Royal again. Surely Darrell was too well established at Texas by now. He wasn't going to leave Texas. He had had the chance to come to Oklahoma when Jim MacKenzie was hired, and another chance before Chuck got the job. Certainly he wouldn't move this late in the game.

But you never know what those seven regents, the ones who have the power to hire and fire, will end up doing. Many of them really do not know anything about football (And why should they? Running a major university is a bigger part of their job.), but it did create a great deal of uneasiness and uncertainty.

I didn't think they would go outside the staff. We had a terrific staff put together, with two very successful seasons, and it would be foolish to break it up. Chuck felt the same way. But you just couldn't be sure about the regents. The suspense was driving me and the staff crazy.

On the evening of January 28, 1973, the suspense heightened when I was called to a meeting at the president's home. Present at the meeting were the president, Dr. Paul Sharp, who has since retired, Jack Santee, a Tulsa lawyer and regent, and regent Houston Huffman, an attorney and businessman from Oklahoma City. As it turned out, Houston Huffman and Dr. Sharp had very little to say. Jack Santee conducted the meeting.

Jack was a highly respected regent, well thought of by the

faculty and the administration, and he was one of the regents who did understand something about football; he had played for Bud Wilkinson in the 1950s. In later years Jack and I became good friends and he was very supportive of me and of our program. At that time, however, we really did not know one another.

The regents had two areas of concern. First, they were particularly concerned about an incident that had occurred back on April 26, 1972, five years after Jim MacKenzie had died. Jack Santee asked me to tell him what had happened.

Each spring during that era, the athletic administration would give a spring dance and invite former players, alumni, and their wives and dates. At one point in the evening I happened to be in the restroom when one of our ex-players came in who had had too much to drink. He was a kid who had been highly recruited out of high school but who, it turned out, just wasn't good enough to play at Oklahoma's level of competition. Well, someone happened to mention it was the anniversary of Jim MacKenzie's death, and then this kid said, "Yeah, and I'm glad the son of a bitch is dead."

What he said instantly flew all over me, and really before I knew it, I had hit him two or three times. But since he was much larger and younger than I was, I should probably be glad that Steve Zabel, Steve Owens, and Mike Harper then came in and pulled us apart.

When I had finished telling this story to Jack Santee on the night of January 28, 1973, he asked me whether that could happen again. I told him, "Only if the son of a bitch says it again." I have a feeling that's not the answer Jack wanted to hear. But he knew it was the honest one.

The second point that concerned the regents was that I was only an assistant coach, not a head coach, but they resolved that concern by only giving me a one-year contract. I told them it was absolutely necessary, however, that the contract be announced as being for four years, since I needed it for recruiting purposes and to give my staff (Jim's and Chuck's staff, too) a sense of continuity. As for the real one-year contract, that didn't concern me because I knew we had some great players and a great staff. And I really felt great because all of the staff felt that I should be the head coach.

Ironically, I learned later that although I was being appointed as the University of Oklahoma's seventeenth head football coach, all of my predecessors (other than Jim Tatum, who came out of the military) had also been assistant coaches at the college level.

The next day, January 29, 1973, the regents held a big meeting at the Memorial Union on campus to announce my appointment—and my "four-year" contract. I remember distinctly walking out of the Union that day with Frank Boggs, a reporter with *The Daily Oklahoman*. I was hungry as hell, and as Frank and I walked by a candy counter on the way out, I stopped and told the girl behind the counter, "I'm really hungry. Do you have a candy bar that tastes like a steak?"

On January 29, 1973, they had named me head coach at Oklahoma. I was thirty-five years old.

You know how I celebrated the news? I ate my candy bar and ran straight to the telephone and began calling every recruit on our entire list. It was my top priority to talk to the kids, especially the ones who didn't know me. And that was most of them, because Chuck had been in the homes of kids in every recruiting district, but my area was strictly Texas.

I had hardly finished putting the pictures on the walls in my new office when we got blindsided by the Big Eight Conference and the NCAA.

This event was really difficult to live with. A lot of people think Chuck Fairbanks knew what was coming and jumped ship just before the storm hit. Personally, I have never believed that. I believe Chuck just had it in his blood that he had to try coaching in the NFL.

What happened was that the previous year, freshmen quarterback Kerry Jackson and defensive end Mike Phillips, of Ball High in Galveston, had enrolled in Oklahoma with transcripts that had been altered.

I think a lot of you may need a little bit of a history lesson at this point. Transcripts were altered all the time back in the late 1960s and early 1970s, but not by the college coaches doing the recruiting—it was the black coaches and principals in the black high schools who, out of the most sincere and compassionate of motives, wanted to help some of their kids have a chance to get out of the ghetto and better themselves.

This was before total integration, and there were still a lot of those Booker T. Washingtons, Cashmires, and Dunbars, inner-city schools that were totally black. The principals and high school coaches would often tell coaches when they would come to see one of their good players, "Don't worry, coach, our boy will qualify for your program." You learned not to ask any questions.

Well, it was internal feuding at Galveston Ball High School between the different coaching staffs that brought to the attention of the NCAA the fact that Kerry Jackson's and Mike Phillips's transcripts had been changed. The NCAA couldn't have found out any other way, since transcripts were not the whole story, even at that time, to determine eligibility for admission; they were but one part of a formula in which tests figured to determine a "predictor" of whether the young man could succeed in college academics. And since the kids were given several chances to take the tests, other college coaches who knew a kid was marginal could think, Well, Kerry finally made the grade.

Phillips's transcript had been altered only to the extent of raising his class standing so that Jackson, who ranked below him, could become a "predictor." Phillips was, however, always a predictor and was not declared ineligible.

But the feud at Galveston Ball High School and all of the bad feelings that came out when the transcript allegations became public led to Head Football Coach Joe Wooly's resignation. And he sure as hell did not change the transcripts. I am glad that things turned out well for Joe. He is now director of player personnel for the Philadelphia Eagles in the National Football League.

As you would expect, the NCAA found Oklahoma guilty of a major violation. And Billy Michaels, one of our coaches, a great friend and college teammate of mine at Arkansas, was forced to resign because he *knew* the transcripts had been altered. What happened to Billy and his family because of that incident still bothers me. But I am glad that Billy, an excellent coach, is on Fred Akers's staff at Purdue today.

At that time in NCAA history, the NCAA utilized the services of the Big Eight Conference as its investigative arm on problems that came up in Big Eight schools. The relatively new Commissioner of the Big Eight Conference was Chuck Neinas, a gentleman who is today the executive director of the College Football Association and unquestionably the premier athletic administrator in the country. He and his gorgeous wife, Patty, are now two of my best friends, but in 1973 during the transcript investigation, Chuck and I were bitter enemies.

I do not believe that at that time Chuck, or anyone on the NCAA justice committee (which simply rubber-stamped the Big Eight recommendations), really understood the situation that existed in the real world out there in those high schools or they would never have hit us with such a heavy punishment. But the NCAA rightly views academic violations of this nature as the most serious of NCAA transgressions. And that's why we got a jail term instead of a speeding ticket.

The first thing this news meant was that we had to forfeit the three Big Eight games Jackson had played in, thus Nebraska was now the champion instead of us. I'll never forget Bob Devaney's classy remark after Nebraska had been officially awarded the conference championship. He said, "We don't want the damn trophy. We know who won the game."

But the forfeitures and the probation really staggered us. Then the NCAA threw what could have been a knockout punch. They jerked us off TV and out of bowl games for two years.

As our punishment for accepting the falsified transcripts, the Big Eight and NCAA put us on what was supposedly a two-year probation that actually ran for four years. We were banned from bowl games for the 1973 and 1974 seasons and banned from television appearances for the 1974 and 1975 seasons. They couldn't start our TV blackout in 1973 because ABC already had contracts for two national telecasts of our Texas and Nebraska games.

The "experts" in the media were already picking us to finish fourth in the conference, especially with our coaching disruption, and now the newspapers began saying we were going to lose players who would quit and go to other schools because of the probation.

I know people who look at an obstacle and see a barrier that means defeat. I have always believed in looking at an obstacle as a challenge and an opportunity to grow from the experience of overcoming it.

I remember addressing a group of alums in Tulsa shortly after the probation was announced. "I'm a fighter, I'm a competitor, I'm a winner, and nothing is going to stop our team," I said. "I'd better go now. I'm double-parked, and I may get another year for that."

Our coaches and players knew we were a hell of a lot better than fourth place. The Big Eight and the NCAA had put us on probation—but they hadn't forbidden us to win the Big Eight championship or go undefeated. So that became our goal.

During recruiting that spring, I ran into my first serious personal head-knocking with Darrell Royal. To this very day, seventeen years later, I think Darrell still believes I lied and cheated trying to sign a player he wanted. And it was Darrell who won the contest for the player.

Darrell had accused us of spying on his workouts before his game against us in 1972. We blocked a quick kick that Darrell claimed we had somehow illegally found out he intended to use. In fact, we did expect him to quick kick at some point—one of Larry Lacewell's friends had tipped us off—but we really didn't know they were going to quick kick then and weren't trying to block the kick. When our defensive backs saw what was happening, starting from their normal alignment, they started flying backward to field the ball. But one of our linemen broke through and knocked it down. I might add that it's not like blocking a quick kick makes a hell of a lot of difference in our 27–0 victory.

I do not believe that at this early time, before the incident I am about to describe, Darrell had it in for me personally. He may have known my name, since I had recruited in Texas for a number of years. But the other Oklahoma coaches and I, with our emphasis on the great black athletes, had hurt Darrell and the Southwest Conference a lot. I've read that he was particularly upset about the loss of Jack Mildren, a great white player from Abilene, but whether Darrell realized it or not, Texas was never in the hunt for Jack even if Jack hadn't decided to go to Oklahoma.

The Wishbone had brought Texas back after a slight

slump. Darrell's 1969 Longhorns were very clearly the last all-white national football champions the world will ever see.

But now Darrell wasn't getting the skilled blacks to run the Wishbone that we had, and he didn't have much chance to beat us unless he could land some of them.

Every time Oklahoma would sign a Joe Washington, a Greg Pruitt, a Billy Brooks, a David Overstreet, a Thomas Lott, a Billy Sims, or a Mike Thomas (who later transferred to UNLV and played for the Washington Redskins)—the official line that came back from Austin was, "Well, you know why those black kids go to Oklahoma, don't you? The kids are poor and need money. Oklahoma buys them, simple as that."

That was the simple, easy, and stupid way to explain why Texas lost those players. Texas wasn't outrecruited, according to the Texas coaches and fans. The fact that Oklahoma was first and that blacks felt comfortable with us and knew we would give them every chance to play at any position, this didn't count. No, the Texans said the only reason blacks went to Oklahoma was for money.

Bullshit. They came to us for the same reason the whites did—to be winners, to be champions. And more important, they wanted to be part of our family.

My first personal encounter with Darrell had its source the last week of recruiting in 1973. A running back named Ivey Suber from O. D. Wyatt High School in Fort Worth had already told everybody he was going to the University of Texas. Jimmy Dickey was recruiting Fort Worth for us, and he told me he thought the kid was going to Texas mainly because his parents wanted him to, and he thought that I might have a chance to change his mind with a visit to the Suber home.

I never did go to the Suber home. But I did have a conversation with Ivey in the locker room at his high school. I talked to him about the difference between Texas and Oklahoma. I painted a picture of him being one of a few black athletes in an environment that wouldn't be as compatible for him. I told Ivey he would step in a huddle and look to the right, look to the left, and there might be another brother lined up there with him in the backfield; and he would look in front of him and see all white faces; and when he broke the huddle to go to the line of scrimmage in practice, he would see a white defense except for maybe a brother or two in the secondary.

I told Ivey that he would be a great player, but there was a lot more to the four or five years of college than the hours you put in on the practice field or in a game. I said the difference was that at Oklahoma he would see brothers everywhere at all positions, and they would make it so much easier for him to adjust to the pressure of playing big-time athletics while he made his acquaintance with big-time academics.

Ivey said he had already promised Darrell Royal in front of his parents that he would come to Texas. But I asked him to visit us at Oklahoma first, and he said he'd come the next weekend. He walked me out to the car and said he was really glad I came by, that he was looking at things a little bit differently now. On my way out of town, I stopped by the cafe where Ivey's mother worked and visited with her. I left feeling that we might have a slight chance to get him.

But Ivey didn't show up in Norman that weekend. Jimmy Dickey got a phone call from Ivey's high school coach, who said the kid was going to Texas. I was kind of disappointed, but I didn't think about it long. We already had several running backs as good or better than Ivey Suber.

A few weeks later I received a visit from David Swank, who came to my office in his capacity as our faculty rep to the Big Eight and NCAA. Swank told me I faced serious allegations. Darrell Royal had told NCAA investigators that I had offered Ivey Suber a 1973 Pontiac, $1,000 in cash, a new wardrobe, and $250 monthly payments if he would attend Oklahoma.

Swank said Ivey Suber's father and mother gave Darrell this information on, or a few days before, signing day, and Darrell ran to the NCAA and turned me in. I didn't know Darrell other than as an assistant coach who'd seen Ivey a few times. But if the parents had told me the same thing they told him, I would have done exactly what Darrell did.

The NCAA had prepared an affidavit, Swank said, for Ivey to sign, swearing to this charge so that the NCAA could launch an official inquiry. Swank told me that Ivey was under a lot of pressure, but he still wouldn't sign.

Why wouldn't Ivey Suber sign that affidavit? He didn't owe me anything.

Why would Ivey Suber go ahead to play football at Texas—including the 1976 game against us in the Red River War in the Cotton Bowl—for four years and never relent and sign that affidavit?

I mean, Texas had started recruiting more blacks by the time they signed Ivey. They had Roosevelt Leaks by then and had started a run of great defensive backs with Raymond Clayborn. But we were beating Texas fairly consistently when Ivey Suber was in school there. With Oklahoma on probation for the falsified transcripts, all Ivey Suber had to do to put us out of business and end my career before it began was to sign that affidavit some lazy afternoon down in Austin.

The reason Ivey never would sign it is that he and I knew it had never happened.

The day that David Swank first told me of the Ivey Suber allegations, I had the feeling from his manner that he didn't believe me when I denied them.

I don't believe in lie-detector tests. Darrell Royal used to love them and call for me to take them frequently. But polygraphs are only about 70 percent accurate. Good criminal lawyers may use them on their own clients to try to get an indication about their truthfulness, but polygraph evidence is not accepted in any court, primarily because it is not reliable.

But this was my first year as head coach. Hell, I hadn't even coached a single game yet.

If I got Oklahoma in trouble again while we were already on probation, I would be fired faster than you can fry an egg.

It almost goes without saying that I expected to be fired if we didn't win at least eight or nine games. But I sure as hell didn't want to get into a shaky situation with the faculty rep and the president and the regents just because a high school kid told a lie.

So I took a polygraph. Instead of asking me specific questions like did I offer Ivey a 1973 Pontiac, I got the two polygraph operators to ask me each question in a broad sense—like, Did you offer to buy any recruit any car at any time? And did you offer any recruit any money? And on down the line with any other charge that could be made.

After I passed the polygraph, we filed away the results. Darrell was yelling for me to take a polygraph, but I had already done it in secret. Two years later, I ordered my whole coaching staff to take the same test at the end of recruiting season.

The polygraph operators asked each coach, "Did you offer a car, clothes, money, paid transportation, or help in the selling of tickets to any recruit as an inducement to attend the University of Oklahoma, and did you ask anyone (a booster) to provide these inducements to any recruited athlete?"

Our coaches were not laughing and joking when they went in to take the test. A lie detector will make anybody nervous who is not a total sociopath, just like you get nervous when you see the police in your rearview mirror and wonder if you missed a stop sign someplace.

Every so often over the next four football seasons—until he retired in 1976—Darrell would demand that I take a polygraph test.

When it was eventually announced that the whole staff and I had passed the polygraph, Darrell said the operators must have screwed it up. He never would cut me any slack.

Before the start of my first season as head coach, I told the team, "I've been to eleven bowl games in thirteen seasons. I've been around a lot of success, a lot of great players. Bowl games and playing on TV are fine incentives. But I'll tell you what, people—the greatest reward in football is winning. That's why they have scoreboards. When they put us on probation, they made one mistake. They didn't tell us we couldn't win the Big Eight championship, and nobody said we couldn't win the national championship. Men, that is our challenge."

We opened my first season by beating Baylor 42–14. Sophomore quarterback Steve Davis, the Baptist preacher from Sallisaw, scored twice, and so did Joe Washington.

The next week we faced the defending national champion, USC, in the Coliseum before a crowd of 84,000 at night. USC had won nineteen in a row. We fumbled and lost the ball on our first two possessions, including one at our 25-yard line that set up Pat Haden to throw a pass for USC's only touchdown. We missed two field goals and went in at the half down 0–7. In the third quarter we went on a 70-yard drive to tie the score. In the fourth quarter we drove to the USC 11, where we missed another short field goal. The game finished in a tie, 7–7.

In the locker room afterward, I told our players, "Hold your heads up high. We didn't get the breaks tonight, but we proved that we are the best team. I'm proud of every one of you."

We showed the whole country that night that we were a great team. We held USC to 161 yards of total offense, and Lee Roy Selmon—the best defensive lineman in OU history—missed the game with pericarditis, which kept him out the first half of the season. USC had Anthony Davis at tailback, Lynn Swann and John McKay as receivers. But we put a junior-college transfer named Tony Peters on Swann man-to-man the whole game and shut him down, and they couldn't get anywhere running against our defense. Peters later played twelve years of pro ball with the Washington Redskins, but prior to that night no one from USC, or anywhere else, had heard of him.

We came from behind to beat Miami 24–20 the following week—which set up my first head coach meeting with Darrell Royal. Both teams were unbeaten. I think Oklahoma was the only team Darrell lost to in a stretch of thirty-seven games.

I was really pumped up for my first game against Texas. Only once in my whole career did I ask my football team to win a game for me—and that was fifteen years later in the Orange Bowl, when we hammered Arkansas in the revenge match—but my players knew how much this 1973 Texas game meant to me. Hell, it meant a lot to them too, of course, since half of them were Texans, but I was the one roaming the locker room making a speech.

Tinker Owens taped what I told them before the game.

"Defense. We've got to gang tackle. Swarm Roosevelt Leaks. Swarm Marty Akins, intimidate him . . . fifty million people watching you play today on national television . . . 75,000 people out there in the stands . . . a 12 o'clock shootout. We'll strap the irons on at 12. That's what these Dallas papers like to write. Comments. Sell newspapers . . . poise. Keep your poise . . . Texas is not good enough, people, to take the football and beat us. They've got to have things happen good for them . . . There's no bigger ball game you'll ever play than this one right here. Nothing means more . . . Let me tell you, people, you're a great football team!"

We startled the hell out of everybody, including me, that day by throwing passes of 40, 63, and 47 yards for touchdowns in the first half. We completed four of six passes for 225 yards. Steve Davis threw two touchdowns—a 63-yarder to Tinker Owens and a 47-yarder to Billy Brooks, a junior-college transfer from Austin. Brooks caught it on a streak pattern thirty seconds before the half. In my mind I can still see Billy Brooks, a 6-foot-3 9.5-second sprinter, just flying past Texas's white cornerback. Our fullback, Waymon Clark, was from Austin, too, and he wound up gaining more than 1,000 yards that year.

Even Little Joe Washington got in on the aerial act against Texas by throwing a halfback pass for a touchdown to Tinker Owens.

The sportswriters wrote that we beat Texas throwing. But we didn't beat Texas throwing. Hell! We beat Texas *catching* the ball. We only threw it six times.

Oklahoma that day scored the most points ever against a Darrell Royal team—52–13—and piled up 508 yards in total offense.

Our freshmen on that team would never lose to Texas in their entire careers.

In the locker room following the victory, some of my players, who loved Billy Michaels just as I did, asked me to give a game ball to him. I said, "No, we can't flaunt it. That's just for us, and we can do it next week." We actually had a private awarding of a Texas-OU game ball to Billy at practice the next week. It was not for publication. But, somehow, it got out and some raging asshole reporter, wanting to be cute and controversial, printed the story. As you would expect, Darrell was furious about it, I heard, and some of the coaches in his peer group took it as an insult, like I was thumbing my nose at the charges that had put us on probation—which couldn't be further from the truth. But Darrell had the ear of respected coaches like Ara Parseghian, John McKay, and Joe Paterno, who didn't know anything about me except that I was a somewhat brash rookie coach—and that their good friend Darrell thought I was a crook.

In order after Texas, we demolished Colorado, Kansas State, Iowa State, Missouri, and Kansas. This brought us to the game against Nebraska for the Big Eight title. It was on national TV, our last TV appearance for the next two years. Nebraska had its usual powerhouse, averaging 418 yards per game on offense.

I'll tell you how brilliant our defense was that day. Nebraska never snapped the ball on our side of the 50-yard line all afternoon. We beat them 27–0.

Since we were ineligible for a bowl game even though we were the champions, we took it out on Oklahoma State, 45–18, in the last game of the season.

We ranked third in the national polls with a 10–0–1 record, and with no bowl game, we couldn't hope to improve our position. Alabama finished number one in the final voting.

If I had made my debut with a 6–5 record and perhaps a more modest attitude, I might not have gotten the reputation as the guy in the black hat. But of course, if I had gone 6–5 at Oklahoma, I would have been fired after my first season.

At the end of the 1973 season, the American Football Coaches Association passed a rule that no coach of any team on probation could ever be honored as coach of the year. I learned from Bob Blackman, former head coach at Dartmouth College and then head coach at the University of Illinois, that Darrell had indeed been a "strong voice" in favor of the adoption of that rule.

I did not go to the AFCA's annual convention in San Francisco in January 1974. Defensive coordinator Larry Lacewell was there in the middle of it because I sent him to represent me and the University of Oklahoma.

At that convention, the AFCA announced that no team on probation would be considered by them in the national polls in the future. That meant that the UPI—the coaches' poll—would bar Oklahoma and a few other schools also on probation from being ranked in 1974 or thereafter. It didn't make a damn to the others. They had no chance to be ranked in the Top 10, or Top 20; the rule had clearly been a personal slap at me and the Oklahoma program.

When Lacewell saw the convention pass the rule, he understood what it meant, got very upset, and called me. He first told me what had happened, and then he said, "Barry, I don't feel right going to the banquet and sitting on the dais representing Oklahoma as conference champions in front of a bunch of coaches who feel this way about us." I replied, "Yeah, if we had gone seven–four and lost to Texas, that rule would never have been put in. Come on home."

The funny part about all of this is that I really support the rule—it's a good one. What hurt about it all was the timing of it and the fact that it was directly aimed at me and Oklahoma because of the unfortunate Kerry Jackson transcript affair, the Ivey Suber problem, and because Darrell Royal believed me to be a Red River bandit. And I guarantee you that if Oklahoma hadn't been undefeated and ranked number two in the country while on probation, this rule would never have been implemented.

12

NATIONAL CHAMPS, MEET THE MOLECULES OF THE UNIVERSE . . .

My 1974 team was probably the best all-around group I ever coached. Because of our TV ban, we were often called the greatest team nobody saw. I had a powerful group of players who stayed together for three or four years in the 1972–75 period. Seven offensive starters and six defensive starters from this bunch made all-America during their careers. And we had the same quarterback, Steve Davis, to run our offense for three straight years, a tremendous help in maintaining our continuity.

If we had been on television in 1974 and 1975, Joe Washington would have won the Heisman Trophy at least once. Archie Griffin of Ohio State won the Heisman back to back during Joe's career, which is a testament to the power of national television exposure.

I've coached as many first-round NFL picks as anybody. In 1977 I had Billy Sims, Kenny King, Elvis Peacock, and David Overstreet, all first-rounders, playing in my backfield at the same time. In 1972 I had Greg Pruitt, Joe Washington, and Mike Thomas all playing the same position.

In fact, during the 1974 season I was approached by Lamar Hunt's Kansas City Chiefs to see if I would be interested in that head-coaching job. I decided, however, because of the great success we were having on the field and in recruiting, not to pursue the position. When they asked me why, I said, "Because Oklahoma has more number-one draft picks than the Chiefs."

But I have to say that Little Joe Washington was to me the ultimate running back. He didn't have the strength or the great speed, but he was just a pure runner. Darrell Royal said Joe was like smoke through a keyhole. Joe did things I have never seen any other back do.

The way you can tell a great back from a good back is that the great back will make something happen when it looks as if there is nothing for him. He heads into a black hole and gets swallowed up—and suddenly here he comes again, zigging left, zagging right, jumping over a couple of tacklers, and breaking free. The really great back like Joe Washington can turn chickenshit into chicken salad. Like Darrell once said, "All great backs look the same when there's no place to run." They all make something happen.

I have always believed there is a strong correlation between great rushing teams and winning. The great rushing teams in college football have been the consistent winners. There are exceptions—like the Miamis, with their string of top quarterbacks and fast wide receivers—but basically the teams that can run the ball are the winners.

And as I have said many times already, the Wishbone is the greatest rushing offense ever designed.

It helped a hell of a lot that we could put offensive linemen on the field like John Roush, Jerry Arnold, Terry Webb, and Mike Vaughan, and that Steve Davis could throw the ball to Tinker Owens or Billy Brooks when necessary.

In 1974 Oklahoma led the nation in three major offensive categories, had a total offense average of 570 yards per game, and finished with a rushing *average* of 438 yards a game—our 1971 Sooners still hold the all-time rushing average of 472 yards per game. That is a record I really believe will never be broken, because it was set at the birth of the Wishbone.

We finished the season voted number one by the Associated Press (AP) as national champions—and not even mentioned by the coaches' poll of the UPI, because we were on probation.

I don't want to give you the impression that there was anything shabby about our defense.

Lucious Selmon had finished his eligibility, but brothers Lee Roy and Dewey returned for two more years, joining stars like Randy Hughes, Rod Shoate, Jimbo Elrod, Zac Henderson, and others, an unbelievable assembly of talent.

But I kind of felt like it all started with Little Joe Washington.

Every time Joe tucked the football under his arm there was a sense of anticipation, like you were about to witness something that you had never seen before. We called it "Showtime!"

If you couldn't see him you couldn't touch him, and if you couldn't touch him you couldn't tackle him. Joe and I were laughing about this the other day. He is the smallest player in stature drafted the highest in NFL history. Five-foot-eight, 169 pounds—and he was the fourth pick in the entire country. Lee Roy Selmon was first that year, Steve Niehaus of Notre Dame went second, and for the third pick New Orleans debated 15 minutes before they screwed up and chose big running back Chuck Muncie, 6-foot-4 and 230, over Little Joe. The San Diego Chargers grabbed Joe with the fourth pick and he played pro ball for ten years with the Chargers, and Baltimore Colts, and the Washington Redskins. He was one of the most elusive and exciting backs ever to play the game, and just this past year the staff of ABC's *Monday Night Football* selected Joe to their all-time Monday night team for an incredible all-purpose running display he put on for them while playing for the Colts.

Let me take you on a tour of our back-to-back national championship seasons of 1974 and 1975. When I reach 1975 I'll tell you about one unsettling case of football fan behavior that actually shook the Christian faith of our Baptist quarterback, and I'll tell you of two consecutive plays when our second national title was in the hands and feet of Little Joe Washington in what had seemed a fairly insignificant game until suddenly it could have turned into our total downfall.

We opened the 1974 season ranked number one in the AP poll, but we had an unexpectedly tough time putting away Baylor, 28–11, with three touchdowns in the fourth quarter. Baylor had a good team that year, and won its first Southwest Conference title since 1924. We gained 438 yards rushing—

156 in seventeen carries for Little Joe—but we lost four fumbles and dropped eight rungs in the AP ladder.

Utah State came to Norman the following week and picked up their biggest paycheck of the season before a full house at Owen Field. Our starters only played the first quarter, which gave freshmen like running back Elvis Peacock a chance to show their stuff. We won, 72–3.

Wake Forest fell, 63–0, and we went into our annual Red River War against Texas undefeated and a three-touchdown favorite. But Darrell Royal had the Longhorns ready for a fanatical effort and showed us his freshman fullback, Earl Campbell. Earl, meet the Selmon brothers.

In the fourth quarter Texas led 13–7. When I heard offensive coordinator Galen Hall call a reverse to Billy Brooks, I didn't think it was the right time or place and I started to change the play. But something told me to shut up. The next thing I knew, Billy Brooks was in the open field and running 40 yards for a touchdown. Then we missed the extra point. With the score tied, 13–13, Texas drove to midfield. On fourth and one, Earl Campbell smashed into the middle for a first down, but he was blindsided by Jimbo Elrod and fumbled the ball. Tony DiRienzo kicked a 37-yard field goal with about five minutes to play, and we escaped with a 3-point win.

Bill Mallory, the new Colorado coach, had criticized Oklahoma as an undisciplined team and said he could not imagine allowing one of his players to wear silver shoes. Little Joe put a fresh coat of silver on his shoes each week and trimmed them in red. Mallory's comments didn't bother me, but I do remember visiting with Joe just before the kickoff against Colorado and teasing him, "Now, you be sure not to make us look silly in your pretty shoes. You couldn't stand to lose to these guys twice in your career." (Our loss to Colorado in 1972, when Eddie Crowder was its coach, was one of only two games we lost in Joe Washington's entire career.) So Joe laced up his silver shoes and ran for 200 yards and four touchdowns as we whipped Colorado 49–14.

The next week Kansas State quarterback Steve Grogan completed 14 of 29 passes for 119 yards, but Little Joe had rushed for 133 by halftime and we won 63–0.

Iowa State was at home and played us tough but lost,

28–10. It was a memorable day for Steve Davis. When the captains went to the middle of the field for the coin toss, there were several Iowa State girl cheerleaders out there and one of them pinched Steve on his rear—just the sort of thing a Baptist preacher would remember. (At least that's the story that Steve told us. He always thought he was a good-looking preacher boy.) Our eighth victory was a 37–0 shutout of Missouri as we rushed for 498 yards. The following Saturday, Kansas surprised us with a 73-yard touchdown run on the third play of the game—the first touchdown Oklahoma had given up in the first half all season—and we had to rally for a 45–14 win.

I declared the Nebraska game in Lincoln to be our bowl game. Cornhuskers' coach Tom Osborne used an 11-yard throwback pass to quarterback David Humm for a touchdown that put Nebraska ahead 14–7 in the third quarter. When Elvis Peacock fumbled the ensuing kickoff and gave Nebraska the ball at our 20, it looked as if they had us on the ropes. But our defense held, Nebraska missed a field goal—and then Steve Davis took over and directed three long touchdown drives that were as good as you will ever see a quarterback execute the Wishbone. On one drive it was third and sixteen. Steve rolled out as if to pass—he didn't complete one all day—and ran for 19 yards. He later called it his best run of the year.

Safety Randy Hughes had complained to me before the game that teams wouldn't try to pass against us. If they called a pass, Lee Roy or Dewey barged in and mangled the quarterback. We didn't even need to blitz. Nebraska quarterback David Humm challenged us in the fourth quarter, and Randy intercepted two passes to give him a career total of fourteen—one shy of the school record, held by Darrell Royal.

Our final opponent of the season, Oklahoma State, was going to the Fiesta Bowl, but we didn't seem to take them seriously. Late in the third quarter, the Cowboys were leading us 13–10 in Norman and our offense looked totally stalled. Suddenly I heard Randy Hughes yelling at offensive linemen John Roush and Jerry Arnold, "You guys better get off your ass and start playing!" It was very unlike Randy to do that, but he certainly caught the attention of our offense. In each of

Randy Hughes's first three years, Oklahoma had a shot at the national championship but didn't make it—losing to Nebraska in 1971 and to Colorado in 1972, and tying USC in 1973. Now it looked as if Oklahoma State was going to knock us out of still another chance at being number one, and Randy wouldn't stand for it. The offense answered his challenge by scoring 34 points. One touchdown was a 57-yard punt return by Joe Washington that is hard to believe even today when I see it on tape. Eight tacklers had Joe surrounded and completely covered up on the sideline at about the 50, and suddenly he appeared out of the mob, running free. We won the game 44–13.

Strangely enough, it was a recruit I lost in a real struggle who helped us win the AP poll. Ike Forte, a junior-college transfer, had promised to come to Oklahoma but wound up at Arkansas, really making me angry at the time. However, Ike Forte had a great game in Arkansas's 1974 opener—a 22–7 victory that spoiled what would have been an undefeated season for the USC Trojans.

As it was, USC finished number one in the UPI coaches' poll and we were number one in the AP writers' poll.

Steve Davis was the ideal Wishbone quarterback. He had fullback legs, halfback speed, and quarterback mentality. He only completed twenty-six passes in 1974, but eleven were for touchdowns. Our receivers—Tinker Owens, Billy Brooks, Joe Washington and Wayne Hoffman—caught a total of thirty-three passes, and thirteen were touchdowns. Critics were already saying I was lax on discipline and "ran a loose ship"—which almost any of my players will tell you is far from the truth—but I had kicked Waymon Clark, a 1,000-yard rusher, off the team for disciplinary reasons. His replacement at fullback, Jim Littrell, ran for 837 yards, finishing second on the team to Little Joe's 1,321.

That was the final season for Hughes, Shoate, linebacker Gary Gibbs (now the Oklahoma head coach), Tony Peters, Ron Waters, and the left side of our offensive line. To tell the truth, every team coming up on our 1975 schedule scared me.

But to hear our fans tell it, we had another national championship in the bag.

Both major political parties were courting Steve Davis as a

possible future candidate for governor or senator. In the summer, Steve leased an airplane and flew to preaching engagements around the country. He appeared on the bill with Billy Graham before crowds of 60,000 in towns like Lubbock, Texas.

We opened the 1975 season with a terrible game against Oregon State in the rain in Norman, fumbling twelve times and drawing eleven penalties. I had held Joe Washington and Steve Davis out of contact drills and scrimmages to keep them from getting hurt, and they both looked rusty. But running back Horace Ivory gained 104 yards and scored two touchdowns on nine carries, and we drowned the Ducks 62–7.

The second game was touted as a contest between Joe Washington and Pittsburgh's Tony Dorsett. Little Joe won the battle by rushing twenty-three times for 166 yards and three touchdowns while Dorsett picked up 17 yards on twelve carries, which was his all-time career low, and was knocked rubbery by Randy Hughes's replacement, strong safety Scott Hill. We beat Pittsburgh, 46–10. You may recall that the very next year Johnny Majors's Pitt Panthers won the national championship, and Tony Dorsett won the Heisman Trophy.

The next week Miami was a 35-point underdog, but Joe had a touchdown called back just before the half, and Miami scored 10 points in the fourth quarter to give us a fright, 20–17. It was our twenty-third straight win and our thirty-second in a row without a loss, but we did not play well and were worried about it.

In the fourth game, we were flat lucky to beat Colorado, 21–20, in Norman. Weird, though, is another way to describe that one. Little Joe had scored twice in the first half, once on a dive and once on a punt return, and with 17 seconds left in the half, we led 14–0. A Colorado punt had just rolled dead on our 2-yard line, and I sent our offense in with orders to simply kill the clock. But Steve Davis fumbled the snap and Colorado recovered on our two. Colorado's Billy Waddy scored on the next play—a 2-yard drive—and we led by only 14–7.

Later in the third quarter Joe let a punt trickle off his fingers and Colorado recovered on our 24. It took six plays for Colorado to score, but they did. Elvis Peacock scored for us, with three minutes remaining in the third quarter, to make it 21–14. But late in the game, the Colorado players and coaches put it all together, really for the first time all day, and made a long 68-yard march for a score, this time a pass to Billy Waddy, to make the score 21–20. Only 1:23 remained on the clock. Instead of going for the 2-point conversion and a victory, Bill Mallory chose to kick the extra point and take the tie, which would surely have cost us the Big Eight championship and eventually the national title. But their kicker missed it! Like I always say, you've got to be lucky—and we had our share in 1975.

After we got the ball back with a 1-point lead against Colorado, I ordered Steve Davis to run out the clock and save the win.

What do you think I heard from the capacity crowd at Owen Field? Boos, that's what. A 1-point victory would nowhere near cover their bets.

Our luck held the next week in a heart stopper against Texas, which entered the game leading the nation in rushing, total offense, and scoring. With the score tied late in the fourth quarter, Horace Ivory ran 33 yards for a touchdown to put us ahead 24–17. Then Joe Washington got us out of a hole with a 76-yard quick kick from our goal line with only three minutes to play. The Longhorns went on to a 10–2 record and tied for the SWC championship.

Steve Davis and Little Joe still hadn't come up to their level of play from the year before, and against Kansas State our Wishbone struggled for the fourth week in a row in a 25–3 win. Iowa State came to Norman the next week, and we set a school record with thirteen fumbles (we had a record fifty-eight for the season) but won easily, 39–7. In the fourth quarter, a freshman named Billy Sims scored his first of many touchdowns for the Sooners.

We blew past Oklahoma State 27–7 for our eighth victory of the season. We had now won twenty-eight straight and had gone thirty-seven without a loss. My personal record was 29–0–1. I bring this up to prepare you for what happened the next week right there on our own home field.

Kansas was a damn good team that year. They had Nolan Cromwell running the Wishbone for coach Bud Moore. Kansas controlled the ball on us. The Jayhawks did not throw a single pass. Steve Davis had the worst day of his life. He threw twelve passes—our side caught three of them and Kansas caught four—and we lost four fumbles, all on eight consecutive possessions.

On the banquet tour I told the story that Steve Davis was after me for four years to let him call his own plays, and I let him do it once—against Kansas in 1975. It got a laugh, but it sure as hell wasn't funny the day Kansas beat our ass 23–3.

I'll always remember our halfback Elvis Peacock going in for an early touchdown when we were leading 3–0 and it would have made it 10–0. But the ball was raked from his arm at the 1-yard line and it bounced twenty yards back upfield—where Kansas recovered it.

It was just that kind of day.

I was standing beside Steve Davis late in the game, and we heard the boos starting.

Here was a kid who had quarterbacked at Oklahoma for three years and had never been beaten in twenty-nine games, and now some of the home fans were booing him.

The clock was ticking down and it was inevitable that we were going to lose the ball game by twenty damn points, and nobody in the world hurt worse than Steve did. It was hard to believe that our fans would boo the whole bunch of us, who had had such success.

I put my arm around Steve on the sideline and told him, "These people we hear are really insignificant. We can't let them influence us or anything we have to do. These people are just molecules in the universe."

In our locker room afterward the players and several of the coaches were crying. I saw Larry Lacewell sitting on a bench with Dewey Selmon, both of them with tears streaming down.

I told the team, "Hold your heads up. You are a great ball club. We rode this train a long time, and it had to stop sooner or later. But we have nothing to be ashamed of. When you talk to the press, be sure to give our opponents their due. They played a hell of a game and deserve the credit. This is not the end of the year for us."

Johnny Keith, OU's sports information director in those days, used to hire a motel suite after every home game. I would go to the motel to talk to all the sports writers who might have been writing their stories right after the game and not have had a chance to visit with me.

Some of the writers would come on to my house after we left the suite. My assistant coaches would show up, libations would be poured, and if we were lucky Kay might heat a pot of duck gumbo. Newspaper guys and magazine writers from out of town were always invited to my house after home games—which is how I got the reputation for throwing a constant party.

When I walked into the motel, I knew they were waiting to see how I would react after a painful defeat. I remembered what Jim MacKenzie had told the press after unbeaten Oklahoma had been demolished by Notre Dame. "It's a very short distance from the castle to the outhouse," Jim had said.

I looked at the empty chair that faced the roomful of press with a few Oilys mixed in.

"I guess I'm going to be like that skunk—and sit down and see how much of this I can take," I said.

I held court much longer than was customary. I didn't want anybody to say I had flinched or been a sour loser. Finally Jim Billings, an official from the Orange Bowl, spoke up. "I've never been in a press conference before with a guy who had won twenty-seven in a row."

"Twenty-eight," I said.

As a result of the loss to Kansas, we dropped to seventh in the national polls and faced a real gut check the next week at Missouri.

I got a letter from a guy in Tulsa telling me any fool could see we ought to abandon the Wishbone and go to a new offense that our opponents hadn't caught up with yet. He didn't mention that it was the Kansas Wishbone that beat us.

You really don't know how a team will react to a devastating loss like ours to Kansas. Steve Davis came to me and said, "It's taken me three or four days to get over the team—and me personally—being booed like that. It sort of confused my Christian faith for our people to act like that. Those people have got the wrong idea of what this game is all about."

The team was emotionally down on our trip to Columbia. Missouri had beaten Alabama 20–7 in their opener. That's how good Missouri was.

Steve Davis played the best half of his life and we led 20–0 at the intermission, but Missouri came back to go ahead 21–20.

Bob Devaney told me later that the stands went crazy in Lincoln when that score was announced, because Missouri beating us would put Nebraska in the Orange Bowl.

Then Missouri scored again but missed the extra point and led us 27–20. With four minutes left, it was fourth and one at our own 24-yard line. I called time out. I was staring at the grass field and saw Missouri replace their standout safety Kenny Downing with a lineman. I was talking on the headphone with Galen Hall. Steve Davis came to the sideline and got on the headphones, too. We were talking about what tendency had Missouri showed on fourth downs and where will they line up in short yardage.

Finally, I said, "Never mind what the hell Missouri is going to do. It's obvious what we are going to do. We are going to run our best play and that is the option. Steve, call the option with Little Joe as the pitchback."

As Steve trotted toward the huddle, I called after him, "Steve, you make sure Joe gets that ball."

Missouri was crammed inside, looking for a sneak. Steve slid down the line and pitched the ball to Little Joe, who cut inside Missouri's left end and spurted into the secondary. Maybe Downing could have caught him, but I don't believe it. Little Joe hit inside the cornerback, planted a foot and cut back against the grain. The Missouri guys are all chasing him full speed one direction, and instantly Little Joe is going in another direction. He sailed 71 yards for a touchdown.

Now it was 26–27 and clearly we can't kick the extra point. We need two to win. I called another time out. Steve Davis ran over and said, "I know, coach, I know. Run the option and make sure Little Joe gets the ball."

Steve pitched it to Little Joe going right and he hurdled two tacklers into the end zone and we had won, 28–27.

The press quizzed me on why we ran two high-risk plays on vital downs.

I said, "What's high-risk about giving the ball to the best back in the country?"

Before our final scheduled game—against undefeated

Nebraska, to see who went to the Orange Bowl—as our seniors were being introduced for the last time to their home crowd, Steve Davis said to me, "We're going to win this one for ourselves." He was still thinking about the booing.

Our defense ate up Nebraska, caused six turnovers, and we scored 21 in the fourth quarter to win 35–10 as the crowd pelted the field with oranges.

The Sooners moved up to third in the national polls at the end of the regular season. Our Orange Bowl opponent would be Michigan, which had two 1,000-yard runners in Rob Lytle and Gordon Bell. I sensed that our team was looking at their first bowl game as a day at the beach. But I shook them up when I kicked Horace Ivory off the team because of a dormitory incident, and he was our second leading runner behind Little Joe. I chewed the players' asses out in our first team meeting because of their poor attitude over the Horace Ivory incident.

And I stunned everybody by ordering a full scrimmage on the first day of practice. It was the first time all season our number-one offense had faced our number-one defense. Nobody was excused. On the first play, Jimbo Elrod knocked the devil out of Steve Davis. The next play, Lee Roy Selmon grabbed Joe Washington and slammed him to the ground.

"Look at that," I told the Michigan sportswriters, who were surprised they had been invited to watch our workouts. "Nobody knows more about the Selmons than we do, and we can't block them either."

That year Lee Roy had won the Lombardi Award as the outstanding college lineman and the Outland Trophy as the outstanding interior lineman.

After we finished our pregame warmups, Steve Davis gave the pregame prayer to the Orange Bowl crowd, but the public-address announcer broke in with the news that UCLA had upset top-ranked Ohio State in their Rose Bowl rematch.

Steve was praying and the crowd was going crazy. Everybody realized that suddenly this game had become much more important. We were playing Michigan for the national championship!

Michigan knocked off Little Joe's headgear and gave Steve Davis a headache in the first quarter. But then Steve hit

Tinker Owens with a 40-yard pass that was a spectacular catch. On the next play we ran the reverse to Billy Brooks, and he scored.

In the fourth quarter, Steve ran 10 yards for another touchdown to put us ahead 14–6, and our defensive studs rose up and kept it that way.

Bo Schembechler told the press, "Oklahoma is a great team with the best manpower we've ever played against. I will vote them number one."

This time, all the polls agreed with Bo.

13

THE RED RIVER WAR

Before I describe my last meeting with Darrell Royal in the Oklahoma-Texas game, otherwise known as the Red River War, let me go back in time a little more than a year—to the summer of 1975.

I released an official statement to the media that summer, and I would like to quote it here so you will understand some of the hysterical events that followed:

"During the past year Coach (Darrell) Royal has made inferences that the University of Oklahoma has possibly used illegal recruiting practices in recruiting high school prospects from Texas.

"On April 29, 1975, our entire coaching staff voluntarily submitted and was given a polygraph test on this past season's recruitment.

"The pertinent questions asked each coach were: Did he offer cars, clothes, money, paid transportation, or selling of tickets to any recruit as inducements to attend the University of Oklahoma and did he ask anyone to provide these inducements to any recruited athletes? All coaches answered 'no' to these questions, and it was the opinion of two professional polygraph examiners that there was no deception and that all coaches had answered truthfully.

"The results of this examination are known to our president, Dr. Paul Sharp, vice-president, J. R. Morris, and faculty representative, David Swank. It was not my intent to divulge the results of this examination, but because of Coach Royal's recent challenge to both our coaching staffs taking a polygraph test, I feel it is necessary at this time.

"The University of Texas and the University of Oklahoma both enjoy one of the greatest football programs in this part of the country. I truly believe that the success each has incurred in recruiting high school athletes is based on that fact alone and not on illegal recruiting methods."

What brought on that statement was an interview the day before in the Tulsa paper quoting Royal as saying I was un- ethical, and challenging the Sooner staffs to take lie-detector tests.

This was really nothing new for Royal to say. In Novem- ber 1974, he was quoted in *Sports Illustrated* as saying, "I resent even playing them (Oklahoma) when they develop a monster team with illegal tactics."

I didn't take Royal seriously in 1974. We had just finished beating Texas four years in a row, and he had to explain it somehow. Texas has its rabid, idiotic fans just like the Okla- homans who booed Steve Davis in the Kansas game.

Besides, there was more than just a little hypocrisy in- volved in Royal's constant damn accusations. He was a really powerful, respected coach, and his attitude toward me made me avoid coaching conventions for years. I felt paranoid and unpopular with most of the leading coaches who were friends of his. I believe Darrell never bought a player or cheated in recruiting. On the other hand, I believe UT's fire-breathing football fan alums are every bit as quick to hand out party favors to players as the OU alums are. It happened behind Darrell's back—just like it happened behind mine—but Aus- tin was no monastery. Their violations were fairly petty stuff, like some of those we were charged with in 1988. But rules are rules, and the NCAA has a million of 'em.

But in 1975 I disagreed with Royal over a proposal to cut back on the size of college coaching staffs and the number of visits allowed to a recruit.

Then, something I said to a group of OU alums in Tulsa made Darrell so mad he started spitting like a cat. I mean, I really struck him on a nerve.

I told the Tulsa group that Darrell supported the cut- backs because they would weaken Oklahoma recruiting in Texas.

"If Oklahoma could only visit a prospect in Texas twice in

seventy days—as this proposal says—I have to think Darrell Royal has a better chance to sign a Texas recruit than I have," I said.

"Some coaches don't want to coach anymore. They would rather sit home and listen to guitar pickers. They want to make it where you can't outwork anybody."

Darrell got so hot when he read this that he telephoned Bill Connors, sports editor of the *Tulsa World,* and called me unethical and challenged us to the lie detector.

Mind you, Darrell Royal was president of the Football Coaches Association of America at the time. If a respected leader of your club tells the world you are a liar and a cheater, it is bound to make an unfavorable impression with your peers.

And on top of everything else, Darrell Royal is a hero in Oklahoma, where he was born and made all-America.

Darrell told Bill Connors it was that remark about the guitar pickers that "really got me wild-eyed."

Although I hadn't mentioned any coach's name, and the newspaper story reported I "said it smilingly and without malice," Darrell told Connors there wasn't any doubt which coach I meant—I meant him.

Well, he was right. I did mean him. I knew Darrell liked to hang out with Willie Nelson and a bunch of those pickers. Hell, I would like to hang out with them myself. I'm a country music fan. But I didn't realize my remark would sting Darrell so hard. I thought it was funny.

Looking back at it now, I can better understand Darrell's feelings. He had turned the corner past fifty years old in that summer of 1975, and I was still a young man of thirty-seven. After the age of fifty it is much harder to work up your enthusiasm for chasing seventeen-year-old recruits, who might stand you up at the hamburger drive-in. I know that feeling now, like wanting to slap an arrogant recruit's face, but I didn't know it when I said some coaches—meaning Darrell—would rather listen to guitar pickers than go out recruiting. Looking back on it, now that many years of experience have soaked in, I have to ask, "Who the hell *wouldn't* rather hang out with Willie Nelson than watch TV in a recruit's living room while the dog hunches your leg?" What seemed funny at thirty-seven is not necessarily funny at fifty-two. To the old bull, the young bull is no joke.

Anyhow, Darrell gave the press a statement that said, "First of all, Barry Switzer does not know why I am in favor of cutbacks on recruiting, because I have never discussed it with him. I am in favor of cutbacks because I feel the aggressive recruiting programs in their present form do irreparable harm to the prospects being recruited.

"For Barry to indicate I am in favor of cutbacks because I do not want to work and would rather listen to guitar pickers, instead, is highly unethical.

"Since he has felt free to inaccurately express my reasons for favoring cutbacks, I have a proposal to make—again. Have the two coaching staffs at Oklahoma and Texas take a lie-detector test based on the recruiting programs of the last two years. If both pass, I will concede I have been outworked and will quit listening to guitar pickers."

Darrell went on to tell Bill Connors, "I wouldn't object if they went back twenty years for a lie-detector test on me. I have never cheated. But I know an awful lot of cheating goes on. I don't think many right-thinking people have any idea how much. If they did, they would want to shut everything down. I'm disturbed by people who excuse cheating by saying every school does it. It rankles me when they say we don't have to cheat because we're Texas. Well, I didn't cheat at Mississippi State or at Washington, either. All state universities have a recruiting advantage. That's why I never did any button-bustin' bragging when we won a good share.

"But as distasteful as it is, if the cutbacks don't pass I will load up my staff with as many recruiters as it takes and raise money and we'll meet our competition. We haven't been outworked. We have been outnumbered. This is not an old lazy coach who doesn't want to work talking. I promise you we will meet the competition."

Darrell had a pretty straightforward solution to the quandary of how to face the results that my staff and I had already passed the polygraph. He said it was bullshit, the tests were rigged.

And the next year he quit his job as head coach at Texas.

But first we had to play each other one more time and

walk down the ramp in the Cotton Bowl together with President Gerald Ford walking between us.

And Darrell was even angrier by now, because before the 1976 game we had our big spying scandal.

Let me go straight to the heart of this "scandal."

It did happen. As it turned out, although I didn't know it at first, Darrell was right to accuse us of that. It was my fault because I was the head coach, it happened, and when I found out about it, I denied that it had happened. The ironic thing about it is that it was not an NCAA violation of any sort, and the NCAA wasn't even interested, but it was a bad, embarrassing deal that should never have happened. I wish I'd said that at the time. When Richard M. Nixon did the same thing I did, they called it Watergate.

A friend of Larry Lacewell named Lonnie Williams, who lived in Texas, slipped in and watched a practice and reported to Larry what he saw. Darrell claimed the vital information the spy passed to us was how he planned to align his defense. Larry was my defensive coordinator (and assistant head coach), so he was more concerned with how we aligned our *own* defense—which simply amounted to strapping two Selmon brothers to Earl Campbell on every play. The only chance to stop Texas was to stop Earl Campbell. This was no secret, by any means.

As you will see by the score, if we learned anything about how to defeat the Texas defense from spying on them, we forgot to take that information onto the field.

We had started the 1976 season by beating Vanderbilt 24–3, with junior Dean Blevins replacing the departed Steve Davis as our Wishbone quarterback.

The next week we rushed for 490 yards and polished off California 28–17. We beat Florida State 24–9 as reinstated Horace Ivory got loose on two long touchdown runs and Elvis Peacock scored another. At Iowa State we didn't look so good. It took two touchdowns late in the game for us to win 24–10.

So this brought us to the Red River War undefeated, two-time defending national champions. We were number one in the nation. Texas had lost by a point to Boston College and had barely beaten North Texas State. The Longhorns were fired up high to knock us off—it was their chance to save what had begun as the kind of season that even legends like Darrell don't survive.

They claim the Red River War is played at a neutral site, even though every time I look at a map, Dallas is still in Texas. And the game is always played the first Saturday of the Texas State Fair.

But Dallas is about halfway between Norman and Austin. A parade of Big Red drives south to collide with an army of Big Orange coming up from the south. The Friday night before the game, downtown Dallas was like a combination of Mardi Gras and a prison breakout. Horns blaring, people screaming, drunks and fistfights everywhere, cops hauling students off to jail.

This game was for serious bragging rights. Oklahoma had a great geology department and had turned out thousands of Oilys who got rich in the Texas oil patch. You didn't see many Texas grads moving to Oklahoma, but Texas was full of Sooners.

Sooners are proud people. "I'm Sooner born and Sooner bred . . . and when I die I'm Sooner dead," is the song they sing, and with the drums and the trumpets it really gets your heart to pumping. Anybody who could go down the ramp at a Texas-Oklahoma game and not feel extremely excited must be legally dead.

They split the ticket allotment to the two universities—37,500 to each.

But the split is in Oklahoma's favor, because Texas gets the north half of the bowl and Oklahoma gets the south half. The north half is solid Orange, and the south half is solid Red.

How is this in our favor? Well, the entrance ramp is at the south end, so that when Oklahoma players leave the locker room and come onto a field in that enormous uproar of noise and emotion, they are at first totally among their own, almost like at a home game.

Well, this Saturday in 1976, Darrell and I are standing in the tunnel on either side of President Ford, waiting to go on the field. President Ford is going to flip the coin. Darrell wasn't speaking to me and I had nothing to say to him, but both of us were trying to conduct a conversation with President Ford.

As we became visible walking toward the field, there is some old redneck drunk Okie (obviously) who stands up several rows behind us and roars in this voice you can hear all the way out to the 50-yard line on both the east and west side.

"Who are those two assholes with Switzer?" is what he roars.

I wanted to step in a hole from embarrassment. I didn't give a damn what Darrell thought, but in front of the president of the United States, this was . . . well, to tell the truth, it was funny. The whole crowd at the south half of the bowl was screaming with laughter. As the remark was passed from mouth to ear, the whole place started laughing.

Texas played our ass off that day. Dean Blevins had suffered an unusual injury a few days earlier, and sophomore Thomas Lott made his debut as our Wishbone quarterback. Against a great Texas defense led by guys like tackle Steve McMichael and safety Johnnie Johnson, we gained only 95 yards in 50 rushes and made a miserable six first downs.

Texas kicked two field goals and led 6–0 late in the fourth quarter. Then a Texas halfback named Ivey Suber fumbled and we took over at midfield and drove for a touchdown that would tie the game and an extra point that would win it.

But our snapper was a little high and hard with the ball, it bounced out of our holder's hands—and the Red River War wound up a 6–6 tie.

Our players were crushed. In their minds we were going for a third straight national championship, and this had derailed us. In the locker room I told them we still had time to win it all, that there was no reason to be ashamed for tying Texas. "It took twenty-two of us not to win this game. No one player is at fault. You've got too much character to let this get us down."

We went to Kansas the next week and took revenge for what they'd done to us in 1975. The score was 28–10, but it wasn't easy. Kansas led 10–3 in the third quarter. Thomas Lott gained 102 yards and scored twice, and still the team was kind of shaky.

Then Oklahoma State came to Norman and beat Oklahoma for the first time since 1966. Oklahoma State is often called Tailback University because of its long line of great tail-backs like Barry Sanders and Thurman Thomas. Well, the one who got us this day was Terry Miller, who ran 73 yards for a touchdown on the third play and gained 154 yards for the game as we lost 31–24.

The following week it got worse. Colorado whipped us 42–31 in Boulder. It was the first time Oklahoma had lost two in a row since 1970. We gave away four fumbles and let Colorado score the final 22 points.

Thomas Lott got going with 195 yards rushing to beat Kansas State 49–20. Against Missouri the next week we won 27–20 as Lott, Kenny King, and Horace Ivory all rushed for more than 100 and we didn't try a single pass.

At Nebraska in the last game on the schedule, we pulled some Sooner Magic to score 13 points in the fourth quarter and beat them 20–17—our fifth straight win over Nebraska— and force a three-way tie for the Big Eight title with OSU, Colorado and us.

Colorado received the Orange Bowl invitation and ended up losing to Woody Hayes and his Ohio State Buckeyes . . . a team we would play for the very first time ever the next year.

Oklahoma was invited to the Fiesta Bowl to play Wyoming, coached by my old Arkansas athletic-dorm social chairman buddy Freddy Akers. We had Wyoming outmanned and won easily, 41–7, without ever punting.

It was the first time I faced Fred as a head coach. But it was a long way from the last.

At the end of his 5–5–1 season, Darrell Royal resigned after twenty years' service at the University of Texas as the winningest football coach in their history (167–47–5, with eleven SWC titles). Royal expected to be succeeded by his defensive coordinator, Mike Campbell, who would keep the program intact.

Instead, the regents at Texas launched their own search, led by a man named Frank Erwin, who was a master promoter of buildings (the Erwin Center is the official name for the Texas basketball arena that the fans and press call the Super Drum) and a master manipulator of people. With a former Texas governor, Alan Shivers, now a regent and an opponent of Darrell's, the board voted not to listen to the old coach's advice.

So to replace Darrell Royal they hired—Fred Akers.

While all this hunting and hiring was going on, I received a phone call from Frank Broyles. The University of Arkansas was changing head coaches. Did I want to return to my home state university in the job I didn't even dare dream of as a kid?

I asked Frank to give me twenty-four hours to think it over. You don't want to drag out something like this at the end of a season, because you and your staff are heavily into recruiting by then.

I think everybody has an urge to go home, where your roots are. But I had been in Oklahoma ten years by then and had known almost nothing but success. My wife, Kay, would have been happy to pack up and move back to Arkansas, but I was looking at the kids we were recruiting for 1977, all these top blue-chippers and everybody coming back from 1976, and I knew we were going to be a great team for the next two or three years at least.

After twenty-four hours I called Frank back and turned him down. He then hired Lou Holtz.

Less than a year later, Lou Holtz would help to cause the worst night of my entire life.

14

SOONER MAGIC

I may have given you the impression that Texas was Oklahoma's most important game of the year. This is not true. Texas is not a conference game. I was expected to beat Texas, of course, but it was even more important to win the Big Eight and go to the Orange Bowl—which meant beating Nebraska.

Oklahoma State was a big game for intrastate recruiting. Missouri and Colorado were big games. But nothing compared to Oklahoma vs. Nebraska. Almost always when we played Nebraska it was for the conference championship, and one or the other of us, if not both, was in the running for the national championship.

In my sixteen years as head coach we played Nebraska seventeen times—yes, that's right, twice in the 1978 season—and beat them twelve.

Nebraska coach Tom Osborne and I each became head coach at our institutions for the 1973 seasons. I coached a total of sixteen complete seasons through the 1988 campaign and finished with a record of 157 wins, 29 losses, and 4 ties, a winning percentage—best in the nation—of .837. Although Tom is still very active, through the same sixteen seasons, Nebraska's record was 158–36–2 for a winning percentage of .811. [Readers might note that Nebraska played more NCAA-approved twelfth games and went to more bowl games than we did.]

When you consider that twelve of Tom's total of thirty-six losses came at the hands of Oklahoma, that tells you how Tom did against everybody else.

But we had something going for us at Oklahoma that our

fans started calling Sooner Magic. Eight times in really major games, sometimes when it didn't seem remotely possible, Oklahoma came from behind to defeat Nebraska in some kind of a magical way. I would add that in my total career in games that were decided by three points or less, our record was 17–1. You Nebraskans will take pleasure in knowing that that one loss was a 17–14 loss to Nebraska in 1978, one that clearly cost us the national championship for that season.

The 1975 game with Nebraska did not itself involve Sooner Magic, but it was set up by something close to it—our great comeback win over Missouri, 28–27. Nebraska came into that game undefeated and ranked second in the nation behind Ohio State. We ran all over them, 35–10, on our way to our second national title. But Bob Devaney, Nebraska athletic director, told me after the game that Nebraska was already psyched out and beaten before they ever made that trip to Norman.

The week before, the Nebraska team had been in their locker room celebrating their tenth victory. Somebody ran in and yelled that Missouri had beaten Oklahoma 27–20. Everybody in the locker room started cheering and shouting, "Beach! Beach! Beach!" None of those Nebraska players had ever beaten Oklahoma, and now it looked like they were going to Miami and the Orange Bowl without having to beat us. They were really celebrating. Then they heard the true final score. Oklahoma had won, 28–27. Devaney said the locker room suddenly became like a morgue. We had taken something away from them that they thought was already theirs—but now they would have to fight for it. Bob said all week he could feel the drastic emotional effect of the mood change caused by that score. He wasn't surprised when we knocked Nebraska out of another undefeated season.

Our kids always rose to the occasion when they played Nebraska. The Nebraska people called it a jinx. We called it Sooner Magic.

It started in 1974, when we came back from a 14–7 deficit and won 28–14. There wasn't all that much magic involved, but it was a comeback victory. The term Sooner Magic really came into use in 1976. We were a young team, and Nebraska was clearly better than we were. I asked Scott Hill, team captain and defensive back, to say a prayer in the locker room before the game, as is customary. Scott said, "Please, dear Lord, don't let any injury or harm come to any player. And please, please, please, dear Lord, please don't let the best team win."

With three minutes left on a cold afternoon in Lincoln, we had the ball on our own 16. Nebraska had led by as much as 17–7 and was still up by 4. Woodie Shepard threw a 50-yard halfback pass to Steve Rhodes, a freshman from Dallas, who made a miraculous catch. A couple of plays later, Dean Blevins passed to Rhodes on the old hook-and-lateral play, Rhodes pitched it to Elvis Peacock, and Elvis was knocked out of bounds at the 3. We scored, with thirty seconds left, to win the game 20–17, and join a three-way tie for the conference championship—without Nebraska being in the trio.

In 1978 the Cornhuskers turned it around on us—they thought. We were 9–0, going for a perfect season and another national championship. We fumbled nine times and lost six of them. Billy Sims gained 153 yards in 25 carries on his way to winning the Heisman Trophy. But with 3:27 on the clock, we had the ball at the Nebraska 3-yard line and trailed 17–14. Billy fumbled it away. We never got the ball back. Nebraska was offered the Orange Bowl bid that afternoon.

But the next week we crushed Oklahoma State 62–7, and Nebraska was upset by Missouri. I told our kids in the locker room that it looked as if we would go to the Sugar Bowl. They were all excited, whooping and hollering. The trainer came and told me I had a phone call from the Orange Bowl committee. The Orange Bowl said they had not spoken to Nebraska about it yet, but wanted to know if we would accept an invitation to a rematch. I said, "Well, let me ask our players." I put down the phone and gathered the team.

"We have our choice," I said. "We have the Sugar Bowl and there's a chance at the Cotton Bowl and there's several other bowls that want us. But the Orange Bowl is on the phone right now wanting to know if you all would like to play Nebraska again."

The team went bananas.

On the television news later, we saw Nebraska's reaction when the Orange Bowl people told them who they had to play in Miami. They had somber faces. There was no cheering. I didn't blame them. I've seen those rematches in college football—like in 1959, when Billy Cannon made his 89-yard punt return to beat Ole Miss in Baton Rouge and then Ole Miss just killed L.S.U. in the Sugar Bowl. In fact it had been UCLA revenging an earlier defeat by Ohio State in the Rose Bowl rematch that opened the door for our national championship in 1975.

In the Orange Bowl rematch when we only fumbled once, we led Nebraska 31–10 in the fourth quarter and ended up winning 31–24. Nebraska scored a meaningless touchdown on the game's last play long after we had started celebrating the victory. The Sooner Magic was in getting us another shot at them.

The following season, 1979, Nebraska was unbeaten again when they came to Norman. We had lost one game—to Texas and Fred Akers and Earl Campbell, a nonconference game. It was the final appearance in Norman for Billy Sims, who should have won the Heisman again as a senior, but the voting was done before he exploded against Missouri and Nebraska. Billy broke 74 yards for a touchdown up the middle on our first play, but it was called back for a penalty. And still Billy gained 247 yards on 28 carries against the Cornhuskers, who led the nation in rushing defense. With eight minutes to go, OU was leading 10–7 with the ball at the Nebraska 3 on fourth down. I first sent the field-goal unit onto the field, but changed my mind and sent the offense back in. Our junior quarterback, J. C. Watts, scored a touchdown on a keeper. Nebraska drove 86 yards to come within 17–14, but that's as close as they got.

The 1980 Oklahoma-Nebraska game is memorable because of things that happened both on and off the field. Let's set the stage for that game by recalling some of the events that preceded it. In order for you to understand why it was so funny, you need to understand that since Oklahoma and Nebraska were almost always playing for the conference title and the right to go to the Orange Bowl, we almost always made a two-team deal with the bowls. The winner would go to the Orange Bowl and the loser would go to another good bowl, such as the Fiesta Bowl in Phoenix.

In 1980, however, I had personally promised Jimmy
Rogers, executive director of the Sun Bowl in El Paso, Texas,
that if we did not go to the Orange Bowl, I would bring the
Sooners to the Sun Bowl. But the Nebraska folks wanted none
of El Paso or the Sun Bowl. They adopted the position of
Orange Bowl or bust.

On my regular Thursday-night television show from
KTVY-TV in Oklahoma City, I joked that the only reason
Nebraska didn't want a tie-up with the Sun Bowl was that they
didn't like Mexican food. I had no idea at the time, but a TV
station in Lincoln, Nebraska, had picked up the feed from
KTVY-TV, and my show was shown live in Lincoln!

Well, when we arrived in Lincoln on Friday afternoon,
every marquee and sign in front of every motel and convenience store in Nebraska had signs like SWITZER AND SOONERS
LOVE TACOS. The Nebraska press had a big day with us,
ridiculing us for tying up with what they considered to be a
minor bowl.

Lee Allen Smith, currently an advertising executive in
Oklahoma City and a close friend of mine, was the general
manager of KTVY-TV at that time. Lee Allen had asked me
to do a live shot back to Oklahoma City from Lincoln's NBC
affiliate. It just happened to be the same television station that
the Nebraska athletic director Bob Devaney did his weekly
show from.

When I finished doing my live show back to Oklahoma
City and was starting to leave the studio, I noticed that there
was a lot of activity, moving around sets, cameras, and the like.
I happened to ask Dick Janna, the producer for both Bob Devaney's and Tom Osborne's TV shows, what was going on.
Dick told me that Bob Devaney was going to be doing his live
show from this studio at 10:30 P.M. I looked at my watch, saw
that that was in about twenty minutes, and had an idea.

I asked a stagehand whether he would run out to a Taco
Bell that I had noticed a few blocks from the station and pick
up a sack of tacos. He said he would, and I handed him a few
bucks. Then I asked Dick Janna whether I could hide behind
the set of Devaney's show and choose my time to come out
during the show. Dick said it was a great idea and a lot of fun.
The stagehand arrived back in the studio with the tacos just

before Bob got there, and I was just able to hide myself behind the set before Bob walked up.

Bob arrived on the set with Ray Hong, a restaurateur from Honolulu, whom I later met and enjoyed visiting with on several of my Hula Bowl trips. Then, as Bob began the show, he said, "I wish I knew where Switzer is now. I'd present him with this pineapple, because where he'll be going after tomorrow's game there will only be Mexican food."

There couldn't have been a better cue than that! I immediately walked out onto Devaney's set. You should have seen Bob's expression! It was one of total unbelieving shock . . . that there I was! He was totally speechless . . . but I said, "Bob, I've got something for you." I took the pineapple out of his hand and handed him the sack of tacos. "These are for you just in case you need them—since you guys won't be going anywhere for New Year's."

Bob Devaney, long the old pro, had by this point gathered his composure. We shook hands and visited for a while on camera, saying all the right things about each other and the great programs at each of our schools.

I'm certain that all the Nebraska fans who were watching that show, especially the coaches and players, became convinced that this Switzer guy was nuts. I guess this is one of the reasons people have always said that Switzer's Sooners are a loosey-goosey bunch. What it really is, is just having fun and a belief that fun is what it all should be. But to tell you the truth, I don't know that I would have had the nerve to pull that stunt if Nebraska hadn't been a two-touchdown favorite. They were the ones with the pressure on them—and they were expected to win.

As it turned out, the game was another thriller in which Sooner Magic played a decisive role. Cornhuskers' running back Jarvis Redwine ran 89 yards for a touchdown in the first quarter, and Nebraska scored another touchdown with 3:16 to play to go back in front 17–14. But super J. C. Watts took us on an 80-yard drive in eight plays, and freshman Buster Rhymes dived in for a 1-yard touchdown with only 56 seconds left, to give us a 21–17 win.

As a footnote to the 1980 game and the TV taco show, Nebraska ultimately relented and decided to accept the Sun

Bowl invitation. I have heard that my friend Jimmy Rogers made sure the Nebraska family enjoyed their stay in El Paso. It was not much of a "bust" for them after all, because they beat a good Mississippi State club 31–17.

In 1984, Nebraska had the nation's top rushing offense and we were tops in the country in rushing defense. Nebraska was ranked number one in the country and was a solid 6-point favorite. They really showed why they were the favorites when they took the opening kickoff and moved impressively down the field against our very good defense. They stalled, however, and on fourth down from about our 20-yard line, they lined up and attempted a field goal for what would have been an early 3–0 lead. They kicked it, but the ball hit the left up-right of the goalpost, bouncing back into the end zone! I couldn't believe it! But then I could. I knew we couldn't lose. I was jumping up and down and I grabbed my nephew Bryce, who was there on the sideline with me and screamed, "It's our night." And it was. That damn, beautiful old goalpost shook all night, signaling the Sooner Magic in Lincoln, Nebraska.

Later in the game we were ahead by 10–7, and Nebraska made what was obviously a last-ditch drive. They drove literally to our 1-inch line. But on fourth down, when they tried a pitch sweep to our right, our defense swarmed the ball carrier. Our defense made its own magic! Then our quarterback, Danny Bradley, ran 29 yards for the touchdown that put us up for good at 17–7.

But the greatest example of Sooner Magic probably came in 1986, back in Lincoln.

A few weeks before the Nebraska game, I had been in Oklahoma City and was rushing back to Norman for a team meeting when I saw the lights flashing behind me and recognized a state trooper car.

A big, fine-looking black patrolman—about 6-foot-6 and 250—got out and said, "Coach, you're in an awful big hurry." I had seen this patrolman before and knew he was stationed in Norman, and his name tag read Jerry Cason.

I said, "Jerry, I've been looking for a guy like you."

Actually, I had. Coach Bryant used to have Alabama state troopers around him at games, and that had always looked like a cool and safe thing to do. I had noticed, too, that a lot of the SEC coaches, including Pat Dye and Vince Dooley, used troopers in this way. But on that afternoon Jerry looked at me, puzzled, so I took control of the conversation.

"I've been considering taking security with me to all road football games. If your supervisor approves it, would you be interested in the job?"

In short order, Jerry and I were friends and traveling companions. He was quite impressive in his state police uniform with his .357 Magnum on his hip. He had been a gunner on a helicopter in Vietnam. Jerry asked what he should do in various situations. I told him, "What do you think I have you traveling with me for? If anybody grabs me or puts their hands on me, I want you to shoot the son of a bitch." Obviously, Jerry knew I was joking.

Well in 1986, Nebraska was leading at the half, and when I walked toward the north-end zone where we entered the visitors' locker room, the crowd of Nebraska fans, all dressed in red, were screaming and taunting and busting my ass and telling me what they were going to do to me in the second half. Some Nebraska drunk reached over the rope and pulled me up into his face unexpectedly. I jerked back and grabbed him by his parka and shouted, "Jerry, shoot this son of a bitch!"

Jerry grabbed at his pistol! (Faking it, of course.) I was hiding a smile, but the crowd didn't know if I meant it. People started ducking and running and falling over each other, and we escaped to the locker room!

The second half of that game was astonishing Sooner Magic.

We scored 10 points in the last 1:22 of the fourth quarter. On our own 6-yard line with four minutes to play. Jamelle Holieway hit Derrick Shepard with a 35-yard pass—I later read in the story of the game written by Wayne Bishop in *Sooners' Illustrated* that just as Derrick caught that pass, a voice in the Nebraska press box cried out in anguish, "Oh no, they're going to do it to us again!" Then on third down, Jamelle threw a 20-yard touchdown pass to our great tight end Keith Jackson, who wrestled it away from the defensive back. We kicked the point and tied the score 17–17.

Nebraska went one, two, three, punt and we got the ball back with less than a minute to go. It was third and twelve on our 45, with 18 seconds left. Jamelle passed to Keith Jackson down the sideline. Keith made a fantastic one-handed catch and raced down the boundary and was finally knocked out of bounds at the 13. Six seconds on the clock. Tim Lashar went in and kicked the field goal and we won, 20–17.

Nebraska was stunned. The crowd was almost silent. Jerry the policeman and I walked off the field toward that same tunnel where I had been grabbed. On the right side of the end zone, the Nebraska fans in red were deflated and frustrated. On the left side of the end zone, the OU fans in red were deliriously happy.

I nudged Jerry and pointed at the Nebraska fans and said, "That bunch is awful damn quiet."

Just as if I had been a movie director giving them a cue, the 15,000 Nebraska fans in that section all rose as one person—men, women, grandfolks, little kids, they all stood up and gave me the finger.

Yeah, 15,000 Nebraskans all shooting me the bird.

"God, Jerry, I'd love to have a picture of that to hang on my wall," I said.

What had stunned those wonderful Nebraska diehards was not only that their team had lost, but that in the last five minutes of the game, Oklahoma had the ball 3:32 to Nebraska's 1:28; Oklahoma ran 17 plays to the Husker's 3; Oklahoma scored 10 points to Nebraska's 0; we picked up 6 first downs to Nebraska's 0; we gained 150 yards in total offense to only 4 for Nebraska; and we rushed for 49 yards while they were rushing for 4 yards. But . . . I guess that's why they call it Sooner Magic.

Before our 1987 game with Nebraska (again to be played in Lincoln, because of a Big Eight Conference schedule adjustment) Nebraska athletic director Bob Devaney finally got his chance to get back at me for the taco joke of 1980. In 1987, I was doing my Thursday-night television show from Tulsa with host Dean Blevins, my old quarterback. As part of the show, we planned to have a live hook-up with Bob Devaney in a studio in Lincoln by remote. Bob was my guest on my show.

But totally to my surprise, right during the middle of this segment of the show out walked this incredible stripper from some Tulsa nightclub, and then, right there on live television, came over, hopped into my lap, and did whatever it is those girls do—when they are dancing! To say that I was shocked would be an understatement. But I guarantee you that I enjoyed that more than Bob enjoyed the tacos. That's what's great about the coaching profession—the great guys in it. Thanks, Bob.

People around the country need to remember that Bob Devaney was one of the really great men of college football history. But for reasons that totally escape me (Bob was never on probation, and I don't think he offended any of the powers in the American Football Coaches Association), he was never selected as AFCA's coach of the year. Bob is considered by those who really know the game to be one of the best coaches and molders of fine young men that the game has known.

But back to Sooner Magic. Our 1987 Nebraska game was called the Game of the Century Two. Nebraska was a 4-point favorite, and a lot of their players were really talking it up in the press about how badly they were going to beat us. Their great defensive end Broderick Thomas was quoted as saying that Nebraska's stadium was "our house" and that they weren't going to let those guys from Oklahoma come in and take it over. What Broderick didn't know, however, was that we had the "key" to their house. It was great players and something called Sooner Magic.

Nebraska took a 7–0 lead on their second possession with a splendid 10–play, 84-yard drive, and was leading by the same score at the half. But they then began a streak of going twelve straight possessions without making a first down.

If we hadn't fumbled eight times, we would have beaten them a lot worse than 17–7. Jamelle was hurt, and redshirt freshman Charles Thompson started at quarterback with another reserve, Rotnei Anderson, at fullback. Both gained more than 100 yards rushing. Broderick Thomas had predicted they would beat us by four touchdowns. I said, "Hell, Nebraska hadn't scored but three touchdowns against us in three years. What made them think they could do it this year?"

Tom Osborne called that the most disappointing defeat of his life. He said, "There's not a lot I can say. We just got whipped."

I'll guarantee you that there was no one in the world happier than my daughter, Kathy, that we had just beaten Nebraska. Even though all of the coaches other than I and most of the players already knew about it, she had been dreading telling me about something that had happened to her two nights before the game and she really wouldn't have known how to do it if we had lost. But there we were in all of the joy and uproar of having won with the incredible comeback and then Kathy picked her moment to tell me that she had run into and destroyed a Porsche 911 on the way to Norman to catch the flight to Lincoln, Nebraska.

The timing couldn't have been better for her. I was so thrilled with the Nebraska win, I couldn't even chew her out. What the hell's a 911, anyway?

At that point we had won twenty-five straight Big Eight Conference games and twenty straight victories over all. Obviously, great and talented players were responsible, but a lot of people figure that a little bit of Sooner Magic was involved, too.

15

FROM THE PENTHOUSE
TO THE . . .

On September 24, 1977, Oklahoma and Ohio State played a classic game in Columbus, Ohio. It was one of the greatest things I ever saw or participated in—90,000 people screaming in the stadium on that big old campus with row after row of academic buildings. That campus is so big we would call it a city in Oklahoma. The legendary Woody Hayes standing on the other side of the field, glancing appraisingly at the Oklahoma players. It's like Woody was thinking, How did I ever get talked into *this*?

I remembered something Larry Lacewell had said. "We try to keep this game of football fun, but on Saturday 90,000 people interfere."

Oklahoma was ranked third in the nation, and Ohio State was fourth. It was the first-ever meeting of the two football powers. The whole country was curious to see what Woody Hayes would do to an upstart like me.

We built a 17–0 lead in the first half that could have been one touchdown more if David Overstreet's run hadn't been called back for a penalty. But Thomas Lott, who had been injured all year, was knocked out of the game with a hamstring pull. I replaced him again with senior Dean Blevins. But Billy Sims was injured and had to leave the game with two quarters to play. You don't replace Billy Sims.

Oklahoma went ahead 20–0 in the third quarter, and then chaos broke loose and Ohio State scored 28 unanswered points.

140

Trailing by 8 with fourth and goal at the Ohio State 1 yard line, 1:29 left in the game, we scored on an option. We went for the 2-point conversion on another option but were stopped. Now Ohio State led 28–26.

It may sound like we found our kicker, Uwe von Schamann, in Prussia, but he was a high school star from Fort Worth, Texas. Uwe punched an on-sides kick that Oklahoma recovered barely across the 50-yard line.

Dean Blevins hit Steve Rhodes, number 24, with a pass to the Buckeye 24. I called time-out with three seconds on the clock. I felt confidence in Uwe. He could kick it from 61 if he needed. All we had to do was keep the Ohio State rush off of him.

Our players went back to huddle, and now Woody Hayes called time out. They wanted Uwe to think about the feat he was facing—kicking a 41-yard field goal to beat *Ohio State*.

The whole 90,000 people chanted, "Block that kick! Block that kick! Block that kick!"

Uwe was one cool character. He stepped out to the center of the field and knelt, with his head bowed as if meditating. Then he stood and waved his arms to the crowd like an orchestra leader conducting their chanting.

"Block that kick! Block that kick! Block that kick!" And Uwe is making like Toscanini.

It was an electric, eerie feeling when the ball was snapped perfectly to a perfect hold, and von Schamann kicked it right through the middle of the posts with so much power it landed in the back rows of the stadium.

You never heard 90,000 people so silent.

Oklahoma 29, Ohio State 28.

The most famous field goal in Oklahoma history.

After the game, I told the press, "I've got to be the luckiest guy alive."

Woody Hayes said, "The hell with the most exciting. I'd rather be dull as hell and win."

We beat Kansas easily the next week and were 4–0 and first in the nation when my old buddy Fred Akers ambushed us 13–6 in the Red River War. Replacing Darrell, Fred had gone to the I formation to let Earl Campbell have the ball thirty times a game and break records. And Fred inherited one of the best group of defensive players in the country.

Don't forget that Fred Akers had an 86–31–2 record and two SWC titles in his ten years as head coach at Texas. In 1977 he was 11–0 until he lost the national championship to Notre Dame in the Cotton Bowl. In 1981 he was 10–1–1 and beat Alabama in the Cotton Bowl. In 1983, Fred's Longhorns came within one fumbled punt at the end of the Cotton Bowl game from being 12–0 and winning a national championship. But that fumble gave Georgia a 10–9 victory, Fred's season fell to 11–1, and three years later he was fired in an outcry of angry alums. Fred beat me five times and tied me once at Texas, but that first one really hurt because it was our only loss of the regular season.

We needed an interception late in the game to beat Missouri the next week. But then we rambled through the rest of our schedule—rushing for more than 400 yards against both Colorado and Nebraska and running up big scores. Nebraska had a tailback named I. M. Hipp, who was supposed to be the greatest thing since plumbing, and he gained 33 yards against us.

Oklahoma was Big Eight champion again. The question was, Who would we play in the Orange Bowl?

The Orange Bowl committee asked if my team would like to play the SWC runner-ups, and we phoned our friends in Arkansas to load up on suntan lotion.

Arkansas had lost only one game—a 13–9 squeaker to Texas—and had finished second in the Southwest Conference in Lou Holtz's first year as head coach.

The bowl situation set up with Texas rated a big favorite over Notre Dame, which was ranked seventh in the nation. Oklahoma was ranked second in the nation, behind Texas. If Texas beat Notre Dame as expected, the title went to Fred Akers.

Somewhere in all this speculation, people were losing sight of the fact that Arkansas was a damn good football team, with some great players like Dan Hampton. A few days before the Orange Bowl, Lou Holtz had some disciplinary problems and kicked off his best halfback, Ben Cowens, who was leading the conference in rushing, along with his fullback Michael

Forrest, and his best receiver, Donnie Bobo—three starters who had to stay home.

The suspensions suddenly shot us up to an 18-point favorite over Arkansas.

I remember sitting in the hospitality room in Miami in the afternoon and watching the Cotton Bowl on television with the press and media. My players were in their rooms watching the game. If Texas whipped Notre Dame that afternoon, it didn't matter how much we beat Arkansas that night, we wouldn't have a shot at the national championship.

But Notre Dame upset Texas 38–10.

The trap was set for us. We went into that night's game the most overconfident team I ever saw. In football it is no question but that the mental and physical preparation are a given, but the emotional plays a bigger part than either of those.

We were the poorest prepared emotionally of any team I ever coached. It was my fault. It was a combination of things, but I was the guy in charge. On the TV, after Texas lost, the announcer said, "This means Oklahoma wins the Orange Bowl tonight and takes their third national championship in the last four years."

That's how everyone looked at it except the people on the Arkansas side of the ball.

I lost my head, I guess. Here I was playing my alma mater, with the national championship practically in my pocket again, and all my old pals from Arkansas were eating their hearts out.

It had rained off and on all day and it was drizzling just before kickoff. The Orange Bowl had a grass field at that time, and although it was not muddy, it was slick. We had developed a pattern of usually choosing to kick off if we won the toss, because we felt our defense was so dominating that we would usually end up in better field position for our offense than if we simply received the kickoff. But this night my offensive coaches are saying, "Come on, coach, we gotta go win, we gotta go score, we gotta take the ball. We've gotta make something happen."

I don't give a damn what's at stake, to win the ball game you had better do the things that are conservative, that you believe in, that win for you percentage-wise. You'd better keep doing what got you there.

But that night I chose to receive. God, I knew it was a mistake. The minute I saw them lining up to kick the ball, I wanted to run out and stop them. We didn't drop the kick, thank heaven, but we did take a loss on our first two plays. From back at our 10, we ran a draw on third down and Billy Sims fumbled it.

Arkansas recovered at our 7 and went in and scored.

Emotionally, Arkansas was miles higher than we were. Lou Holtz had done a hell of a job. He beat me on both sides of the ball. I was solidly outcoached on offense and defense and probably in the kicking game, too, if it mattered.

Arkansas surprised us on defense. We had prepared for a certain scheme that Arkansas had played all year against other Wishbone teams—Texas A&M, for example. But Holtz changed his defensive alignment and how he supported with his secondary, things he had not done before, and we never could get unconfused. We just didn't have the focus. We couldn't concentrate on the different looks we were seeing. That was the worst example of preparing a team for a game that I ever gave in my life.

In the first half, we had an eight-minute drive and wound up punting from our own 46. That's how pitifully we were executing our offense. Arkansas running back Roland Sales, a substitute, gained 205 yards on 23 carries. Everything Oklahoma tried, Arkansas stuffed us.

The final score was Arkansas 31, Oklahoma 6.

I have never been so humiliated.

For the rest of my life, every time I went home to Arkansas I would have to hear jokes and jabs about this night.

Not to mention what I would have to hear when I went home to Oklahoma.

After the game was over and we were dressed and I had handled the press, I was left with my son, Greg, who was about ten.

I said, "Let's go to the Arkansas dressing room, son. I want to congratulate Coach Holtz."

Greg said he would rather not.

"Suck it up," I said. "You've got to learn to do things like this in life."

The Arkansas locker room was full of coaches I had played with and worked with. I knew them all. I shook hands and congratulated them, and pretty soon Lou Holtz comes walking in from the shower.

Lou is a skinny little guy who can't see his shoes without his glasses. If Woody Allen were a football coach, he'd be Lou Holtz.

I introduced Greg to Lou, and Lou said all the nice, complimentary things, all the gracious things, like, "Your daddy has the best record in college football and you ought to be very proud of him." Greg just kept nodding, never saying a word.

Later, Greg and I were walking down the tunnel to board the bus back to our hotel. I was holding his hand and he still hadn't said a word, as if he was in total amazement.

Finally, Greg said, "Daddy, did he play football?"

"Who?"

"Coach Holtz. He's the same size I am."

Back in Norman, nobody had put a FOR SALE sign in my yard or killed any of my cats. But the rumor factory was cranking full blast with the gossip that Larry Lacewell and I had conspired to throw the Orange Bowl game.

Can you imagine? Two boys who grew up in Arkansas and me with a chance to beat my alma mater for the *national championship*. We would throw the biggest game we had ever coached?

I mean, if you had given either of us a choice at 8 o'clock that Orange Bowl night of losing to Arkansas or jumping naked into a pit of starving wolverines, we would have started stripping.

The gossip and insinuations were all around town, and spread throughout the state. They said Larry and I had major gambling debts in Las Vegas and this was how we repaid them.

The rumors never did appear in print, but they were on many thousands of lips. My brother, Donnie, and his family (his wife, Linda, and their twins, Alison and Bryce) moved to Oklahoma in February 1978, right in time to receive this greeting from their new neighbors.

I guess one reason none of the fiction writers printed the

rumors is that the only thing they could find to really pin on me was the decision to receive instead of kick off.

This is awfully circumstantial as evidence, but sooner or later, if you stay in Oklahoma long enough, somebody will eventually tell you about the great Switzer-Lacewell Orange Bowl conspiracy.

It became part of the folklore. "You know why Switzer decided to receive in the rain on grass? He knew Sims would fumble."

It reminded me of four years earlier, when Randy Hughes, our all-American safety, went to some big city back East to accept an award.

The very first question some sportswriter asked Randy was, "How does it feel to be an outlaw playing for an outlaw school?"

Randy Hughes was an academic all-American and as straight an arrow as you will find outside anywhere.

And that reminds me of something more recent. A few months ago, Oklahoma offensive coordinator Jim Donnan, who coached four years for me and one for Gary Gibbs, left Norman to take over as head coach at Marshall University, where the football team is known as the Thundering Herd.

The first week Donnan was there, a couple of football players got thrown out of some saloon. About twenty football players armed with baseball bats went back to the same saloon and demolished the place.

Newspaper headlines the next day said: "DONNAN BRINGS OKLAHOMA OUTLAW TRADITION WITH HIM."

I've sort of gotten away from the subject of my most agonizing football loss, but that's because I can't stand to think of it for long.

Until 1989, that Orange Bowl defeat to Arkansas was the low point of my career.

I'm still liable to wake up in the middle of the night and mumble, "No, no, let's kick the ball . . ."

16

BAPTIST QUARTERBACKS

In the spring following the 1973 season, the town of Eufaula, Oklahoma, put on a parade and a special day to honor Lucious Selmon.

The parade started at the high school. They had an old tractor with a big flatbed trailer behind it. There were seats on the trailer, with Lucious right up front and me close beside him and banners fluttering in the wind.

Eufaula had about two thousand residents at the time, and every shop and store was closed for the occasion. Everybody in town lined along the one main street and waved and cheered as the tractor pulled the grinning Lucious toward the place where we were going to give speeches.

The town fathers had also said that they were going to name the street that ran out to the Selmon home Selmon Road. When I heard that, I told Lucious, "I wouldn't accept that if I were you, Lou." He looked at me with a puzzled look and asked why. I said, "Hell, I'd make them pave it first." (It was just like one of those old gravel roads I had to walk home on when I was a kid.)

As we passed the pool hall on Main Street, Lucious turned around and yelled at me.

"See that kid standing over there?"

I looked over there and saw a husky black kid about six feet tall.

"You mean that one?" I said.

"Yeah. That kid is a great football player. He's going to be your quarterback someday. His name is J. C. Watts."

"If he's a great player, how come I never heard of him?"

"Because he's only a sophomore in high school," Lucious said.

Long before he watched Lucious and me go past in that parade, J. C. Watts knew he was going to Oklahoma. There was no real recruiting problem with him. Oklahoma State made a run at him, but Lucious, Lee Roy, and Dewey Selmon were his heroes, Thomas Lott was his favorite quarterback, and OU was his favorite school.

Quarterbacking is so important, and I was lucky to start off my head-coaching career with three great quarterbacks in a row. Not only were they great players—they also stayed healthy, except for Thomas Lott in his junior year with a pulled hamstring that limited him early in the 1977 season.

First Steve Davis ran our Wishbone to three straight Big Eight (and two national) championships. Then Thomas Lott took over and quarterbacked us to three straight Big Eight titles. J. C. Watts was the backup for Lott in 1978, became the starter the next season, and won two Big Eight championships and was voted the most valuable player in the Orange Bowl two years in a row—the only time that has ever happened.

I know I have said the 1974 team was the best I ever had at Oklahoma, but on further reflection, the 1978 bunch might have been the best. Or maybe my 1987 team was the best of all. I don't know how I would really compare them, but I do know the 1978 team could have won the national championship as easy as not, and the 1986 and 1987 teams would have both won it had it not been for Miami.

We finished third in the AP poll in 1978. It was the year Billy Sims rushed for 1,762 yards to lead the nation as a junior and win the Heisman Trophy. It was the year we played Nebraska twice—as I discuss in Chapter 14, "Sooner Magic"—and won the rematch in the Orange Bowl.

A last-second end-zone interception helped us survive eight fumbles and beat Stanford 35–29, to open the 1978 season in Palo Alto. We came home the next week in 95-degree heat against West Virginia, and Sims had 114 yards on 8 carries in the first half as we won 52–10. After that game, I told the press that Thomas Lott was the best Wishbone quarterback Oklahoma'd ever had.

Our third game was against Rice, and it was almost embarrassing. Oklahoma was leading 52–0 and had the ball on the Rice 2 when the gun sounded—and that was at the half! I walked across the field at the half to Rice coach Ray Alborn and said, "I'm sorry. I'm not trying to run up the score. I can't tell my kids just to take the ball and fall down." Alborn knew I was telling the truth. He had no bitch against us or the final score of 66–7.

There were lots of times during the 1970s when scores got out of hand like that, but by and large, the only people who raised hell about it were those sportswriters who didn't understand the game or know what was going on. First of all, teams like Rice wanted to play Oklahoma if they could because it meant a great deal to their programs financially if they could get the guarantee we were offering with our 76,000-capacity stadium sold out—as it always was. They knew they were overmatched, but it was good for their programs and for the kids, too, because they got to compete at a higher level. Athletes always want a chance to compete against the best.

Scores did not mount because we wanted to embarrass our opponents. You don't do that in the football business, because, really, "What goes around, comes around." There were two basic reasons for those scores. One was the Wishbone. In the early years when we were running the Wishbone, a lot of coaches were scrambling simply to learn how to tell their players to line up against us. But when they figured that out, no matter how good their players might have been, we had an advantage because their kids simply didn't have enough repetitions in practice to become familiar enough with all the variables so that they would be able to react instinctively in a game. If you have to think about what you are going to do defensively, the other team (if it's running the triple option) has probably already scored.

But obviously, the most important reason for the scores that got out of hand was the same reason we beat a lot of great teams, too: We had more players and better players. Even if a defensive player has learned his responsibilities, there were only two or three schools in the country that could provide truly realistic practice simulation of game conditions. That is, with a scout team or B team practicing against a first team, when the scout team had 4.4 and 4.5 speed backs running at you. You simply can't simulate speed. You have to see it in the flesh.

Also, because of the strength of the Oklahoma program and the higher scholarship limits (fifty per year and ninety in a two-year period), we were often in a situation where our second- and third-team players were quite a bit better athletes than the first-team players of our opponents. By the time our second and third teams hit the field, generally in the second or third quarter, they were fresh and raring to go, while the opponents' first-team players were dead tired. If the over-matched teams put in their second- or third-team players, it would become absurd, because I could not tell our players to quit or lie down.

The reduction in the number of scholarships down to ninety-five over four years was designed to reduce this disparity in talent—and it has, to a great extent. It has reduced the talent edge that Oklahoma, Miami, USC, Nebraska, and Notre Dame had. But obviously, because of their tradition of success, those schools will continue, year in and year out, to be among the best.

But to get back to 1978 in particular, Rice coach Ray Alborn didn't gripe, and other coaches in his situation didn't either—because they knew what was going on—unlike a lot of national sportswriters, who didn't see us play and simply formed their impressions based on the scores.

The first three times we had the ball against Missouri in the next game in 1978, Lott and Sims led drives of 82, 81, and 82 yards for touchdowns. We won 45–23 and Uwe von Schamann broke the record of 88 consecutive extra point kicks.

We intercepted seven passes and beat Texas 31–10 in the Red River War.

It was major weirdness when we played at Lawrence, Kansas, the next week. Thomas Lott and fullback Kenny King were out with injuries. Billy Sims gained 192 yards on 30 carries as we ran a lot of I-formation plays to get Billy the ball more and also to make up for the inexperience of J. C. Watts at option quarterback.

With 15 seconds left, Kansas scored on a 6-yard touchdown pass to close the score to 17–16. Naturally, I figured they would go for 2 and try to beat us. But they lined up to kick the extra point, and I groaned. A tie would be as good as a victory for Kansas but as bad as a loss for OU. Then Kansas got a delay penalty that moved the ball back to the 7-yard line. Now, I thought, they are bound to kick the extra point. We are doomed. Instead, Kansas tried a pass for 2 points, it failed, and we won the game 17–16.

At Iowa State the next week, Sims rushed for 231 yards in a 34–6 win. Billy picked up 202 in the following 56–19 victory over Kansas State, although our team didn't look very sharp. At Boulder, Billy rushed for 221 yards—the most ever allowed to a single back by Colorado at that time—and we won 28–7.

We were undefeated and ranked number one in the nation before going into Lincoln, Nebraska, the next week, on a particularly cold Saturday afternoon. Our backs' hands must have been cold, too, because even though we had a great offensive day, we fumbled nine times and ended up losing 14–17. I'll never forget the last fumble. Our Heisman Trophy winner Billy Sims made a great 19-yard run to the 3-yard with about a minute left and, while putting out a Heisman-like extra effort, had the ball stripped loose.

That fumble, without question, cost us the 1978 national championship. After the game, during the press conference, some dumb-ass reporter referred to Billy's fumble late in the game and asked, "Should he be considered for the Heisman now?" That made me hot, because Billy Sims was one of the greatest backs ever to play the game. I said, "Well, hell no! Since I'm sure no other Heisman winner ever fumbled!"

Sims rushed for 209 yards and four touchdowns on 30 carries in the first half in a 62–7 victory over Oklahoma State to close out the regular season.

In our Orange Bowl rematch against Nebraska, which I've already talked about, there was a huge difference. We had lost six fumbles when they beat us in Lincoln. We lost one fumble in the Orange Bowl and Sims gained another 134 yards as we won 31–24. The game wasn't that close. Nebraska scored a touchdown on the final play. We had led 31–10 going into the fourth quarter.

J. C. Watts came into his own in 1979. It was Sims's senior year and should have been his second Heisman Trophy, but Billy was bothered all season with injuries and didn't really explode until the last couple of games after the voting was done.

The only game we lost in 1979 was to Texas, 16–7. J. C. Watts was the best passer I ever had at Oklahoma (until Troy Aikman in 1985), and he started that Red River War with a touchdown throw. We had a 7–3 lead with about a minute left to play in the half and the ball on our 10-yard line. I should have sat on it. Instead, we called a streak route to our wide receiver. J. C. threw the ball 50 yards, the Texas cornerback made a great play, intercepted it and ran it back for the only Texas touchdown of the day.

Two fourth-quarter field goals wrapped it up for them.

After that, Kansas State, Iowa State, Oklahoma State, and Kansas fell by large scores and we came to two nationally televised games in a row—against Missouri and Nebraska.

Billy Sims put on a great show against Missouri with 282 yards rushing, including a 70-yard touchdown run in the third quarter. Missouri missed a 37-yard field goal with three minutes left, and we escaped Columbia with a 24–22 win.

On Thursday afternoon before Nebraska, we were in shorts working on the kicking game and I saw Billy Sims sitting by himself. I went over and sat with him. We reminisced about all the things that had happened since he came down the road from Hooks to OU. "Let me ask you," I said. "Have you got one more big one in you?"

"Coach, this will be the last time I play at Owen Field. You just watch me. It'll be the best yet," he said.

Nebraska was unbeaten and we had lost once. Our TV audience was the biggest of the year. Nebraska led the nation in rushing defense, giving up only 68 per game.

I believe there were times in 1979 that Billy didn't really cut loose like he had in 1978. He was ricochet romance in

1978. In his senior year, an obvious number-one pick for the pros, many people, including me, felt Billy would pull up or take it easy or protect himself a little bit in those games that we won easily. He already had some small injuries and didn't want to make them worse. He wanted to stay healthy. I didn't blame him.

But when it was nut cutting time, the real Billy Sims showed up. He proved it the very first time he touched the ball, when he broke 70 yards for a score. Billy stood in the end zone, raising his arms to the cheers of 76,000 fans, only to see that there had been an unnecessary clip back upfield. We ended that drive with a field goal for a 3–0 lead.

In the fourth quarter, with Oklahoma only leading 10–7, Billy broke a 71-yard run to the 8-yard line. We scored to make the score 17–7 and ultimately win 17–14. He had 247 yards rushing for the day against the best defense in the country. All those people who had already voted for Charles White of USC for the Heisman Trophy had a chance to see who was really the best back in the country—number 20 from Oklahoma.

At the Orange Bowl our opponent was Florida State, 11–0 and damn good . . . but not good enough. Before the kickoff I was on the field talking to Florida State coach Bobby Bowden.

"Barry, I had a chance to hear J. C. Watts speak," Bowden told me, "and I am really impressed. He preached at the University Baptist Church in Coral Gables on Sunday. I went back and told my coaching staff, 'I'm gonna warn you, if that kid can play football as well as he can preach, we are in for one hell of a night.'"

Bowden was right. J. C. scored our first touchdown on a 61-yard run off the option. Sims rushed for 164 yards to finish his college career—his last touchdown was on a pitchout from J. C.—but Watts was so outstanding he was voted most valuable player. We beat Florida State 24–7 and were ranked third in the nation in the final poll.

J. C. Watts is now a youth minister at a church in Oklahoma City and gave religious testimony all through college. This sincere, devout young man was my children's second baby-sitter after Joe Washington. J. C., who played pro ball in

Canada for six years, is as upstanding and righteous a person
as you will ever meet.

It's kind of funny, isn't it? Here we were in the 1970s
kicking everybody and getting a national reputation as a
bunch of outlaws playing at an outlaw school—and two of our
three top quarterbacks of that era were Baptist preachers!

J. C.'s senior season, 1980, was a strange year.

We beat Kentucky 29–7 in the opener. The next week
Stanford came to Norman with John Elway at quarterback.
Elway was a sophomore and our fans didn't know too much
about him. But the coaches and I had seen miles of film of
Elway, and we were in awe of his ability. A great player is a
great player when he arrives in college. A coach doesn't teach
him how to be great. Joe Washington and Billy Sims were
great when they first set foot on the OU campus, like Earl
Campbell at Texas and Eric Dickerson at S.M.U. A good coach
will do things to enhance the player's talent, maybe make him
bigger and stronger and a little smarter, but you don't coach
greatness.

And Elway was great. My respect for his talent caused me
to make a big mistake in my game plan.

It was a rainy day on a slick field. A lot of people think
the defense has the advantage on rain-slick artificial surfaces,
but it's just the opposite. The quarterback and the receiver
know what the pass route is supposed to be, whereas the defensive back has to react. On a wet, slick field, the defensive
back loses a step on coverage.

I remembered Jim MacKenzie's philosophy. Jim believed
you should try to defend against the passing of a great passer,
but you should rush a poor passer. So my defensive plan was
to rush three men and drop eight back into coverage.

Elway, with his terrific scrambling ability, ran away from
our three-man rush and held the ball so long that his receivers
eventually got open. We were trying to make him throw on
rhythm, but he threw it when he damn well pleased. Elway hit
three touchdown passes and ran for another as we gave up
237 yards in the air and lost a home game for the first time in
four years, 31–14.

One week later Oklahoma set an NCAA record for most
yards rushing in a game (758) and most total offense (875).

And who did we do it against? Colorado and my old Oklahoma boss Chuck Fairbanks.

Before the 1979 season I had received a call from Jack Vickers, a big Colorado supporter, who wanted to know if I would be at all interested in taking the head job in Boulder. I told Jack I would be crazy to leave Oklahoma. Then I was shocked—hell, everybody in football was shocked—when Chuck Fairbanks turned up with the Colorado job.

Chuck didn't realize the impact the thirty-scholarship limit had had on college football while he was off coaching in the pros. In Chuck's days at Oklahoma, we could recruit twice as many. The scholarship limits would eventually tend to level out some programs, but to rebuild a program in a short time with lower numbers was devastatingly difficult. Besides that, Colorado had raised its academic standards while Chuck was gone. And Chuck didn't have the solid backing he needed from the alums. And on top of everything else, *Sports Illustrated* did a hatchet job on him, blaming him for OU's earlier probation over the falsified transcripts.

The 124 points and the 18 touchdowns in the game were also NCAA records. OU fumbled nine times, had eleven penalties, and missed two extra points, or there's no telling what the score might have been. We could have scored 100 easily. But at the half we were leading only 34–21.

Here are a few other random numbers from that incredible day. OU running back David Overstreet rushed for 258 yards. Our second-string quarterback, Darrell Shepard, carried the ball three times for 151 yards and two touchdowns. Buster Rhymes scored four touchdowns. Jerome Ledbetter completed our scoring with a 97-yard kickoff return. We averaged 10.4 yards per rush, made 35 first downs, and didn't punt.

The final score? OU won 82–42.

I felt bad that the score got out of hand.

But of course I didn't feel as bad as Chuck did.

Early in the fourth quarter, one of Chuck's assistant coaches on the headsets up in the press box walked down and knocked on the door of the room where Galen Hall was calling plays for Oklahoma.

"I have a message from Coach Fairbanks," the assistant said.

"What is it?"

"Coach Fairbanks says, 'Damnit, Galen, you tell Switzer just to give the ball to his damn fullback from now on.'"

It wasn't like Chuck was saying please. It was like he was still my boss—ordering me to give the damn ball to my fullback from now on.

Down on the sidelines, I got the message. I waved across the field at Chuck. "I hear you, Chuck," I yelled. "Here comes our fullback on every play!"

That's what kept us from reaching 100 points.

I guess my team must have had visions of 82 points per week dancing in their heads, because the following Saturday in the Red River War Freddy Akers and his undefeated (at the time) Texas Longhorns upset our dreams 20–13.

Texas has been down in football for so long now that people forget what great teams Fred had in Austin until 1986, when he committed the horrible crime of actually having a losing season (5–6–0) and those rabid UT boosters in the orange neckties fired him. No matter how well Freddy did at Texas, a large faction never forgave him for not being Darrell Royal's handpicked successor.

The Longhorn program has really taken a nosedive since they chased Freddy Akers off to Purdue after the 1986 season, even though they did beat OU in Dallas in 1989 in a freakish game right out of *Twilight Zone,* including a play where OU's great running back Mike Gaddis blew out his knee without being touched.

Freshman Buster Rhymes returned the opening kickoff 100 yards for a touchdown as we turned the ball over five times but beat Kansas State 35–21. We breezed past Iowa State 42–7, and our next opponent was undefeated North Carolina.

North Carolina was 6–0, leading the nation in defense with a tackle named Donnell Thompson and an end named Lawrence Taylor. Amos Lawrence was their tailback. They were a really good team.

But I remember I was kind of shocked that day as we warmed up on the field. I was standing in the end zone with

our linemen, and as North Carolina came down the ramp
Lawrence Taylor and a bunch of other players started shouting threats at us, taunting us. I looked around and I could see
that our whole team was shocked to hear the trash the North
Carolina players were laying on us.

I had watched Lawrence Taylor on film and had brought
all my assistants in to see him because he was a real difference
maker. North Carolina's first-team defense hadn't been scored
on in six games, and the films showed us why.

But hearing Lawrence Taylor and the others daring to
taunt the Oklahoma football team right there in our own
backyard at Owen Field—this was too much.

It made me think about that Jim Croce song that says if
you come into Superman's home, you had better not tug on
his cape.

That's what it made my players think of, too.

North Carolina hadn't faced the Wishbone and had never
seen speed like ours. J. C. Watts, David Overstreet, Stanley
Wilson, and the rest rushed for 495 yards and beat North Carolina, 41–7.

Something happened during this North Carolina weekend that I'm not proud of but which was pretty funny. When
Coach Crum and his North Carolina players arrived in
Norman on Friday and began working out in our stadium, I
went out to meet Coach Crum, whom I had never met
before. I went out to the middle of the field and said,
"Denny, I really look forward to playing your great team." It
was "Denny this" and "Denny that" for about ten minutes.
But Crum gave no expression at all about anything. He
never said a word. I began to think he must be an unfriendly
guy.

Before the game on Saturday I tried to say a few more
nice things to Denny about his team and his program, but all I
would get back was a cold stare. Then after the game, when
we had just busted their undefeated bubble 41–7, I went out
to midfield to try to say something nice. But before I could get
a word out, Crum said, "Coach, the name is *Dick*!" That was
the only thing he said to me in two days, and I felt about two
inches high. I had been calling him *Denny* Crum for two days,
which is the name of the University of Louisville's basketball

coach! I'm sure that to this day Dick Crum thinks I was doing that to psych him out.

Later, in our locker room, I told our coaches what had happened and how embarrassed I was. One of them said, "Hell, coach, that's all right. North Carolina's a basketball school anyway!"

Our Kansas game looked like a rout when we scored touchdowns the first two times we got the ball, but then we had to hang on to win 21–19. Buster Rhymes ran for two touchdowns the next week in a 17–7 victory over Missouri.

Leading the team onto the field before the Nebraska "taco" game in Lincoln, my shoe got caught in the artificial turf and I tripped and rolled up like a ball. The Nebraska student section loved it. They jeered and razzed me, so I jumped up and moved my feet real quick to try to look like some kind of an athlete.

Then it was Sooner Magic again in Lincoln, coming back from being down 10–0 to beat Nebraska again, this time on a 1-yard run by Buster Rhymes with 56 seconds left. The score was 21–17.

The last week of the season we managed to play a whole game without fumbling, and beat Oklahoma State 63–14. J. C. and Jerome Ledbetter scored three touchdowns each.

So we were Big Eight champs again, ranked fourth in the nation and headed for the Orange Bowl to face Florida State and Bobby Bowden for the second year in a row.

Florida State was a much better team the second time.

They only gave up one fourth-quarter touchdown all year, and that was to us with 1:27 on the clock—an 11-yard touchdown pass from J. C. Watts to Steve Rhodes at the end of a 78-yard drive mostly in the air.

Going for the two points, J. C. ran a play action pass and found Forrest Valora in the deep corner of the end zone.

Florida State tried a 62-yard field goal on the final play, but it fell short. We won the Orange Bowl 18–17 with J. C. the MVP again.

"It was ridiculous to get beat by a Wishbone team throwing the ball," Bobby Bowden said afterward.

The real difference in that game was not the passing, it was everything J. C. Watts did.

Eight straight years of three great quarterbacks with a combined record of 83–9–2 had just come to an end for Oklahoma. I knew we were going to miss them (and their great supporting cast), but I didn't realize how much.

17

THE MARCUS DUPREE
TRAGEDY

The 1981 season was a disaster by Oklahoma standards.

We beat Wyoming in the opener and went to Los Angeles to play USC ranked number one in the nation, with the Trojans ranked second. USC had Heisman Trophy winner-to-be Marcus Allen, who rushed for 208 yards in 39 carries against Oklahoma, but despite fumbling ten times, we would have won the game if one of our defensive backs had not dropped an interception right in his hands in the end zone as the clock ran down. USC scored, with two seconds left, to beat us 28–24.

The next two games were even more painful.

We were damn lucky to get out with a 7–7 tie against Iowa State when the Cyclones missed four field goals, including a 23-yarder with about a minute to go. Iowa State's unlucky coach that day was my good friend Donnie Duncan. Then a good Texas team (eventual Cotton Bowl victors over Alabama) stomped us 34–14. That made Oklahoma 1–2–1— the first losing record of my career.

Kansas, Oregon State, Colorado, and Kansas State fell, in order, and we were still in the Big Eight race with two weeks to go. But Missouri beat us 19–14 in Columbia, and Nebraska came to Norman and whipped us 37–14. With a 5–4–1 record, I accepted a Sun Bowl invitation. We closed the regular season by beating Oklahoma State 27–3 as freshman fullback Fred Sims ran for three touchdowns. In the Sun Bowl, Sims came in again to replace injured Stanley Wilson and gained

160

181 yards on 15 carries in the second half. I was planning on a bright future for Fred Sims. We beat the University of Houston 40–14, to finish with a 7–4–1 record, ranked twentieth in the polls.

At Oklahoma, one season with a 7–4–1 record was just barely sufficient to keep the staff and me employed, as long as we promised to do better next time.

Over in Philadelphia, Mississippi, at that moment was a young black Hercules named Marcus Dupree. Comparing Marcus to Hercules might be unfair, because I'm sure Marcus was a hell of a lot faster than Hercules.

You take Earl Campbell, Herschel Walker, Bo Jackson, Eric Dickerson, Billy Sims, Joe Washington, and all of the rest of the great running backs—and I am here to tell you that Marcus Dupree could have been the best of them all.

What happened to Marcus was a pure tragedy.

Sports Illustrated blamed his downfall on me, of course. The truth is, *Sports Illustrated* was as much to blame as anybody.

Really, though, the flaw—which is what we'll call it to keep this on the tragic level—lay within Hercules himself.

Marcus Dupree just didn't like to play football as much as all the rest of the world wanted him to.

It takes a peculiar breed of cat to play football at the big-time college level. It is a harsh, violent, sometimes brutal game. And playing the game is the glorious fun part of football. The practices are where you suffer and sweat and fall hurt and exhausted and get up to do it again. During two-a-day scrimmages and drills is when you question your dedication. Many fine athletes drop out. I used to wonder what it would be like to go to college on a golf scholarship. The coach tells you, "Tough work today, boys. You have to play thirty-six holes, and it's kind of windy." Or even basketball. I know basketball players run their asses off and knock each other down in practice. But guys love to play hoops. My football players were always organizing hoops in the gym. You don't see a bunch of athletes out on the field on their own organizing a game of tackle football.

It's no disgrace not to love to play football. My brother, Donnie, was good at the game, but he quit as soon as life would let him and he then concentrated on books and throwing the hammer and discus.

However, it is different if you are a 6-foot-3, 230-pound black Hercules who runs a 4.3 in the forty and a 9.4 in the hundred-yard dash. People feel this Hercules is depriving them of pleasure if he doesn't love the game enough to pay the price to play at the top level of his awesome capabilities.

The first photograph I ever saw of Marcus Dupree was an AP photo of him at age seventeen, bench-pressing 400 pounds.

Lucious Selmon went to Philadelphia, Mississippi, to meet him during Marcus's senior year in high school. Lucious called back with stories like you used to hear about Paul Bunyan or some other mythical hero. Marcus had always played sports with kids older than himself, but still it was nowhere near equal. As a child he pitched in a teenage league and threw such a fastball that the catcher howled in pain, took off his glove, and quit in the middle of a game.

Marcus was born in 1964, the year Philadelphia was in the news for the murders of three civil rights workers. While his mother, Cella, finished school, Marcus was raised by his grandparents, the Rev. and Mrs. Major Dupree. All of them helped care for his younger brother Reggie, who had cerebral palsy.

The first time Marcus touched a football in a game for Philadelphia High he was only in the ninth grade, but he returned a punt 75 yards for a touchdown.

He carried the ball more than three miles in high school games.

Every school in the country wanted him, of course. UCLA, Texas, and Oklahoma were in the lead. A local preacher named Ken Farley became his agent—in fact, Marcus is the only kid I ever saw who brought his agent to college with him as a freshman.

Recruiters knew damn well the NCAA and every coach were watching closely for illegal inducements to Marcus. When I was trying to recruit Earl Campbell, the only thing I offered him was a coffee can to spit tobacco juice in when he was visiting in my home. I told Lucious to be especially careful he didn't innocently slip up. When Marcus went to Austin for

his official visit to the University of Texas, he wanted to see a
place that sold cowboy boots. Marcus tried on a beautiful pair
of $600 boots and then walked out, leaving an assistant coach
to pay the bill. At least, that's the way Texas explained it when
the NCAA took away some of their scholarships as punishment.

I went to visit Marcus in Philadelphia, but his mother,
Cella, was sort of cold to me. My charm seemed lost on her.
But Marcus was a nice kid, much brighter than his grades
would have you believe.

He told me he was leaning toward Oklahoma. You know
one big reason? We had a game scheduled in Honolulu in
1983 and Marcus wanted to go to Hawaii. The most glam-
orous road game on the Texas schedule for that year was
against Oklahoma in Dallas. The next year it would be Fayetteville, Arkansas, where they go every other year.

Time came for Marcus's official visit to OU. Without
warning Marcus, I sent a private jet to pick him up. (NCAA
legal at the time!) The jet had one passenger in it—Billy Sims.

When Billy Sims showed up in Philadelphia, they let all
the school kids out of class to come meet him. Marcus was very
much impressed. Flying back to Norman, it was just Billy and
Marcus in the passenger seats. No coaches. And especially, no
agent.

On signing day, Marcus chose Oklahoma.

He arrived on campus in the fall driving a 1982
Oldsmobile with his agent, Ken Farley, in the car. I don't know
how Marcus got the car or who really owned it, but you can
bet the NCAA investigated it immediately.

Marcus weighed about 235, and I told him to lose fifteen
pounds. He didn't like the idea and didn't do it. After his performance in his first scrimmage—six carries for 154 yards and
three touchdowns—Marcus felt like he could do as he pleased.
Me too!

There were a couple of side effects to signing Marcus that
caused instant trouble. Some of our best backs, like Freddy
Sims, quit the team and transferred to other schools. Not only
did Marcus's arrival run off a bunch of backs, his exodus the
next year really left us short of good running backs.

West Virginia came to Norman and handed us our first

opening-day loss in thirteen years, with Jeff Hostetler passing
for 321 yards. The score was 42–27. The next week at Kentucky, reserve quarterback Danny Bradley replaced senior
Kelly Phelps, who was injured, and led us to a 29–8 victory.

Back in Norman the following Saturday against USC, it
was a horror show for our offense. We had such a struggle
moving the ball against USC's future pro stars that the crowd
began cheering for first downs. We gained only 43 yards rushing—the all-time low for one of my teams—and were shut out
12–0. It was the first time Oklahoma had been scoreless in 181
games and sixteen years.

The Daily Oklahoman, the only statewide newspaper, began
to question my character and my sanity. Our headline said,
"SWITZER HAS OUTLIVED HIS USEFULNESS TO THE UNIVER-
SITY." Another paper wrote, "As a winner, Switzer was tolera-
ble to many. As a loser, perhaps it is time for him to move on."

For our next game I put in the I formation and moved
Marcus to tailback behind Stanley Wilson. Wilson scored our
only touchdown, but we won 13–3 over Iowa State.

Then came the real debut of Marcus Dupree—on national television against Texas in the Red River War.

The first touchdown he ever scored for Oklahoma was a
63-yard run in the first quarter as we beat the Longhorns
28–22. Marcus carried the ball nine times for 96 yards that
day, and suddenly this freshman was in the headlines as the
top running back in the country.

And can you believe *The Daily Oklahoman?* The next week,
after our great team victory over Texas, the newspaper actually took credit for the victory, saying its negative editorials
had inspired the team to victory. Talk about fiction writers!
We may have had two players who even read the editorial
page.

"DUPREE SAVES SWITZER'S JOB" was what another newspaper said.

At Kansas, Marcus rushed for 158 yards and averaged
17.6 per carry in a 38–14 victory. Oklahoma State came to
Norman and held Dupree to only 83 yards, but we stopped
their star tailback—Earnest Anderson—with 59 and won
27–9.

At Colorado, Marcus ran a punt 77 yards for a touchdown and we won 45–10. I thought this run by Marcus was a very good sign, because I believe it takes more courage and concentration to return a punt than any other play in football.

Against Kansas State, Marcus ran for 118 yards, and Stanley Wilson for 143, as we won 24–10. In the Missouri game the following week, we gave the ball to Marcus nineteen times and he responded with 166 yards to break the OU rushing record for freshmen. He looked so good that day I told the press Marcus "plays in a different league than everybody else."

Now we had won seven straight games since I had switched to the I formation. We went to Lincoln to play Nebraska for the Big Eight championship, as usual. It was a hell of a battle in 20-degree weather. Dupree carried 25 times for 149 yards and two touchdowns. He broke an 83-yard touchdown run in the third quarter. But Nebraska won 28–24.

I accepted an invitation to play in the Fiesta Bowl against Arizona State.

That game would be the beginning of the end of Marcus Dupree's relationship with the Oklahoma football team.

By anybody's standards except what should have been his own, Marcus had a fantastic day against Arizona State. He rushed for 239 yards on 17 carries—14.1 per pop—and wound up with 1,143 in a season in which he didn't start until the sixth game.

But Arizona State beat us 32–21 in the Fiesta Bowl, and Marcus was caught from behind on three long runs. Marcus had made more long touchdown runs that year than any back I ever had. Nobody in the country could catch him from behind. But in the Fiesta Bowl, they did.

Marcus should have had more than 400 yards rushing that day. He said he had a sore hamstring. Oklahoma had the ball for 69 snaps on offense. Marcus was in the game on 34 of those plays and carried the ball on 17 of them. His hamstring didn't look sore to me. It looked to me as if Marcus was too heavy and out of shape. He was up to 240 by now and had lost that tiny fraction of speed that was the difference between an 80-yard touchdown and being caught 20 or 30 yards downfield.

I lost my head and criticized Marcus in front of the

sportswriters afterward. I should never have done that. The teacher should never criticize the student in public. Marcus, his agent, his family—all of them were angry at me. I hurt their feelings.

But now I had the 1983 season to prepare for.

You build a football team starting in January. The off season is what most coaches call the fourth-quarter program. You have running and agility drills, weight lifting, sessions with the trainer to cure your injuries. A kid learns how to work and push himself until it becomes part of his personality. Soon it's a habit. He knows no other way than to bust his ass when he goes onto the field.

So my staff and I started our off-season program in 1983, *and Marcus wanted no part of it.* He said his hamstring still hurt. I told him to get his big butt into the training room. He did do that. The trainer told me Marcus had a knot in his hamstring but not as bad as those of several other players who were on the field every day.

Spring training started, and Marcus did not suit up for practice a single day. He had asthma, he said. He had a headache. He had a sore shoulder. He did not take one snap. Marcus hadn't hit a lick since the Fiesta Bowl, and now he sat out spring training. I saw the other players watching him. Having been a player, I knew what they were thinking and feeling: Here we are working ourselves half to death and getting the crap beat out of us, and over there sits the prima donna. You can't fool the players.

I remembered Billy Sims in his first spring training after his freshman season, in pain from an injured collarbone. Everybody knew Billy was a star, too, but he didn't expect special treatment. He ran scout team, B team. Billy was a member of the *team.* He knew he wouldn't be successful without the help of the guys around him, and he didn't consider himself above any of them. Billy took everything that we dished out to him, and he responded like a champion.

All Marcus did was go home for the summer and eat fried chicken.

One day just after school let out for the summer I got a call from Mike Treps, the sports information director. Mike said *Sports Illustrated* wanted to open the 1983 football season with a cover story promoting Marcus Dupree for the Heisman Trophy as a sophomore.

I told Mike to let me think it over.

I have never denied my players any publicity. I've always been very vocal, even outlandish, in trumpeting the virtues of my players. I believe the first thing that makes a player perform like an all-American is knowing his coach thinks he's that good. Publicity helps the players. Their families love it. Good publicity is great for recruiting.

But I had to think of the good of the team. I didn't know if the team would accept Marcus or not. They're out there busting their asses every day and wanting to have a good football team. They know Marcus is a great player, but they also know he hasn't been part of the team. He hasn't paid the price like they have. They resented him.

So I don't want my players to be at home dispersed all over the country and pick up a preseason issue of *Sports Illustrated* and see Marcus on the cover being promoted for the Heisman Trophy—because they knew he hadn't "pissed a drop" in six months. They wanted him to be a team member. They wanted him to do the same things they did. They knew what I thought of Marcus's work ethic and probably resented me for letting him get away with it. For me to hype him for the Heisman Trophy this early would be the utmost in hypocrisy. It would ruin our team morale. I couldn't do it.

The next day I told Mike Treps, "It is not in the best interests of our football program at this time for us to promote Marcus Dupree for the Heisman Trophy."

The next thing I heard about it, Mike told me, "Hey, coach, Doug Looney is doing a hatchet job on you. He's going to do a cover story on Marcus Dupree, but it won't be to promote Marcus for the Heisman—it'll be a controversial story pitting you against Marcus."

I tried to phone Doug Looney, the *Sports Illustrated* writer who would have done the Heisman Trophy cover story. I had given Doug Looney carte blanche to my program for several years. He went in my meeting rooms, my locker rooms. He traveled to ball games on the team plane. I had him as a guest on my TV show several times. Doug had been at my home for dinner with my family. Any time Doug phoned for information, I gave him what he wanted. I really thought he was a straight guy.

I called Doug at home in Westport, Connecticut. I called him at his office. I left messages everywhere. Doug would not return my calls. I told Mike Treps to get word to Doug to please wait and see how Marcus starts the season before we start talking Heisman Trophy. If Marcus is as good as a sophomore as he was a freshman, he deserves it. But let's allow Marcus to help our football team first.

I guess Time Inc. wasn't going to let some damn football coach dictate to them what they could write, so they decided just to turn and pit Marcus against me.

On June 20, 1983—two and a half months before the first game of the season—the cover of *Sports Illustrated* was a color portrait of Marcus wearing his red No. 22 Sooners jersey with Fiesta Bowl emblems on the shoulders. Marcus wore his wire-rim eyeglasses (he wore goggles in a game) and a sort of sullen look and was leaning his forearms against a weight like I wish he had been lifting.

The cover of the magazine said CLASH OF WILLS AT OKLAHOMA . . . Heisman Hopeful Marcus Dupree: Can He Coexist with His Coach?"

The story was about how Marcus loved to work hard and play hurt in high school, and if he'd changed, it must be Switzer's fault. Bullshit!

And my players knew this was bullshit. Magazine readers and a growing number of enemy alums may have believed it, but it really put the pressure on Marcus when he arrived to start practice for the fall.

His teammates had slaved and suffered all spring and many had spent the summer on the track and in the weight room. Marcus was a superstar. Everything came easy for him because of his great physical talents, but this gave him an attitude, through his immaturity, that he didn't have to pay the price the same way other players did. As a result, he never really was part of the team.

Merv Johnson, my assistant head coach and offensive-line coach, looked at Marcus one afternoon in an early scrimmage and said, "It appears Dupree is much more fond of adulation than he is of football."

Fatigue makes cowards of us all, and when you are not physically prepared to perform in athletic endeavor, then you are going to get tired, you're going to quit, you'll be embarrassed, and you may even get hurt.

I tried often to explain this to Marcus, how hard physical preparation could help him and help the team. But his attitude, his conviction that he was a superstar different from all the others, kept him from ever really listening to me.

Looking back on it seven years later, I think Marcus's agent, Ken Farley, might have already been working on a plan to get Marcus away from Oklahoma and into professional football.

In those days, the NFL didn't draft a player until his class graduated. You realize that if Marcus Dupree had graduated with his class, it would have been with our 1985 national championship team.

But Herschel Walker of Georgia was about to change all that by declaring himself eligible for the draft as a junior.

There are very few college football players who have the strength, talent, and maturity to jump into pro football without several years of growth and training.

Herschel was the first one who could who actually did it. I believe Ken Farley might have already been in the process of negotiating for Marcus to be the next.

We teed it up at Stanford to open the season and Marcus ran for 138 yards. The sportswriters were already calling him "Heisman Trophy candidate" in every opening paragraph. Our defense held Stanford to minus one in rushing. We won 27–14 and were ranked second in the national polls.

Then it started. Ohio State came to Norman. They were fired up to get revenge on us for beating them at home six years earlier. Ohio State had some big, tough linebackers who had probably read *Sports Illustrated* and just couldn't wait for the joyful moment when they could beat the cold shit out of a Heisman Trophy candidate.

Marcus left the game limping in the second quarter. He had gained 30 yards. The Ohio State players had spoken very unkindly to him. Life didn't look so damn great anymore. Ohio State and their really good quarterback Mike Tomczak whipped us 24–14, but they whipped Marcus a lot worse than that.

The next week against Tulsa was the worst exhibition of offensive football one of my teams played in my sixteen years as head coach. Oklahoma won the game 28–18, but Tulsa didn't have anywhere near the talent we had. Marcus sat out that game with a sore leg that he had picked up in the Ohio State game a week earlier.

Marcus suited up again the next week and ran for 151 yards and three touchdowns on 19 carries in a 29–10 victory over Kansas State. We had a freshman running back, Spencer Tillman, who gained 131 in 21.

Then came the Red River War again.

Texas was strong that year. It may have been Freddy Akers's best team. The Horns had an 11–1 season and missed the national championship on a fumble in a 1-point Cotton Bowl loss to Georgia.

They were already 4–0 and looking for Marcus when they came to Dallas. The year before, remember, Marcus had been a big surprise to their players and had helped win the game with a long touchdown run. Now they were taking dead aim on him.

This kind of situation is faced in every game that every great back plays against a strong, well-coached team. The great back knows he is going to be the target for many blows. The great back summons all his skill and courage and keeps hammering and makes something good happen for his team.

Marcus carried the ball 14 times for 50 yards, and we lost 28–16. Marcus had the shit knocked out of him, play after play.

After the game he went to Philadelphia for the weekend. No one had any idea where he was. He hadn't told anyone.

On Monday afternoon when he hadn't returned to Norman, I phoned Marcus and ordered him to get his ass back on campus. He told me he'd be back. But later he said he couldn't get a ride to the airport. On Tuesday I heard he went to the airport but didn't get on the plane. On Wednesday he phoned Scott Hill and said he was returning, and he phoned Spencer Tillman to check that his car was safe.

Lucious Selmon went to Mississippi to visit with Marcus

and had a sort of tug-of-war with Ken Farley. Lucious was trying to persuade the kid to come back to school, and Farley kept telling him he wasn't happy in Norman and that he should not go back.

Farley was working at the time as a counselor at Mississippi Southern. So on Friday he took Marcus to visit with Southern coach Jim Carmody. Marcus phoned coach Emory Bellard at Mississippi State to see if he would be welcome there.

Marcus had given me no choice. So I had to call him and tell him he was dismissed from the team, on the Thursday before our next game against Oklahoma State.

Our team traveled to Stillwater to play Oklahoma State. The Aggies really loved all of the trouble that we had had with Marcus. Some of their fans had hung banners that read BARRY IT'S 1:30. DO YOU KNOW WHERE YOUR PLAYERS ARE? and ROSES ARE RED, VIOLETS ARE BLUE, MARCUS IS HISTORY AND SO IS OU.

Sports Illustrated printed photos of both banners.

At halftime, Oklahoma State was leading 20–3. They only had three first downs, but our offense kept giving them the ball. I was busy at the half talking to my staff—you don't make speeches at halftime, you make adjustments—and I was shocked to look around and see OU president Bill Banowsky standing there.

"Barry, I want you to know everything's okay," Banowsky said.

It damn sure didn't look okay to me—trailing by 17 points, getting our asses kicked, and my superstar tailback sulking in Mississippi, eating Cella's good cooking and gaining weight.

"What do you mean?" I said.

"I don't want you to worry. The regents are okay," Banowsky said.

Yes, this was the same Bill Banowsky who was soon to tell me that if I won the national championship, I could smoke dope and not get fired.

Here was Banowsky in the Stillwater locker room at half-time, talking politics! He had been sitting in the stands with some of my bosses—the regents—and he was bringing me a message.

I didn't give a damn what Banowsky thought at that moment. I had urgent problems to face in a few minutes. But he kept following me around until I took the team back on the field.

With about three minutes to play, Derrick Shepard got us back into the game with a great individual effort, breaking several tackles and running 73 yards for a score after catching a short pass that cut the lead to 20–18. Oklahoma State coach Jimmy Johnson expected me to try the onside kick. But I sent instructions to kick it deep.

However, all my players got this news except freshman kicker Tim Lashar. The Sooners went flying down the field, and Lashar kicked the ball sideways.

The ball hit the headgear of Oklahoma State's Chris Rockins and ricocheted back into the hands of our Scott Case on the dead run.

Lashar kicked a field goal with 1:57 left. We won the game 21–20. Thousands of Aggie fans had left the stadium several minutes earlier, already relishing their first victory over Oklahoma since 1976 and what would have been only their fourth since 1946! They all sat in their cars, unbelieving, as their Aggies lost again—and this time to an average Oklahoma team in the middle of great turmoil and without its superstar.

That game was the last time I beat Jimmy Johnson. I should add, however, that it was only because he didn't stay in Stillwater.

Back in Norman, I heard from the athletic department athletic adviser, Jin Brown, that Marcus Dupree had been failing every class and had mostly stopped even attending. One of the classes he had skipped was Philosophy 1203—taught in part by OU president William S. Banowsky. It then became obvious to me that Marcus and his agent had planned all along to go pro—that they had never intended for Marcus to try to complete his college career.

I consider not being able to communicate with Marcus as a real failure in my coaching career.

But I still had six more games to play in 1983, and now

the outcry was getting a lot louder that it was time for Barry Switzer to be fired as the head coach at Oklahoma.

Spencer Tillman and freshman Earl Johnson both ran for more than 100 in our victory over Iowa State. We pounded Kansas the next week. Then Missouri shut us out at Columbia 10–0, and their fans tore down the goalposts. We bounced back to beat Colorado with Earl Johnson rushing 28 times for 258 yards and two touchdowns—the best day ever for an OU freshman, breaking Marcus Dupree's record.

I guess we should have started touting Earl for the Heisman Trophy.

Nebraska was averaging 50 points per game, was ranked number one in the country, and had their usual great team with players like Turner Gill, Mike Rozier, and Irving Fryar, the *real* "triplets." I talked to my squad and we decided not to accept a bowl bid unless we beat Nebraska. It was a terrific game, but this time, when Nebraska was clearly the better team, they won 28–21. We actually did have a chance to win when late in the fourth quarter we took a drive from our own 26-yard line to the Nebraska two. Great, strong runs by Earl Johnson and Spencer Tillman had brought us to that point. Then, the CBS national television audience saw us, with second down at the two, have an offensive tackle jump offsides and put us back to the seven, where we then suffered a loss and fired two incomplete passes.

I've often thought that we had lost an opportunity to tie or win that game, but as I look back on it, I remember how great Turner Gill, Mike Rozier (their Heisman Trophy winner), and Irving Fryar really were. Those guys might have been able to score again anyway. That Nebraska team was the team that, had the breaks gone their way, would have won the national championship in the Orange Bowl following that season. That was the game they lost 30–31 to Miami by going for the win on a 2-point conversion on the last play of the game.

The 1983 season, Marcus Dupree's second (and last) season, would be the first time Oklahoma hadn't been to a bowl since our 1974 probation, and it was the only time in my career we finished a season out of the top twenty even though an 8–4 record wasn't all that bad—at least by the standards of most programs.

I declared our last game of the season as our bowl trip.

It was, after all, against the University of Hawaii in Honolulu and it was the game that had attracted Marcus Dupree to Oklahoma in the first place.

We beat them 21–17 without you, Marcus, and we had a hell of a good time on the beach.

I'm sorry you eventually had to take Ken Farley to court to try to collect your money from your USFL contract and insurance policy. I'm sorry you tore up your knee, and I hope you're happily rocking on the porch.

Damn you, Marcus, you gave me some great thrills in a short time, and I'm really sorry for the way things have turned out for both of us. Marcus, you could have been the greatest ever to play the game.

18

THE GREAT CONSPIRACY

My situation now was somewhat similar to how it had been with Chuck Fairbanks in 1970 when CHUCK CHUCK bumper stickers had been popular in Oklahoma.

But I knew there would never be a BURY BARRY bumper sticker.

The reason I knew it is that I had copyrighted the slogan, and I damn sure wasn't going to let anyone have permission to use it.

I didn't need a bumper sticker to make me understand that I couldn't have another four-loss season at Oklahoma or it would be adios to me and my whole staff. Jakie Sandefer, former halfback from Breckenridge, Texas, now a wealthy oilman in Houston, had phoned me around Thanksgiving to warn me that certain people were out to get me. The week I returned to Norman after our game in Hawaii, I got a call from my sportswriter friend Bill Connors, sports editor of the *Tulsa World*, with the same sort of warning.

But I didn't have time to sit around and indulge my paranoia. There was only one thing that would bring Oklahoma football back to the top—players. My staff and I were working hard to fill our sack with blue-chip recruits. These recruits would join a redshirted class that included Brian Bosworth, Dante Jones, Darrell Reed, and Troy Johnson. The best set of linebackers I ever recruited. We would have Tony Casillas back at nose guard, so I knew my 1984 defense would be stronger than I had had in years. On offense there was an Oklahoma-born kid we were going to sign who could run the option fairly well, but he could throw the ball with the all-time

best. His name was Troy Aikman. We had Danny Bradley and
Spencer Tillman returning, and we were going to sign freshman fullback Lydell Carr and tight end Keith Jackson.

My opponents didn't realize it, but I was loading up
again.

Goodbye to the I formation. I threw it out when I fired
Marcus Dupree. I hired coach Mack Brown from Appalachian
State, one of the top young offensive coaches in the country,
to join the staff and reeducate us in the art of the triple option.

I felt good about the way things were going with the football team.

But things weren't going so well for me or for the state of
Oklahoma.

Oklahoma had been accustomed to leading the nation in
football.

Now Oklahoma was leading the nation in going broke.

For a while there had been no way a smart, well-connected Oklahoman could avoid the showering of money. You
have to understand the atmosphere around Oklahoma City in
the first few years of the 1980s. The oil wealth was staggering.
People were flying to ball games in jet helicopters. It was nothing to fly to Las Vegas for dinner. Jackie Cooper, probably the
state's largest car dealer, opened a Rolls-Royce dealership in
Oklahoma City. It was fantasyland, that's what it was. I guess
we thought it would never end.

The Penn Square Bank in Oklahoma City collapsed in
July 1983—the first bank to fail in what became a nationwide
disaster involving thousands of banks and savings-and-loan institutions. The so-called energy crunch that helped bankrupt
most of Texas three or four years later hit Oklahoma first, at
the same time the banks were flopping. Guys who had been
flying around in Lear jets now couldn't pay their mortgages or
their country-club dues.

I got caught in this financial mess, myself.

Two partners and I had borrowed almost $2 million from
Penn Square Bank, which we found impossible to pay when
the price of oil, and drilling rigs, hit bottom. Because of the
failure of Penn Square, we had to deal with an ever-changing
cast of players for the FDIC in Oklahoma City in an attempt

to settle the debt, and at least two separate deals were reneged upon by the FDIC.

Finally, I actually had to go to the Washington offices of the FDIC and make a settlement arrangement that stuck. It certainly wasn't easy, but I was able to pay off the debt several years later.

The immediate effect of financial troubles in Oklahoma hit Bill Banowsky hard. He wasn't really a college president as much as he was a fund-raiser and Church of Christ minister. In better days he had raised $100 million to build Pepperdine College in Malibu, California.

Now Banowsky was trying to raise $60 million to build the Energy Center, which was supposed to tower over Owen Field on campus. For many years the University of Oklahoma had the finest geology school in the world. You found Sooner geologists from Alaska to Persia to Argentina and they covered Texas. Foreign students came from places like Arabia and Indonesia to study geology at OU.

But Texas A&M, Texas, and a few other schools had muscled into OU's turf with strong geology departments of their own.

There is a school of thought among a lot of academicians at Oklahoma and elsewhere to the effect that a strong academic program is inconsistent with a strong athletic program.

I never understood how it would improve academia if athletics were to be diminished. Would the professors and students get smarter if the football players got slower and the coaches got fired?

Banowsky was caught on a hook here. He had to try to please the people who wanted to have the best Energy Center in the country, but they weren't happy with 8–4 seasons. But at the same time he had to try to please rich people who liked football and wanted a winning team.

For example, Bill Saxon, a graduate of OU, had promised Banowsky his company would give $30 million toward the Energy Center. If Saxon came across, Banowsky would be half-way home. Saxon was a football fan who had helped me recruit Jack Mildren in the days when that was allowed.

I didn't think all these politics had much to do with me, but I quickly found out how wrong I was.

My ex-wife, Kay, and I had gotten divorced in 1981. All divorces are painful, but we had parted as friends. I was dating Janet Gibson, who was twenty-six years old, and a lot of gossips thought it was disgraceful. I really didn't give a damn about that, because I didn't feel it was any of their business. My coaches and I were working hard to bring our program back up to our expectations.

I read in the paper that Spencer Tillman said he had seen my office light on at 2 A.M. I asked Spencer, "What the hell were you doing up at 2 A.M.?" I had put in stricter rules governing class attendance, curfews, workouts, the dormitory, study halls, monitors, tutors, and grades. I had graduate assistants who would literally walk a player's ass to class and stick him in his seat and watch to see he stayed there and took notes. Our football team, in most years, led the university in average percentage of graduates, but by God I was going to graduate every player from now on if I possibly could do it.

I guarantee you that for the last six years I was head coach at Oklahoma, my football team lived by dormitory rules that if you had tried to enforce them at a fraternity house or even a regular student dorm, you would have had another student revolt like in the 1960s, when the kids took over buildings and shouted, "Off with the fascist pigs!"

Football coaching was no longer two hours on the field, blocking and tackling and running and catching the ball. Football coaching now was trying to control, direct, and manage a hundred players. It was a difficult—make that impossible— situation because for twenty-four hours a day, I was accountable for making sure everything ran smoothly and that there were no problems. Tough to do, isn't it, Jim Valvano?

I told the newspaper we just left the lights on in the offices to fool the players or anyone who drove by. But we didn't fool the players. They knew the staff and I were working hard and committed to the job at hand.

The Oklahoma Sooners were headed for the top again immediately. Call it Wishbone Two, the Sequel.

But, on December 9, 1983, I was working in my office at 5 P.M. when Bill Banowsky phoned. He said he wanted to visit with me at my convenience, and I replied that this was as good a time as any. I was preparing to go on a recruiting trip.

I went to his office. Banowsky opened the conversation by saying he had written down three categories that we needed to discuss. One was personal, one was business, and the third was coaching. I grinned at the last one, like he would know something about that.

"Someone with a different background might not be as sensitive to your life-style as I am," he said. "But this isn't Los Angeles, Barry. People see that young lady's car parked in front of your house, and they speculate." I had been dating Janet for about two years, she went with me on bowl trips, and there was no secret about our relationship. "You know I'm a preacher and I'd be happy to marry the two of you and remedy that," he said. I laughed and said, "Hell, Bill, I don't know if she'll marry me! Let's move on."

The next category was regarding my personal business problems, which he said were embarrassing him and the University and, he believed, interfering with my ability to run the football program. (Oklahoma City business associates Jack Hodges, Bob Hoover, and I had bought $4 million of stock in a company that we felt would sell, and did, and after we made a profit, the Securities and Exchange Commission was all over us, particularly me, for supposedly violating insider trading rules. I didn't, and we eventually won the case in dramatic fashion when the United States District Judge from Kansas City dismissed the government's case for lack of evidence. At the time of this meeting with Banowsky, however, the case was leading to stories in the local and national press almost every day.) Banowsky said that with an 11–1 record my outside businesses were no problem, but at 8–4 they were a "real difficulty."

Finally, he got to the most important thing on his list— pressure from the regents.

He said the regents wanted to talk to me about my coaching. Two regents were on my side, two were against me, and three were in the middle, according to Banowsky. He said they would vote 7–0 if he should recommend my dismissal. But if he supported me, they would vote 7–0 to renew my contract. I didn't believe him. I knew three of them were solidly on my side, and I was sure I could swing one or two more votes if it came to that.

I asked Banowsky where he stood personally. He proposed a one-year contract that he wanted me to accept for 1984, and then he would have a group of people raise the money to buy out of the regents' "moral commitment" for $240,000. "I'm not going to do that, Bill," I said. "I intend to coach at Oklahoma as you and the regents have committed to me that I can—five years."

Then Banowsky picked up a stack of letters that he said had been pouring in from around the state asking that I be fired as head coach.

"I don't even know these people who are writing all this mail," he said.

"You know who I am," I said. "That should be what makes the difference to you, not the opinions of people you never heard of. There's always going to be these kind of people out there."

"Also I had a phone call from Cy Wagner in Midland," Banowsky said. "Cy wants you dismissed. Cy says you should not even come back to Midland, because you will receive no support from him."

That cracked me up. Cy Wagner is one of the richest men in Texas. The last time I'd heard from Cy was before our previous Texas game, when he called and asked me to send him eight tickets (which I did) and then asked if Oklahoma had a chance to win. "If you win this football game, Barry, I'll own half of Midland," Cy told me. I hung up the phone and thought, Shit, I thought Cy already owned *all* of Midland.

Cy saying he wouldn't help me recruit in Midland was preposterous. Alumni were no longer in the recruiting process. Their influence was not allowed by the NCAA. (Now it is a two-year felony crime for a booster to take part in recruiting in Texas). What determined whether I would be going back to Midland was not Cy Wagner, it was whether Midland had any players I wanted. And if I went, I wouldn't be calling on Cy Wagner anyhow. I'd be visiting the players, coaches, families, and high school principals.

Later Banowsky told me he was under tremendous pressure because he had to go ask Cy Wagner for a couple of million dollars' donation to the Energy Center. That was another laugh. Cy Wagner's donations to OU had been what I will call insignificant. But still, Banowsky—a fund-raiser at heart—had to keep acting as if Cy would eventually come up with something. This was obviously the bottom line of the whole discussion—the football team had not won enough for the "big cigars" who were Banowsky's fund-raising targets.

Obviously, when a college president is primarily in the fund-raising business, it has a great influence on the athletic department. Our development office told me in 1985, during the depths of the oil bust, when times were really hard, that winning the national championship in football led to the second best year OU ever had in donations. Some so-called experts deny it, but there is a tremendous correlation between a winning athletic program and contributions from alums.

The dilemma Banowsky faced in 1983 was not unusual. It is simply part of the pressure faced by any college president who is directly involved in fund-raising at an institution with a rich athletic tradition such as Oklahoma's. Part of the problem is that the rich alumni who are the prime "targets" for major contributions are heavily interested in athletics, particularly football. There is nothing evil or sinister about it; it is simply a part of their lives and something they are interested in.

Another aspect of this constant pressure to raise money, and not to jeopardize well-established sources, can be seen in the decisions that had to be made in the 1988 recruitment of Tulsa, Oklahoma's Tony Brooks. Tony was a great running back from Booker T. Washington High School who was wanted by most major programs in the country.

Assistant head coach Merv Johnson and I learned in the eleventh hour before the national signing date that Tony had narrowed his choices to Notre Dame and us, and we visited with him. It didn't take long to figure out that we had no chance for Tony because he began asking us whether we could make the same promises to him that he said had been made to him by representatives of Notre Dame's interests. We couldn't "match the offer," because we felt that what had *apparently* been promised to Tony would constitute improper inducements under NCAA recruiting guidelines.

I told Tony and his family of my concerns and that I intended to report what they had told me to the NCAA.

This incident really concerned me, depriving us of a great

player like Tony in our own state, and I immediately went to the athletic director Donnie Duncan to tell him what had happened, and I asked him to report this apparent violation to the NCAA for investigation.

A few days later, however, Donnie told me he had received a phone call from President Frank E. Horton, Bill Banowsky's successor, who faced the same sort of fund-raising pressures that Bill had faced. Donnie said that Frank had voiced his concern that this incident might jeopardize major contribution sources and constitute a major public embarrassment to a well-respected private foundation in Tulsa that had donated millions of dollars to the University of Oklahoma. President Horton was my boss, I'm a team player, so we dropped the matter.

How did President Horton discover that we were about to report our concerns about Notre Dame's recruitment of Tony Brooks to the NCAA? Obviously, Tony and his family had told representatives of Notre Dame what we were about to do, and Frank was told of it all by friends of Notre Dame.

For those of you who don't know, I should note that Tony Brooks became a starting halfback for Notre Dame as a freshman in the 1988 season—the year Notre Dame won the national championship. Again, this is an example of the type of pressure placed upon college administrators because of the constant need for money and the impact that it has upon athletics.

But back to 1983 and Banowsky's office. At the time, I didn't pay any attention to all those "anonymous" letters on his desk, or I would have noticed the pattern of the post marks.

Instead, I said I wanted to visit with each of the regents in person.

The first two I met with were Elwood Kemp and Tom McCurty, in Banowsky's office. They were definitely in support of me. I answered all of their questions and felt I was a good enough judge of human nature to be able to rely on those two in hard times.

A few days later I met with regents Dan Little and Ron White at the president's home. Banowsky left us alone to talk. Ron told me it was unfortunate that Banowsky wasn't strong enough to deal with negative criticism. Hell, I knew that already. I always thought it would be great to have a relationship with my college president like Bob Devaney and Tom Osborne had with their president at Nebraska.

Little and White told me that three straight four-loss seasons had put pressure on them and all our alums. They said I would have to win in 1984. I asked, "Don't you consider 8–4 as winning?" They said it wasn't just them, it was everybody. I said, "I work for seven regents and the president. The president works for seven regents. So it is your opinion that counts. How many games do I have to win in order to have a winning season?" They couldn't say. I said, "Is nine enough?" They couldn't answer. "Ten?" I asked. They still couldn't answer the question. I didn't feel as good about this meeting as I had about the first one, but I respect Dan Little and I knew he wasn't really all that interested in athletics. Many regents live for winning athletics, but some, quite properly, have different priorities.

My next meeting was with one regent I considered an enemy and one I knew was a friend. We met at Banowsky's office. When I walked in that day, Banowsky told me the seventh regent—Charles Sarratt—had sent word he didn't need to meet with me. Charlie was the only regent who had played football for Oklahoma—he was on Jim Tatum's 1946 Gator Bowl team—and he understood my problems and supported me.

Julian Rothbaum had been a regent before, during the Bud Wilkinson era. I really liked him. He stayed at the meeting long enough to shake my hand and tell me, "You don't need to worry about me, Barry. I've got to leave to go to another meeting, but I wanted to see you and tell you that you have my support."

That left me with Mickey Imel.

In front of Banowsky and Rothbaum, Imel said he wanted to help turn the program around and get it back on track and that he supported me. I didn't trust him or believe him.

Lee Allen Smith, a good friend of mine who was general manager of the TV station where I did my shows, was also a friend of Imel's. Lee Allen had told me he'd called Imel to raise money for the Pride of Oklahoma Band. They give $500 scholarships to band members, and I contributed every year. But Imel told Lee Allen that he would not support the band as long as Barry Switzer was head football coach. "What does this have to do with Barry and football? The band plays for basketball games, too," Lee Allen had said, but it didn't change Imel's mind.

One explanation that he gave Lee Allen was that I had made fun of his golf game and embarrassed him at an annual alumni function at Southern Hills Country Club in Tulsa in the spring of 1983.

It was a big stag dinner with steaks and lots of drinks. I played in a foursome with Mickey that day. It might have been at his request; it certainly wasn't mine. I sat at a round banquet table with Imel and some other guys, and we were joking and carrying on.

When it was my turn to speak, I said, "I played golf with Mickey Imel today. Watching Mickey play golf is kind of like watching someone masturbate. Everybody watching gets sick. Mickey's the only one that gets any enjoyment out of it."

The room broke into laughter, including Mickey. I mean, this was a stag dinner, where you can say anything. I went back to the table and the rest of the evening was fine.

But Imel later told Lee Allen Smith that I had humiliated him in public and that he had gotten up immediately and left. That was a damn lie.

Incidentally, after 1983 OU won four straight Big Eight championships and a national championship and went to four straight Orange Bowls—and there was Mickey Imel's big ass sitting in the front of the plane and demanding an ocean-view suite at the Fontainebleau Hotel in Miami Beach. He didn't support me or the team, but he damn sure liked to ride, eat and suit up with us.

In my mind I counted the votes. Kemp, McCurty, Sarratt, and Rothbaum would vote for me. Little might. Imel wouldn't. Again, I didn't know which way Ron White would go.

Anyhow, January 22, 1984, was when Wade Walker and I went to Bill Banowsky's house and the president told me if I won the national championship, I didn't have to get married and I wouldn't get fired if I was caught smoking dope. That statement amazes me even today.

On January 27, I received a letter from Mickey Imel saying he was not on my side after all and was not going to help me with my recruiting program, because he was "disenchanted."

I phoned him and asked why he had changed his mind since our meeting in Banowsky's office.

"I guess it all happened over the Christmas holidays," Imel said. "People beat on me about you everywhere I went, and I just feel it is time for a new coach."

Meanwhile, I had started finding out about the Great Conspiracy.

All those "anonymous" letters on Banowsky's desk demanding that I be fired? They were orchestrated by Leon Cross, our associate athletic director in charge of fund-raising, who happens to be a very close friend and associate of Mickey Imel's.

Jake Sandefer had tried to warn me. Bill Connors had tried to warn me. But Bill hadn't really known what was going on until later, when he got a call from Steve Davis.

Leon had the audacity to phone Davis—my first quarterback, winner of three Big Eight and two national championships—and ask him to denounce me on the air. Steve was by now a television personality, doing network color commentary. Leon Cross asked Steve to speak up during the Blue-Gray game in Montgomery on national television and say it was time for a coaching change at Oklahoma.

Steve didn't do this, of course, but he did confirm to me that Leon had asked him.

Bill Connors said he was getting calls and mail from people who told him they were "authorized by Leon Cross" to speak out against me and my program. He may have felt that his close ties with regent Imel gave him some sort of immunity.

The backstabbing, traitorous son of a bitch. There sat Leon Cross right in the middle of the athletic family and he was trying to get everybody in football fired except himself.

Because that's what it would have amounted to. Wade Walker had already been gut-shot and deprived of any real power as athletic director. Oklahoma needed a strong athletic director, but instead we had a guy who was constantly worried about survival. I'll tell you how little authority Wade Walker had. Before Dave Bliss was hired as basketball coach, Wade phoned Ron Danforth, the Syracuse coach, and told Ron he was OU's number-one man and should come to Norman for the press conference to announce he had been hired. By the time Danforth's plane landed, the regents had changed their minds and contacted someone else, leaving Wade to tell Danforth to go back home.

If I'd been fired, Wade would have been swept out with me, and so would twelve assistant coaches and their wives and children . . . after an 8–4 season.

Leon Cross had been kind of a mystery to me. He had played guard for Bud Wilkinson and made all-America in 1962. He was more interested in the gymnastic team than in the other sports, but his real job was to seek contributions from the alums. Once on a flight I had asked Leon what he wanted to do with his life, and he said the only job in the world he wanted was to be the athletic director at Oklahoma.

That sure as hell was never going to happen with me as coach, no matter how soon Wade Walker left.

Leon Cross's chief protector and supporter was Mickey Imel.

I started putting it all together—the summons from Banowsky in December with the pointed reference to the "anonymous" letters, the demand that I visit the regents, the offer of a one-year contract, the threats from Cy Wagner and Mickey Imel . . .

Leon Cross thought he saw a weakness in me that he could turn into a fatality, and he had started making his move. If they fired me, Wade would be gone too, and his dream of being athletic director would be realized.

I went to my secretaries, Shirley Vaughan and Kay Day, two ladies who had been loyal and trusted employees and friends for fourteen years. They said they had been hearing about an organized letter writing campaign but weren't sure if it was accurate, but told me to talk to Kathy Sukenis. Kathy had just resigned as Leon Cross's secretary, and she told me she had placed a lot of calls for Leon and had heard a lot of conversation and it was all highly disloyal. She didn't like it, and in the meantime had quit and decided to go to New York and become a writer.

The next day I went to my friend J. R. Morris, the provost of the university. I told him the whole story. I sat in J. R.'s office while he walked down the hall to talk to Banowsky. J. R. came back and said, "Barry, I told him about Leon orchestrating the letter-writing campaign. He picked up the phone and reamed Leon's ass out. Banowsky told him if he was involved in this, it was very disappointing and for him to cease at once."

I told J. R. that I had suspicions that Bill Banowsky was aware of what Leon was doing. At the time I thought this might be pure paranoia, but years later Stan Ward, then a Norman attorney but in 1983 legal counsel to the university, confirmed to me that Banowsky had known all about Leon's activities.

Later I was told the post dates on the letters would be two or three on the same date from Tulsa, Ardmore, Duncan, Oklahoma City. Then a flood on December 19, 20, 21, and 22, in a totally orchestrated pattern from around the state.

Really, there weren't all that many letters. If I had known about this and started a KEEP BARRY letter writing campaign I could have outdrawn them ten to one.

With everything confirmed, no secondhand information, I went to Leon's office and stuck my head in the door and said, "I want to see you in Wade Walker's office right now."

Wade was sitting at his desk smoking his pipe. Leon went in and sat down. I closed the door and kept standing. I knew Wade had been neutered by the regents over the day-to-day grind and for years Wade had just been a figurehead—but now Leon Cross wanted the job, and he would be Mickey Imel's puppet.

I told Leon and Wade everything I knew about the conspiracy. And I also knew it wouldn't accomplish anything because Wade couldn't have fired him even if he had wanted to. The regents ran the show.

Leon's only comment was, "Did you tell the president?"

"Damn right I did," I said.

I said my piece, called Leon every name I could think of. Then I walked out and left them together and went back to work building my football program and winning a national championship.

But let's not leave the Leon Cross story there. Let's skip

ahead two years, to the late summer of 1986, when Wade
Walker resigned from the athletic department and moved to
Palm Springs to work for Landmark, the big development
company. [God, I hope you're happy now, Wade. I knew you
weren't when you were here. Don't anyone play golf with him;
he is probably a two-handicapper by now.]

There were two candidates for the job of athletic director—Leon Cross and Donnie Duncan. There had been many
others, but they had been weeded out.

Donnie Duncan was obviously the strongest and most
qualified candidate. It wasn't like he asked for the job. Donnie
was executive director of the Gator Bowl, with a nice setup
down in Jacksonville, Florida. Tom McCurty, chairman of the
board of regents, liked Donnie, who had been an assistant for
me at Oklahoma and had a winning record in four years as
head coach at Iowa State, which is no small feat.

Soon as I learned Wade was leaving, I had started work-
ing in Donnie's behalf. I knew that McCurty already knew
Donnie and was impressed with him, and I felt certain that
Elwood Kemp and Charlie Sarratt would be convinced by
Donnie's impresssive credentials and intellect.

Three regents were supporting Leon. They were his old
protector Mickey Imel, Ron White, and Sarah Hogan, a friend
of Ron White's who also lived in Oklahoma City.

The swing vote would be new regent Sylvia Lewis, who is
black. And guess who's the best recruiter of blacks in the
country? Me. You didn't have a chance, Mickey. Today I consider Sylvia to be a close friend. A very sweet, able, and intelligent lady.

When I heard Donnie was coming in for an interview on
Monday or Tuesday, I got on the phone on Friday night and
called him at home in Florida, where he was watching TV. He
already knew about Leon's betraying me and the athletic family with the '83 letter-writing campaign and the rest of it.

I looked forward to Donnie's coming and to visiting with
him, and I told him that I felt like he would have at least four
votes, maybe more. Even though I knew that Ron and Sarah
were very much influenced by Mickey, I really didn't know
how they would vote. Obviously, I knew that Mickey Imel
would do everything he could to push Leon into the job.

I knew that I really couldn't do it, but I did tell Donnie that I wanted to have a press conference and tell the world what Leon had tried to do to me and our coaches, but Donnie said, "Barry, if you do anything like that, you can scratch me off the list. I will not show up for an interview under those circumstances," he said. "Whatever the situation is, I can handle it."

I had already spent time with Sylvia Lewis, calling her and taking her to lunch. Sylvia and I got along well. She had seen what I had done for the black athletes in Oklahoma and was appreciative of it. I told Sylvia that when she came to know Donnie, she would realize he was the man the university needed. "If he's the man you want, he's the man I'm sure I will want," she said.

It looked to me as if Donnie had four votes locked, and it was a done deal.

But Leon's backers weren't ready to quit without a fight. Some of his most enthusiastic supporters were a group called the 49ers—a bunch of guys who played football at Oklahoma back in the '40s and '50s. A few of these guys were old, bigoted white racists. I want to qualify this by saying a few, because a lot of these fellows were friends of mine and our coaches. Leon had played ball about ten or twelve years after most of the 49ers, but he was their man. They wanted him as their athletic director.

One of the loudest of the 49ers was J. D. Roberts, a former all-American guard who had been head football coach of the New Orleans Saints in the early days of that NFL franchise. After he left coaching, J. D. had tried his luck in the oil business, and it was rumored that he wanted a job as assistant athletic director at Oklahoma, but he had no chance of getting that unless Leon became the boss.

A couple of the 49ers started phoning Sylvia Lewis at home, threatening her and making racial slurs. She told me this in the aftermath of what they had put her through.

Donnie came to town and was interviewed. The board of regents met at the Embassy Suites Hotel in Oklahoma City. The media was there in force, filming everything. The 49ers were out on the sidewalk and tried to intimidate Sylvia Lewis when she walked through to the meeting room.

I was waiting down the street at the Hilton with Donnie's son, Mark.

They announced Donnie was the new athletic director by a 7–0 vote, but Donnie looked sort of subdued and drained to me when I met with him later at his room. I knew the 7–0 was just a cosmetic announcement; the real vote was 4–3. It had been a tough week on Donnie and he was disappointed not to have had a real 7–0 vote. I learned later from another source, someone else who was in the private meeting, that regent Mickey Imel had made a point about the fact that Switzer has a strong personality "and so does Billy Tubbs [the OU basketball coach]." And then, in addressing Duncan, he said, "You're a strong person, too. Don't you think that perhaps a weaker person might be a better athletic director?" Donnie had replied, "I don't think weakness is an advantage in any position."

When the regents came out of the meeting after their vote, they were heckled by a few of the 49ers. Some people in the crowd yelled racial insults at Sylvia Lewis. She had to be escorted to her car. J. D. Roberts got up in the face of regent Elwood Kemp, who was seventy-two years old, and started jawing at him. But Elwood is an old lion. You don't jaw at Elwood.

Remember now, all this stuff happened nearly two full years after the letter-writing conspiracy and Banowsky's offer to buy up the last four years of my contract.

In the meantime, instead of getting fired, I had won two Big Eight championships and one national championship.

No, I did not take up President Banowsky on his statement that I could get caught smoking dope and not lose my job if I won the national championship.

Even if I had wanted to try it, Banowsky was already gone. He had quit the year after that meeting in his office when he had told me how worried he was about my social values and my SEC problems and my outside business interests.

And whatever became of Leon Cross? You can still find him in his associate athletic director's office unless he's out at an athletic fund-raiser, a booster-club meeting, or at a gymnastics meet.

19

WISHBONE TWO, NATIONAL CHAMPS

When the Big Eight Conference Skywriters Tour—a band of sportswriters who visit each school and write their predictions for the season—came to Norman just before the start of the 1984 schedule, what do you think was the main thing they wanted to know in the press conference?

"Hey, Barry, how many games do you have to win this year to keep your job?"

That's what the sportswriters were yelling. I had to grin. Just a few months ago I had tried to pin down the regents on this very question, and they couldn't answer it.

"You're asking the wrong guy," I told the writers. "I really don't know."

There I was, the winningest coach in the nation at that moment (106–21–3 in eleven years), and everybody was wondering what number it would take to get me fired.

"Right now on our schedule I can see three teams—Pittsburgh, Texas, and Nebraska—that are better than we are," I told the sportswriters. "If we beat the teams we are supposed to beat and play lights-out against those other three, I can live with that. I plan on winning them all, of course. But if the coaching job at Oklahoma is based on beating Texas every year, I'm in trouble. Go check the record. OU wins about one out of four [Texas led the series 47–28–3 at the time.] Last year our Texas and Oklahoma State games were the two worst games one of my teams ever played back to back, even though we won the second one. When we lost Marcus Dupree in the middle of the year, we had to search desperately for something to hang our hats on. We were just floating and scrambling.

"I know that we'll be better in '84 because of these factors: 1) the recommitment of our players and coaches; 2) going back to the Wishbone; 3) because of a group of redshirt players on defense that you guys don't even know about yet. But you'll be hearing about them in the future."

But the headline in the *Tulsa World* the next day said: "SWITZER ADMITS JOB ON LINE."

There was no getting away from that subject.

Actually, the 1984 season was the debut of a great young defensive team—freshmen, sophomores, and redshirts—who finished second in total defense in 1985, 1986, and 1987, the only time any team has ever accomplished that in college football.

I knew we were going to be studs on defense. Our gun was loaded. And I felt very comfortable back in the Wishbone offense. Now our recruiters could go scour the country for option quarterbacks and sign brilliant young players like Jamelle Holieway of Los Angeles, Eric Mitchel of Pine Bluff, Arkansas, and later Charles Thompson from Lawton, Oklahoma.

With Danny Bradley back as a senior quarterback, the offense was in pretty good hands. Danny didn't make many mistakes, even though he threw the ball nearly twice as often as any quarterback I'd ever had.

I was counting on redshirting our freshman quarterback from Henrietta, Oklahoma, a big white kid with 4.6 speed and a major-league arm. I am speaking, of course, of Troy Aikman—who wound up his college career at UCLA as an all-American and being the first pick in the NFL draft.

When Troy was recruited, we were running the I formation, but by the time he arrived on campus to play ball, we were back in the Wishbone. I promised him we would throw the ball more and use his talents, but I wanted him to sit out a year and let Danny Bradley play quarterback.

Stanford came to Norman to open the 1984 season and drove 71 yards for a touchdown on their first possession. People in the stands were screaming that I would be lucky to survive the first game, let alone the season. But our young defense—guys like Casillas, Bosworth, Paul Migliazzo, Keith Stanberry—shut Stanford down cold after that first drive, and OU won, 19–7.

Pitt was a one-point favorite at kickoff, but we massacred them, 42–10. After the game, Danny Bradley told the press, "The old OU is back."

The next week Baylor scored in the last few seconds of each half to make our 34–15 victory seem closer than it was. OU was now 3–0 for the first time since 1979.

We had to overcome five turnovers to beat Kansas State 24–6 as Steve Sewell gained 295 yards of total offense.

Now came the Red River War against Texas—a game that still eats at my stomach. It was pouring rain all day. The rain must have blinded the officials. We recovered a Texas fumble that the officials took away from us. Steve Sewell made a great run, bouncing out of a stack of bodies for a touchdown that gave us a 15–12 lead. Then, with a few minutes left in the game, Texas fumbled near midfield and we recovered. But the officials ruled no fumble. The films confirmed that the officials had blown the call. Then again Keith Stanberry clearly intercepted a pass in our end zone that would have ended the game, but the official on the spot waved it off and yelled that Keith was out of bounds—a wrong call, as shown again and again on television around the country. On the last play of the game, Texas kicked a 32-yard field goal in the rain to tie the score 15–15.

We traveled to Ames, Iowa, for a game that was moved from afternoon to night so it could be televised on ESPN. It was raining again, and this time it was also miserably cold. Our team was not anywhere ready emotionally to play. Midway through the fourth quarter, Iowa State was leading 10–3. We kicked a field goal to pull closer. Then Danny Bradley pitched out to Spencer Tillman, who sailed into the end zone for what became a 12–10 victory after we missed the extra point.

The seventh week of the season OU was ranked second in the nation, but Danny Bradley was hurt prior to the game. Troy Aikman had been running our scout team, not even working with the varsity. I had been hoping to redshirt him, but suddenly I had to have him prepare to start against Kansas. I realized Troy couldn't run the Wishbone very well yet, but I thought we could give him enough protection to show his passing ability. And, really, I thought our defense would win the game.

Well, none of that happened.

Troy looked pitiful that day. Nobody watching would have dreamed he was a great prospect. He went 2 for 14, passing for a total of 8 yards—both completions were shovel passes—and had three interceptions in the first half. It devastated Troy. But I didn't blame him a bit. The rest of us didn't give him a damn bit of help. Kansas kicked our butt 28–11.

We bounced back against Missouri and beat the Tigers 49–7. Troy didn't enter the game until it was 42–0, so he had a chance to relax and try to get some of his confidence back.

At Colorado, freshman fullback Lydell Carr ran 64 yards for a touchdown in the first minute and finished with 143 yards on 15 carries in our 42–17 victory. Colorado was a minus-three yards rushing.

Nebraska was a hell of a lot better team than we were and was properly favored to beat us in Lincoln. The Nebraska defense dominated our offense except for about four plays, but one of them was a 50-yard run by Danny Bradley for a touchdown in the fourth quarter. A few minutes earlier, Nebraska had the ball with a first down on our 2-yard line, and we stopped them with inches to spare on maybe the top goal line stand of my career. Danny's run iced it 17–7.

But we still had to beat Oklahoma State to win the conference championship and go to the Orange Bowl.

The Cowboys scored two odd touchdowns. At the end of the first half the officials stopped the clock to let the players unpile and gave Oklahoma State an extra play, which resulted in a touchdown. In the third quarter Rusty Hilger, their quarterback, fumbled the snap, picked up the bouncing ball, and threw a 77-yard pass that was a one-handed catch by Malcomb Lewis for a touchdown. The rest of the game they were fairly helpless against our defense and had a rushing total of minus-four yards. The score was Oklahoma 24, Oklahoma State 14.

I took my team to Miami two weeks early for the Orange Bowl game against Washington and put them through two-a-day workouts. I doubted this game would be for a national championship, but I tried to build it up as being that important.

Undefeated Brigham Young was ranked number one in the nation and was playing a Michigan team with a mediocre 6–5 record in the Holiday Bowl.

NBC wanted me to promote the Orange Bowl game like it was the national championship. I went to New York and did the *Today Show* and was taken out to dinner several nights by TV executives. Sure, I played along with the hype. I was hoping Michigan would knock off Brigham Young and leave the national title for Oklahoma.

Brigham Young coach Lavelle Edwards is a friend of mine, but I told the press and TV that Brigham Young was by no means the best team in the country. I said OU was a better team than Brigham Young. Partly I said these things to pump up our TV ratings for the Orange Bowl. Mostly I said them because I believed them, but I should add that Bobby Proctor, our defensive secondary coach, would have had a heart attack if we had had to play them.

The Mormon press and the Utah papers ridiculed me. This is when that sewage treatment plant in Midvale, Utah, was named for me.

However, my players and I may have spent too much time hoping Michigan could upset Brigham Young and too little time wondering if Washington could beat us.

My critics said I did a poor job of preparing the team for the Washington game, but I don't really agree. I have prepared ten Orange Bowl teams. I know how to do it. But this was a very young team, and some of the players may have felt deep down that just arriving at the Orange Bowl was enough. I'm not sure how much that may have had to do with it. Washington played a hell of a game. They scored two touchdowns early in the first quarter and two touchdowns late in the fourth quarter. In between, they didn't do much. But it was enough to beat us 28–17 and drop us to sixth in the nation.

In that game we had kicked a field goal to take a 17–14 lead and possibly the momentum, but a flag was thrown for illegal procedure. Then we were hit with an additional 15-yard penalty when our pep club's Sooner Schooner covered wagon, not seeing the flag, raced onto the field celebrating.

The Schooner cost us 15 yards, but I have always felt that that was a chickenshit call by the referee because we had talked about the Schooner before the game, and he welcomed and encouraged its use as part of the spirit of the game. I found later that the call had never ever been made in the history of The Schooner's participation in OU football games.

I have found that often the best things in life happen when you are not really expecting them.

And I certainly didn't expect a national championship in 1985. I thought we were still a year away. We had everybody back on defense, so it was a given that we would be great on that side of the ball. But I wasn't so sure about our offense. No matter how great he looked throwing the ball or what an impressive athlete he was, Troy Aikman still had to prove he could run the Wishbone.

Suppose I had gone to a gypsy with a crystal ball before we kicked off to start the 1985 season.

What if that gypsy had looked into the crystal ball and predicted:

My two most experienced running backs would get hurt in the opening game, and one of them would miss the rest of the season, and . . .

Starting guard Jeff Pickett and tackle Greg Johnson and center Travis Simpson would go out with injuries, and . . .

Troy Aikman would break his ankle, and . . .

Tony Casillas would miss three games with a bad knee, and . . .

All-American free safety Rickey Dixon would miss four games because of injury, and . . .

A freshman would lead the team in rushing, and . . .

In the Orange Bowl we would need to beat the number-one team in the nation to have a shot at the top ranking, while all Miami would need to do was beat underdog Tennessee in the Sugar Bowl . . .

Every one of those predictions would have been correct.

Spencer Tillman and Earl Johnson got hurt early against Minnesota under their new coach, Lou Holtz, in the dome at Minneapolis on September 28, but our defense won the game 13–7. Minnesota didn't make a first down until near the end of the third quarter, and their only touchdown was the result of a fumble at our 19.

Kansas State managed six first downs and Lydell Carr gained 131 yards rushing for our side in a 41–6 victory. But I still wasn't happy with our Wishbone. I don't want to sound greedy, but 41 points against this Kansas State defense was no cause for optimism.

In the Red River War, our defense stuffed Texas, holding them to four first downs and 70 yards total offense. But the Texas defense scored a touchdown by picking a fumble out of the air at our 7-yard line. Aikman threw a 43-yard pass to Keith Jackson to set up a 1-yard touchdown by Carr, and Patrick Collins raced 45 yards for a touchdown on an option. OU won 14–7. But I was yet to see Aikman really move our Wishbone on one of those 500-yard track meets I always loved so much.

My old associate and rival Jimmy Johnson brought his Miami Hurricanes to Norman the following week. Jimmy had been at Miami only a couple of years since leaving Oklahoma State. He hadn't been able to beat me when he was at Stillwater. But he never had the players there that he had at Miami.

Football schedules are drawn up years in advance. I had been consulted, of course, when Oklahoma athletic director (at the time) Wade Walker put Miami on our schedule three years in a row. Fortunes of football teams sometimes change at schools. When Miami had been placed on our schedule they were not nearly as formidable as they are now.

Jimmy had a junior quarterback named Vinny Testaverde, who threw a 56-yard pass to Michael Irvin for a touchdown in the first quarter.

But all of a sudden Troy Aikman started playing the greatest game of his Oklahoma career. Troy ran 49 yards on the option for a touchdown that was called back on a penalty. Then he hit six out of seven passes—a 50-yarder to Jackson and a 14-yard touchdown to Derrick Shepard.

With nine minutes left in the second quarter, Troy rolled right to throw deep to Shepard, and two Miami linemen smashed into him, one from either side.

Troy was carried off the field with a broken ankle.

I looked around on the sideline, and there was this eighteen-year-old Los Angeles kid with his eyes big as silver dollars.

"Okay, Jamelle," I said. "Go run their ass crazy."

The Miami players looked at little Jamelle, a true freshman, trotting out to the huddle, and they started laughing. I mean, Miami looked so damn huge and Jamelle looked so young and small.

There was no miracle finish for us this day, no Sooner Magic. Miami beat us 27–14, and Testaverde threw for 270 yards.

But from that day on, with Jamelle at quarterback, we became a truly great option football offense.

(After the season I was coaching the West team at the Hula Bowl. We practiced on alternate days at Aloha Stadium, and I watched the East quarterback, Jim Everett of Purdue, a number-one pick in the NFL draft.

(I turned to a group of pro scouts and said, "I've got a quarterback at Oklahoma who's better than this guy, has more speed, and a better arm." They looked at me and said, "Switzer, what the hell would you know about a quarterback?"

(Troy came out for spring practice at Oklahoma, but he knew his talents didn't fit our offense. After about a week, he came to my office and said he would like to transfer. "I'd like to go to the West Coast to some school that throws the football a lot," he said. He was thinking about Stanford, UCLA, or Arizona State.

(I phoned Arizona State coach John Cooper, who had seen Troy in high school and was excited to set up a visit. I called Jack Elway at Stanford, and he never returned my call. I called Terry Donahue at UCLA. Terry had never heard of Troy and wasn't very enthusiastic about a transfer. Most coaches don't want to gamble on transfers. My old college line coach, Dixie White, always use to say that they didn't like to hang out someone else's "dirty wash."

(OU's first game in 1986 was against UCLA. I told Terry that if he took Troy, he couldn't have him on the squad until after that game. Troy wouldn't have been eligible to play—transfers have to sit out a year—but I didn't want anybody insinuating that Troy helped the Bruins prepare a defense for our Wishbone. I said, "Terry, I don't know what kind of quarterbacks you have out there, but I am telling you about the top draft choice of his class."

(Donahue invited Troy to Los Angeles for a visit. You probably know the rest of the story. Aikman led UCLA to the Pac Ten Championship and was the top pick in the entire NFL draft—for the Dallas Cowboys, now coached by Jimmy Johnson!)

But back to 1985. If Troy hadn't broken his ankle, I don't know how long it would have taken Jamelle Holieway to hit the field as our quarterback. But once he took charge, our offense was suddenly racing up and down the field on people, like our Wishbone of old.

In Jamelle's first start, our Wishbone cranked out 542 yards in an old-fashioned 59–14 win over Iowa State. Eric Mitchel entered the game as Jamelle's backup and rushed for 135 yards himself.

Against Kansas, Jamelle ran 19 times for 162 yards and we outrushed the Jayhawks 424 to 63 to win the game 48–6.

The major suspense in our Missouri game the following week was if Jamelle would break Jack Mildren's school record for total offense in one game. Jamelle did it with 324 (156 rushing, 168 passing). Keith Jackson caught five passes for 133. The score was Oklahoma 51, Missouri 6.

Colorado had started running the Wishbone in 1985, but our defense wasn't impressed. The Buffs snapped the ball twice on our side of the field and punted ten times as we shut them out 31–0.

We were ranked seventh in the nation when Nebraska came to Owen Field. Oklahoma State had lost to Iowa State earlier in the day, so the winner of our game would be Big Eight champion, with an Orange Bowl bid, and the loser would go to the Fiesta Bowl. Nebraska had the top rushing offense in the nation. Our defense held them to ten first downs and would have shut them out, but with 26 seconds to play, Nebraska defensive tackle Chris Spachman took a loose ball away from one of our reserve halfbacks and ran 76 yards for a touchdown. Our leading rusher was tight end Keith Jackson, who ran the reverse three times for 136 yards. The first one was an 88-yard touchdown in the first quarter. Jamelle showed a national TV audience his remarkable quickness on a 43-yard run for our second touchdown. The score was Oklahoma 27, Nebraska 7.

The Oklahoma State game the next week in Stillwater was played in the worst conditions I ever saw. The game was switched from afternoon to night to accommodate ESPN and Chuck Neinas, the president of the College Football Association, who *promised* me great weather. Snow and sleet swirled in the lights. The field looked like an ice-hockey rink. Jamelle stood beside me, shivering on the sidelines, and said, "Coach, you lied to me. You told me if I came to Oklahoma I would never have to play in weather like this."

We restricted our offense pretty much to giving the ball to Lydell Carr between the tackles. Our walk-on junior from Texas, Tim Lashar, kicked two field goals, and Spencer Tillman skated in for a touchdown. We won the game 13–0.

Before the season, S.M.U. had been regarded as a candidate to win the national championship. The Mustangs had the finest offensive talent we had faced, with Reggie Dupard, a first-round draft choice, who had rushed for more than 1,000 yards. At Owen Field, S.M.U. drove 82 yards for a touchdown the first time they touched the ball.

Then we got serious. Jamelle ran for 126 yards and two touchdowns, and our defense threw a net over Dupard and the rest of their great athletes. We beat S.M.U. 35–13.

Now the national championship could be ours.

All we needed was for UCLA to beat Iowa in the Rose Bowl, for Tennessee to upset Miami in the Sugar Bowl—and for Oklahoma to beat Penn State in the Orange Bowl.

Oh, there was one other thing. I had to hope the voters in the major polls wouldn't notice that Fresno State was undefeated.

Also unbeaten, Penn State was ranked first in the nation, Miami second, and Oklahoma third.

At the end of November, when it was announced that Penn State would be Oklahoma's opponent in the Orange Bowl, Beano Cook and *Sports Illustrated* both tried to revive a "feud" between Joe Paterno and me that never existed in the first place.

Way back in 1980, before I had ever met Joe Paterno, the Penn State coach was hosting a group of reporters in his home and one of them asked Joe if he would be interested in a pro coaching job.

Thinking this was off the record and he was making a little joke, Joe replied, "No, I can't leave the college game to the Barry Switzers and Jackie Sherrills of the world."

A real gentleman and a stand-up guy, Paterno phoned me when the quote hit the papers and apologized. Joe didn't apologize to Jackie, because there was some true bad blood there. But Joe knew Jackie was a friend of mine, and for years Joe had been hearing Darrell Royal telling the establishment coaches that I was a crook and so Joe said it flippantly and without really even thinking about it.

Joe offered to make a public apology, but I told him it wasn't necessary, to forget it. Later, when Chuck Neinas, former Big Eight commissioner, became head of the College Football Association, Chuck urged me to come out of my paranoid social shell and get involved with the group. At the first meeting I went to, Joe Paterno was the moderator.

In the following years Joe and his wife, Sue, went on Nike trips, and on occasion I would have dinner with them. We had many fun evenings together and developed a genuine mutual respect and friendship.

Through the years, we became friends. We were all a part of a group of twenty-five coaches and wives who came to call ourselves the Nike family, obviously because our teams wore Nike shoes.

Because of this experience, I had the opportunity to establish meaningful and lasting friendships with some of the top coaches in the country. And I have to say that no longer being able to go on these trips and losing a lot of these associates is one of my greatest regrets at no longer coaching college football.

In Joe's recent autobiography, *Joe Paterno, By the Book*, he commented about his association with me and again apologized, in print, for having made that flippant remark back in 1980. He also said that Barry Switzer is no hypocrite, he is a fun guy to be around, and a real practical jokester.

One of the events that Joe may have had in mind took place on one of our Nike trips. Our "Nike girl," Karen Moreland, and the folks at Nike take this group of coaches and wives on a trip in late February of each year. On the trip we took in 1983, we all rendezvoused in San Juan, Puerto Rico, for a week's cruise in the Caribbean on the *Sun Princess*. About the fourth day out, we anchored offshore at a small private island and ferried ashore in small boats.

Janet Gibson, who accompanied me, and I were sitting at one of those thatch-roofed bars having piña coladas, while a lot of the coaches and wives were lying out on the beach enjoying the sun and the surf. Joe and Sue were lying about twenty yards away from Janet and me, toward the water. While Janet and I were talking about something or another, we were both suddenly amazed to smell the distinct aroma of marijuana cigarettes. We looked around and there, about ten feet away, were these island natives leaning up against a palm tree and openly smoking dope. They saw that Janet and I were laughing, and one of the natives immediately came over and asked us if we would like to purchase some of his island-grown "good dope." He reached into his swim trunks and pulled from his jock strap a cellophane package with four or five rolled "reefers." He obviously wanted to sell us all his stash, but I had a better idea.

I told him that we had all we needed, but there was one guy on our ship who had been asking me for several days if I knew where I could get any "good shit." I said, "Do you see that black-headed guy with the thick dark-tinted glasses sitting down there?" And I pointed at Joe and Sue, twenty yards away. "I think he'll take everything you've got."

The native immediately jogged off in Joe's direction, convinced as he ran, I'm sure, that he was about to make a big sale. Janet and I both watched as he tapped Joe on the shoulder. Obviously, we could not hear the conversation, but as Joe looked up, we saw the native reach into his trunks and pull out his stash and show it to Joe. We then saw shock and bewilderment on Joe's face. He asked a question of the native and the native "fingered" Janet and me at the bar. Joe and Sue turned to look at us, and by that time Janet and I were laughing so hard, we literally fell off the bar stools. As you would expect, Joe waved at us and ran the native off.

You know, though, later that afternoon, as we were getting ready to reboard the ship, I happened to see some guy who looked a lot like Joe talking to that same native . . . and just for an instant thought it was him! Gotcha, Joe! Of course, it really wasn't, was it! Joe is a hell of a good guy.

But getting back to the 1986 Orange Bowl, Joe and I were facing each other as head coaches for the first time. We were the two winningest head coaches active in the game. Joe had a 183–47–2 record in twenty years, and I was 124–24–4 in thirteen seasons.

By an eerie coincidence, Bud Wilkinson's record at Oklahoma through 153 games of his career had been 125–24–4, with three national championships. Obviously, then, if we were to beat Penn State, my record would become identical to Bud's at 125–24–4! But still, all of the other things mentioned above had to fall in place for this to come about and for us to win three national championships.

In the first quarter of the Orange Bowl, Penn State was stopping our option stuff pretty well, with their all-American linebacker Shane Conlan chasing Jamelle and belting him on every play. We went backward on our first possession. Penn State took the ball and drove 62 yards for a touchdown against the best defense in the country.

I felt shell-shocked. But my coaches noticed Penn State's regular safety leaving the game with a limp, and we called a deep pass. It was a 71-yard throw from Jamelle to Keith Jackson for a touchdown.

In the second quarter, we heard the public-address announcement that Tennessee was leading Miami 14–7.

Sonny Brown intercepted a pass and returned it to the Penn State 15. Lashar kicked his first of four field goals that day. A few minutes later, Tony Rayburn intercepted a pass and ran it back to the Penn State 14. Two more Lashar field goals in short order put us up 16–7. Jamelle fumbled on our 11 with nine seconds left, and a Penn State field goal made it 16–10 when we went to the locker room.

Penn State drove the third-quarter kickoff back to our 21 before Sonny Brown intercepted again. We had to punt, Penn State fumbled at their own 4, and Mike Mantle—Mickey Mantle's nephew—recovered for Oklahoma. Paterno was out on the field raising hell with the officials on a couple of calls that went our way. Lashar kicked his fourth field goal, and we led 19–10 as the fourth quarter started.

That's when the announcement came over the speakers that Tennessee had beaten Miami 35–7. Thanks, Johnny Majors, my old coaching buddy. You helped it all fall into place.

If we could hold our lead, the national championship was ours.

We knocked each other back and forth for a while, and then Penn State took the ball to our 10-yard line. OU's great defense stopped them, and the Nittany Lions missed a 27-yard field goal that was their last chance to get in the game.

Lydell Carr ran 61 yards for a touchdown—he had 148 yards on 19 carries for the night—with 1:42 remaining.

The score was Oklahoma 25, Penn State 10.

I was so happy I didn't know if I was laughing or crying. I barely remember shaking hands with Joe. Jeff Tupper and Tony Casillas picked me up on their shoulders and carried me off the field.

And who do you think came to the locker room to congratulate me on winning the national championship?

Sue Paterno, Joe's very charming and classy wife.

We finished on top in all the polls, of course. But in the UPI poll—which is voted by the coaches—it failed to be unanimous by one vote.

The only coach who didn't vote for Oklahoma was me. I voted for Fresno State as national champion and Jim Sweeney as coach of the year.

Frank Mays Switzer, the bootlegger, as he appeared in the late 1920s or early 1930s. AUTHOR'S PRIVATE COLLECTION

Mary Louise Wood, my mother, as she appeared in the same era. AUTHOR'S PRIVATE COLLECTION

This is the way I looked as a player at Arkansas in 1959. I couldn't have made any of my Oklahoma teams from 1973 through 1988! AUTHOR'S PRIVATE COLLECTION

Below, Merv Johnson (*left*), Frank Boyles, and me on the sidelines at an Arkansas game in the early 1960s. Frank seems to be after Merv, not me! COURTESY OKLAHOMA PUBLISHING COMPANY

My mentor and great friend, Jim MacKenzie. President Cross knew Jim could bring to Norman the talent necessary to feed the "monster." AUTHOR'S PRIVATE COLLECTION

Above, the new 1966 Oklahoma staff.
Left to right: Galen Hall, me, Homer
Rice, Jim MacKenzie, Pat James,
Chuck Fairbanks, and Swede Lee.

Pat James—the last of a breed.

Chuck Fairbanks as Oklahoma head football coach, 1967–1972. AUTHOR'S PRIVATE COLLECTION

Steve Davis, my first quarterback after I was named head coach. This young man, also a preacher, quarterbacked the Sooners to two national championships. AUTHOR'S PRIVATE COLLECTION

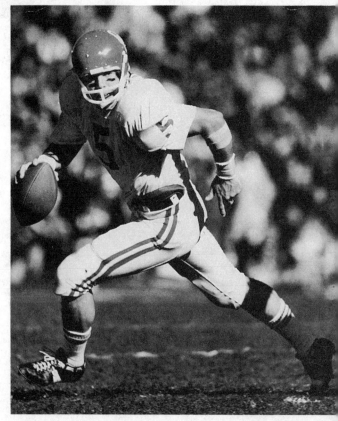

Above left, Thomas Lott (6), the second great quarterback of the Switzer era at Oklahoma, from San Antonio, Texas. COURTESY OKLAHOMA PUBLISHING COMPANY

Above right, J. C. Watts, another of the quarterback preachers—two-time most valuable player in the Orange Bowl, 1980 and 1981. AUTHOR'S PRIVATE COLLECTION

Showtime. "Little Joe" Washington was certainly one of the best and most exciting running backs ever to play in the college game. AUTHOR'S PRIVATE COLLECTION

The Switzers in the mid-1970s. *Left to right:* Greg, Kathy, me, Doug, and Kay. COURTESY OKLAHOMA PUBLISHING COMPANY

Bobby Bell and me holding a few that didn't get away. Bobby was my "hunting and fishing coach" and got as much TV exposure as I did. AUTHOR'S PRIVATE COLLECTION

Below, the *real* "brothers"—LeRoy Selmon, Lucious Selmon, and Dewey Selmon. AUTHOR'S PRIVATE COLLECTION

Above, Billy Sims and me just before the 1979 game with Nebraska. Billy set a few records that day. AUTHOR'S PRIVATE COLLECTION

Left, Wendell "Deadset" Mosley. He was a great judge of athletic talent, a "smooooooth operator," and a good friend. AUTHOR'S PRIVATE COLLECTION

20

OH, BUT FOR MIAMI . . .

I believe that except for the University of Miami, Oklahoma had the best team in the country in 1986 and 1987. Oklahoma unquestionably had the two best defensive teams that had ever played modern college football. NCAA stats stand with me on that. In 1986 our defense led the nation against rushing, passing, total offense, and scoring. In 1987 we were tops on defense against passing, scoring, and total defense. We led the nation in total defense and pass defense for three years in a row.

And how was Wishbone Two doing all this time? In 1986, with sophomore Jamelle at quarterback all the way, we led the nation in rushing and scoring. During our Orange Bowl game at the end of the season, Don Criqui, calling the plays in the booth for NBC-TV, told America that "this Oklahoma rushing offense is the most ferocious in college football history."

Hearing that statement later on videotape, I smiled inwardly and took a bow to OU teams of 1971, 1973, and 1974. I thought of the players on those teams. Now they were "old" guys in their thirties. They had truly been the most ferocious rushing offenses in college football history, but television had already forgotten them.

You college players out there, you guys who are real studs right now, I wish you would take this to heart. In ten years television may well have forgotten you, too. So stay in school and get your degrees.

In the summer of 1986, before the season, I received the first notice of any possible problems with incoming freshman Charles Thompson. He was caught shoplifting in a shopping

213

center in Tulsa. My critics have recently said that I should have gotten rid of Charles right then, that I'm too easy with kids and give them a second chance too often, but I don't agree. I visited with Charles Thompson. His family was devastated. The kid had been punished enough. I talked to him about his future responsibilities. I told him we weren't selling dreams at Oklahoma, we were selling reality. He could live his dreams here, because Oklahoma could make them come true with a little help from Charles.

Should I have dismissed Charles from the team over the shoplifting incident? I didn't think so then, and I still don't. Probably the main thing you deal with as a coach is the personal problems of your athletes. Over the years we have had a number of kids like Charles who got into minor trouble that could have cost their futures, but nearly all of them pulled out of it. I recall Kenny Pope, a defensive back in the early 1970s. Kenny was a problem maker. One day in a staff meeting when I was an assistant coach, we had an opportunity to discipline him and get rid of him. Some coaches wanted to give him the boot, but I wouldn't go along with it. It's always easy to give up and fire someone. It's a hell of a lot tougher job to stick with someone who we know is wrong and reeducate him into being a better person. Kenny later graduated and became a very successful college coach. If we had sent him back to his ghetto in Galveston, it could have ruined him. But as his coaches, it was important for us to stick with him. As I've told many since, "Don't ever quit on yourself and we won't ever quit on you."

Kids go through great emotional swings, especially in athletics, because they think it's so important to them to have instant success. They're all in a hurry. And some of them will make mistakes.

Well, I didn't have instant success. I had to pay a price. I understand completely what the kids are going through.

But, back to 1986.

Looking back on it, I get a sort of painful joy out of realizing how easily Oklahoma could have put together three national championships in a row in 1985, 1986, and 1987— during three of the four years Bill Banowsky had wanted to buy up my contract. And, but for a missed field goal against USC in 1973, we would have been national champions in 1973, 1974, and 1975.

Each of those three years our record was 11–1. Our Orange Bowl games following the 1985, 1986, and 1987 seasons produced the national champion in two of those three years, and in the other game the Orange Bowl gave me one of my greatest personal satisfactions. It allowed me to go home to Arkansas again as a winner.

If it just hadn't been for Miami . . .

Brian Bosworth, whom I talk a great deal about elsewhere in this book, made an ass of himself before our first game of the season against UCLA by saying to the press that "UCLA plays girls' football." Actually, UCLA (with transfer Troy Aikman sitting out a year of ineligibility) had a damn good ball club. But Oklahoma was awesome. We outrushed them 470–34 and would have shut them out except for a late interception and a field goal. The score was Oklahoma 38, UCLA 3.

My running backs that year were a really outstanding group. Lord, what talent they had—Jamelle at quarterback, giving the ball to Lydell Carr or Earl Johnson or pitching it to Spencer Tillman or Patrick Collins (a great blocker as well as runner) or keeping it himself on one of his spectacular runs. He was constantly surprising tacklers. They expected him to be quick and fast, but they were shocked when he lowered a shoulder and knocked them on their butts. Jamelle was physically very strong.

We also had Eric Mitchel, Anthony Stafford, Leon Perry, Rotnei Anderson, and others to carry the ball in 1986 behind an offensive line that had three all-Americans—Keith Jackson, Anthony Phillips, and Mark Hutson—and several others who would have been stars at most schools.

In case you think we had laid off recruiting in Texas after my struggles with Darrell Royal in the 1970s, consider that there were more than thirty-five Texans on our roster in both 1986 and 1987. One of them—defensive end Darrell Reed from Houston—made all-Big Eight four years in a row.

The second game of 1986 was a total rout of Minnesota, 63–0.

Finally, we flew down to Miami to take our revenge on the Hurricanes for upsetting us the year before. My coaches, players, and I were no strangers to Miami. The Orange Bowl was where we expected to go every year at the end of the season.

But this was the first time we had played in the Orange Bowl in a regular season game with Miami as the home team.

Ask Notre Dame; ask anybody who ever played there. That Miami home crowd of 70,000 was the most unruly mob Oklahoma played in front of in my entire experience. Those people were just insane—truly intimidating to our fans in their mental and verbal abuse, spitting on them, throwing things at us. The kindest thing they called us was "stupid Okies." When the captains met for the coin toss, the Miami guys wouldn't shake hands with us. They just kept glaring and cussing. They truly tried to intimidate football players, but our guys had played in too many big games against great teams to let that kind of bullshit shake them. It's all an act anyway.

I'm not blaming any of that for what happened on the scoreboard. Miami quarterback Vinny Testaverde—the best quarterback Oklahoma ever faced during my career—had an outstanding game. He hit 21 of 28 passes for 261 yards and four touchdowns and is so big and strong that he was really difficult to bring down when we had his receivers covered and he had to scramble.

For the second year in a row, Miami beat us. This time it was 28–16. We didn't play well. Our offense snapped the ball 69 times and made 19 busts, or mistakes. The incredible crowd noise had a real impact on our lack of performance since we use many audible play calls at the line of scrimmage.

The score against Kansas State the following week—a 56–10 Oklahoma victory—made it seem we were back on the track, but I was worried. Again, we didn't play well. "People, we can't play like this next week and beat Texas," I told the team afterward.

So we came back and beat Texas 47–12, the worst whipping we'd given them since 1973.

In our sixth game, Tim Lashar kicked four field goals and linebacker Dante Jones ran 55 yards with an interception for a touchdown in a 19–0 shutout of Oklahoma State. First time our offense hadn't scored a touchdown in thirty-two games.

Iowa State went down 38–0. Then we mangled Kansas 64–3 in Lawrence. We had 566 yards rushing against a minus-52. After we scored 37 points in the third quarter, ABC-TV switched to a different game. Our third-string quarterback, Glenn Sullivan—a left-handed baseball star—had a touchdown run called back in the fourth quarter.

If Kansas had been a mismatch, what did that make our Missouri game? We rushed for 681 yards while Missouri never crossed midfield. The score was 77–0. Our defense kept the shutout string going against Colorado in a 28–0 victory.

Then we beat Nebraska 20–17 in that fantastic comeback with 10 points in the last 1:22 that I describe in Chapter 14, "Sooner Magic."

As the host coach, I was asked by the Orange Bowl selection committee what I thought of inviting Arkansas. The Razorbacks had finished tied for second in the Southwest Conference.

For nine years I had been telling the home folks back in Arkansas that someday I would get them another Orange Bowl bid to meet Oklahoma and would wipe out that personally humiliating loss that cost Oklahoma a national title.

This was my chance.

Not that the 10–1 Razorbacks figured to be easy. Coach Ken Hatfield ran an offense called the Flexbone—which looks like the Wishbone except for the line spacing, and mostly runs between the tackles instead of attacking the corners like the high-risk, high-reward Wishbone.

There was no way we could claim another national championship, because Penn State knocked off Miami in the Fiesta Bowl and won the title for Uncle Joe Paterno. But I wanted to beat Arkansas really bad—this is the only game I ever asked any team to win for me.

The 1987 Orange Bowl against Arkansas was the game Bosworth was ruled out of by the NCAA for steroid use—as I will tell about elsewhere.

In the first quarter, to my amazement, Arkansas stuffed Jamelle and the Wishbone. They held us without a first down. Then Jamelle struck—a beautifully handled pitchout to Spencer Tillman, a tremendous block by Patrick Collins, and Spencer scored on a 77-yard run.

Moments later, the same play. Jamelle to Spencer, block by Collins, touchdown.

We led 14–0 at the half. I knew if we could score at the beginning of the third quarter, we had the game won. Because a three-touchdown lead would force Arkansas into a passing game that would be like duck gumbo for our defense.

Jamelle scored two touchdowns on the option in a three-minute span in the third quarter. We intercepted five Arkansas passes. Arkansas couldn't score until there were 20 seconds to play.

The score was Oklahoma 42, Arkansas 8.

I was accused in the press of running up the score on my alma mater. They wrote that I was running trick plays and throwing deep passes with the outcome well in hand.

All I can say is the trick play was a 49-yard touchdown run on a tight end reverse by sub Duncan Parham, who had spent his career behind All-American (now All-Pro) Keith Jackson. I couldn't tell Duncan he shouldn't make himself a touchdown in the Orange Bowl.

And as for my calling deep passes, our quarterback at that point in the game was baseball player Glenn Sullivan, who was having the thrill of his life getting to throw four left-handed passes in the Orange Bowl.

Hell, I don't call deep passes to run up the score. At Oklahoma that year, we used the deep pass to hold the score *down*, if anything.

So we finished the 1986 season ranked third in the nation. But we were loaded for the next year. I really believed that with any luck at all, 1987 would bring our fourth national championship.

Jamelle broke his thumb in the spring and missed the whole practice schedule. This was not the kind of luck I wanted to start off with, but at least I could work rookie Charles Thompson at quarterback. Offensive coordinator Jim Donnan and I spent a lot of time preparing Charles, just in case. Jamelle had just been named most valuable player in the Big Eight as a sophomore and had two more years to go. It looked as if he would be the best of my long line of great option quarterbacks.

I knew a football coach was never more than a week away from instant humility. But I looked closely at our schedule, and Miami wasn't on it anywhere.

North Texas State was our first victim of the year, 69–14. No way they should have scored twice. A good North Carolina

team came to Norman the next week and we shut them out
28–0. No telling how much we might have scored if we hadn't
been penalized nineteen times, a school record.

The sportswriters asked me if I would let my team score
100 points against Tulsa the following week, and I swore I
wouldn't. Oklahoma won 65–0.

The fourth game was at Iowa State. With a 35–3 lead,
some of our starters took off their shoulder pads for the second half and signed autographs while the subs were finishing
the game with a 56–3 victory.

For the fourth year in a row, we had not lost the Red
River War. This was another blowout of Texas, 44–9—and my
first encounter with David McWilliams, who had replaced
Freddy Akers as head coach. Nineteen eighty-seven was the
season Oklahoma had five AP all-Americans—first time any
team had that many since the great West Point teams of World
War II—and three of them were from Texas. They were defensive end Darrell Reed (who was about to graduate with a
business degree), linebacker Dante Jones, and safety Rickey
Dixon, who broke Darrell Royal's old interception record with
15. Our other two AP all-Americans were Keith Jackson and
Mark Hutson, a 285-pound offensive guard who was destined
to score our final touchdown of the season.

The newspapers said we were 57-point favorites the next
Saturday against Kansas State. If you bet on the Sooners, you
lost. We beat Iowa State 59–10. On an 81-yard pass they
scored their first offensive touchdown against us in five years.

Oklahoma was a 35-point favorite against Colorado on
ESPN at night in the seventh game. We fumbled nine times
and pulled out a 24–6 victory. The next week, though, we
covered the spread with a 71–10 win over Kansas.

In our ninth victory of the season—29–10 over Oklahoma State—luck started turning against us.

It was win number 146 for me, putting me one ahead of
Bud Wilkinson, but the price was high.

Jamelle tore up his knee on what I call one of those self-
tacklization injuries. Nobody hit him. He just caught his foot
the wrong way and—pop!

Charles Thompson ran out there to run our Wishbone
wearing his neck collar that had .HANTA YO—which is Sioux

for "clear the way"—printed on it, but it took two interceptions returned for touchdowns in the final four minutes for us to win the game.

With Jamelle out for the rest of the season—actually, he was never as good a player again—the Wishbone really struggled against Missouri, the team we had beaten 77–0 a year earlier. This time it was only 17–13. On top of that, a Missouri tackler missed Charles Thompson along the sideline, crashed into me, and tore up *my* knee! It was more serious than any injury I had ever received as a player.

Nebraska was ranked number one in the nation and we were number two the final week of the regular season, when we met at Lincoln. Broderick Thomas and some of those Nebraska studs were threatening in public to demolish us by scores like 42–10. I told my players, "These Nebraska guys have only scored three touchdowns against us in three years. What the hell even makes them think they can score on you guys? If I were on their team, I'd be worrying whether I could even score on this bunch."

Oklahoma dominated the game and beat Nebraska 17–7. Patrick Collins took off on a long touchdown run, and I could hear him yelling, "Hello-goodbye, Nebraska," with his 4.35 speed.

At the end of the regular season, Oklahoma was 11–0 and ranked number one in the nation.

Who do you suppose was 11–0 and ranked second? Yeah, you already know.

Miami.

It was the perfect matchup for the Orange Bowl and for NBC-TV. No matter what happened in any of the other bowl games, the Oklahoma vs. Miami winner would be the national champion.

The NCAA drug squad that had hit the Boz the previous year didn't get to any of our players this time—but they banned two Miami players from the game, including middle linebacker George Mira, Jr., the Hurricanes' leading tackler, who had done a hell of a job shutting down Lydell Carr the year before. Mira, whose father had been a star quarterback at Miami, was charged by the NCAA with using a diuretic that could possibly conceal the presence of steroids. I was sorry it happened. I wanted Mira to play.

At a luncheon, I told the crowd, "Brian Bosworth urinated in vain."

Testaverde was gone, and in his place Jimmy Johnson had a lanky sophomore named Steve Walsh. Scouting him, we didn't consider Walsh as being in the strong arm category with Testaverde. But one thing about Walsh stuck out—he didn't make mistakes. The kid called audibles at the line of scrimmage about 80 percent of the time. Maybe Walsh didn't look like a really great athlete, but nobody had been able to beat him.

Critics had said my teams of the last few years didn't play good defense against great passers. What they really meant was we had lost once to Elway and twice to Testaverde. But I felt that if we played a zone against Walsh, we could stop him and pick off a few Oskies. I thought Walsh couldn't throw deep against us.

(You may have heard players or coaches referring to interceptions as Oskies, like we did at Oklahoma. It is a term with an old-fashioned football bloodline. General Bob Neyland, coach at Tennessee, had a bird dog named Oskie, and he liked defensive backs who could go straight to the ball like a champion bird dog.)

Just before the kickoff, I glanced over at Jamelle. Both of us were on the sideline wearing casts on our knees. Miami's defense was quick and big. I was wishing the team had Jamelle's physical strength running the option. Jamelle could tear away from tackles. With Charles Thompson—for all his speed—if you got a grip on him, he was down.

Lydell Carr was back at fullback after missing two games with a knee injury, but Miami started hammering him on every play and pretty much took our fullback out of the action. If you don't have a fullback threat up the middle on the Wishbone, you can't attack the corners.

Everybody knew we had one of the best pass receivers in the country—Keith Jackson—but one of the least effective passers in Thompson. Taking away our fullback put us into long yardage situations on second and third down, the worst thing that can happen to a Wishbone.

Meanwhile, Walsh was shouting audibles constantly when Miami had the ball. In the first quarter he caught us shifting our defense—actually, we had twelve men on the field, but it didn't help—and threw a 30-yard touchdown pass to fullback Mel Bratton to put Miami ahead 7–0.

Thompson took us on a 15-play drive in the second quarter. No long runs. We scratched for every inch. Anthony Stafford scored from the one, and R. D. Lashar (Tim's brother) kicked the point to tie the score at the half.

In the third quarter, Miami lined up to try a 56-yard field goal—the longest in Orange Bowl history—and many thought it was a fake. But Greg Cox kicked the hell out of that football. It went between the posts a good ten feet above the crossbar.

So we were down 10–7, and it started pouring rain. We had our chances, but Miami made the big plays. On a fourth and four at midfield, they went for it and made a first down. On a third and ten, Walsh threw a touchdown pass to Michael Irvin.

In the fourth quarter, Charles finally completed a pass to put us in scoring position, but as tight end Keith Jackson was struggling for extra yardage he fumbled the ball. Miami recovered. Cox kicked a 48-yard field goal and they took a 20–7 lead.

With 2:05 left, we pulled the old fumblerooski.

Charles took the snap, deftly laid the ball on the ground, then everybody took off as if it were an option wide to the left. Everybody except guard Mark Hutson, who reached down and picked up the ball and ran 29 yards for a touchdown.

Now it was 20–14, with Miami on top and two minutes to play.

We needed a big shot of Sooner Magic. But Miami recovered our try at an onside kick, kept the ball—and the clock ran out on my chance at a fourth national championship.

21

THE STORM GATHERS

After three consecutive 11–1 seasons, the natural cycles of the game dictated we were bound to fall off somewhat. Even at Oklahoma, a coach is allowed to have a rebuilding year every decade or so.

I knew my 1988 team was a little weaker than the three that had preceded it. A number of players who were real difference makers graduated after that bitter Orange Bowl loss to Miami. You take away three great players on offense and three great players on defense, and when it's fourth and one on either side of the ball, not having those three players will cost you that crucial yard just enough times to get your tail beaten against strong teams.

We had a tough schedule coming up—North Carolina, Arizona, USC, and Texas were our nonconference games. In the conference, Nebraska would be making its usual bid for the national title. And the rest of the league looked stronger than usual, except for Kansas and Kansas State, where basketball was king. I hoped Iowa State would be an easy win, too. You need a schedule with a few easy wins in it. The reason is that this helps your team stay healthy.

I shake my head in wonder at the people who keep proposing a Super Conference, where every week would be a meeting of giants. This is completely ridiculous. Talk about exploiting the players (and the coaches) for television profits, a Super Conference would be the worst thing that could possibly happen.

Let's suppose Mike Tyson, Muhammad Ali, Sonny Liston, Joe Louis, George Foreman, Rocky Marciano, Jack Dempsey,

Larry Holmes, Jack Johnson, Archie Moore, and Jersey Joe Wolcott were all in their prime at the same time. A Super Conference would be like making these guys fight each other every Saturday for eleven weeks and then having the ones with the best records fighting again for a twelfth week—every year.

This kind of football would destroy itself.

Even the best team in the country needs a soft spot or two or three on its schedule—to let the subs play, allow injuries to heal, build up morale, and throw peanuts to the fans waving their banners in the stands.

I have to make a bowing gesture in the direction of Notre Dame. The schedule the Irish play year in and year out is certainly the toughest in the country.

But I wasn't begging for mercy as I planned for the 1988 season. I didn't say we were going to be bad—just that we weren't quite as good as we had been the last three years.

Hell, *nobody* was as good as we had been the last three years . . . again, except Miami.

Jamelle missed spring practice following knee surgery, but the doctors said they had rebuilt his knee and he could possibly be good as new. Charles had a good spring practice. We had a running back named Mike Gaddis who had been a redshirt in 1987. At Midwest City Carl Albert High, he had been named Oklahoma player of the year. Mike was 6-foot-2 and 210 and looked like the best all-around running back we'd had since Marcus Dupree was a freshman.

And we had had a good recruiting haul.

We went on our Nike trip in February 1988, and I took my girlfriend, Ann Jones, and my kids to Italy early in the summer, looking at all the cathedrals and museums and eating in those wonderful Italian cafes.

When I returned from our trip in late June, the NCAA hit us with the official announcement that Oklahoma's football program was under investigation for sixteen alleged violations of its regulations.

The way the NCAA handles this is that they inform you of the violations they think you have committed, your institution conducts its own investigation, and then your CEO and faculty representative go before the NCAA committee on infractions and present your defense.

Nobody can deny there is a certain amount of politics involved in the judgment and punishment handed down by the NCAA. A school with a really strong, respected, well-connected CEO can promise the committee, "Anything we did wrong was not orchestrated, we won't let it happen again, trust me." Because of their old-time friendships in the NCAA, the representatives of Texas A&M and Texas, for example, can often straighten out problems on the strength of their word.

Reading the allegations against us, I really wasn't very worried. Even the newspapers were predicting Oklahoma would draw a wrist slap at worst.

The only thing that scared me about it was that our representative before the NCAA would be our *interim* president—a position of weakness, not of strength.

Andy Coats, our outside counsel, was the attorney who would argue Oklahoma's case, along with our faculty representative Dan Gibbens, an OU law professor.

Swank became interim president when Dr. Frank Horton resigned. Swank had been faculty rep to the Big Eight and the NCAA and been removed from that position by our regents a decade earlier.

Oklahoma's internal investigation would be under the direction of athletic director Donnie Duncan, faculty rep Dan Gibbens, and Ron Watson, assistant athletic director in charge of keeping us in compliance with NCAA regulations. In fact, Watson's job description was compliance officer. He had been an enforcement agent for the NCAA and assistant athletic director at Tulane before coming to Oklahoma in April.

Some sportswriter asked Tony Casillas, who had graduated from OU as the number-one draft pick of the Atlanta Falcons, if he thought his alma mater was guilty of illegal recruiting or paying players.

Tony was quoted as saying, "I never got anything at OU myself, but I used to look around me at the other guys and wonder how some of them got their cars and spending money."

Tony was only the greatest lineman in America. My Lord, Tony, if I were going to pay anybody, it would have been *you*!

I hardly need say that football players are full of macho. It's not unknown for them to get a few beers under their belt

and start bragging about how much they were wanted by recruiters. One player will say, "Yeah, Bonehead University offered me his and her speedboats for my folks, a BMW, and
$3,000 a month for me." The next player will say, "Is that all?
Hell, Bonehead U. offered to buy me my own small town in
Switzerland. Some place called Gstaad."

I tried to put the investigations out of my mind. There
was an eleven-game schedule for 1988 to play before the infractions committee would meet.

Wearing a specially built brace on his knee, Jamelle
started against North Carolina in the opener. But he wasn't
the Jamelle of old. Where he once had been able to cut
through a momentary opening or stiff-arm a tackler, now
Jamelle ran more like an ordinary mortal. He was still better
than the average option quarterback, but the fairy dust was
gone. Now a sophomore, Charles Thompson relieved Jamelle
on alternate series.

Our defense played tough and we beat North Carolina
28–0. It was Oklahoma's sixteenth win without a loss against
the Atlantic Coast Conference.

In the second game, against Arizona, Jamelle led OU in
rushing for what would be his last time. We overcame seven
fumbles at home to win 28–10. Arizona was running the
Wishbone now, too. In the first quarter, each team had the
ball once.

The next week took us to the Los Angeles Coliseum for
the home opener of USC's hundredth football season. The
crowd of 86,000 was the biggest that had ever seen Oklahoma
play.

The Trojans were loaded that year with a strong defensive team and a quarterback named Rodney Peete. The defense was too quick for the slower version of Jamelle. We
gained only 89 yards rushing. Jamelle lost two fumbles inside
our 12-yard line in the second quarter. We were down 20–0 at
the half. I put Charles in at quarterback in the fourth quarter,
but USC finally beat us 23–7. As a starter, Jamelle had had a
30–2 record.

In the locker room afterward, I told my team, "USC is a
great team, but we did not quit. We beat them in the second
half, but we helped them beat us in the first half. We'll get
better."

Jamelle hit five of five passes for 113 yards and two touchdowns against Iowa State in a 35–7 victory in Norman. My team still had a lot of mysteries. I saw some good things on defense. We made some big plays on offense. But I couldn't get a feeling for what this team would do.

At the Red River War in Dallas, we ran into a Texas team that featured superquick Eric Metcalf on offense. Jamelle led a 93-yard touchdown drive in the first quarter but sprained his ankle and was out for the rest of the day. Anthony Stafford broke an 86-yard touchdown run—longest in series history. Linebacker Kert Kaspar from Houston grabbed an interception and made such a good run for a touchdown that I told the sportswriters I was moving him to fullback. Another of our Texas recruits, Kevin Thompson, intercepted a pass and also chased down a Texas receiver to prevent a score. Oklahoma won the game 28–13.

Did I say I hoped for a breather against Kansas State? Whatever I wished for, I didn't dream we would set the all-time NCAA record for rushing in a single game. We ran for 768 yards and broke the record Oklahoma had set against Colorado in 1980. Our backs averaged 10.6 per carry against Kansas State. A walk-on freshman named Joe Muti ran 34 yards to break the record and score our last touchdown with a minute to play.

But I wasn't happy with the score. The 70 for Oklahoma was all right, but the 24 for Kansas State looked dangerous. A sophomore quarterback named Carl Straw threw for 347 yards!

At Boulder the next week, Colorado tried wearing their black uniform pants to put a jinx on us. Before the game, I told my players, "If they think the color of their pants will help them, these guys have got a big surprise coming. You know, men, the ESPN cameras are over in the Colorado locker room right now, and their players are telling the nation how they're gonna whip your ass tonight."

They damn near did it.

The score was tied, 14–14, with eight minutes to play. R. D. Lashar, whose brother had won several games for Oklahoma, kicked a 22-yard field goal to put us ahead 17–14. A Sooner fumble gave them the ball at midfield with two minutes on the clock. It wasn't over until Colorado missed a 62-

yard field-goal try. It made us 6–1 for the season and 5–0 on ESPN, career.

The eighth game—against Kansas—was stopped for a ceremony when Jamelle threw a 22-yard touchdown pass that made him Oklahoma's career leader in total offense. Jamelle's 4,893 yards was the best since the 4,818 by Jack Mildren, the father of the OU Wishbone, in 1969–71.

But the bad news is that Jamelle had not been the starter for three games now. His knee just wouldn't cut it. Charles Thompson had moved ahead of him.

Kansas had us tied 14–14 in the second quarter and owned the ball at our 7-yard line. But we held them. If they had scored at that time, the final would have been 63–21 in our favor.

Before the Oklahoma State game, their coach, Pat Jones, said, "If we stand around on defense, Oklahoma will keep running right up the ramp and out on the street and will run all over Stillwater."

For a while it looked like he was right. We scored three quick touchdowns—two on strong runs by Mike Gaddis—and took a 21–7 lead. This game was a real basher on national TV. You could hear the banging and grunting all over America. Oklahoma State had Barry Sanders as the current chairman of Tailback University, and his second touchdown put the Cowboys ahead by 24–21.

This was a wild one, with Mike Gundy throwing to Hart Lee Dykes and making big plays for OSU. Down 28–24, Charles Thompson guided the Wishbone on an 80-yard drive that ended with him running it in for an 18-yard touchdown. Now we led 31–28 with 2:33 left. Oklahoma State zipped back to our 19, where it was third and one. Barry Sanders time. Our guys stopped him short. It would have been fourth down and inches. While the players were unpiling, an official penalized the OSU fullback Garrett Limbrick 15 yards on a dead ball personal foul for apparently telling that official to go "do" something to himself. I'd heard a lot of insults out there, but I was glad that particular one outraged the official.

With the penalty, the Cowboys had the ball fourth and fifteen-plus instead of fourth and inches. One of their receivers couldn't hang on to a tipped Gundy pass. We escaped with a 31–28 win.

On his way to the Heisman Trophy, Barry Sanders gained 215 yards in 39 carries. Our freshman Mike Gaddis had 213 on 18.

I didn't think Missouri could score on us the next week, but they did. It was a rainy day in Columbia, and we won 16–7—my thirty-first straight Big Eight victory. And my last.

We were 9–1 when Nebraska came to Norman. The weather was awful. Drizzle, thirty-mile-an hour winds, nine-degree chill factor. Nebraska had the better, more experienced team with a defense led again by Broderick Thomas.

For the benefit of our youngsters who hadn't been part of Sooner Magic against Nebraska before, I reminded them, "Six times we've been behind these guys, and we've come back and won. When things go against you, keep your poise. They're gonna hammer you! They're gonna assault you! Come right after you! But you keep your poise and play hard for sixty minutes and good things will happen."

Nebraska took the opening kickoff and drove 80 yards for a touchdown. And that was it. The only touchdown of the day. If you had told me we were only going to score three points, I would have thought we'd get the hell beat out of us.

But our defense played their hearts out. We lost the game 7–3.

And Charles Thompson got tackled hard and broke his leg on our last offensive play of the game.

"Hey, we're nine and two! That's a great season!" I shouted in the locker room. "Give Nebraska their due. They're a hell of a team, and so are we."

After every OU-Nebraska game, Bob Devaney has always made it a point to come to see me, win or lose. He walked into our coaches' locker room just as I was coming out of the shower, and as I was joking with one of the few coaches remaining, I'm sure that Bob was surprised at how jovial I was. I told him, "I damn sure don't like losing, but there's one good thing that comes out of losing. You bastards gotta go play Miami. We've had our bats against them!"

And then they had theirs . . . and were totally dominated by Miami. They found out what I had learned: Miami was just on a different plane from the rest of us.

We accepted an invitation to play Clemson in the Citrus

Bowl. My staff and I hit the road recruiting. We burned the office lights late at night preparing for Clemson.

On December 18 came the news that instead of a wrist slap, the NCAA had whacked us with a two-by-four.

With the probation began a gathering storm of troubles.

At the Citrus Bowl, with Charles on crutches, Jamelle made his first start since the Texas game. Compared to the Jamelle of a year and a half ago, this guy with the ugly brace on his knee moved like an old man. He had some kind of mental attack in the first quarter with the ball on the Clemson 1-yard line.

In the Wishbone, we run the fullback play at least a thousand times in practice. When players asked why they had to run a rather simple play—like 12 or 13, for example—so many times, I said because 999 is not enough.

We called 12 at the Clemson 1-yard line on second down. Fullback Leon Perry hit the middle, expecting Jamelle to slip him the ball. Perry crashed five yards deep into the end zone.

But Jamelle had pulled the ball away from Leon and started limping backward like it was a play action pass. Clemson players started chasing him, and he wound up being tackled for an 18-yard loss. At last Lashar hit the field goal. You see, practicing the play a thousand times wasn't even enough! Football is a game of repetitions. That play was probably the difference in the ball game.

For the day, Jamelle carried the ball 15 times for a gain of 17 yards. It was the worst game of his career. Four years previously, when he took us to a national championship as a true freshman, who could have guessed he would go out on such a sad note?

Clemson scored in the fourth quarter to take a 13–6 lead. With three minutes to play, Jamelle produced one more great effort. Starting at our 20, he completed seven passes in a drive to the Clemson 14. On fourth down the last pass of his career was thrown into the end zone. It was one of those balls that could have been caught with a little luck.

But it wasn't caught.

We lost the Citrus Bowl to Clemson.

Obviously, this was not the result our fans and we had expected.

Coming only two weeks after the NCAA probation was announced, the loss in the Citrus Bowl was a major disappointment. My team had a 9–3 record—a success at many schools.

But I could feel the OU Football Monster growing angry and hungry again. We flew home ready to go to work. We needed to fill our emotional buckets and put that loss behind us. All teams need to do this to recover from defeat. But even at Oklahoma, and with Dr. Cross's Monster, coaches and their families are not run out of town after 9–3 seasons ending in bowl games.

As I said at the beginning of this story, I thought I would triumph again . . .

PART TWO

ON THE SUBJECT
OF FOOTBALL

22

HEY, BOZ

And now for a few words to Brian Bosworth.

Brian, you were one of the greatest players ever to play for the University of Oklahoma. You were a dominating force on the field. There have been very few linebackers in the history of the game who could play in your class.

You helped take the Sooners to the Orange Bowl three straight years and to the national championship in 1985. I know how much that national championship meant to you. In the locker room after we beat Penn State, you were laughing and crying with joy and relief and pride just like I was.

I am honored to know you, Brian. You are a scholar who graduated from the University of Oklahoma in four years with a business degree and a 3.6 grade-point average. You have guaranteed your financial future through your professional-football contract and your other commercial tie-ins. You are an outstanding example of the possibilities that await a true scholar-athlete.

Congratulations and good luck to you, Brian.

But I have some problems with this guy you call the Boz.

The Boz was an asshole who strutted around Norman like he owned the place, both stiffing and intimidating people. The Boz took some stereo equipment for his Corvette, purchased for him by a fan on the promise that he would pay for it when he became a rich pro football star. And the Boz never

paid the fan a dime, even after he signed with the Seattle Seahawks for $11 million, until the guy sued him on January 19,
1988. The Boz was an obnoxious, overbearing loudmouth and
deadbeat.

Hey, Boz, I read your book.

I don't understand what all the uproar was about. I
thought *The Boz* was basically the poignant story of a young
man in love with his haircut. I wish there had been more in it
about Brian, but naturally the Boz got all the publicity.

The Boz hit the headlines as "a devastating exposé of the
Oklahoma football program."

Suddenly people like David Swank were denouncing your
book and getting very defensive. I hadn't even read your book
yet, but I was saying things like "grossly exaggerated" and "a
stab in the back." This wasn't very smart of me, but when you
get microphones shoved in your mouth all the damn time and
reporters yelling questions about *The Boz,* you don't always say
the intelligent thing.

Now that I have read your book, I come to the conclusion
that most of the people who cried the loudest must not have
read it.

The public perception is that your book somehow
branded our players as a bunch of outlaws and severely
wounded me personally as a cheater and a renegade.

With permission, I would like to quote from page 76 of
the paperback updated edition, the one with the extra chapter
that dwelt on our problems of 1989 (two years after you left):

> Switzer isn't a cheater. Switzer doesn't have a
> slush fund and doesn't set up payments to players or
> any of that. Switzer just turns his back and lets his
> players fend for themselves. He never wanted to
> know how it was that I was living in a nice $500 a
> month condo, watching a big screen TV, driving a
> Jeep and a Corvette, and always operating with
> $2,000 in my checking account. And he never asked.

Thank you for testifying that I am not a cheater. But,
Boz, you weren't a kid from a poor background. Your folks
are solid middle-class people from Irving, Texas. They could

have bought you a car and sent you spending money—and we know how far you could stretch a dollar. Was that any of my business? Your bank didn't mail your statement to my address. I imagine you stuck somebody with the bill for the big-screen TV. As for your renting the condo, I knew about it. We paid all our scholarship players $390 a month if they chose to live outside the dorm and not eat at the training table. You chose the money. That is perfectly legal. It was common for two or three players to share the rent on a place or for a player to move in with a girl, who might have a job. If you were big enough to live off campus, you were big enough to fend for yourself.

I didn't go around with a stepladder and look in your windows.

I kept on reading *The Boz,* searching for the devastating exposé.

I came to the part where you saw some players smoking cocaine on the day of a game and you went up to them and made them stop it.

Sorry, Boz, but this sounds like bullshit to me. I can't deny that some of our players did use cocaine despite our warnings and our testing. But even as fierce as you got when you were all pumped up on iron and steroids, I don't believe you would have broken up any so-called coke smokers. I wish you had just told me instead, and I'd have thrown their asses off the team.

But that was the only cocaine incident mentioned in the story of your four years at Oklahoma.

I kept searching for the devastating exposé and finally found the part about Buster Rhymes firing his Uzi out the window of Bud Wilkinson Hall.

In the first place, it was a pistol, not a submachine gun. And Buster was shooting into the air.

I had to kick Buster off the team later, but it wasn't for shooting his pistol out the window.

If I had a dollar for every round of ammunition that has been shot out the windows of athletic dorms at universities all over the country ever since there has been such a thing as an athletic dorm, I would be rich enough to buy myself a kingdom in the Alps.

There is something about playing football and loving to go hunting that just kind of fit together and always have. I won't try to explain it, but everybody knows it is true. The next thing you know, a guy is wanting to show his pals his new shotgun, so he goes to the window and blasts away. Why, Boz, this very thing happened at a Southwest Conference school the same year. You could have given me a break and told on them instead of us.

I'm not picking on the SWC here. All I'm saying is I have heard of this happening at every school in the NCAA. It happened when I was a player at Arkansas.

The shooting that happened in our dorm in January 1989 was totally different from what Buster did, but you were gone by then, Boz.

You say in your book that you were born in Oklahoma City. Your parents met at OU. After they moved to Dallas, you remained a Sooner fan. You say I visited your home and walked down the hall of your high school with my arm around your shoulder and told you I wanted you to come to Oklahoma and be great.

This is where a devastating exposé should have said I took you out to the parking lot and handed you the keys to a new Jaguar with $50,000 in an alligator briefcase in the front seat.

But let me quote again from *The Boz*.

> . . . the first time I walked into Owen Field in Norman, I got goose bumps the size of golf balls. I was awed by it the first time I saw it and most every time I walked into it after that. You see all those national championships on the scoreboard. They've got that Hall of Fame. They've got the All Big Eight players on the wall beside the locker room. And when I saw the weight room, I was hooked. . . . I knew I was going to be a football player for the University of Oklahoma.

That's why you came to Oklahoma, Boz—to be a champion, with your picture on the wall with our other champions.

It's a sad thing that the day came when we had to take

your picture off the wall. I was sick that Brian's picture had to come down at the same time as yours, Boz.

But we took your picture off the wall because the other Hall-of-Famers demanded that we do it, not because I demanded it.

You know why too, Boz. It came down at last to that stupid damn T-shirt you wore on television at the Orange Bowl game against Arkansas.

For those readers who don't remember what I'm talking about, let me give a quick summary. Bosworth had been a great linebacker for us for three years as we won three straight Big Eight championships and won two of three Orange Bowls.

Anybody could tell the Boz had used steroids at some time or other just by looking at him. He was 250 pounds of anger and muscle that covered 40 yards in 4.5 seconds, which is halfback speed. We coaches knew he must have taken steroids (on his own), but felt that he had cleaned up his act. We tested him before the Orange Bowl revenge game against Arkansas, and, as we expected, he was clean. Then the NCAA did its own test while Bosworth was sick in the hospital, and he came out dirty, as I will explain elsewhere.

I think Bosworth and Oklahoma got a raw deal the way the NCAA tests were done. But it didn't matter what I thought. The NCAA ruled Bosworth ineligible for the Orange Bowl.

Bosworth's worst enemy was his mouth. At the sight of a TV camera, he would break into an outrageous song and dance.

I didn't try to muzzle him. That's not my style. I let my players express themselves. Long before the Boz fell in love with his haircut, we had a great quarterback named Jack Mildren whose long hair hung out below the back of his helmet back when few coaches would allow it. We had headbands, bandannas, Afros, earrings, gold teeth, silver shoes—and we didn't censor what our players said to the press.

At one place in your book, Boz, you say I should have given you more guidance when you were in school, and in another place you say you had to pound it into my head to make me keep out of your business and leave you alone.

The truth is, I spent hours talking to you and your folks about your outlandish mouth, which created your problems. I begged you not to play the jerk for the media. I wanted you to wear the white hat. I know what it is to wear the black hat.

I definitely tried to interfere after you were suspended from our Orange Bowl team. You had been a heavy contributor to our success. Even though you couldn't play in the game, the team and I wanted you to go to the Orange Bowl with us. It was okay with the NCAA if you stood on the sidelines.

When you got to Miami, we treated you like a comrade—not an outcast.

Before the kickoff, I walked up to you and looked you right in the eye and said, "This ball game is going to be played on the field, not in the newspapers. I am telling you do not do anything to embarrass this football team and this university today. Do you hear me?"

You kind of smiled.

I said, "Damnit, Bosworth, do you hear what I'm telling you?"

In street clothes, you went out to the middle of the field for the coin toss with our other captains.

We had already cleared this with the officials. You could go out as a captain and shake hands. But you had to leave just before the coin toss, because that's when the game officially begins.

I later learned that on national TV, NBC's Bob Trumpy didn't know what was going on (and didn't try to find out), but decided to go ahead and tell the audience the officials didn't want you on the field and ran you off. But that wasn't the story at all. The protocol had been agreed on with the officials.

In the third quarter we were leading 28–0 and the TV cameras were looking for human-interest pictures—and here came the Boz.

I was involved with the game on the sideline. I didn't know that a TV camera was showing a guy twenty yards away who wasn't even playing.

It was the Boz on national TV wearing a T-shirt that said NCAA: NATIONAL COMMUNISTS AGAINST ATHLETES.

The storm broke all over us. What kind of tasteless trick were we trying to pull? How could I let such a thing happen?

I didn't say much until I looked at a tape of the game to see for myself.

Then I phoned Donnie Duncan and said, "Bosworth is through here. He will not play for Oklahoma his senior year."

Obviously, since you had redshirted as a freshman, your class was graduating. You were eligible to enter the NFL draft, although you had another year of college eligibility.

Being kicked off the team for good meant you would be turning pro for sure. This cost you some of your bargaining chips with the NFL. You came to me and asked if I would reinstate you to the team, just to keep the NFL in suspense and help you negotiate a bigger contract.

I said first you had to write a letter and apologize to everybody in Oklahoma.

You did it.

I announced that you might have a chance to be back on the team, but I didn't really mean it. I'd had more than enough of the Boz. He would never play at Oklahoma again.

In the spring you declared yourself available for the draft, were picked number one by Seattle, and signed a long-term deal for a lot of money.

Good.

But no amount of money will buy a place for your picture on the Hall-of-Fame wall. You were up there with Heisman Trophy winners and other players as good as you were or better.

The guys who wanted your picture off the wall carry more weight at Owen Field than you ever will, Boz.

Sorry, Brian.

23

WHO'S NUMBER ONE?

All national college football championships are mythical.

Without a national playoff—which I am against, but not as much now that I'm out of the game—the question Who is number one? often comes down to whose mythical judgment you want to believe.

During my career as head coach at Oklahoma, there were yearly number-one polls by the AP and UPI, the national wire services, which were generally thought of as the most authoritative and prestigious. I don't know why. The AP poll was voted by a selected group of sportswriters and editors around the country. The UPI poll was voted by a panel of coaches and might have been the least reliable of all. It's a natural thing for coaches to tend to vote for their friends . . . or have their sports-information directors really do it for them.

There were other polls that were just as valid as the AP or UPI.

The Football Writers Association, the Hall of Fame, the Helms Foundation, the Dunkel ratings, and the *Sporting News* also named a number-one team.

Bear Bryant always counted his team number one if he won any of the polls. So did Notre Dame. As Bear said, "If you win one, you can play like you won them all."

He meant it only takes one to make a bumper sticker.

My friend Dan Jenkins, who proudly admits he has never met a list he didn't like, points out in his book *You Call It Sports, But I Say It's a Jungle Out There,* and by his way of counting, that my Oklahoma teams really won seven national championships!

We received official AP or UPI recognition for finishing number one in 1974, 1975, and 1985.

But we won the Helms and the Dunkel in 1973, my rookie season as head coach, when the *Sporting News* named me coach of the year. In 1978 we won the Helms and Dunkel, while USC and Alabama split the wire-service polls. We won the Dunkel in 1980 and the Helms in 1986.

What does this mean?

According to Dan, it means there are three coaches in history who have won seven national championships—Howard Jones (at Yale, Iowa, and USC before World War II), Bear Bryant during the sixties and seventies at Alabama, and me.

If I were immodest, I could point out that I went seven for sixteen in national championships. Dan told me that on the telephone.

"And here's something else," Dan said. "Anybody can make all-America now. There are dozens of teams. But the only all-America team that really counts is the *consensus*—where a player makes every major team.

"In that regard, you coached twenty-eight consensus all-Americans in sixteen seasons, and that's some kind of record. Bud Wilkinson had seventeen consensus all-Americans in seventeen years at Oklahoma. Darrell Royal had fifteen consensus all-Americans in twenty years at Texas."

My Oklahoma consensus all-Americans:

1973—Lucious Selmon, DT; Rod Shoate, LB
1974—John Roush, OG; Rod Shoate; Joe Washington, OB
1975—Lee Roy Selmon, DT; Dewey Selmon, DT; Jimbo Elrod, DE
1976—Mike Vaughan, OT
1977—Zac Henderson, DB
1978—Billy Sims, OB; Greg Roberts, OG
1979—Billy Sims; George Cumby, LB
1980—Louis Oubre, OT
1981—Terry Crouch, OG
1982—Rick Bryan, DT
1983—Rick Bryan, DT
1984—Tony Casillas, DT

1985—Tony Casillas; Brian Bosworth, LB
1986—Brian Bosworth; Keith Jackson, TE
1987—Keith Jackson; Mark Hutson, OG; Dante
          Jones, LB; Rickey Dixon, DB
1988—Anthony Phillips, OG

Another thing Dan told me is that I am the only guy who ever coached winners of the Heisman, Outland, Lombardi, Butkus, and Thorpe awards, plus a national championship.

Back to the polls for a minute. In the Associated Press poll—the most respected by sports-information directors, television talking heads, and many sportswriters who don't really follow football—my Oklahoma teams ranked in the Top 10 in twelve of my sixteen seasons. We were in the Top 20 all but once.

That once was 1983, when our record was 8–4 and there was a strong movement to get me fired. As a comparison, Coach Jim Wacker was 8–4 at T.C.U. in 1984, and they gave him a raise and a new seven-year contract, and the Moncrief family built a new law library for the school.

After three seasons as a head coach, I had lost only one game, having won three conference and two national championships. In the first five seasons, I lost a total of five games, having won five Big Eight championships. After sixteen seasons I had the highest winning percentage of any active coach and had won twelve Big Eight Conference championships, three (AP and UPI) national championships, and had a record of 157–29–4. Obviously, this was accomplished by reason of outstanding assistant coaches and great players.

And still I got blindsided and run out of the profession I loved.

If there's a moral at the end of all these statistics, I guess it's in how you keep score. I keep it in my heart, along with my feeling for our players, many of whom remain close friends of mine—like Steve Owens, Grant Burget, Dean Blevins, Joe Washington, and Billy Sims—just to name a few. That's the score I'm more proud of than all of the victories—the coach-player relationships that grew into genuine friendships. They last a lifetime.

I also score and savor the opportunities that coaching at a great institution like Oklahoma made available to me. If I had not been OU's head football coach, I would never have been able to work with Terri Kerr, the executive director of the Oklahoma Special Olympics and have been its head coach. That has long been a favorite project of mine. One thing I noticed again and again was that Special Olympics kids are totally unaffected by our world. They haven't been corrupted. They don't know deceit, and are so feeling, compassionate, so full of love.

And I also score and value all the great friends I have made in the American Football Coaches Association, and in the Nike Family. Mind you, I really will not miss college football . . . but there are parts of the life it made possible that I will miss.

24

THE MAN WHO MADE THE MONSTER

Dr. George Cross is a distinguished gentleman and scholar who served as president of the University of Oklahoma from 1944 until he retired in 1968.

Now eighty-five years old, Dr. Cross maintains an office in the Botany Building, where he has written several books on the history of OU. On the wall in his office is a portrait of his beautiful wife of sixty-three years, Cleo, who looks like the movie star Olivia DeHavilland. Cleo, I can personally attest, is a marvelous lady and worthy companion to a man like Dr. Cross.

I went to see Dr. Cross recently to ask about the birth and early years of the Oklahoma Football Monster. He is *the* authority on the subject. Dr. Cross was president throughout Bud Wilkinson's reign, and he is the man who saw to it that Jim MacKenzie was hired in 1966—so, ultimately, Dr. Cross is the one who brought me to Norman, too.

They were pretty wild years after World War II and through the 1950s. During that period sportswriters called the stroll from Owen Field to the athletic dorm the Million-Dollar Walk because it was widely believed that wealthy OU boosters would line up to press handshakes padded with cash on the football players.

In the course of Bud's 47-game winning streak, Oklahoma beat Kansas State one day by 13 points. The Sooner faithful couldn't believe it—only 13 points! Jay Simon, the sports editor of *The Daily Oklahoman* at the time, was working on the news desk that Saturday night, writing headlines and answering the phone. For hours he kept repeating the OU score into the phone and then listening to the fans scream, curse, and demand to know what the hell was wrong that the Sooners won by only 13 points? Finally Simon put down the phone and said, "I wonder how much rice a damn Chinaman can eat?"

OU fans were called the Chinamen by sportswriters and coaches for many years after that remark was widely repeated. I used the term one time, myself, and got jumped on for being a racist, so I dropped it.

The reason I started off about Dr. Cross, whom I deeply admire and respect, and then drifted into the Million-Dollar Walk and the Chinamen—two stories of football excess—is that Dr. Cross created the conditions for these things that grew and grew until they became the Oklahoma Football Monster.

He did it with the very noblest of intention.

It is often remembered that it was President Cross who told the Oklahoma legislature, "I want to build a university of which the football team can be proud."

This is exactly what he said, but when you learn the situation you will see that this remark, like other things President Cross innocently set in motion, became the fodder and the electrical sparks the Oklahoma Football Monster needed.

Dr. Cross wore a sports coat and a Countess Mara tie at his desk the day I visited to ask him some Oklahoma football history. In his 1977 book called *Presidents Can't Punt,* Dr. Cross had told the OU football story in fascinating detail. But what I asked of him was a condensed version, plus any items he might have needed to scratch out of his book thirteen years ago that he would like to talk about now.

Leaving off the quotation marks, this is what Dr. Cross told me:

Yes, I'm the guy who did it. I created this monster.

When I took over as president in 1944, Oklahomans had a mass inferiority complex and pictured themselves as creatures out of the *Grapes of Wrath,* you know, John Steinbeck's great novel. I was trying to counter this depression and give the people a source of pride in their state. And we did give them a source of pride. But they eventually took too much pride in us, as a matter of fact.

We really started it growing in the fall of 1945. Snorter Luster, our football coach, was resigning because of poor health. His poor health consisted of the fact that he couldn't beat our sister institution, Oklahoma A&M (now Oklahoma State), and he couldn't beat Texas, either. The fans had made Snorter's life so miserable that he just decided to quit before it killed him.

In a board meeting with the regents, Lloyd Noble—for whom our new basketball arena is named—was talking about this feeling of Dust Bowl inferiority around the state. Lloyd was wondering what the university could do about it, and suddenly he had an idea.

"The war is ending and there will be a four-year crop of fine high-school athletes, all with four years of eligibility, coming out of the service all at once," Lloyd said. "If we can just get enough of them to come here, we can have a good football team right away. A good football team at the University of Oklahoma will give the whole state something to take pride in."

Someone asked, "How do you find these fellows?"

Earl Deacon, a member of the board who had played guard on the 1929 team, said, "Every branch of the armed forces has football teams. They have coaches who have coached the best athletes in the armed forces. Let's hire a coach who has been in the military with the athletes."

I called Jap Haskell, our athletic director, who was in the Navy, and Haskell came up with several names—including Bear Bryant and Jim Tatum. He thought the best man for our situation would be Tatum. I phone Tatum at the Iowa Seahawks, a Navy team. Tatum said he would be interested, and asked whether he could bring a potential assistant coach. This was an All-American lineman from Minnesota who had a master's degree in English from Syracuse, I believe. His name was Bud Wilkinson, a brilliant chap. I said, sure, bring him along.

Tatum and Wilkinson arrived the same week the NAACP decided to challenge our state's segregation laws with a test case, a young woman who had graduated from Langston University and wanted to study law.

The board had a rather busy week, but we spent time with the two coaches. Frankly, we liked Wilkinson much better than Tatum. Tatum was boisterous and had little charisma. Wilkinson was quiet, a gentleman, obviously a person of distinction.

After the coaches left, the regents asked me if it would be ethical to offer the job to Wilkinson instead of Tatum.

I said, "No, this would compromise our ethics. But if Bud Wilkinson would even give a thought to accepting in such circumstances, he wouldn't have the ethics for the job, anyway, and I would have nothing to do with hiring him."

We waited a few days and then offered a package deal—a three-year contract at $10,000 per year for Tatum and a three-year contract for Wilkinson at $6,000.

Tatum exploded on the telephone. "I have the right to name my own damn assistants," he shouted.

"Well, Jim, there's just nothing I can do about it," I said. "It's both of you or neither of you."

In the meantime, Wilkinson had decided to go into the real estate business in Minneapolis with his father and his brother. Tatum decided to phone him and try to talk him into taking the $6,000-a-year job at OU. Jim asked Bud to do it for just one year—1946—so that he could get the job, and then Bud could quit and return to real estate. Wilkinson agreed to the proposal just to help his old friend get the job, and that's the true story of what happened.

That first team of Tatum's included many players you still hear about today—Jim Owens, Wade Walker, Buddy Burris, Darrell Royal, Plato Andros, Stan West, Jack Mitchell, and Charles Sarratt to mention a few.

We did have what you might call instant success.

I can best explain it by saying that A&M College—now Oklahoma State—had whipped us in our own stadium 47–0 in 1945. The next year, 1946, Oklahoma A&M had the same team, with some additions, and we went to Stillwater and beat them 73–12.

I was up there watching, saw us goof up at the beginning and fall behind 12–0. One of the *Daily Oklahoman*'s sportswriters was sitting in the stands. He had seen our boys play and knew what we had, and also he may have had too many scotch and sodas. He stood up and said, "I have twenty dollars that says OU will win by fifty points." Well, he made his bet and had a 10-point margin.

An Athletic Council was developed early in the history of OU to support the football program. It was a private corporation at first, which enabled it to issue bonds that were used to expand the stadium. It was a booster group with no official connection to the university.

We were invited to play in the second Gator Bowl game in Jacksonville, Florida, with a $25,000 guarantee. Jim Tatum asked me if it would be all right for him to give the boys some presents. He thought they might be more enthusiastic and do a better job of playing if we gave them some presents.

At that time you couldn't even give a ring or a wristwatch to an athlete. I pointed out to Jim that gifts would be a violation of the conference and the NCAA rules and asked him not to do it. He went off grumbling, but we beat North Carolina State 34–13 in the Gator Bowl.

Even though the Athletic Council was a private corporation, I asked for a financial report on the Gator Bowl trip, and there was a $6,000 item for "miscellaneous" that I couldn't figure out. I looked to see if they had bought some liquor, and they had, but it had been paid for separately.

I realized that Tatum must have given the boys some presents.

I drifted out the north door of the administration building one day and ran into Joe Golding, one of our fine halfbacks. Just playing a hunch, I asked, "Joe, what kind of gifts did the squad get at the Gator Bowl? Tatum was talking about giving golf clubs or shotguns or something. What did you get?"

"President Cross, we voted on that and decided to take the cash," Joe told me.

"How much cash?"

"Each player received $120."

To be sure I was hearing correctly, I asked, "Did everyone get paid, or just those who played in the game?"

"Oh, we voted on that, too. Every man on the squad got $120."

I did some mental calculating. We had fifty players. At $120 each, here was the miscellaneous $6,000.

I called Tatum to my office for a visit. I said, "After I told you it would be a violation to give our players presents, you gave them $120 each. How come?"

"The boss man said it was all right," Jim said.

"Just who is the boss man?" I asked.

"Why, it's Neil Johnson, the chairman of the Athletic Council," Jim replied. "Remember, the council is a private corporation over which you have no control."

I made two mental notes to myself—get that corporation dissolved, and get rid of Jim Tatum.

The regents were of no mind to let Tatum go. But fortunately for me, Jim's arrogance gave me an opening. Jim demanded a ten-year contract at $15,000 per year and the firing of Harold Keith, our sports publicist, and Jap Haskell, our athletic director.

I went to work putting together a kind of deal that would look good but that Jim wouldn't accept. I had been talking to Curly Byrd, the president of the University of Maryland, and I knew approximately what they were offering Tatum to come there. I recommended to our regents that we offer Jim a six-year contract at $15,000 but refuse to fire Keith or Haskell. Our regents were worried about losing Jim, but they voted 4–3 to make the offer.

Jim turned us down as I had hoped (and planned) and jumped to Maryland after one year at Oklahoma.

In the meantime, we found out that Tatum had overspent his budget by $113,000. I asked Haskell where the money went, and he didn't even know it was missing. So we fired Haskell.

A week or so later Tatum phoned from Maryland with a most unusual request and threat. I've never told about this before, but Jim said, "I'm having a little trouble with the sportswriters back here. They're saying I caused Haskell to lose his job. It's kind of embarrassing. I want you to issue a statement saying I had absolutely nothing to do with Haskell being fired."

"I can't do that," I said. "Indirectly, you were responsible. Haskell lost his job not because you overspent your budget, but because Haskell didn't know you had done it."

"Listen, Dr. Cross, you *are* going to issue this statement," Tatum warned me.

"Why?"

"Because if you don't, I am going to tell the newspaper that OU paid its football squad six thousand dollars to play in the Gator Bowl. You like good football, and you always liked Bud Wilkinson better than you did me, but when I talk to the newspapers you won't have a single member of your squad eligible to play football next season."

I told Tatum I would think it over, as this was a very serious matter. I phoned Curly Byrd. Curly had been the football coach at Maryland before he was promoted—or maybe demoted—to the job of president.

"President Byrd," I said, "if Tatum releases this statement it will deeply hurt the University of Oklahoma. But remember, Tatum is your boy now. How's it going to look for you to have a coach who announces he broke the regulations of the NCAA and our conference? If you could just persuade . . ."

Curly broke in and said, "Persuade, hell, I'll tell Tatum to keep his damn mouth shut, and he will."

I also managed to get the Athletic Council changed from a private corporation to a department of the university under our control.

But the next year, 1947, Big Boy Johnson of Norman came up with the idea for the Touchdown Club, Inc., for the purpose of receiving, holding, and disbursing money for the support of athletics, especially football, at the University of Oklahoma.

The Touchdown Club started because of a high school athlete from Muskogee who was supposed to come to OU but didn't show up. Big Boy Johnson hired a detective to find the boy. He was located in Little Rock, where an assistant coach at Arkansas was keeping him hidden. Posing as a coach, the detective invited the Arkansas coach to have coffee in the coffee shop, thus giving an accomplice a chance to persuade the boy to come back to Norman.

It turned out the boy's father had been given $5,000 for his son to attend Arkansas, money which needed to be refunded. Well, Big Boy, Paul Brown, Harrison Smith, Luther Delaney, Boston Smith, and some others organized the Touchdown Club and immediately raised $75,000. Paying the $5,000 ransom was the club's first act.

Their idea for the Touchdown Club was to meet the recruiting competition financially. They were a bit overly enthusiastic. In 1954 the Touchdown Club took the entire Muskogee High School football team to the Orange Bowl as guests and gave all Muskogee athletes a scholarship to OU.

Now the Touchdown Club is a respectable agency. All the money the club raises is turned over to the university. The club no longer gives scholarships. We have the Touchdown Club under pretty good control. Not perfect; some members of the club, I'm sure, cheat a little. That has always been the case and always will be as long as so much stress is put on winning. Coaches know if they don't win they'll get fired, so coaches aren't too quick to interfere in dealings of this kind.

Our plan to revive Oklahoma's state pride by playing winning football worked so well that I could ride into a gas station in any little town and someone would see my car tag and come over and ask how the Big Red was going to do that fall. The old *Grapes of Wrath* image was fading—and the monster was taking its place.

The 1949 OU-Texas game marked the turning point in overinterest in Oklahoma football—for the worse, that is.

After we beat Texas 20–14, our fans just went totally out of control.

Wilkinson had put together a staff of six assistants, including Gomer Jones and Bill Jennings. In 1948, Bud had his first great team with a 10–1 record and a victory over North Carolina in the Sugar Bowl. He was undefeated (11–0) in 1949 and stomped L.S.U. in the Sugar Bowl 35–0. In 1950, Bud went on to win his first national championship.

But it was that 1949 win over Texas that made our fans somehow sense that the old defeatist attitudes were over and happy days had truly arrived for OU football . . . and for the state of Oklahoma.

On Sunday night after the Saturday game, about five thousand fans gathered outside my house shouting, "No school tomorrow! No school tomorrow!" It seemed that nearly the whole student body was there trampling the lawn, along with others who weren't students. I knew I had to get rid of them, so I announced, "I have no authority to dismiss school Monday, but why don't you go over to Bud Wilkinson's house and show him how you appreciate this victory?" So at least they moved off my lawn and onto Bud's.

On Monday the students didn't go to school. They and about half of Norman went to Oklahoma City to celebrate at the capitol and got the governor out to join them. I thought, Well, this is just too damned much. This emphasis on winning has gotten out of hand.

Even now, there is no school on the following Monday when we play Texas on Saturday.

It was quite interesting for me when Wilkinson and Tatum met at the Orange Bowl game at the end of the 1953 season.

Maryland was number one in the nation—in those days they named the national champion before the bowl games, not after, as they do today—and we were number three.

I had been wondering about the secret of Wilkinson's success because he was so different from Tatum and most other coaches I had known. Bud would never shout at or curse an athlete. Tatum had done it frequently. I couldn't figure out why Bud's mild treatment was working so well.

Before the kickoff at the Orange Bowl, I went into our locker room to see how Bud would get his team ready. The players were stretched out on mattresses, resting. Wilkinson wasn't saying a thing. He sat at the front of the room looking at big charts of plays. He would look at a chart, study it carefully, and then move it. The team was watching him, and while he wasn't saying anything, you could feel the tension.

When it came time to go on the field, Bud had the team stand up.

"Now you are going out to play the number-one team in the nation," Bud told them. "At least, the Associated Press thinks they're number one, but we're going to find out about that this afternoon."

Not emotionally but carefully, Bud said, "I want everyone who gets into this game to play as well as he can every minute. I'm not asking you to do it for the crowd. Forget the crowd. I'm not asking you to do it for the university, although that would be reason enough. But I want you to do it for each other and especially for yourselves, so that twenty-five years from now if you should happen to think of this game you will be able to remember with satisfaction that you played as well as you could.

"Remember, if you play as well as you can in every game, you always win as a person, although your team may lose. And if you don't play as well as you can, you never win as an individual even though your team may win.

"Now, go out and beat the national champions."

We beat Maryland 7–0.

A couple of years earlier, 1951, I had made my often-quoted statement that is still as widely used by OU football detractors as if I had made it last week.

The statement was made before a meeting of the combined appropriations committees of the House and Senate of Oklahoma.

I was defending OU's request for an increased budget. I explained in great detail why we needed the money to operate the university effectively. As I spoke, I gathered confidence and felt I was doing an exceptionally good job. I had never made such a brilliant presentation.

When I finished, the chairman thanked me and asked if there were any questions.

A sleepy old senator on the front row, about three feet from me, rubbed his eyes and said, "Yes, I'd like to ask the good doctor why he thinks he needs so much money to run the University of Oklahoma?"

Boy, was I deflated. I thought, Well, I haven't done a damn bit of good here. This senator hasn't heard a word I said. All I could think of was a cynical remark: "I'd like to build a university of which our football team can be proud."

I got a laugh, but not much additional money for the school. The quotation, however, went all over the world. *Reader's Digest* picked it up, printed it twice, and sent me a check for $15. A newspaper in Europe printed it. There were a few nasty editorials chastising me for emphasizing football over academics. But some understood how the remark had been prompted and intended.

Bud Wilkinson's illustrious career as coach ended when he resigned after the 1963 season. Bud lost only to Texas and Nebraska in 1963 but had a constant problem with a halfback named Joe Don Looney, who punched one of the coaches.

The assassination of President Kennedy the day before the Nebraska game weighed heavily on Bud's mind. The team finished eighth in the nation with an easy victory over Oklahoma State, but some of the regents became critical of the program—for some reason, critical of Wilkinson and of me.

Bud came to my office one day and told me he was no longer able to get himself into the "proper frame of mind" to prepare for a football game and therefore would be unable to get his staff or his players ready. He was quitting and intended to run for the U.S. Senate.

Immediately, Darrell Royal's friends and fans put a lot of pressure on us to hire him away from the University of Texas, where he was extremely successful. But it was decided that Gomer Jones was entitled to the job. Some expressed doubt that Jones would make it as a head coach, but he had been incredibly hardworking and loyal and had turned out some wonderful players. He had earned the chance.

Jones lasted through 1964 (6–4–1) and 1965 (3–7) before it was decided to change coaches.

Now again came the cries of "Bring Darrell back!"

The pressure on us was extremely intense to bring our all-American native son back to Oklahoma.

Royal had won the national championship at Texas in 1963. In 1964 his team was 10–1 and beat Alabama in the Orange Bowl. His 1965 team fell off to 6–4, but Darrell remained very much a public hero. I realized that the pressure to hire him would never go away until he was made an offer.

While I was an admirer of Royal and considered him to be a close friend, the man that the council for athletics and I wanted to hire was Jim MacKenzie, an assistant coach at Arkansas, whom we thought would be perfect for OU.

I phoned Darrell and asked what it would take to bring him back. He was pretty well satisfied with Texas. He had tenure there as a full professor, which meant his salary would continue when he was finished coaching. He told me how much money he was making from television, business opportunities, and other benefits.

I did a little figuring and came up with an offer of a six-year contract at $32,000 per year. This was more than any coach had ever been paid at Oklahoma. The regents made the offer publicly in the newspapers so the people who were pressuring us to hire him would know about it.

Royal, of course, had a much better thing going at Texas than we could give him. We offered him nothing but a coaching job—no possibility of tenure, no outside arrangements. He would have to set up his own television and radio shows and make his own business deals. Of course, if he would accept under these conditions, everything would be fine.

After a few days, Darrell replied that he was deeply touched by our offer, but he was going to stay in Austin. He was very gracious about it.

We then proceeded to hire the young, vigorous Jim MacKenzie, who would bring with him a remarkable group of smart, energetic assistant coaches—five of whom later became head coaches.

Jim was an excellent judge of coaches and players.

And furthermore, Jim and his staff agreed with me that we needed to recruit black athletes vigorously, something not yet being done in Texas.

Why? Well, let me say in admiration that the black race is superior physically. They are great in any kind of game that involves jumping or power. They're not much for golf or pole vaulting, but they can certainly play games like football and basketball.

Remember I mentioned that the NAACP was testing OU's segregation laws the week Jim Tatum and Bud Wilkinson arrived in 1946? After four years of litigation, the U.S. Supreme Court broke down our segregation laws, which should have been done much earlier. Wilkinson and then Jones, however, did not recruit black athletes.

Bud had one great black player—Prentice Gautt. But Prentice was not recruited by our coaching staff. Prentice was just a fantastic athlete at a black high school in Oklahoma City, and a group of blacks in Oklahoma City raised the money to send him to school here.

It took tremendous courage, patience, and wisdom on Prentice's part to be the only black on the Oklahoma football team. Certain hotels, like the Skirvin in Oklahoma City, wouldn't let our team stay there on pregame nights because of Prentice.

At one of the two Orange Bowls he played in for us, Prentice ran wild, gained more than 200 yards, and we won by a large margin. The next morning, in the hotel lobby, Prentice came walking through with a teammate. A corpulent fan who must have had several Bloody Marys for breakfast, looked up at Prentice and said, "You black son of a bitch!"

Prentice stiffened perceptibly. If he had hit the man, he might have killed him, since Prentice was a tremendous man—I mean powerful. He looked grim and the whole lobby became quiet.

The drunken fan then walked over and put his arm around Prentice and said, "You black son of a bitch, you're the best damn player I've ever seen on a football field. I congratulate you on what you did yesterday."

Well, everybody relaxed—but Prentice didn't. He looked as if he wasn't breathing. Prentice stood there for several seconds, then finally said, "Thank you very much, sir," and walked on.

Prentice's times required a hero, and he was one. Not only was he an all-American football player and built like a Greek statue, but he had a superior mind. He and his wife, Sandy, got their doctorates at the University of Missouri after graduating from Oklahoma.

But it had been ten years since Prentice was a freshman and I still didn't see many blacks on our athletic teams. Jim MacKenzie and his crew set out to change all that.

Glenn King was our first black cocaptain in 1971. This had an impact on recruiting such superb black athletes as Joe Washington, Rod Shoate, the Selmon brothers, and many others. Working in harmony with our white players, our talented blacks were perhaps the decisive factor in OU's return to national prominence in football.

At the end of my book, *Presidents Can't Punt,* published when Barry Switzer was fresh from his first two national championship teams, I wrote that he was now in the unenviable position of knowing he could not continue to win national championships indefinitely, and Oklahoma fans have little tolerance for merely placing in the Top 10.

Barry was a superb coach. Being from a poor background himself, he was very compassionate toward underprivileged youngsters. Perhaps a little too compassionate for his own good, sometimes.

All those unfortunate things that happened to Barry might scarcely have been noticed if they'd been spread out over a year. Such things happened in other institutions right along. But they happened to Barry in a very short time, and it was more than our interim president, David Swank, could take. As I told *The New York Times,* the situation was not peculiar to Oklahoma at all. It's simply that we were providing an example of what is wrong with big-time college athletics.

The fans are the main problem. Many of them, disappointed with their personal performance in life, start living their lives through the football teams and the athletes. When the teams win, the fans win. And when the teams lose, the fans lose as individuals because they are imbued with the idea that the team is a part of them. This brings out the worst in them.

The impact of the game on the fans is a serious matter—in what it does to people and their attitudes. I don't know of any way to cope with that problem. You can't make the fans any more successful personally. That's limited by their genetics.

What you see in Oklahoma, you see in Arkansas, you see in Alabama, you see in states that are, let us say, less developed than certain areas of the east and west coasts. There, areas may have a broader lower middle class. They are the less sophisticated places, which I think identify too emotionally with their college football teams.

Having said this, I bow to those who point out similar problems at Notre Dame, California, USC, and UCLA, to mention a few.

It's just that in the *Grapes of Wrath* period in Oklahoma, when the terrible dust storms swept our state, our people were so desperate for something to take pride in that they embraced the idea of a great football team with too much passion.

As the man who helped to create the football monster at Oklahoma, I would like to offer my opinion on the future of the game.

I think these billion-dollar TV contracts are bound to influence college athletics in a very undesirable way. Money has become the dominant factor in the game now. There is no way to restrain television or turn back the clock, because this is what the people want.

The game is about big money. I dislike the thought, but the only thing I can think of to make it a little more palatable is to pay the college athletes.

Father Hesburgh of Notre Dame and I are the two who are largely responsible for the present athletic scholarship plan. I persuaded our conference and Father Hesburgh persuaded the NCAA. The plan eliminated part-time jobs, for which no work was done, a situation that had corroded the ethics of coaches and athletes alike.

Now may be the time to come right out and pay our athletes a reasonable stipend—I don't know how much, but enough so that an underprivileged player can afford to go home for occasional visits, or buy a new coat, or pay his own check in a restaurant.

The way the game is run now, there will always be dishonesty. The coaches might not always be aware of the extent of it, but the players always will be.

I think we should experiment with paying the players. If this doesn't work, I think we should discontinue big-time football in college and universities.

25

THE RECRUITING WARS

"Recruiting is the worst part of college football. I no longer look forward to it. I can't wait until it's over. It makes me feel like a pimp . . . a player's word doesn't mean a damn thing any more . . . I'm sick of it."

That is not me talking. It's Bo Schembechler in his book that was published in the fall of 1989, a few months before he retired after a long and successful career at the University of Michigan.

But I pretty much agree with you, Bo. I believe recruiters run into a different type of kid today than they did a few years ago.

Blame it on TV, sports agents, a general air of corruption in our society, or whatever else you want to blame it on. Maybe you can blame it on Bo and me being middle-aged now. I think when Darrell Royal quit coaching in 1976, he said one reason was because kids weren't like they used to be. Hell, maybe kids never were like they used to be.

But I know I finally got tired of recruiting, something I really used to enjoy. Recruiting has always been something like pimping, I guess, but it never really bothered me until I looked around one day and said to myself, Hey, Switzer, what is a fifty-year-old man doing chasing eighteen-year-old boys around the country?

I didn't have a satisfactory answer for myself. It was kind of a shock, too, because I used to look at recruiting as exciting, a challenge and a welcome break in the steady grind of coaching.

Recruiting now is probably no dirtier than it ever was—

just more expensive. Some recruiters have always used every trick from lying to bribery to outright kidnapping.

To put this recruiting business in historical perspective, let me tell you about legendary coach Fielding H. "Hurry Up" Yost, who became famous for his "point-a-minute" teams at Michigan.

Yost was in California—and out of a job—at the turn of the century when a halfback named Willie Heston, who is listed on many of college football's all-time teams, asked him for help. Heston's team, the San Jose Normal School (now San Jose State) was preparing to play Chico State for the normal-school championship. Yost agreed to do the coaching if Heston would do the running and tackling. San Jose won.

After drifting to other schools, suddenly Yost got the coaching job at Michigan. He contacted Heston, who was by now twenty-three and teaching in Oregon, and invited him to come to Michigan and play some more football.

Though Yost's opponents cried that Heston was "hired help" because he held a part-time job on the campus as an ad salesman for a magazine, Heston played four more years of football at Michigan while the Wolverines were winning two national championships and never losing a game.

In Heston's first season at Michigan, they outscored the opposition 501–0 and won the very first Rose Bowl, beating Stanford 49–0 while Heston gained 170 yards on 18 carries.

They called Heston the Wolverine Thunderbolt. He later became a prosecuting attorney and then a judge and lived happily into his eighties.

How old are recruiting and "improper inducements"?

I say they go back at least as far as the Wolverine Thunderbolt, and more likely all the way back to Walter Camp and Pudge Heffelfinger.

But it was disgusting, the crap that Gary Gibbs and his OU staff had to put up with during 1989 from competing recruiters, who warned kids if they signed with Oklahoma they stood a good chance of getting shot or thrown in jail. For every two hours with a prospect's parents, OU coaches had to spend nearly an hour and a half defending our program against slander.

In the many years that I was one of the top recruiters in

the game, I didn't need to stoop to negative recruiting. I was always recruiting for winning programs—Oklahoma and Arkansas are the only places I ever worked—and the best players wanted to play for winners. They wanted to hear how we would surround them with great talent, help them be all-Americans and at the same time get their education. Negative recruitment was never my bag. Most kids didn't want to hear that kind of crap anyway.

During one period I did use what might be called negative recruiting, but it was the absolute truth. It was back in the late 1960s and early 1970s, when I would tell a black recruit in Texas, "If you were to sign with a Southwest Conference team, just think how lonesome it would be to look around in the huddle and see nothing but honky faces."

Actually, the Southwest Conference played right into our hands when I was a young assistant coach under Jim MacKenzie and Chuck Fairbanks and my main recruiting responsibility was in Texas.

For one thing, the SWC just wasn't really interested in recruiting blacks in those days. And for another, the SWC legislated itself out of a real chance to land the best white high school player in the state in 1968—quarterback Jack Mildren of Cooper High School in Abilene.

The Southwest Conference put in a recruiting rule that allowed its coaches to visit a prospect's parents in their home only one time. This rule didn't apply to recruiters flying in from out of state, and it lasted just one year, but that was long enough for our purposes.

In the spring of 1968, I was hot after two Texas prospects in particular—Jack Mildren and Glenn King of Jacksboro.

Glenn King had led the state in scoring and rushing for Jacksboro coach Chuck Curtis, but the SWC wasn't interested in Glenn because he was black. I remember going to the dirt-floor shack where Glenn lived in a shanty town outside Jacksboro the night before signing day, and his mother told me, "Glenn ain't here. The Missouri coaches come and taken him away."

"What do you mean? Where'd they take him?" I said.

"I heard Glenn say he might be going to Dallas with Prentice Gautt."

I realized Prentice, who was then a first-year assistant coach at Missouri and who probably didn't know the rules then, had driven Glenn to a motel and would be staying all night with him until he got Glenn's name on the dotted line. But Glenn's mama didn't want him to go to Missouri. She wanted her boy to go to Oklahoma. First thing, though, I had to find him. The NCAA required that he be in his home on signing day.

About 10 o'clock that night I finally hunted down Chuck Fairbanks. Chuck had worked with Dan Devine, the Missouri head coach, for some great years at Arizona State. Chuck phoned Dan and Dan denied they were hiding Glenn. "We wouldn't do a thing like that," Dan said. (Bullshit, he wouldn't.)

"Well, Barry is at Glenn King's house in Jacksboro and is spending the night," Chuck told him. "If Glenn King is not back home by 8 A.M., I am calling the NCAA."

At about 2 A.M. I'm trying to sleep in my rental car in front of the King house, and sure enough up drives Prentice Gautt and lets Glenn out. Six hours later, Prentice and I were both inside the house, and Glenn signed with Oklahoma because his mother wanted him to. Glenn King became OU's first black cocaptain.

To get Jack Mildren, I practically moved in with his family three days a week. I would recruit in the Dallas area on Monday and Tuesday, and then on Wednesday I'd climb aboard one of those old DC-3 puddle jumpers and fly out to Abilene in West Texas.

Jack was the top player in the state of Texas, and he was white. We had a lot of things going for us with him. Jack knew our quarterbacking situation was going to be wide open, plus his high school coach, Merrill Green, had been a great player at Oklahoma and had been on the staff at Arkansas when I played and coached there.

The main thing, I think, was my chance to be constantly exposed to Jack and his family. I would stay at the home of Jakie Sandefer, an Abilene Oily who had played halfback at OU for Bud Wilkinson, but I'd spend the afternoons and evenings visiting and watching TV with Jack's daddy, Larry, and his mother, Mary Glen. We loved watching Dolly Parton and

Porter Waggoner. It came on at 5:30 in the afternoon. We'd have dinner together and I would help with the dishes while Jack did his homework.

One night while I was there, Beebs Stallings—now the head coach at Alabama (his real name is Larry, but he's Beebs to his old friends)—showed up at the door with his staff from Texas A&M. They were in two cars.

Mary Glen Mildren and I were washing dishes when we heard the doorbell. "I guess that's the A&M coaches, Mary Glen," I said. "Why don't you just leave these dishes and go visit with them? I'll come back and help you finish them later."

Two hours later, I was sitting out front when Beebs and his staff came out and drove off at the end of the only visit their conference allowed at the Mildren house. Beebs wasn't all that happy to see me. As if I gave a damn. I went back inside and did the rest of the dishes with Mary Glen, a really neat lady.

It happened more than once that I'd be driving someplace with Jack and we'd be talking about quarterbacking techniques. I would stop the car at an intersection at night and in the headlights people would see Jack Mildren and me out there practicing handoffs, fakes, and drop back techniques.

On Friday nights I watched Jack play football. The next week we'd discuss his game, talk about theory and the mechanics of football, how he could be more proficient, things like that.

S.M.U. really wanted Jack. They busted their rear ends trying. I don't think Texas was ever really in the picture with him. There were world war-size headlines the day Jack Mildren signed with Oklahoma.

Greg Pruitt and Joe Washington were a couple of black all-American halfbacks we took out of Texas in 1969 and 1972 with the help of Wendell Mosley.

Wendell was Greg's high school coach, the school was segregated, and Greg was so little at that time he almost looked like a midget. Texas wasn't interested in him. The only Texas school that wanted him was Houston. He was so small it was kind of hard to think of really offering him one of our fifty scholarships, but Wendell knew how great Greg was and knew we would treat him right, so he sent Greg up to Norman to see us.

Billy Michaels was in charge of recruiting the Houston area for us. He told us he had this kid Pruitt on the field and we had to see him. Well, it was against the rules to work out a kid officially, so we told them to get up a touch football game in shorts and we told Jack Mildren to throw a lot of passes to the runt.

Maybe the only more striking first impression I ever had was Joe Washington's 80-yard run on 46 Counter the first time he touched the ball at Owen Field—as I've already told you about.

I mean, Greg Pruitt was about 5 feet 6 inches tall in those days, weighed probably less than 150. You can't take a truck-load of players that size or you'll go out of business. For every one who turns out to be a Greg Pruitt, there are thousands of little, quick guys who can't play.

But Greg caught every ball Jack threw in his direction that day, and he made some incredible runs. Chuck Fairbanks didn't watch him, but he called me later and asked if Pruitt was as good as Billy and Wendell said.

I said, "Chuck, he is as good as anybody we've got. I think he's even better than Eddie Hinton."

When it came time to look at Little Joe Washington in the fall of 1971, Wendell Mosley had gone to work for us as an assistant coach. Little Joe's daddy—Big Joe—was a great player at Prairie View A&M, a black college, and had played against Wendell at another black college, Texas Southern. Big Joe coached at Bay City before going to Port Arthur Lincoln High, where he has been for twenty-five years. Wendell had played and coached against Big Joe and gone to clinics with him. He knew Little Joe's girlfriend, Meadowlark, now his wife, who enrolled at North Texas State, which is right down I-35 and across the Red River bridge from Norman, at most a two-hour drive. Believe it or not, Meadowlark has a sister named Robin.

Everybody knew Little Joe Washington was going to leave the Southwest Conference. The coaches down there had just barely begun recruiting blacks and didn't really know how to go about it, whereas we had been doing it with great success for years.

Joe Washington was the top player in the state of Texas that year and never gave a serious thought to playing college ball there. I asked him why he really wanted to come to Oklahoma—I'm always curious about that—and he said as a black athlete he felt at home and comfortable on our campus with so many of his brothers. He knew we would let him be himself and wear his silver shoes. I didn't give a damn. The way he ran with the ball, I didn't care if he played barefoot.

I've told you that Joe Washington baby-sat for Greg, Kathy, and Doug and told them nursery tales while they were young. I can't remember if I mentioned that I pay my baby-sitter $100 an hour. I've always wondered if that violated the NCAA rules.

I asked Keith Jackson, our all-American tight end who is now an all-pro star with the Philadelphia Eagles and who had graduated with a 3.00 average in three and a half years, why he chose to come to Oklahoma from Little Rock, Arkansas. As I say, I'm always curious—and kids pick schools for the weirdest of reasons.

Keith told me, "I came to Oklahoma because when you visited our home, my mother said you were the only coach that made her feel comfortable in her own home."

Mamas are always going to be factors. Very few kids make a decision that their mother isn't part of, especially in black families.

Keith's mother, Gladys, is a nurse. They had a nice home in a black community in rural Little Rock. I came in and sat on the couch and placed my feet on the ottoman, talking to Gladys and her daughter, Gwen. I took off my loafers and started scratching my stockinged feet. Gladys told me that I was the only coach who had ever taken his shoes off in her house. Gladys is from south Arkansas, like me. We started naming all the little old towns like Altheimer and Humphrey, and we understood each other and knew each other. I was like her and she was like me. There was a comfort zone.

Recruiting comes down to the bottom line of how people feel about you, the comfort zone they have with you, the honesty, the genuine feeling that you are the person their son should spend his next four or five years with.

Being able to communicate your sincere feelings to the family and the student-athlete is the key to the whole deal.

A lot of country kids and introverted kids, kids who aren't sophisticated or street-wise, have in them the same values and feelings that I have in me, and I always knew I had a good shot at signing that type of kid.

It's the con guys who are difficult for me to communicate with or even be around, because they have other priorities that I can only guess at.

But there are some big-city street-smart kids I did very well with. For example, Jamelle Holieway, who was the best high school quarterback in Los Angeles and wound up quarterbacking our Sooners to a national championship in 1985 as a true freshman.

When I signed Jamelle, rumors and gossip went flying around the country—like, what the hell did Switzer have to give that kid to make him leave Los Angeles and go all the way to Norman, Oklahoma, to play football?

Let me ask a different question.

If you were eighteen years old in 1985 and you knew damn well that you were the best high school Wishbone quarterback in the United States, where *else* would you go to college except Oklahoma?

Washington, UCLA, California, and a number of other first-class schools were hot and heavy on the trail of Jamelle. It was no secret that he was a truly great athlete. But the other schools all viewed his size—about 5-feet-10 and 175—and said, No, Jamelle, you can't play quarterback for us. We see you as a wide receiver or a defensive back.

On the other hand, I looked at Jamelle and said, "You are just exactly the right size to play Wishbone quarterback at Oklahoma. The height factor has never been a criterion for us."

And I used Greg Pruitt's line: "At Oklahoma we open holes from side to side, not up to down."

Jamelle was a middle-class kid. His mother, Charlie, was a nurse, and his father made a good income. He didn't have his hand out. He wanted to be a great quarterback.

Jamelle was a product of a great high school program at Banning, where we had recruited Stanley Wilson. Jamelle's coach was Chris Ferragamo, the brother of former Nebraska and LA Rams quarterback Vince Ferragamo. Jamelle was smart and had a deceptively strong passing arm. He knew what he could do, and he wasn't going to play cornerback or receiver for anybody.

At the same time, we were recruiting Eric Mitchel from Pine Bluff, Arkansas, a quarterback who weighed 210 and was an awesome natural athlete. If we got Eric and Jamelle both, we would have two great quarterback prospects—and they weren't even thought of as starters. Our number-one quarterback going into the 1985 season was Troy Aikman.

Scott Hill, our national recruiter, and I both worked on Jamelle, but we were pretty sure all along that we had him. If Colorado had had its Wishbone running well at the time, they would have had a good chance at him—the way they scored a few years later, when Bill McCartney recruited Darian Hagan, the second coming of Jamelle—off the playing fields of Los Angeles.

Just like a football, a coach's life can take odd bounces.

When we were still coaching at Arkansas, Jim MacKenzie had just about wrapped up a big stud high school back from Miami, Oklahoma, named Steve Owens. Miami is closer on the map to Fayetteville than it is to Norman. Remember, Arkansas was at its zenith at the time. We had won the SWC, were undefeated for twenty-two games in a row, and had a top program. But Oklahoma was at its lowest ebb.

The first thing Jim did when he got the Oklahoma job was to change gears and start selling Steve Owens on the true story that we were beginning a winning program at Oklahoma and that Steve would be our leader, our bell cow, the one who could come to Norman and make it all happen. I believe if it hadn't been for Jim MacKenzie's great personality, Steve Owens would have gone to Arkansas.

I never watched a film of Tony Casillas in high school. Merv Johnson was recruiting him out of Tulsa, and the first time I saw Tony was at the high school all-star game at Owen Field. It only took a glance to see he was much stronger than anybody else on the field. He was a dominating force at nose guard. Tony was a superstar the moment he came to us, but he had his problems like most of us do. He was keen, quick, emotional, and as a freshman growing up he had to fight through some disappointments and disillusionments when everything in life didn't work exactly as he thought it should. Tony quit school, left, and we had to go get him again.

But he stayed and earned his degree and won both the Vince Lombardi Award and the UPI Lineman of the Year Award in 1985. And he was the second player drafted in the NFL draft that spring, by the Atlanta Falcons.

Another great player we found in Oklahoma was linebacker Rod Shoate, from a little town named Spiro. That was 1971, and Darrell Royal was telling everybody that we were raiding his state like the U.S. Cavalry, capturing or—he claimed—buying their best players. But we were soon to reach the point where we had nineteen starters from Oklahoma.

We never "bought" any player from anywhere, but we sure as hell didn't need to buy an Oklahoma high school player. These kids were growing up watching us playing winning, exciting football. Take Steve Davis, the preacher; the white kid who quarterbacked our national champions in 1974 and 1975. Steve grew up in Sallisaw and got the last scholarship given in 1971. Hell, we started not to take him. And Rod Shoate, the 1974 all-American, wasn't highly recruited. All we knew was he was a fast-ass linebacker, so we took a gamble on him.

OU can't recruit just in Oklahoma, the same as Nebraska can't recruit only in Nebraska or Colorado only in Colorado. There is simply not enough home-grown talent. We have to recruit coast to coast, and especially in Texas—which year after year turns out the best high school players in the country.

But we did, and still do, keep finding gems in our own backyard. Like Randy Hughes, from Tulsa. Randy was the high-school back of the year in the state of Oklahoma, and he didn't even play offense. A big white kid, about 6-feet-4 and 200 pounds, he would dominate the game at safety on defense. You run your tailback off tackle, Randy nails you for a 2-yard gain. You throw a pass, he intercepts it.

When we brought Oklahoma back to the top and began winning bowl games, the Oklahoma-born kids naturally wanted to come to us.

In 1971 the University of Texas finally recruited a black star, Roosevelt Leaks, a Wishbone fullback who set a UT rec-

ord by rushing for 342 yards against S.M.U. in 1973. Leaks
was the type of kid to be a trendsetter, a barrier breaker. Roosevelt was a progressive thinker, like a Prentice Gautt. He had
two 1,000-yard rushing seasons at Texas and paved the way
for one of the best players in the history of the game—Earl
Campbell.

In high school at Tyler, Texas, Earl was just totally unfair
to the opposition. He was a man playing against children. In
high school Earl was 220 pounds and ran a 4.5 forty. He
would take the football and move the whole pile of players
down the field with him. It was awesome. It was close to
murder. Nobody could tackle him. I think Earl is the only
player I have ever seen who could have gone straight from
high school into the NFL and become a starter and a star immediately.

Lucious Selmon and I worked on Earl really hard. We
were as nice and charming as we could be to his mother, Ann,
who was employed by a banker with connections at the University of Texas. In Earl's senior season in high school (1973),
we beat Texas 52–13. We asked Earl to picture how great he
could be surrounded by our players, who went on to win national championships in 1974 and 1975. Just think of it—the
Selmons and Rod Shoate and Randy Hughes and those other
studs on defense; and Joe Washington and Earl Campbell in
the same backfield.

Earl told us he was coming to Oklahoma.

Of course, we couldn't appear on television in 1974 and
1975 because of the NCAA punishing us for the 1972 Kerry
Jackson false-transcript affair. But I don't know if this had any
bearing on Earl's final decision.

What Earl told us at the end was it had come down to
either us or Texas. He said when he went to bed the night
before he signed, he prayed to God for something to tell him
what to do. If I had known that, I would have crouched under
his bed and sung "Boomer Sooner" all night long.

But God must have said for Earl to go to Texas, because
that's where he rushed for 4,443 yards in his career and won
the Heisman Trophy in his senior year, when Fred Akers took
over from Darrell as coach and installed the I formation espe-

cially for Earl, as we had done a decade earlier for Steve Owens.

Would we have changed from the Wishbone to the I just to get Earl at Oklahoma? No. Earl was the greatest, but we had a couple of guys at fullback those years named Jim Littrell and Horace Ivory who would knock your hat off. I mean, nobody could beat us, Earl or no Earl.

Most fans don't understand how the recruiting system operates. It is the assistant coaches who do the hard work day in and day out. They are the key in recruiting. Back in the golden less-restricted years of the 1970s, we could hire special coaches strictly for recruiting. I had a staff of fifteen, and five of them did nothing but recruit. Bear Bryant did the same thing. So did most schools that could afford it. I had a fleet of airplanes at our disposal from our Oily supporters—this was before the great oil crash and the banking and savings-and-loan disasters—and we could fly in to pick up a recruit in a Learjet if we needed to impress him.

So it is the assistant coaches who get the players. All I did as head coach was to keep from screwing it up. In the world of salesmanship, you would call me the closer, the guy who gets the contract signed.

Before I went to see a kid as head coach, I would be thoroughly prepared by the assistant coach on what to say and what not to say. I would have read a scouting report on the kid, probably seen him play ball on film. I would be informed about his academic prowess, or the lack of it. In the last couple of years, I might have been shown a psychiatric evaluation of him. I would know all about his parents, his brothers and sisters. I would visit a lot of kids in their homes before I ever saw them on our campus, so I had to be pretty well educated by my assistant coach, who was probably working on six kids at the same time, whereas I, as head coach, was actually going to visit the homes of seventy.

From my long experience as an assistant, I knew what the head coach had to do on his visit. I had to make them like me. Sometimes the kids, or even the parents, would have put me on a pedestal because I was the head coach at mighty Oklahoma, and it was up to me to kick aside that pedestal and talk to everybody in the house as just another human being with the same needs and desires as the rest of them.

The truth is, I didn't run into all that many kids with their hands out when I was head coach. The kids didn't tell me what they had been offered by other schools. Occasionally, I would hear about a case like Darrell Shepard, a quarterback we wanted from Odessa, Texas, who was given a car by a banker booster to attend the University of Houston (and was ruled ineligible by the SWC and transferred to Oklahoma), but usually it would be the assistant coach who heard such things and dealt with them at ground zero.

I do remember one kid who came into my office and sat across the desk from me and told me another school was offering him inducements, and he wanted to know what I would do for him.

I pointed at the portrait of Billy Sims on my wall.

"You know who that is?" I said.

"Yeah, that's Billy Sims," he responded.

"You're right. He's one of the greatest players to ever play here. He was an all-American. He won the Heisman Trophy. And he rushed for more yards than any other back in the school's history. And besides that, I didn't give him a dime to come here. And he didn't ask for it. And here you sit. You haven't even broken a huddle yet. You haven't made a yard— or a tackle—and you want me to do something for you. I'll tell you what you can do. You get up and get your ass out of this office and go to that other school, and I promise you, we'll kick your ass just like we do every year."

The kid left, thought it over that night, came back the next day with his high school coach, and signed with us. His name was Tony Rayburn. He later, as a junior, intercepted two passes for us in the Orange Bowl when we beat Penn State for our third national championship. A neck injury in his senior year prevented him from ever playing football again. Had that not happened, he would surely be playing in the pros today.

I'll tell you later about how I gave Billy Sims an illegal "extra benefit" in violation of NCAA rules to keep him in school. But I *never* gave him or anyone else any financial inducement to come here. But I'll tell you the one thing I did when I was recruiting him that I think made the biggest impression on him.

I saw Billy Sims on film before he started his senior year

in high school at Hooks, Texas. It didn't require any genius to tell that this kid had everything it takes to be a superstar. I got on the phone and called his high school coach, Jack Coleman, in that little old hole-in-the-wall office of his at Hooks. I said, "Coach, I want you to know Billy is going to be our number-one recruiting priority this year. I hope you allow me to come see Billy play and give your permission to visit with him."

I was laying the groundwork for my assistant coach, Bill Shimick, who would be working the east Texas area.

To Billy's coach, I said, "I wonder where I can get hold of Billy."

"He happens to be sitting right in front of my desk," the coach said, and he put Billy on the phone.

I said, "Billy, I've seen some great ones in my time, and if you come to Oklahoma and let us surround you with a great supporting cast, every dream you have about college football can come true. I want you to start thinking about being a Sooner."

Billy lived on a little country road outside of Hooks with his grandmother, Miss Sadie. His real mother, Mrs. Washington, lived in the housing projects in St. Louis where the Spinks boys, the professional boxers, grew up. Until the eighth grade, Billy would just spend summers in Hooks. But then he started getting into a little trouble in the projects and his family moved him out to Hooks, the best thing that ever could have happened to him.

Before most of our home games that year, I would fly down to Hooks to see Billy play on Friday nights. One night I remember Frank Broyles, another coach, and I all huddling together in their tiny press box to stay warm—Billy was that special. He had rushed in his high school career for nearly 8,000 yards, the second best in Texas high school history.

Then every Saturday morning I would call Billy and talk about his ball game.

That in itself is not unusual. A coach will be sitting around in his hotel room before a game at East Lansing or South Bend or someplace, and he'll telephone his recruits and say, "I'm sitting here thinking about you, and I wish you were playing for us today." The coach usually will hang up and call the next recruit on his list and say the same thing. The kids know the coaches are doing this, but what the hell? It's what they want to hear.

But one Saturday we were playing Colorado at Boulder, and Little Joe Washington was in the process of rushing 18 times for 200 yards and four touchdowns.

At the half we had them 28–0, and I noticed a pay phone on the wall in the visitors' locker room. I asked my old hunting and fishing buddy Bobby Bell for a dime.

See, I had already phoned Billy Sims from the hotel before the ball game and told him to be sure to listen. Billy pumped gas at a Conoco Service Station on Interstate 30 on weekends to make spending money. I knew he would have the radio on at the station.

I phoned him from the visitors' locker room. "Aren't you listening to the game?" I said.

"Sure I'm listening," he said. "But you all have only played a half."

"We've got their ass whipped," I said. "Let me tell you what we're going to run on them in the second half, so you can listen for it . . ."

I talked to Billy on the phone for twenty minutes—the whole rest of the half—and finally the officials came up and tapped me on the shoulder and yelled, "Coach, it's late, you got to get your team back on the field!"

On the phone, I said, "You heard 'em, Billy. We got to go finish this ass kicking. Wish you were here."

This time Billy knew damn well I hadn't been calling anybody but him. He really liked that—standing at that gas station in Hooks, Texas, and talking to me in the locker room at Boulder, Colorado.

You would have thought the University of Texas would have been our biggest rival for Billy Sims, but in truth it was Baylor that came closest.

Baylor coach Grant Teaff is one of the greatest recruiters I ever ran across. Grant is a preacher; he can really operate in the pulpit or in your living room in a most convincing way.

But I had one argument that Grant couldn't overcome. Oklahoma had lost but two games in five years, and in fact, we had just gone for thirty-eight wins without a loss, and we wouldn't lose again until Billy was a freshman. So when I told Billy I would surround him with great talent, he could see it was true.

When Billy came to Oklahoma for an official visit, he came to my house and my kids Greg and Kathy, who were five or six years old and both wore glasses, met him wearing Oklahoma jerseys with the number 20 on them and the name SIMS stenciled on the back, which I happened to have made the day before his visit. "Look here, Billy. They're already selling your jerseys in the stores," I said, and he broke up laughing.

Of course everyone knows that Billy was one of the greatest players ever to play the game. He was all-American two years, won the Heisman Trophy as a junior, and should have won it again as a senior, but finished second to Charles White of USC. He was the first player picked in the NFL draft, was NFL's rookie of the year for the Detroit Lions, which were two feats that Oklahoma State's Heisman Trophy-winner Barry Sanders duplicated in 1988.

Those exploits were well known, but this one isn't. Bob White, a close personal friend and business associate of mine from Texarkana, Texas, who was a door-to-door vacuum-cleaner salesman when I first met him, built a $40 million television-leasing company in the short span of eight years called Crown Home Entertainment Centers. Bob told me this story after Billy had been an all-pro running back for the Detroit Lions.

Since Bob had several stores in the Detroit area and did a lot of TV advertising, he asked Billy to do an ad for him. Billy agreed to do it and did an excellent job. Later, and because Bob is a professional, he sent Billy a $5,000 talent fee. Billy had not asked for or expected to receive a fee for the ad. A week later, Bob received a telephone call from the Hooks High School principal, who told him what a generous financial gesture Billy had just made. Coach Jack Coleman had just received a check from Billy for $5,000, drawn to the Hooks athletic department.

But back to Billy Sims and his senior year in high school.

As national signing date approached, I had a problem. Halfback Kenny King, from Clarendon, Texas, wanted me to sign him at 8 A.M. on signing day, or else he might go to Texas A&M.

I really wanted Kenny, but I knew I had to be with Billy. That was one year we really mopped up in Texas. Of the nineteen high school players on the *Dallas Times Herald*'s blue-chip list, we signed thirteen!

In fact, the starting backfield for one team in the Texas high school all-star game at Fort Worth—Thomas Lott at quarterback, Kenny King at fullback, and Billy Sims at tailback—all signed with Oklahoma.

I had a private jet ready to fly me to Hooks and Clarendon and San Antonio and other places on signing day and was trying to figure out how to please Sims without offending Kenny King. But then Billy announced he had decided not to sign on the national signing date. He wanted to take an extra twenty-four hours to think about his decision. Billy was older than the ordinary recruit, being twenty years old—he was twenty-six when he graduated from OU—and more inclined to reflect on his options.

Instead of this making me nervous, it reassured me. I knew the more Billy thought on it, the more certain he was to come to Oklahoma.

I'll always remember flying to San Antonio from Clarendon that day to sign Thomas Lott. It was my second year as head coach and the third year since Wendell Mosley had left his high school job to join the Oklahoma staff as an assistant coach recruiting in Texas, where he had hundreds of friends.

We thought Thomas Lott from San Antonio Jay High School was the top option quarterback in the country. Thomas, whose trademark later became his bandanna, knew we were his kind of people.

Why did Thomas wear a bandanna? Well, it wasn't for the reason most people thought. Thomas wore his hair in a huge Afro. You take a football headgear and put it down on an Afro during practice or a game, and when you take off the helmet, it has created so many indentations that the hair looks like a waffle. So Thomas would tie a bandanna over his hair to hold it down beneath the headgear, and later when he removed the bandanna, his hair would pop right back up.

After kids saw Thomas wearing his headband for us on national television, there were headbands all over the playgrounds. The bandanna was Thomas's trademark for a practical reason, like Little Joe's silver shoes for superstitious reasons.

But that day we were to sign him, we go to Thomas's house, where all the photographers and reporters and TV are gathered, and Thomas is ready to pick up the pen. I turn to Wendell and say, "Where are the papers?"

"Didn't you bring them?" says Wendell.

"Hell no, Wendell, head coaches don't bring the papers. It's the assistant coach who is supposed to take care of those details and bring the papers."

Wendell leans over and says, "Jesus, don't tell the other coaches, will you?" (No, Wendell, I won't. I'll just write about it someday.)

We phoned Norman and had a set of national signing papers dispatched to us by private jet and signed Thomas Lott inside of two hours.

The next day, when we did sign Billy Sims, I phoned my sportswriter friend Bill Connors in Tulsa and told him we were going to sign a future Heisman Trophy winner. He wrote a column about it then and again years later, when it came true.

The second greatest lie in the world is when a kid's parents tell you, "We want our son to make up his own mind, and we're not getting involved." The parents always get involved.

I remember going into Eric Dickerson's house in Sealey, Texas, with assistant coach Rex Norris. Eric had already told me on his official campus visit that he wanted to go to Oklahoma. I had given him the same pitch I gave Billy Sims about surrounding him with a great supporting cast and becoming our fourth Heisman Trophy winner. Eric was a nice kid and a smart kid. But when Rex and I went into his home, his mom and dad had turned cold and I sensed we were bucking some kind of new odds. We were suddenly out of the picture. We had heard some rumors about why we were out of the chase, but even to this day I really do not know what happened.

But, in all honesty, in all the years I spent recruiting and, admittedly, even in view of all of the dirty things that I heard out there, I never had even one player tell me he got any illegal inducement from any schools other than Oklahoma State, S.M.U., and T.C.U.

As I have said several times now, kids choose schools for the strangest of reasons.

I offer you a prime example of this—Steve Sewell.

Steve Sewell was from Reirdon High School in San Francisco. It's a parochial school. We always checked the parochial schools and found a few good players that way, usually looking at them on 8-millimeter film.

Steve is a very quiet, reserved young man who now plays for the Denver Broncos, and he was just sitting there in his home listening to me without opening his mouth to so much as ask if we had his helmet size.

The phone rang. Coach Joe Kapp of California was on the line.

Steve took the phone and said, "Thanks for calling, Coach, but I'm committed to Oklahoma. I'm going to sign with them next week."

I was stunned but happy. Again I asked my usual question, "Steve, what made you decide on Oklahoma? Why is a kid from San Francisco coming all the way to Norman to go to school?"

Steve just turned and looked at his daddy.

"Well, I'll tell you why," his daddy said. "It's because in the navy in 1955 and 1956 I was stationed in Norman, Oklahoma, and I never missed an OU home game. They won two national championships back to back. I never saw OU lose a game. I always wanted to have a son play football at Oklahoma. Steve here is my son, and Oklahoma is where he's going."

It was rare that we ran into a parent as totally presold on us as Steve Sewell's father. More often, we would encounter the challenge of one like Andre Johnson's mother, who didn't know anything about Oklahoma except that she hated it. I don't think she even liked the musical version of it.

Assistant coach Bobby Proctor was recruiting Andre for us out of Forest Brooks High School in Houston. Andre was a 6-foot-1 200-pound cornerback who we thought could play for us as a pure freshman. But Andre's mother would not allow Bobby to enter her house. She met Bobby at the front door and said, "You get on away from here, you Oklahomas. My boy is not going to Oklahoma, no way is he going to Oklahoma. Now, you get away from our house and leave my son alone, you hear?"

Bobby returned to Norman and told me about it. I said, "Let's go back down there."

"All right, but you've got to go to the door first," Bobby said. The coward!

Mrs. Johnson was blocking the door, a big scowl on her face, when I walked onto the porch with Bobby lurking in the background.

"I recognize you, Barry Switzer," she said. "I know who you are. I know the bad things you do. People have told me about that gang of outlaws you call football players up in Oklahoma. Well, you're not going to take my son, so stop wasting your time around here." (Boy, don't you know some of those SWC coaches had been doing a negative recruiting job on her! But we were used to it. We got that all of the time from them.)

While she was scolding me, my nose picked up a familiar odor coming from her kitchen. It was a smell that took me back to my childhood.

"Is that cracklin' bread I smell? By golly, it is, isn't it, Mrs. Johnson?" I said.

She looked at me suspiciously. "What would you know about cracklin' bread?"

"Irma Reynolds, my black grandmama, made the best cracklin' bread in the world when I was a kid. It's been years now since I had a piece of good cracklin' bread. Mrs. Johnson, I don't know why you hate me. I've never done you or your son any harm. I certainly respect your right to throw me off your property. But you couldn't hate me so much that you'd turn me down for a piece of your cracklin' bread, could you? Have you got any buttermilk?"

(When you slaughter a hog and hang it up to be skinned, the hard layer that comes off the fat is called cracklin'—you know, it crackles. Don't confuse it with chitlins, which is the intestine. But cracklin' bread is cornbread with hard pieces of meat diced up in it. It's delicious.)

Mrs. Johnson softened a little and let me into the kitchen, where I ate two entire pans of cracklin' bread and asked her if she'd bake some more for me to take with me.

"I can't tell you how much I've missed the taste of great cracklin' bread like this. Why, I believe you're a better cook than Irma."

After a while we were out of the kitchen and sitting in the front room with Andre, his brother, his father, and his mother. I was telling them enthusiastically about how I expected Andre to start in our secondary, how he was going to be a great star in our secondary . . .

"Wait a minute, Coach Switzer," Mrs. Johnson interrupted. "I don't want my boy playing in any secondary. If Andre is going to Oklahoma, he is going to play in your *first-dary!*"

Clearly, Mrs. Johnson was not a football fan. But Andre, his father, and his brother got a big laugh out of it. By the time the evening ended, Bobby Proctor and I walked out of the house with an armful of cracklin' bread—and Andre Johnson's signature.

Now, that experience at Andre's house was in no way the kind of recruiting encounter that Bo Schembechler was talking about when he called it pimping.

In fact, this was the kind of recruiting experience that makes you realize all over again the real value of what you are offering to the student athlete.

Andre Johnson did start for us as a freshman. But in the middle of his freshman year, he was involved in a car wreck with Keith Stanberry, another outstanding Texas player, and it tore up all four of their knees. They no doubt would have become number-one draft choices in the NFL, but instead their careers were suddenly over. Neither of them would ever play football again.

But we kept Andre Johnson and Keith Stanberry in the university athletic family on scholarship, and both of them went on to get their degrees.

So the encounter with Mrs. Johnson paid off for everybody. I never would have burnt out if they were all like that.

I wonder if she has any of that cracklin' bread she might send me?

Coaches turn each other in to the NCAA all the time and

clearly should do so. There are also so many NCAA investigators around looking into reported allegations that, if anyone cheats, he is eventually going to get caught. In fact, most of the major universities have by now hired their own former NCAA investigators to keep their own programs within the rules. It's the old revolving-door idea, like retiring generals play with defense contractors—you hire an NCAA guy to keep you straight with the NCAA.

There aren't many secrets in the recruiting jungle. I guarantee you that if any coach is foolish enough to offer an illegal inducement to an eighteen-year-old recruit, everyone will eventually know about it.

We heard about assistant coach Willie Anderson, Oklahoma State's recruiting coordinator, buying a car for Hart Lee Dykes of Bay City, Texas.

The whole damn world heard about it, didn't they, Willie?

Hart Lee Dykes's testimony to the NCAA helped to put four schools on probation—Illinois, Texas A&M, Oklahoma State, and Oklahoma, which I'll explain when I deal with our NCAA problems.

Willie Anderson had recruited for Clemson in the early eighties, when they won a national championship and were put on NCAA probation. After Oklahoma State hired him, a friend phoned me and said, "Look out for trouble." The NCAA had prohibited Willie from recruiting for two years while on Clemson's staff, but the penalty didn't travel with him when he was hired by Jimmy Johnson at OSU.

According to the official NCAA letter of inquiry to Oklahoma State, Willie was responsible for arranging for a gift of $5,000 in cash to Hart Lee, the provision of a new "sports automobile," and a $200 per month allowance. When the investigation was completed, it was revealed that Willie had used some high school coaches as his couriers for the money and that the car, which was arranged for by four specifically named OSU boosters, was a 1986 red Chevrolet IROC-Z purchased from Ayres Chevrolet in Edmond, Oklahoma.

This violated the number-one rule of recruiting—which is, if you give a player a car or money, *the player owns you*. For the rest of your life, you are his hostage, as George Smith held

Texas A&M hostage, and he can turn you in any time for any reason.

It was only two years after Willie bought him the car before Hart Lee Dykes told the whole story to the NCAA.

The reason Hart Lee Dykes ratted on Willie Anderson was to keep his eligibility at Oklahoma State. If a player becomes a witness for the NCAA, he is immune from punishment.

This NCAA tool is, I believe, a necessary evil, but I also believe it sends out a poor message to the kids who are being recruited, because it tells those who have their hands out that they can take all they want yet they will never have to pay any price for it if they are caught. All they have to do is cooperate when they are caught, and they can still play.

In the 1970s, before the NCAA changed the rules, a player could make enough money off his tickets to keep himself in pocket money. We gave each player six books of tickets to home games and six tickets to the Oklahoma-Texas game. Texas players used to phone our players to make deals for their Dallas tickets since the prices were higher in Oklahoma, because we were usually the favorites at this time. I've heard of players selling their Red River War tickets for as much as $200 each and season books for $400 to $500. Obviously, this was a windfall of $4,000 or more to players—all of it "illegal" by NCAA standards, but not for band members, cheerleaders, or anyone else who had access to tickets.

Now, of course, there are no more so-called hard tickets and a player can only put the names of members of his immediate family on a pass list—and they all have to sign at the gate.

I'm sure that some of you who have read the book to this point and who are interested in the recruiting wars are disappointed that I haven't told you that I offered or orchestrated inducements to prospective student-athletes.

That didn't happen. I'm sorry if you're disappointed, but if I had done it, I would have told you, because I don't plan on coaching college football again. I have no reason not to be candid and honest on this point, since I've already admitted to some violations (and will admit to more later), but in the years I coached at Oklahoma, I am not aware of any prospect being offered or given illegal inducements to come play for us.

But . . . I forgot. There was one car I bought for a kid I was trying to recruit to play for me at Oklahoma. He took the damn car and drove it to Fayetteville, Arkansas, where he now plays for the Razorbacks. His name is Greg Switzer . . . so I guess that makes it okay.

26

FICTION WRITERS

Old sportswriter friends like Orville Henry from Little Rock and Bill Connors of Tulsa tell me there was a time, not all that many years ago, when sportswriters were more interested in sports than in money or in being funny.

It was a good thing, according to my friends, that sportswriters didn't care much about money, because they got paid in fun instead of cash.

I know it's hard to believe looking at the sports pages today, but Orville and Bill say they used to go a whole season without writing about, or even thinking about, the salaries of professional baseball players—to cite an extreme example.

These days when you pick up the sports section in the morning, you will read something like this:

"In the ninth inning Rocco Calabresse, the $3,250,000 per year slugger, came up with one out and one on to face $4,575,000 relief pitcher Joseph Greed. Spunky third baseman Orlando Overflight, who has signed a five-year extension on his contract beginning at $2,800,000 this season with balloon payments up to $5,100,00 depending on the inflation index and the condo market in central Florida, was playing deep and on the line when Rocco smashed a hot grounder that Orlando fielded cleanly and fired to $1,950,000 rookie shortstop Ernesto Dinero, who touched second base just ahead of the sliding Dutch Krugerrand, who will ask arbitrators for a raise of $3,400,000 next spring, and threw to $4,350,000 first baseman George Washington Platinum to double up Rocco, who had paused midway to confer with his agent, Mal Merde, and his accountant, Joe Lightfingers—who take 30 percent of

Rocco's gross income—over an offer to do a TV commercial shaving with a Nabisco cookie for $3,000,000 and foreign residuals . . ."

To be fair, really, a sportswriter's byline today ought to say: BY DREW PINCHPURSE ($37,500 per year, plus dental insurance and about $200 a month skimmed from the expense account).

I do not have a lot of respect for many of today's sportswriters. Not only do they come equipped with almost no knowledge of how to play the games they are covering—most never did—they don't even know how to ask an intelligent question about the game or the coaching decisions involved in it.

There are some I call fiction writers, like Tom Weir, of *USA Today*. Bob Hersom, a sportswriter for *The Daily Oklahoman* and one of the few I respect, told me about a conversation he had with Tom Weir after his February 10, 1989, article blasting me personally and the Oklahoma program. For his own information, Bob wanted to know, after having read that article, whether Tom Weir had ever met Barry Switzer or talked to him in person or on the phone. I can answer that question for Bob. The answer is no. But here is a situation where a man has never met someone, doesn't know anything about him, but yet feels free to judge him and assassinate him in print. But this has always been the case. Barry Switzer and Oklahoma have always been used by writers as the worst-case example of what's wrong with college football, and I have never met any of them. It's been that way for years, even in the Bud Wilkinson era.

The sportswriters I like the least are the so-called serious reporters, who think a sports story must involve money, drugs, cheating, or controversy in some form or other.

These people don't go to a game and write, "Oklahoma won the toss and chose to receive . . ."

Their stories will start, "While carefully storing their ill-gotten gold and jewelry in the trainer's safe, Oklahoma's captains got word from a spy that the coin was fixed to turn up heads. They chose to receive so they could fumble. They had all bet the under . . ."

You find sportswriters crouched together in some hotel

saloon, swapping rumors and lies back and forth through the smoke and whiskey haze. They're the ones who tell each other things like, "Boy, you ought to see the parking lot outside the athletic dorm at Oklahoma! Greatest collection of wheels I've seen since Monte Carlo."

Chances are the one saying this has never seen our parking lot either, but that won't stop the tale.

"The parking lot is full of sports cars, I swear. Tinted windows, racing stripes, six-speaker stereos. One guy at Oklahoma has the sheer arrogance to drive a Mercedes right up to the dorm, and he doesn't give a damn who sees him."

Then another writer will say, "Yeah, how does Switzer explain that? Where do all those cars come from?"

This is what I mean about asking intelligent questions. "Where do the cars come from?" might be a good question if the writer asked me instead of asking another sportswriter.

My answer is that I don't know off the top of my head where any player's car came from, but all you have to do to find out is go to the OU athletic department and look it up on our automobile registration form, which is a requirement of the NCAA.

Every athlete's car is registered with the athletic department, along with details of its ownership and financing.

That Mercedes I mentioned? It was featured in a lot of newspapers. The car belonged to Spencer Tillman. The papers didn't report that it was a 1974 model—twelve years old—and that it had a big-time oil leak. But, hey, it's true, we did have a Mercedes in our parking lot.

Quarterback Charles Thompson got a shower of printer's ink when he told some writer that he always traveled in a long silver limousine and his driver parked anywhere he pleased on campus.

Can you imagine how tiny is the brain of a person who would believe this and then, without checking, write it in the newspaper? Fiction writers do.

And let me tell you something else about some fiction writers—they won't write it unless it's dirty, critical, or controversial. Charles Thompson, our quarterback, made the cover of *Sports Illustrated* for doping. Jerry Anderson should have been on the cover for what he did, but he wasn't written about, and basically no one outside of Oklahoma ever knew about him.

Jerry was a defensive back from Murfreesboro, Tennessee, who played on our 1975 national-championship team. He was the toughest, most physical defensive back I ever coached. In fact, he had more to do with our winning our second consecutive national championship than any other person with one play he made in the second quarter of the 1975 Orange Bowl versus Michigan. When Rick Leach, their great quarterback, scrambled down the sideline in front of the Michigan bench in a passing situation, he was hit and tackled so viciously by Jerry that Leach was knocked out and under the Michigan bench. Leach received such a blow that he never returned to the game.

In fact, Jerry was so good that the idea that he might have been seriously injured and lost for the season literally almost caused my secondary coach Bobby Proctor to have a heart attack . . . as a result of a joke. An old teammate of mine at Arkansas from Cotton Plant, Arkansas, Dale Boutwell, who Bobby had coached at Arkansas, came through town and I had an idea how I could get Bobby. All of the coaches except Bobby knew that I had dressed Dale, a man then in his early forties, in a football uniform and had him go through the early practice agility drills with the other defensive backs. He looked just like any one of several walk-on players we had, all dressed in orange jerseys.

We had set it up with Jerry Anderson that at the point they went into tackling drills, Boutwell would pair off with Jerry and go into him, appearing to give him a really good lick. Dale did it as every other coach on the field was watching out of one eye, and as it had been prearranged with Jerry, Jerry fell to the ground and started screaming in pain.

Everyone started running toward Jerry. Proctor got there first, panting and visibly flushed, and yelled, "What's wrong, Jerry? What's wrong?" "My knee, coach, my knee's gone. It's ruined," Jerry cried. Bobby was just about gone—he had vapor-locked—and just then Boutwell ran up to Proctor, who hadn't seen him in ten years, and said, "Is there anything I can do, coach?"

Proctor gasped and grabbed Boutwell by the face mask, yelling, "You walk-on son of a bitch, you've ruined Jerry."

Just at that moment, Dale jerked off his helmet and Jerry Anderson jumped up laughing. Proctor recognized Boutwell then and knew that he had been had. But the one who really nearly had a heart attack was Boutwell, who had to go through all the agility drills before we even got to the tackling drills, which was about twenty minutes of practice. But we all had a good laugh that day with Jerry Anderson, a great player and a great person, and at my good friend Bobby Proctor's expense.

But Jerry's story doesn't end in laughter. It ends in tears and sadness. After a short professional career, Jerry married and moved to Tulsa, Oklahoma. I had helped him get a job with American Airlines in Tulsa. On Memorial Day in 1985, Tulsa experienced a nine-inch rainfall and flooding all over the city. Several people drowned. But on that day, Jerry risked his life jumping into a swollen creek, where three children had been swept away. He was able to save two of them. The third child died, and Jerry often went back to the scene to try to figure out how he could have done it differently and saved that third child. Jerry was given a civic award for his heroism by the mayor of the city of Tulsa.

On Memorial Day 1989, Jerry was back in Murfreesboro on vacation, on a fishing trip with his relatives. Two young boys fell off a spillway. Jerry saw them fall and immediately recognized they were struggling for their lives. Without hesitation, Jerry dove in and got both boys up the bank before the current swept him away. He died saving those two boys, exactly four years to the day after he had saved the boys in Tulsa. All of these boys were strangers to Jerry.

People in Oklahoma know about Jerry. His friends knew him and loved him and miss him. But you never read about Jerry in the national press. He's the one who really should have been on the cover of *Sports Illustrated*, not Charles Thompson. The fiction writers would rather write about dopers, shooters, and rapists. They don't want to write about heroes.

27

HAVE YOU PISSED FOR THE TRAINER TODAY?

For the last five years that I was head football coach at Oklahoma, we had a drug-testing program that was far superior to that of any other school I knew about in the NCAA and made the NFL's drug-testing program look like a total joke.

Our program was in place long before most other schools had one and was such an efficient deterrent that one of our regents, Sam Noble, denounced our test results in 1988 as unbelievable.

For that season, in 2,066 tests for street drugs, we turned up seven football players caught smoking marijuana and zero caught with cocaine in their urine.

Sam Noble said, "Why, you can grab any hundred people off the street, or out of the Noble Foundation, and you'll find more dope users than that."

Hell yes, you can.

But just any hundred people off the street were not faced with being tested for street drugs up to three times a week during the season and once a week during the spring and then at random during the summer, when we'd catch a player on campus and make him pee in a bottle. And three times a year we tested them for steroids. If a player failed any test, it could lead to him losing his scholarship and being kicked off the team.

Go test a hundred fraternity boys, bus drivers, stock brokers, sportswriters, or English professors, and you will find a lot more dopers than you would find on the Oklahoma football team.

Put our drug-testing program into effect at fraternity houses, campus dorms, and faculty offices, and you would see a hell of a lot of people leaving school.

It's not that I want to give everybody a drug test. Far from it. I don't believe in a police state.

But I strapped this heavy testing program on our football team in the spring of 1984 so I would know what the hell was really going on, apart from rumors.

Our head trainer, Dan Pickett, wrote us a program that spring. There weren't really any guidelines at the time. So Dan set up a program the way we thought it should be.

We thought the testing should be weekly and continuous.

By comparison, the University of Texas, in November 1989, started a program that calls for each athlete to be tested once a year for drugs banned by the NCAA. The Southwest Conference conducts random tests for steroids but for no other drugs. Testing once a year for street drugs (cocaine stays in the body only seventy-two hours), you are only going to catch players who are stupid or unlucky. I wanted to put a stop to drugs, not play roulette with them.

But during the 1984 season, a couple of players came to me and said guys were cheating on our tests by substituting other urine samples for their own. We won the Big Eight championship, but in the Orange Bowl loss to Washington, there were two or three stupid mistakes made on the field by one of our players who I had heard was using dope but not getting caught.

After that game, I jumped all over Dan Pickett.

Now Dan, you must understand, has a very big job as head athletic trainer. Not only do he and his assistants tape ankles and care for the injuries and the emotional problems of a hundred football players, they also do it for basketball, baseball, wrestling, track—you name it.

The athletic trainer's profession is old and honorable and vitally important.

But not until January 1985 did it include actually watching streams of urine coming out of the heads of penises thousands of times a year.

I hate to be so gross and blunt about it, but that's the fact of the matter.

Dan protested at first. "This is degrading," he said.

"Yeah, Dan, I know it is," I said. "But if you don't personally eyeball every stream of pee as it pours into the bottle, how can we be sure they're not switching samples or cheating in some way?"

"I won't do it," Dan said.

"Damnit, you sure as hell better do it. And don't be intimidated by any player or anybody else. Your number-one priority from now on is watching young men pee."

"That's sick," Dan said.

"I know it is, but it's the times we live in. Our society is sick. But I'll tell you one damn thing. We are not going to have a team of dopers playing football at Oklahoma."

When Dan first started testing all our athletes, it was the wrestling team that burned holes in the bottles.

One wrestler noticed Dan looking away for an instant and passed his bottle through the fresh water flowing into the urinal as he flushed it. He handed Dan a clear bottle of ice-cold pee.

The relationship of the trainer and the athlete is really important. The athlete has got to trust the trainer and his skills, must have faith in the trainer's judgment. If a player gets hurt on the field and the trainer tells him it is all right to continue playing, the player has to know the trainer knows what he is talking about and that he has the player's best interests at heart.

But the trainer has to put on the black hat when it's time to pee. A player may say, "Dan, I can't pee right now." And Dan has to reply, "That's too bad. You better work up a pee or else work up an explanation for Coach Switzer."

The first few years, we divided our football team into seven groups for testing. Each group had some offensive players, some defensive players, some underclassmen, and some upperclassmen—so we wouldn't be pointing the finger at anyone in particular.

One day I might tell Dan, "Test group two and group six this afternoon. Tomorrow, test group three and hit group six again to see if we can catch anybody falling asleep."

The players never knew when or how often they might be tested.

It's difficult to catch kids doing street drugs like cocaine, speed, LSD, PCP, and other water-based drugs because the body flushes them in three days.

Marijuana is easy to catch. It stays in the system for weeks.

But of course our ultimate aim is not to *catch* kids doing dope. Our goal is to *stop* them from doing dope.

However, I got furious at Dan Pickett for not catching Brian Bosworth with steroids in his system before our Orange Bowl game with Arkansas at the end of the 1986 season. It was the NCAA that caught Bosworth, instead—a major embarrassment to us all.

But let me tell you Dan's side of the story.

Our street-drug test samples were analyzed by a lab in Norman that could give us results in twenty-four hours, at about $5 per pop.

For steroids—a much more difficult test—Dan sent our samples to the Roche Lab in Bloomington, Indiana.

I had announced to the team that anybody caught doing steroids was gone. Goodbye.

The October before that Orange Bowl game in question, we did a steroid test and sent the samples off to Roche at Indiana. Honestly, we were afraid we might have caught some.

But Dan came to my office with the results—and we were clean. I was excited; our weight coach was excited. We had a clean bill from the Roche Lab.

In December, the NCAA crew came to Norman to do their first steroid testing. They collected twenty-eight samples and sent them to the U.S. Olympic Laboratory at UCLA. I wasn't worried about that one at all.

But the results came back with three guys showing positive for steroids. One of them was Brian Bosworth.

I don't know how the UCLA lab could find something they couldn't find at the Roche Lab in Indiana. I went to Dan Pickett and jumped his ass again.

Here's what happened in Bosworth's case.

Bosworth was in the hospital sick as a dog with the flu when the NCAA crew arrived in Norman. He was being fed through tubes. He couldn't keep anything in his stomach. But the NCAA crew chief said, "Well, this guy has got to pee for us by noon or else we turn him in as positive. Get Bosworth over here right now."

"He can't come here. He's in the hospital," Dan protested.

"Then we'll just mark him down as positive for steroids," the NCAA fellow said.

Dan finally talked the NCAA crew into going to the hospital, where they found Bosworth as truly ill as Dan had said he was. You remember how you feel with a bad case of the flu? How would you like to open your eyes in your chills and fever and nausea and see some jerk standing there holding out a plastic bottle and saying, "Hey, you! You piss right now!"

The NCAA crew made the nurses keep pouring juices into Brian for forty-five minutes, until he could finally provide them a urine sample.

As you can imagine, this sample was far more concentrated than usual. It was the very dregs of his kidneys.

It was this sample that UCLA said contained steroids.

Poor Dan had to defend Roche and Indiana for the next forty-eight hours while we all screamed at him.

The positive result came back from UCLA on December 23. Bosworth was out of the hospital by then and had gone home for Christmas. On December 24, I sent Dan Pickett to Dallas to collect another sample from Bosworth so we could get a third opinion.

Bosworth met him at the airport at 1 P.M. on Christmas Eve and peed in a cup. The sample left at 3:30 P.M. on a flight for Chicago, to be tested at an independent lab. Technicians picked up this bottle of pee at O'Hare Airport at 5 P.M. They drove straight to their lab and worked on analyzing this sample until 4 A.M.

They phoned Dan before dawn on Christmas Day and said they had found "traces" of steroids in Bosworth's urine.

I don't know exactly how much a trace is—and they couldn't really explain it—but it was enough to keep Bosworth out of the Orange Bowl.

We paid $600 to have that sample analyzed. Routine steroid tests cost from $85 to $125. Multiply those numbers by a hundred football players by hundreds of NCAA schools, and you can see what a tremendous financial enterprise drug testing has become.

You want to know the ironic thing about all this?

We don't test for the drug that causes far and away more

problems on campus than all the rest of the drugs put together.

That drug is, of course, alcohol.

If the NCAA had the same rules against drinking alcohol
that it has against other street drugs, I guess it would be
Bringham Young vs. Oral Roberts for the national championship.

28

LET'S COME BACK TO THAT ONE

On the morning of December 30, 1989, I was staying at the Anatole Hotel in Dallas, getting ready to watch my son Greg play for the University of Arkansas against Tennessee in the Cotton Bowl game.

Jimmy Sanders, from Pine Bluff, Arkansas, an old friend and now a high school coach in Dallas, came by to see me at the hotel and said, "Barry, if you don't go see Wendell Mosley pretty quick, you'll never see him again."

You readers will remember Wendell Mosley as the assistant coach who told us in the spring of 1972 we were going to have to find another position for Greg Pruitt to play because he had recruited a freshman named Little Joe Washington.

In fact, I've mentioned Wendell several times, but there are a number of stories I haven't told about him yet. I think of Wendell often, like when I'll be walking through an airport someplace and some black person I've never seen before will come up and shake my hand and thank me for what we did at Oklahoma way back at the beginning of the 1970s—playing the black athletes in big numbers far ahead of anybody else in the Southwest, Midwest, or South. The Sooners had black quarterbacks before most schools in the areas I mentioned even had blacks with letter jackets. And Wendell Mosley was a big part of that.

But I had been so wrapped up in my own adventures of late that I had lost track of my old friend Wendell.

"What do you mean I'll never see him again?" I asked Sanders in my room at the Anatole Hotel.

"Wendell is in the veterans' hospital out in South Dallas. He's dying of cancer. His ex-wife, Lois, knows about it, but he hasn't told hardly anybody else. You know how proud he is of his appearance, and now he's all eaten up."

I took my son to lunch after football practice, and then I drove to the veterans' hospital and went searching for Wendell.

I found him in a room, tubes sticking in him, his body shrunken, a mask over his nose and mouth. His eyes showed his pleasure when he recognized me, but they also showed that he was in terrible pain that couldn't be hidden. I stood beside his bed and held his hand.

A young white female doctor came in with a clipboard, checking Wendell to see if he was still coherent.

"Mr. Mosley, I have to ask you a couple of questions," the doctor said. "What is your name?"

"Wendell Frazier Mosley," Wendell said.

"Very good," the doctor said. "Do you know where you are right now?"

"Hospital."

"Good, but we have to be more specific. Do you know which hospital this is?"

Wendell squinted, as if he was concentrating hard. He looked at the doctor.

"Let's come back to that one," Wendell said.

I started laughing. I know it may not seem like an appropriate time or place to be laughing, but I can't tell you how often in the last twenty years Wendell, when stumped for an answer, had said those words to me. Wendell was conning this young doctor. I looked into his eyes and saw a flash of the old Wendell, and I squeezed his hand.

For the next two hours I stood holding Wendell's hand and talking about his great days and the great days we had had together. Wendell could talk a little bit through his mask, but it was enough for me to know he was keeping up with me as the memories came pouring back . . .

Everybody who knew Wendell Mosley was always telling what we called Wendellisms. Some of them may sound sort of cruel, as if we are making fun of Wendell. But Wendell always purposefully set himself up to be the butt of the joke, and by the time you caught on to it, he would have already passed you and be setting up another one.

Wendell was the kind of guy who would lie to you and you would know he was lying and he would know you knew he was lying, but he would keep on lying; but the whole thing was all right because it was Wendell.

Wendell was one of a kind. Back in the early 1970s we had a great all-American receiver named Tinker Owens, who I've always felt was better at his position than his brother Steve was . . . and Steve won the Heisman Trophy. One day during that era, a *Sports Illustrated* writer doing a story on Tinker came into our dressing room after practice one day early in the week. We were talking about Tinker, and then just as Wendell comes into the room and within earshot, the writer said, "That Tinker's got charisma."

Wendell looked shocked, and concerned. "Well, shit! Will he be all right by Saturday?" he said.

Wendell had that faint smile on his lips. He never missed a chance.

I've already told you that we called him Dead Set, because on our sideline during a game he wore a headset that wasn't plugged in. He did it so his several girlfriends, who he had placed separately around the stadium, would think Wendell was really running the show.

Galen Hall, our offensive coach with whom I coached for eighteen years, particularly loved to pull jokes on and with Wendell. One of them happened one day when we were hanging half a hundred on some opponent and just after we had scored our fiftieth point. Galen noticed that Wendell was on the sideline visiting with some high school recruits and not paying attention to the game. An idea occurred to him, and he quickly told Charlie North, an assistant coach who did have a working headset, to "Go tell Wendell to get the receiving team ready." Charlie grabbed Wendell and said, "Galen says get the receiving team ready."

Wendell then started screaming, "Receiving team! Receiving team!" And all of these eleven kids gathered around Wendell with this quizzical look on their faces. Finally, one of them timidly said, "But, Coach Mosley, we just scored." Wendell erupted, "Aw, shit! Galen!"

I always had a habit of walking into the coaches' dressing room before a ball game, while the coaches were getting ready to take the team out on the field. I remember in the early 1970s we were playing Kansas, back when they had a good football team with David Jaynes, a really outstanding quarterback, and I came into the dressing room and walked up to each coach and asked what he thought about the game and what we were going to have to do to win.

Bobby Proctor, our secondary coach, said we had to put on a good, coordinated pass rush to make their quarterback throw the ball early, because they had good receivers that our guys couldn't stay with very long.

Galen Hall said we had to establish ball control. Our offense had to keep the ball for long periods of time to prevent the Kansas offense from entering the game. Their quarterback couldn't hurt us from the bench.

I went around to each coach, and each one had an answer. They all expected it to be a tough game.

Wendell happened to be the last coach as I went around the room. He was leaning back in one of our lounge chairs with his feet propped up on a table.

"What about it, Coach Mosley?" I said. "What do you think we'll have to do?"

Wendell puffed on his cigar, looked up at me, and said, "Coach, all the angels and the archangels in heaven ain't gonna keep Kansas from getting an ass-whipping today."

He was right, of course. We scored 45 points in the first half. Wendell walked the sideline making noises like starting an engine, revving up one of those high-powered Indianapolis 500 cars, like that was us—a Big Red machine.

Wendell and Lois always came over to my house for the then-customary victory party. He usually walked in revving his mouth engine to let everybody know he had arrived. One such evening I was sitting back at the kitchen bar, having a drink with Rex Norris and some other coaches, when Wendell came in.

Rex reached down and picked up a box of Cat Chow that Kay and I fed to our two Siamese cats—Sam and Suzie

Switzer—and poured a bowlful of it. He set the bowl on the counter and hid the cat-food box. Wendell came over and fixed himself a drink, took a place at the bar.

We were all telling stories. In a couple of minutes Rex grabbed a handful of Cat Chow and pretended to be munching on it while we talked. Then Galen Hall took a handful of cat food and acted as if he were eating it. I was sitting there thinking, Oh no, Wendell, please don't.

But Wendell fetched himself a great big fistful of Cat Chow and chomped it right down. We were all talking, looking at him out of the corners of our eyes.

After his third handful in about five minutes, Wendell took a drink and finally said, "God almighty, do you white boys really *like* this shit?"

After he and Lois got divorced, Wendell had lots of girlfriends. He needed football tickets for them. Wendell would go to Jerry Pettibone, who was in charge of our recruiting tickets, and say, "Jerry, I've got four great prospects, all of them fullbacks, who want to see this game. But I don't want these kids to see each other. So let me have two tickets in this section and two tickets in that section and two over here and two over there . . ."

Jerry knew what Wendell was doing. He was keeping his girlfriends apart. One game, Gene Hochevar took charge of the tickets, and instead of splitting them up, he left six tickets at the will-call gate for Wendell's friends in the section behind our bench.

Right before kickoff, Gene, who was on the sideline with Jerry, called Wendell over and pointed to the stands and said, "Wendell, aren't those some great-looking sisters sitting up there together?" Wendell, who had not yet looked up there, turned and to his amazement saw all of his girlfriends sitting together in a covey. He screamed, "What have you sons of bitches done to me?"

One night we were flying back in Riviana Foods' private jet from a recruiting trip to Houston when we encountered some big thunderstorms in the Dallas area. Sam Meason, vice-president of Riviana, was sitting back talking to Wendell and me when the pilot opened the door and said, "Mr. Meason, we're going to have to divert around the storms to reach Oklahoma City and it's going to be close on fuel. Do you think we should land in Dallas and fuel up?"

Before Meason could say a word, Wendell's eyes went wide and he spoke up. "You land this son of a bitch now!" he screamed. "The only time a plane has too much fuel is when it's on fire."

After two hours beside his hospital bed that December day, I said goodbye to Wendell and went back to the Anatole Hotel. I told him I planned to come back the next day.

I phoned Donnie Duncan at his home in Norman and told him about Wendell. Donnie and Wendell had worked together for years on our OU staff.

The next day was December 31 and Donnie had to fly to Miami to represent OU as its athletic director at the Orange Bowl. But he got up at five o'clock in the morning and caught a plane to DFW Airport. I picked him up at seven-thirty and drove him to the veterans' hospital.

Wendell was so happy to see him. We sat for another two and a half hours telling tales about the old days.

We reminded Wendell about 1976, when he came into my office and said, "Barry, my alma mater is calling me. Texas Southern wants me to come back home as head coach."

I said, "Wendell, you're just going to go down there and get your ass fired like the guy they just got rid of. You can't build a winning program at Texas Southern."

"Yes I can, Barry. It's going to be a little Oklahoma the way I run it. They promised me a good salary and a big athletic budget. And on top of that, they are giving me a brand new Cadillac the day I arrive on campus."

Well, Wendell went to Texas Southern. Before long he was on the phone to me. "Barry, I want to put on a clinic for the high school coaches in Houston. How about sending your coaching staff down here? I need your coaches to speak at the clinic."

I said, "Wendell, can you pay them?"

"No."

"Hell, our guys won't come down there for nothing."

"For me they will," Wendell said. "I'll get them rooms in the dorm and take care of them. All I need is somebody to buy their plane tickets."

"Don't you have any rich alums to send a jet for them?"

"You know better than that, Barry. What I was thinking was that you could fly them down here for me."

I did it. When they got to Texas Southern, Wendell showed them his office and his Cadillac and big-timed it pretty strong. Donnie Duncan, a great practical joker, sneaked in and left a message on Wendell's desk pad that said, "Dean Blevins called about transferring to Texas Southern."

You need to understand that Dean Blevins was a white quarterback, the son of the minister of the Trinity Baptist Church of Norman. In high school Dean had been all-state in football and basketball. He had been our starting quarterback until a freak injury just before the 1976 Texas game put him on the bench and brought in Thomas Lott for a long, successful run at quarterback. And Texas Southern was an all-black school, besides.

Later that evening Wendell told Donnie, "We've got a serious problem. I got a message that Dean Blevins called and wants to transfer." Donnie said, "You'd better not call Dean before you talk to Barry about it." Wendell agreed. "You're right." So the matter was dropped for the time being.

They all went to dinner, had a few drinks, and went to bed.

The next morning Wendell picked up Donnie and the other coaches to go back to the clinic. As they were on their way, Wendell said to Donnie, "Donnie, we've got a more serious problem this morning." Donnie, who had completely forgotten about the Dean Blevins message, said, "What the hell are you talking about, Wendell?" Wendell said, "We've got more serious problems. Dean Blevins *called me last night.*" Donnie said, "Dammit, Wendell, I put that damn message on your desk. Blevins hasn't called you." Wendell said, "Aw, Donnie, you caught me again!"

Remember what I told you about Wendell lying.

A couple of years later I was in Houston for the Lombardi Award, a black-tie banquet for about 1,500 people in a downtown hotel. We had Greg Roberts, our all-American guard, as one of the four finalists.

I was standing with a bunch of other coaches at the cocktail reception before the banquet, and Wendell came in. He looked very blue and down. He had just been fired that week.

Wendell said, "I've got to find a job. I'm lower than whale shit."

"At least you've still got your Cadillac," somebody said.

"Yeah, great deal! They gave me the Cadillac and the payments. I've got a three-year-old Cadillac and seven more years of payments on it," Wendell said. "The bastards took out a ten-year loan in my name when they bought that car."

In the hospital, Wendell and Donnie and I all laughed at that story. It was time for me to drive Donnie to the airport so he could catch his flight to the Orange Bowl. We finally had to leave Wendell and told him we'd get back to him.

Wendell Frazier Mosley died that night.

The funeral home got in touch with me and said Wendell's last request was that Donnie Duncan and I speak at his funeral. He had known he was dying and had made arrangements earlier in the week.

There were other football comrades who came in from around the country for Wendell's funeral, too—Greg Pruitt, Billy Sims, Joe Washington, Larry Lacewell, Gene Hochevar, Jimmy Sanders, Billy Lyons (the University of Texas's first black coach), and Wendell's former staff from Texas Southern.

We all had a few words to contribute to his eulogy.

The preacher who spoke just before me started by saying, "Anybody that knew Wendell well knew he was a smooooooth operator . . ."

So when it was my turn to get up and speak, I said, "You've made it easy for me to talk about Wendell. He was the all-time con artist. He used to con us all the time and didn't mind if we knew it. But we all loved him, because as you said, he was such a smooooooth operator."

So long, Big Boy. We'll miss you.

29

THE SIXTEEN NCAA CHARGES . . . AND A LOT MORE

Writing this chapter, in particular, is not a lot of fun. It brings back a lot of memories, mostly angry ones, but it is a necessary exercise for both me and you to go through if the whole story is going to make sense.

The following allegations of rules violations were asserted by the NCAA in its official letter of inquiry dated February 25, 1988. The allegations came from an investigation made by the NCAA, with full cooperation of the University of Oklahoma and its athletic department. The university provided all necessary records, documents, and accounts and made appropriate personnel available for interviews.

ALLEGED RULES VIOLATIONS

1. ALLEGATION In the spring of 1984, an alumnus of the university allegedly provided a prospective student-athlete a used automobile and employed the young man during the summer of 1984 for which he was paid but did not work. Further, a staff member allegedly provided the prospective student-athlete automobile transportation from his home to the alumnus's place of business in Oklahoma, the place of

employment for the prospective student-athlete, where he picked up the automobile in question. Apparently, however, the staff member was not aware that the automobile was provided at no cost or that the young man was not required to work for the weekly payments he received.

1. ANSWER   This involved Kert Kaspar, a linebacker we recruited out of Houston. Kert wasn't a real difference maker, but he was a solid football player who was recruited by nearly every Southwest Conference school. Mike Jones was my assistant coach who did the basic recruiting work on Kert Kaspar. Kert had been here for nearly four years before the NCAA investigators started coming around asking questions about him.

A kid from Tulsa named Richard Davis had transferred from Oklahoma to Arizona State. NCAA investigators routinely go into the field to question transfers about their experience at other institutions. You know, if you find a kid with a chip on his shoulder who thinks he has been treated unfairly at his previous school, he is a good candidate to blow the whistle for the sake of revenge.

The NCAA quizzed Richard Davis about Oklahoma. What did we offer him when we recruited him? How much were we paying him? What had he heard from other OU athletes?

Well, he couldn't think of anything to tell them except that they ought to check out Kaspar. Davis said he'd seen Kert driving a car with an Oklahoma license plate from an Oklahoma dealership, and Davis thought that might be unusual since Kert was from Houston.

The investigation turned up the story that the summer Kert Kaspar signed with Oklahoma, Mike Jones arranged a job for him. Kert was going to work for Bill Lambert, from Lindsey, Oklahoma. Bill Lambert has an oil-field supply service and a pool of company cars. Mike Jones asked Bill if he had any work in the Houston area where he could use Kert. Bill said, "Yeah, I've got some things going personally in the Houston area and energy-related business in other areas, and I can use him."

Unbeknownst to me or anybody else on the staff, Mike

Jones drove to Houston and picked up Kert and drove the kid
back to Lindsey, Oklahoma, to meet with Bill Lambert and
find out what the summer job would be in Houston. Bill told
Kert the pay would be $300 a week and he could drive a
company car for the summer in Houston, like other
employees did. If other employees do it, an athlete can legally
do it. An athlete can't be paid more than anybody else, but he
can be provided the same benefits.

So far the only violation Oklahoma had in the Kaspar case
was the fact that Mike had gone down and driven the kid in
Mike's own car to meet with a prospective employer. That is
an NCAA violation, for sure.

Now Kaspar drove back to Houston in a company car for
his summer job. Bill Lambert put him on the payroll and the
computer started sending him his paychecks. But Bill never
did call the kid and tell him what job he was supposed to do
for the money. Kaspar received checks all summer long from
Bill Lambert's company, and drove the company car, and
never did a day's work.

When it was time to go back to school in the fall, Lambert
told him to keep the company car. Lambert said the company
didn't need it, that Kaspar could take it on back to Oklahoma
and drive it as long as he needed it. So here is another definite
violation. It wouldn't have been a major infraction if we had
reported it at the time on our own, but I didn't know about it
until nearly three years later.

Bill Lambert had established a relationship with Kaspar.
Lambert wasn't even an OU alum. He was just interested in
athletics. He left Kaspar to drive that car for two years. Now,
we had a major violation that wasn't orchestrated by the
university or known to me. I asked Mike Jones why he hadn't
told me much earlier so I could self-report the incident and
thus remove it from the major-violation category into
something far less serious. Mike said he wasn't aware of any
violation except driving Kaspar to Lindsey, Oklahoma.

Guilty.

2. ALLEGATION   During the 1984–85 academic year, a staff
member allegedly twice gave a prospective student-athlete a
ride to the young man's home, where the young man met with

two staff members. On one occasion, a staff member gave the young man a T-shirt and turf shoes, both with the university's emblem on them.

2. ANSWER   This was during our recruitment of Hart Lee Dykes. The coach involved was Mike Jones again. If you, as a recruiter, are in the town of the prospective student-athlete and the kid is at high school, you are not allowed to put him in your car, whether it's a rental car or your personal car, and drive him home from school. I know this sounds ridiculous. The intent of the rule is to say we cannot provide transportation like air tickets home or buying a car, but the rule is so broad that giving a kid a lift to the barber shop, or—in this case—taking him home to his family, is strictly forbidden. The kid has either got to walk, ride with a buddy, hitchhike, take a bus, whatever—he must provide his own transportation. But Mike Jones drove Hart Lee Dykes home, a violation.

And while he was at it, Mike Jones gave Hart Lee Dykes a new pair of Nike athletic shoes that said OKLAHOMA on them, a really dumb thing to do.

This is why it was especially dumb. Hart Lee Dykes was going to be the top recruit in Texas that year. All the coaches knew he had his hand out. Hart Lee's two basketball coaches were handling his recruitment. His football coach stayed totally out of it. Hart Lee was an excellent basketball player, and recruiting comes during basketball season, so basically it was his basketball coaches who had to be dealt with.

I told Mike Jones specifically not to get swept up in the competition over Hart Lee Dykes. This was brought out in testimony before the NCAA in Kansas City. They asked, "Did Coach Switzer tell you not to get involved with Hart Lee Dykes to the extent of breaking any rules?" And Mike answered, "Yes, he did."

The NCAA said, "But you went ahead and violated the rules?" And Mike said, "Yes, I did."

What he was talking about was giving Hart Lee a T-shirt and a pair of shoes.

When I had my one official visit in Hart Lee's home, I

went to his bedroom. In there, he had all the paraphernalia of
the recruiting system. His walls were covered with posters
from all the major football schools. Neatly lined up on the
floor were at least nine pair of brand-new size 13 or 14 athletic
shoes of all types with schools' emblems—Texas A&M,
Oklahoma State, whatever—on them. He had warmup outfits
from all the schools and T-shirts from all the schools. These
things were his trophies. Hart Lee, by the rules, should have
purchased all these items and paid the full price for them.
What a joke. I bet he had a receipt for every one of them,
though.

It wouldn't have made a damn bit of difference in getting
Hart Lee, but Mike Jones did give him shoes and a T-shirt.

Guilty.

3. ALLEGATION   During the 1984–85 academic year, an
alumnus allegedly provided local automobile transportation
and purchased lunch for a prospective student-athlete's
brother.

3. ANSWER   Yes, we did it. Without even a coach around, some
alum drove a recruit's brother someplace and later bought
lunch for the recruit's brother. I didn't hear about it until the
NCAA told me three years later. I'm sure the alum had no
idea he was doing anything wrong. He was just doing a favor
for a kid.

Guilty.

4. ALLEGATION   During the 1983–84 academic year, while
recruiting a prospective student-athlete, two staff members
allegedly led the young man to believe that extra benefits
would be provided to him if he enrolled at the university.

4. ANSWER   This was Lucious Selmon telling a recruit in East
Texas that Lucious would "look after" the kid if he came to
Oklahoma. What Lucious meant was he would help the kid
adjust to life in a major athletic and academic program.
Lucious himself was "taken care of" at Oklahoma, but he
didn't receive any monetary benefits. Hell, Lucious wore the
same pair of wing-tip shoes for three years.

This was a matter of a great black player and coach, Lucious, trying to establish a one-to-one, father-and-son type of relationship with a scared black youngster and reassuring the kid that Lucious would watch over him.

It would have been entirely different if they were sitting in the kid's home in front of all the family and the banker and the car dealer were there telling the kid and his mother and father, "Hey, you go to Oklahoma and we'll take care of you."

Nothing like that happened. Are we guilty? It depends on what you want to believe Lucious Selmon meant by "We'll take care of you." But I would add that if you know Lucious Selmon, you know damn well we were not guilty of this one.

5. ALLEGATION During 1985, a staff member allegedly offered $1,000 cash in an envelope to a prospective student-athlete on high school premises to induce the young man to sign a letter of intent with the university. The staff member allegedly telephoned a relative of the young man and advised that he was planning to give the prospective student-athlete $1,000.

5. ANSWER This brings us back to Hart Lee Dykes. The NCAA charged that Mike Jones was in the high school gym on signing day. We were clearly out of the race by then. Everybody in the recruiting business knew the package Oklahoma State had offered Hart Lee Dykes had a total value of $25,000—it included a brand-new sports car, $5,000 cash for signing, and $200 per month during his career. Do you think that in the eleventh hour Mike Jones would rush to Hart Lee Dykes and offer him $1,000 in an envelope? And then tell Hart Lee's relatives about it on the phone? Hart Lee and his whole family would have laughed us out of town for our miserly gesture. This allegation is downright embarrassing. It makes us sound like fools as well as crooks.

Dan Beebe, the NCAA investigator looking into the Hart Lee Dykes case, interviewed me in the Law School on campus and told me Hart Lee supposedly was insulted at our offer and gave the $1,000 back to Mike Jones.

"Why would he do that?" I said. "Why wouldn't he just put it in his pocket and go ahead and sign with Oklahoma

State? Giving money back is not consistent with the Hart Lee Dykes I know."

Mike Jones denied he offered $1,000 to Dykes, and I believe him. I think this charge came about because of the vindictiveness of Willie Anderson, who had to resign at Oklahoma State after I told the NCAA what I knew about Willie's tactics.

In my opinion this "violation" never occurred; Mike never offered Hart Lee Dykes a dime in cash. It was totally fabricated by the "players" involved and the entire story was absurd, but the NCAA chose to believe it anyway. Which, of course, says an awful lot about the willingness of the NCAA to believe anything negative about Oklahoma, no matter how poor the credibility of the persons making the allegations.

Not guilty.

6. ALLEGATION   During the 1984–85 academic year, during a recruiting contact at the home of a prospective student-athlete, a staff member allegedly made statements to the relatives of the young man that led them to believe the prospective student-athlete would receive extra benefits if he enrolled at the university.

6. ANSWER   This again is an allegation that Lucious Selmon supposedly led Hart Lee Dykes to believe that he would receive "extra benefits" if he came to school at Oklahoma. This is as ludicrous as the other charge related to Lucious. But I'll say this: Hart Lee Dykes sure as hell wasn't going to go anywhere he didn't get something under the table. We just weren't willing to compete for him that way.

Not guilty.

7. ALLEGATION   Prior to and during the 1984 football season, a staff member allegedly sold a season football ticket for each of two student-athletes and gave them the cash received, which was more than the tickets had originally sold for. The staff member allegedly did the same thing for one of the same student-athletes prior to the 1985 football season and offered to do so for another student-athlete.

7. ANSWER   This was back during the period when the NCAA
allowed schools to give the players two season ticket books,
hard tickets, which were, in the right hands, as good as gold.
Years ago, long prior to the 1984–85 year that this charge
relates to, Oklahoma and almost every other major institution
would help its players get some extra cash by helping them sell
their tickets for more than the face value.

So many schools had gotten into trouble for this by 1984,
however, that they quit doing it—at least on an organized
basis. There is no question, however, but that this one
happened. One of our staff members did, as a personal favor
to several players, including Troy Aikman (the great throwing
quarterback I helped transfer to UCLA, now of the Dallas
Cowboys), sell his tickets. Interestingly, and to Troy's credit, in
his initial statement to the NCAA Troy said that the staff
member in question had sold not only his season tickets but
also his Oklahoma-Texas game ticket. He later corrected that
misstatement and remembered that his Texas ticket had not
been sold by or through a staff member.

Thanks, Troy. But we were guilty of most of this
charge. Under new NCAA rules, players are not allowed to
get hard tickets. They have to give the names of specific
close family members they authorize to pass through the
players' gate.

8. ALLEGATION   During the 1984–85 academic year, a staff
member allegedly gave a student-athlete $10 to $20 for
incidental expenses on at least two occasions.

8. ANSWER   Originally, the NCAA charged that our recruiting
coordinator, Shirley Vaughan, had *given* $10 cash to Chris
Richards (another kid who transferred). We disputed that
charge, and then when we were able to interview Chris
ourselves, he admitted that Shirley had only *loaned* him the
money.

Guilty—to the amended charge. When a kid needs help, it
is sometimes difficult to look the other way and not help him.

9. ALLEGATION   In July 1984, a staff member allegedly
arranged for a prospective student-athlete to receive a free

one-way airline ticket to travel from his home to Oklahoma
City, in order to accept summer employment. Finally, in
November 1984, after the young man enrolled at the
university, the staff member allegedly arranged for the young
man to receive a free round-trip airline ticket to travel from
Oklahoma City to his home.

9. ANSWER   This was transfer Chris Richards again. Scott
Hill told me that he arranged for the two airline tickets for
Chris at the request of Chris's parents, Walter and Celeste
Johns.
        Guilty of helping a kid on that one, too.

10. ALLEGATION   On several weekends in January and
February 1985, a staff member allegedly arranged for rented
vehicles to be provided to student-athlete hosts for
entertainment of prospective student-athletes during the
prospects' official paid visits to the university campus. The
rental cost of the vehicles was paid from the staff member's
personal checking account after another staff member
provided funds for the expense.

10. ANSWER   This violation involved me personally and
directly.
        On several weekends during January and February, we
would bring kids in from all over the country to visit our
campus for recruiting purposes. Perfectly legal. But here
comes the ridiculous rule that has to be changed. Imagine
what the weather is like in Norman in January and February.
If you can't, I'll tell you—it is often bitter cold, with blue
northers roaring down across the plains, bringing sleet and
snow. You might spend many thousands of dollars as a
recruiter traveling to the prospect's home, and finally you fly
him in from Los Angeles or Washington or wherever for his
official visit.
        Suppose we have thirty recruits coming this certain
weekend. We get student-athletes who are already on campus
to show them around.
        Believe it or not, a lot of our athletes don't own cars.
During this particular period the NCAA is referring to, the

weather was terrible. We wouldn't have a chance in the world
to sign a kid if we brought him to Norman and then made
him walk around the campus in the snow and cold.

So I rented vans. I personally paid the Ford people $700
to bring us some vans. I didn't know if this was a violation or
not. I didn't ask the athletic department, because they might
have said it was, and I didn't want the recruits to think we
were stupid.

It turned out to be a violation, all right. But the violation
was not that the recruits *rode* in these vans, it was that athletes
who were already enrolled *drove* the vans—and it was not
under "institutional control," because I paid the bill myself.

Guilty.

11. ALLEGATION   From at least December 1984 to May 1985, it
is alleged that a staff member utilized funds from a private
checking account to supplement salaries of other staff
members; to pay for rental vehicles used by student hosts to
entertain prospective student-athletes; to pay money to a
resident of another state who assisted the staff members in
recruiting efforts by providing local transportation in that
other state; and to advance sums on two occasions for other
staff members' recruiting trips.

11. ANSWER   I violated institutional control again. Since we
are a state institution, we have to go through certain red tape
and procedures for everything. I hired Jim Donnan from the
University of Missouri. I sent him to help recruit a kid from
Tulsa. It would have taken a week for Jim to get his expense
check cut by the state so he could go out and hit the airports
and motels and rental-car agencies. You can't hire a coach and
have him sit on his rear end for a week when it is just three
weeks to signing date. I paid Jim $1,000 out of my pocket, not
knowing at that time it was an NCAA violation, and later he
reimbursed me.

Guilty.

In this same charge is another violation that nobody
realized was against the rules until Galen Hall got caught
doing it as head coach at Florida. But I did it first. It goes back
to institutional control again.

I have my own corporation—called Prime Time, Inc.—that received all money from my three TV shows, my radio shows, my speaking engagements, and my shoe contract. Every year I would write Christmas-bonus checks of $1,000 to each of my secretaries and my part-time coaches and give them the checks at my home at the annual Christmas party. Every check was written on the same date. For me to pay those bonuses out of my pocket was an NCAA violation.

In 1984, I hired Mack Brown, the head coach at Appalachian State, as my assistant. Mack was making $80,000 a year at Appalachian State, but I could only pay him $50,000 at Oklahoma because that's all the budget allowed. What I did was supplement his salary out of my corporation in return for his services for that corporation. I paid Mack to do things like be on my radio and TV shows, make speeches, go to banquets, promote our program, appear on talk shows. I paid him a talent fee.

This is an NCAA violation. Why? Because the institution, meaning the University of Oklahoma, did not control that money. I can understand their reasoning. Monies out of institutional control could turn into slush funds or booster-club funds to be used in illegal inducements.

Guilty.

That's what was behind the NCAA charges on lack of institutional control. But there is a funny side to this, too. I have seen at least a dozen articles written by dumb asses in the national press during the 1989 troubles and they were trying to do a hatchet job on me and they would prove their point by saying something like, "Well, what do you expect from Switzer's players other than shooting, raping, and doping? The NCAA found that Switzer doesn't exercise proper institutional control." The bastards didn't even have a clue as to what the phrase meant—but they figured it would be a good one to rap my ass with anyway.

12. ALLEGATION   During the academic years from 1981–86 (except 1982–83), during the official paid visits to the university's campus, a number of prospective student-athletes, staff members, and student-athlete hosts allegedly arranged for the young men (and on one occasion the student-athlete

host) to receive souvenirs (usually clothing items with the
university's name or emblem) at a reduced cost or at no cost to
the prospects.

12. ANSWER   When a recruit comes to visit your campus,
he wants to take souvenirs home with him. He goes back
and wears his cap or T-shirt around his high school and
everybody thinks he's a stud because Oklahoma wants him.
The guy who is showing the recruit around campus is legally
allowed to spend $40 per recruit on entertainment—not on
buying souvenirs. This is a rule I really don't understand. It's
dumb. But it is a rule; it's called "excessive entertainment" and
I'm sure that some of our coaches and player hosts violated it.
So they bought a T-shirt or two instead of a hamburger.
    Guilty.

13. ALLEGATION   During the 1985–86 academic year, a staff
member allegedly arranged for a student-athlete to use the
university's football-office telephone to make free personal
long-distance calls. The student-athlete continued to make
the free phone calls until the end of the academic year.
    The young man has repaid the university for the cost of
the calls.

13. ANSWER   This charge was against Jamelle Holieway as a
freshman in 1985. Usually, it's homesick freshmen who want
to use the phone. Jamelle would go to Scott Hill's office, and
Scott would place the call to Jamelle's mama. Jamelle would
talk to her for half an hour. No rules violation yet.
    But then Jamelle would come back when Scott was out of
the office and place long-distance calls on his own but
charging them to the athletic department. Going through our
phone records, we catch the kids who do this and make them
repay us. Jamelle was ruled ineligible because of this and later
was reinstated after the university got its money back. We self-
reported that one.
    Guilty.

14. ALLEGATION   During the 1984–85 and 1985–86 academic
years, a supporter of the university allegedly made in-person,

off-campus recruiting contacts with several prospective student-athletes and provided transportation and meals for some of the prospects. Specifically:

14A): During the 1984–85 academic year, while recruiting two prospective student-athletes, the supporter allegedly contacted two young men and the family of one of them in person, off campus, for recruiting purposes. In December 1984, he and a staff member allegedly contacted one of the prospective student-athletes at the young man's high school and gave him a ride home. In January 1985, he and the staff member contacted the prospective student-athlete and his family in the young man's home, where he allegedly offered to employ the young man and provide rent-free lodging for the summer. In January 1985, he allegedly provided two prospective student-athletes automobile transportation to the airport in order for the prospects to travel to the university's campus for their official paid visits. After arriving at the airport, he bought breakfast for the prospective student-athletes.

14B): In January 1985, while recruiting a prospective student-athlete, this supporter, accompanied by a staff member, allegedly made an in-person, off-campus recruiting visit with the young man and his parents at their home.

14C): During the 1985–86 academic year, the supporter allegedly provided automobile transportation for two prospective student-athletes round-trip from their homes to the airport in connection with their official paid visits to the university's campus. In January 1986, he and a staff member allegedly contacted one of the prospective student-athletes at the young man's high school. On February 12, 1986, after a prospective student-athlete had signed a national letter of intent to attend the university, he and the staff member allegedly contacted the young man and his family at their home.

14D): In January 1986, the supporter and a staff member allegedly met with a prospective student-athlete and his family in their home. On another occasion, a staff member allegedly arranged for the supporter to provide round-trip transportation for the prospective student-athlete between his home and the airport in connection with the young man's official paid visit to the university campus.

14E): During the 1985–86 academic year, the supporter allegedly twice met in person, off campus, with a prospective student-athlete and, on one of these occasions, provided transportation for the young man. Specifically, on one occasion, he and a staff member allegedly met the young man at his high school, where they had been evaluating his performance by viewing the high school's football game films. In January 1986, on another occasion, he and two staff members allegedly provided transportation and rode with the prospective student-athlete from the airport to the young man's home after his official paid visit to the university's campus.

14. ANSWER   This five-part charge involves Scott Hill's recruiting in Los Angeles.

A young man named Jay Thomas, an Oklahoma fan who grew up in California, contacted Scott and wanted to help us recruit. Jay Thomas said he could provide summer jobs. He owned a limousine company, among other things. Scott would fly into LAX and Jay Thomas would pick him up in a limo and drive him to the recruit's house.

If Jay had waited outside in the car and not spoken to the recruit or his family, it would have been okay. But for Jay to come into the house—even at the invitation of the family— was considered *personal contact by an outsider with a special interest.*

If Scott had said, "Jay, you stay in the car," there would have been no problem. He could have told Jay to go away and come back at a certain time. But Scott thought nothing would ever come of it. Jay went to a high school coach's office with Scott and sat and looked at film. If the prospective student-athlete hadn't been there, it would have been no crime. But he *was* there—a violation.

15. ALLEGATION   In January 1986, during the official paid visits to the university's campus, a staff member allegedly lent his automobile to a student-athlete so that he could provide

local transportation for two prospective student-athletes during their visits.

15. ANSWER   Guilty. A staff member loaned a car to one of our players for forty-eight hours to take two recruits around town. The violation, again, didn't involve the recruits—it was loaning the car to the athlete already on scholarship that was the violation.

16. ALLEGATION   In the fall of 1983, a staff member allegedly arranged to provide a prospective student-athlete one complimentary admission in excess of the three permissible admissions to two university home football games.

16. ANSWER   We are allowed to give a prospect three tickets to a ball game—for his mother, his father, and himself. The recruit in this violation had a brother. One of our coaches gave the brother a ticket, too.
Guilty.

THE "GENERAL ALLEGATIONS"

NCAA bylaws 5–6–(d)–3 and 5–6–(d)–4 are the basis of what the NCAA calls the general allegations. Here's what it's all about:

Each year the president of the university has to sign an affidavit saying the athletic staff is in compliance with all NCAA regulations—a package of rules about the size of the Des Moines phone book.

The president checks with the athletic director and the head coaches, who check with all the assistant coaches. When everybody says the program is in compliance, and the head coaches have signed the form, the president puts his signature on the affidavit and sends it to Kansas City.

Then if the NCAA investigators find your program guilty of something, they charge you not only with the actual violation but *also* with not self-reporting your violation—no matter how minor or innocent they may have been.

But, based on this failure to self-report the specific allegations discussed above, the NCAA concluded that:

". . . staff members of the University of Oklahoma did not on all occasions act in accordance with the generally recognized standards associated with the conduct and administration of intercollegiate athletics. This letter asserts that certain of the allegations would constitute a knowing and willful effort on the part of these persons to operate the university's intercollegiate football program contrary to the requirements and provisions of NCAA legislation.

"It is alleged that during the 1983–84, 1984–85, and 1985–86 academic years, staff members failed to report the above violations to the chief executive officers of the university during these years and these officers certified that the university was in compliance with NCAA legislation. when it was not."

I really have a problem with that letter because it is a conclusion that *as an institution,* Oklahoma was willfully violating *serious* NCAA rules. That is tragically wrong. That sort of conclusion indicts a great many well-meaning, able, and intelligent people who genuinely try to live by the rules and do what is right. Rules violations at most schools are *isolated events;* they happen in particular circumstances, sometimes intentionally, but most often they are simply the result of mistakes and misunderstandings of one individual. And, as I've shown, there are some times the violations don't even really occur. The NCAA just concludes that they do.

So if an assistant coach commits a violation and doesn't know it is a violation, he doesn't "self-report." Obviously, an assistant who knowingly committed a violation sometimes didn't report himself, either. But because the coach, innocently or not, didn't report it, the self-reporting requirement works all the way back up the chain of command to further indict and penalize the institution, as though it were really a separate offense. I'm sorry, folks. It's okay in my mind to charge institutions for the violations that do occur, but to create new, fictitious ones and penalize the institution simply because the higher-ups didn't report something they never knew about in the first place just doesn't make any sense. To use it as a policing mechanism would be fine, but the way it's currently being used is absurd.

It's like being punished twice for the same criminal offense. Even a murderer who kills *one* person doesn't get *two* life sentences because he forgot to run and tell the district attorney what he did.

With regard to the specific NCAA charges listed above, I believe we were guilty of several piss-ant ones—and I've admitted them. But I believe Oklahoma was guilty of two major violations, and only two. They were: (1) the Kert Kaspar incident; and (2) Mike Jones's giving Hart Lee Dykes a pair of sneakers. I do not believe that Mike Jones offered Hart Lee $1,000.

Here's defensive secondary coach Bobby Proctor making a point. It was probably important. COURTESY OKLAHOMA PUBLISHING COMPANY

Marcus Dupree in 1982. This young man from Philadelphia, Mississippi, was *potentially* the greatest running back ever, college or pro. AUTHOR'S PRIVATE COLLECTION

Greg Switzer meets a couple of his idols, former U.S.C. stars O. J. Simpson *(right)* and Lynn Swan, at our 1982 game with U.S.C. in Norman. COURTESY OKLAHOMA PUBLISHING COMPANY

Donnie Duncan, my friend, my assistant coach, my athletic director. AUTHOR'S PRIVATE COLLECTION

Lights, camera, action—"The Boz." Enough said. COURTESY OKLAHOMA PUBLISHING COMPANY

Above, I don't really know what Joe Paterno is doing here. But it was before our 1985 national championship game against Joe's Penn State team. "The Boz" looks on. COURTESY OKLAHOMA PUBLISHING COMPANY

Right, Jamelle Holieway was quarterback for our 1985 national championship team. He was superquick, strong, and a great competitor. AUTHOR'S PRIVATE COLLECTION

Left, 1985 national championship rally in Oklahoma City after we had beaten Penn State in the January 2, 1986, Orange Bowl. COURTESY OKLAHOMA PUBLISHING COMPANY

"You call me that again, and you're outta here." Referee tells it like it is. COURTESY OKLAHOMA PUBLISHING COMPANY

Oklahoma's three Heisman Trophy winners, taken in May 1987. *Left to right:* Billy Vessels, 1952; Steve Owens, 1969; and Billy Sims, 1978.
AUTHOR'S PRIVATE COLLECTION

Tom Osborne, Nebraska's head football coach, and me before some recent game. Tom is one of the game's real gentlemen. COURTESY OKLAHOMA
PUBLISHING COMPANY

Above, *left to right:* Doug, Greg, me, and Kathy at the airport in Oklahoma City in the summer of 1987—just back from Italy. PHOTOGRAPH BY JANICE HIGGINS

My brother, Donnie, and my nephew Bryce Switzer just before Oklahoma's 1987 national championship game with Miami. We lost. PHOTOGRAPH BY JOE GARCIA

That's my daughter, Kathy, wearing the Miami sweatshirt—having fun with Miami coach Jimmie Johnson and me before that 1987 Orange Bowl.

PHOTOGRAPH BY JOE GARCIA

June 19, 1989: the last photo taken of me as head football coach at Oklahoma. This part wasn't any fun.

OKLAHOMA PUBLISHING COMPANY

My niece Alison Switzer at Baylor in the fall of 1989. Baylor with Grant Teaff must have been better than Oklahoma without Uncle Barry.
AUTHOR'S PRIVATE COLLECTION

Below, *left to right:* Me, George Allen, and Hank Stram with Craig T. Nelson on the set of the *Coach* television show in Universal City in the fall of 1989.
AUTHOR'S PRIVATE COLLECTION

30

MORE ABOUT THE NCAA— AND A FEW OF THE THINGS I REALLY DID DO

As I told you earlier in the chapter on recruiting, neither I nor my coaches have, to my knowledge, ever been guilty of any violation of an NCAA rule that gave Oklahoma a competitive advantage in the recruitment of athletes. Those rules that I have knowingly violated in my career all relate to the fact that I have been the head of a "family" with over a hundred "kids." I have always found it difficult not to help my players when they were desperate, when they were in trouble, and when they had no other "father" with the financial ability to help them at the times we are talking about. Simply, it's always been hard for me to say no when good kids, black or white, but mostly black, needed help. Here are a few examples of how I broke the NCAA "law."

In the spring of 1979, Billy Sims came to me with a real problem, both for himself and for me. He had already won his Heisman Trophy in his junior year, 1978 (and almost a national championship for the team), and he was then being hotly pursued by sports agents offering lots of money for him to turn pro. He told me that getting his degree had really been important to Miss Sadie (his grandmother in Hooks, Texas, who had raised him and who had recently died), and it was very important to Billy.

But Billy was also desperate for cash to pay bills he and his wife had built up. I asked him, "How much would it take,

Billy?" He said he needed about $1,500, and I decided then and there to help him. He did stay in school for his senior year, and he did get his Oklahoma University degree before he turned pro.

I remember the joy on Billy's face with his cap and gown on and his diploma in his hand, hugging his wife and his relatives, and how really proud we all were of him at that moment. I didn't give Billy a dime to come here, but I gave him $1,500 to stay here, and it was the best investment I ever made.

If I hadn't given Billy that $1,500, he would have been the first underclassman to come out early and go pro—not Herschel Walker.

In the last fifteen years, not many Heisman Trophy winners—like Herschel Walker, Barry Sanders, Bo Jackson, and others—have graduated. And by God, I'm proud of the fact that Billy Sims did.

The $1,500 was only a "get by" figure for Billy, and I'm really glad that I was able to beat the pull of the sports agents (who I consider the worst aspect of sports today) and keep him in school. You can't call that buying a player. He was already mine. I was just taking care of my family. The NCAA and David Swank might ask if I would have done that for a third-teamer as well as for a Heisman winner. My answer is, "Hell, yes." I've done it. You can even ask some of my walk-on players that I've helped.

Ricky Bryan from Coweta, Oklahoma (actually Tater Hill, a country crossroads community), was a big, great ol' country boy who was as nice a kid as you would ever meet. At 6-feet-5, 270 pounds, he made all-Big Eight Conference at defensive tackle in 1981, 1982, and 1983, and he was an all-American in both 1982 and 1983. He and his wife, Shelby, had just gotten married, and he and Shelby went home one weekend to his parents' home in Coweta. While they were gone, all of their wedding gifts were stolen. Everything. The television, vacuum cleaner—everything they had, amounting to several thousand dollars.

Well, Ricky comes in to see me, crying like a baby. He and Shelby were totally devastated. Ricky's Dad, Jack, was a truck driver, and there was simply no way all of their stuff could be replaced. So I asked Shelby to make up a list of everything they had lost, and then I made a few telephone calls to certain people, friends of the program, and we got everything replaced.

We made Ricky and Shelby's lives a lot more livable and pulled them through a lot of grief. But of course, that was a violation of the extra-benefits rule. A major violation. The rule is you can't help kids who are in trouble.

And then there was Earl Johnson and his wife, Janice. Earl played fullback for us in 1983, 1984, and 1986, sitting out 1985 with an injury. Earl is a bull of a young man who fell victim to an apartment fire in, I believe, 1985. He and Janice lost everything they had, all of their clothes. They literally did not have a damn thing to wear. So I arranged for some new clothes for both of them. The NCAA response would probably be, Well, they should have had insurance. Major violation.

Then when Kenny McMichel, a defensive back in 1986–1988, came in and told me his father, who had just had a heart attack, was about to die at home in Indianapolis, I bought him a plane ticket home. He didn't have any other way to get there. And then, a week or two later, after Kenny had returned to our campus, his father died. I sent Kenny to the funeral. A major violation—although I will say the NCAA did in 1987 relax this rule. Nonetheless, when it happened, Oklahoma could have gotten nailed for helping the kid in a crisis.

Forrest Valora was the strongest and best blocking tight end I've ever coached and who made all-Big Eight conference in 1980. He and his wife, Valerie, had a child, a son, who died four or five days after he was born. The kids had no insurance, no way to pay for their child's funeral. Their families had no ability to bury the child. I called Jerry Greer, Karl Goodall, and Wendell Knox, three friends of mine and of the program in Oklahoma City, and told them the story. They, because they cared, paid several thousand dollars to bury Forrest and Valerie's child. Major NCAA violation. And I don't give a damn.

And it wasn't always football players. I remember driving across the campus a few years ago during the Christmas break, and I saw this young black girl, a track athlete from Canada. I asked her what in the world she was doing around here. And she said she couldn't go home. There was no way. Couldn't afford to. So I sent her home. For her not to have to spend two weeks on the campus all by herself. Another major violation.

Through all the years there were so many things that I had to touch and people to help. There were other guys . . . and girls too . . . from other sports who would sit there crying and not know where to turn. They had problems and their family might not be able to help them, and I would be compelled to. I couldn't turn my back on them. You know, I would get in those situations where I couldn't say no. Those were the things that I did to violate the rules. But I damn sure never bought one player . . . and I don't have a damn bit of trouble sleeping at night.

31

MORE ABOUT THE NCAA— AND MY THOUGHTS ABOUT THE FUTURE OF "BIG-TIME" COLLEGE ATHLETICS

Before closing the subject of the NCAA, there are a few thoughts and concerns that I want to share with you. I believe this book is about a lot more than what happened to the University of Oklahoma in 1989. And it certainly is a lot more than simply the story of a man's life, with a little humor and tragedy thrown in. It is also the story of an institution that has probably gotten a little out of hand but that is now suffering a backlash that could kill the institution itself and have fallout effects, which I do not believe the country would tolerate.

What I am talking about, of course, is the institution of big-time, big-money college athletics, which realistically includes only football and basketball and the hundred or so major colleges that participate in them. College athletics have certainly gotten bigger than the founders of them would have dreamed. I'm sure they have become too big and too important to too many people. That is not to say, however, that college athletics are bad, that the players should be stigmatized or punished as a class, or that fans should not be able to enjoy their favorite teams. It's just that some things need to be brought into balance and into somewhat clearer perspective.

First of all, something must be done about relieving the incredible pressure on college football and basketball coaches to win. It would not be realistic to believe all pressure to win or to succeed could be done away with, because it is human nature for anyone to want to succeed. And the teaching value of competition itself cannot be denied. But it is also undeniable that the pressures of winning placed upon coaches by fans, donors, and college administrators (particularly in their fund-raising roles) must be lessened, to reduce the incentive that coaches have to cheat. Obviously, some coaches are going to cheat no matter what because that is their nature, but the year-to-year unstable existence and the "What have you done for me lately?" mentality of fans and college administrators presents an ever-present motive to cut corners, to cheat, to get an edge on the competition by improper inducements to athletes.

It needs to be understood, too, I believe, that there are lots of times that cheating occurs and it is totally beyond the control of the head coach. He cannot eyeball every assistant coach and every over-enthusiastic alumnus or supporter of his program, twenty-four hours a day. Obviously, if a head coach has clearly orchestrated such things, he is responsible and should be penalized. But by the same token, there are many instances where events beyond the control and responsibility of coaches have forced them out of their jobs.

I have to believe that mandating tenure in some fashion for both head coaches and assistant coaches is a possible answer to this problem. If a coach has been successful enough in his multiple roles as recruiter, tactician, and surrogate-father for a given period of time, he should be granted tenure—not necessarily as coach, but in an administrative position in any event. If a coach isn't constantly worried about being kicked out on the street, he is less likely to be inclined to cheat. But once a coach has proved himself and *hasn't done it by cheating*, he should be granted the same benefits of tenure as any other faculty member.

Second, both Dr. George Cross and I believe there needs to be NCAA legislation enacted to allow universities, based on financial-need criteria, to supplement the normal room and board and tuition scholarship with some reasonable amount of spending money. As I said on June 19, 1989, in my resignation speech, there are many kids who do not have the ability to provide for their basic needs. By giving a lot of them scholarships, we have placed them in a college environment without the ability even to buy a pair of shoes or a new pair of pants.

But the primary area of my concern is also with the kids, particularly the marginal students, who more often than not these days happen to be black. I was hired by the University of Oklahoma to win football games, and when I resigned in 1989, I had the highest career winning percentage of any major college coach in the country. But that wasn't the only part of my job. I was the head of a very large and continually growing family of players, coaches, and administrative personnel for sixteen years and performed a father role to the hundreds of athletes who played for me. By and large—and considering the number of years I coached and the number of players that I coached—I believe I did a good and maybe a superior job in that area of my responsibilities. But often during those sixteen years, the national press—not understanding earrings, long hair, players wearing bandannas, players giving high fives or simply having a good time in football—criticized me for being "loose." What they were also doing, however, was being critical of people who did not happen to fit the image or the mold they wanted them to fit.

In a word, I believe the press and a large part of the public have been intolerant of difference and diversity. We at Oklahoma have always been disliked because of resentment and jealousy over our success, but there has been a great deal of intolerance in the press, in the public, *and* in college faculties and administrations, at Oklahoma and other schools, too, because of these differences and diversity of the players who were coming to dominate college athletics.

Let's think a minute about what I'm getting into here. Is it race? You could say that. I have felt and have often stated in my career that the three most significant events that have affected college athletics have been the emergence of the black athlete, the development of the triple-option offense, and the development of strength-training programs. And obviously, the emergence of the black athlete has had far and away the most dramatic impact.

Since I became a coach at Oklahoma in 1966, college athletics have been totally turned around by the emergence of black athletes. Their abilities, and the desire for success at all NCAA institutions, made that evolution inevitable. In 1965, I would say that at Oklahoma blacks made up approximately 5 percent of the football team and about 20 percent of the basketball team. At that time there were no blacks in the Southwest Conference (Jerry Levias being the first at S.M.U. in 1966), and there were none in the Southeastern Conference. By contrast, in 1989 blacks dominate at Oklahoma, comprising over 50 percent of the football program and 95 percent of the basketball program. These numbers are repeated nationwide. The game has clearly changed, and it has changed dramatically. Just watch television on Saturdays and Sundays if you want confirmation of this.

Cultural or racial differences cannot explain or serve as an excuse for the crimes that took place on the Oklahoma University campus in early 1989. You'll hear no excuses from me about that, because the crimes were clearly inexcusable. What I will say about them, however, is that I am really afraid those isolated incidents have accelerated the process of "athlete bashing" and institutional discrimination against the athlete, both black *and* white, which has been going on in institutions of higher learning in Oklahoma and all across the country for some time.

I worry about what is going on with college athletics now and what has been in process in Oklahoma and in the NCAA as a whole. I am particularly sensitive to the race-related aspects of it, since I was in the forefront of the emphasis upon the recruitment of talented black athletes. I was playing blacks at any and every position, depending totally upon their individual abilities, before other teams would even recruit them.

But a lot of you folks out there do not realize something very critical about the process of athlete recruitment and the state of racial integration in this country. By law, there is equal opportunity for every child in the country, all schools are to be integrated, and every kid (black, white, yellow, or red) is supposed to have his shot at being president. But that's not the reality.

In truth, there are lots of different classes out there—different economic levels, different levels of intellectual ability and, just as important, different life-styles. What has happened nationwide in athletic programs that have mixed all of the races together to achieve success is that you have a mix of colors, values, and life-styles. The problem with that is that all of these kids are viewed and judged by the *same standard*—that of the press and college administrators, both of which professions are dominated by well-educated white men raised in middle- or upper-class homes that had *both a mother and a father*. To some extent that's okay. These kids, who are trying to use the college experience *(whether or not they graduate)* as a way out of the slums and the ghettos and to obtain a little bit of the "good life," need to learn that they are often going to be judged by the white man's standards, values, and standardized tests.

But I strongly believe that the press, the NCAA as an institution, and the academic community, helped along by the tragic events in Norman, Oklahoma, in early 1989, are taking matters too far. Each year the Presidents' Commission of the NCAA enacts some new bit of legislation designed to restrict the number of scholarships available, raise the entrance requirements on athletes, or impose tougher academic-performance requirements on athletes than are required of nonathlete students.

Major tax-supported universities, including Oklahoma, keep raising entrance requirements across the board, applicable to both athletes and nonathletes, which, of course, has the overall effect of prohibiting the entrance into college of the marginal students—and more important, restricting a class of people. The thought has even occurred to me, and I've said so many times, that the universities that have traditionally been the centers of learning in our country and that have allowed our people to achieve excellence are now almost demanding excellence as a condition to admission. I've read about how the universities complain about having to spend time and money in remedial programs because of the poor job being done by the high schools and that remedial education isn't the proper role of the university. Well, my response is that it always has been, and until the public does increase the performance of the high schools, it is not right for the universities to simply close their doors and look the other way—which is exactly the direction they are going in now. I have felt that the proper function of a state university is to have a positive social impact on as much of the population as possible.

This is a very, very important topic in Oklahoma, particularly at this point, for reasons not directly related to me or the program I once headed. The Oklahoma economy has been based on oil and agriculture ever since statehood, and because of the devastation that both of those areas of the economy have suffered, there is a tremendous push in the state toward diversification of the economy and strengthening of the educational system in order to support the diversification. And the Oklahoma legislature wrestled for six months and finally passed a tremendous $230 million tax-increase package designed to finance a dramatically improved public-education system to raise it above the forty-sixth rank in the nation on *per capita* spending for public education.

But in this atmosphere of driving toward excellence we have also seen the state's board of regents for higher education just propose a "no pass, no play" rule for all extracurricular activities, incorporating a mandatory 2.0 grade-point-average requirement, obviously aimed at football and basketball players. This is in part a reaction to an incredible media attack upon Oklahoma State University president John Campbell, who recently readmitted almost one hundred nonathlete students to OSU who did not meet that school's requirements for readmission. His "mistake" was that he included seven football players in that number, and the press screamed about the readmission of the football players—never mentioning the others.

And Oklahoma University's regents have increased the minimum requirement for admission to the university on the ACT test to 21, and is increasing it to 23 in 1993, as compared to the requirement of 18 that is in force in most NCAA schools. And Oklahoma University has scrapped its recreation major, and a lot of other programs that traditionally the marginal student, often black, could perform in.

All of this, may at first glance, appear great. What could possibly be wrong with educators and politicians wanting to improve the quality of education? I would suggest that there is nothing wrong with education itself, and this is particularly true with respect to the blacks because there is, in reality, no way that blacks can pick themselves up by their own bootstraps if it is not through education. The road out of the ghetto is certainly not through college to the National Football League or the National Basketball Association. It has to be through mass education and merging into all areas of our society.

But what is wrong is that in the approach the NCAA, the politicians, and the educators are taking, they are making implicit social choices that combine to *deny the marginal student from having the opportunity to better himself*. It may result in statistics that all of them will like, such as higher graduation rates for those kids who end up on the football or basketball teams, but those are misleading statistics. That approach fails to recognize that in developing these higher numbers, there are two inevitable by-products:

1. It unquestionably lowers the overall quality of athletic competition, since it closes off the largest single pool of athletic talent available (I realize the educators don't care about this); but

2. More important, it freezes a great many kids, who might have been able to better themselves, into a permanent underclass status. (All of us should care about this.)

I worry about those kids out there who are going to be frozen out. How many are there who, with the opportunity to be in a college environment and perhaps get a degree, which is made possible by the athletic scholarship, are going to end up on the streetcorners? Or God knows where?

Sometimes I think that the press, the politicians, and the college educators, when they act in this arena, display a tremendous lack of social tolerance and a basic insensitivity to the problems of the underprivileged. It is as if they are reacting to episodes like that of Oklahoma State's Dexter Manley, who went to school there for four or five years on a football scholarship and who later claimed (maybe he was) to be functionally illiterate. The message I am getting is that the colleges and the NCAA are not going to let themselves be embarrassed like that again. So in reaction, they *overreact* and take steps designed to assure that no more Manley-like episodes occur. At the same time, these steps have the effect of closing the doors of major tax-supported universities to a class of people that is disproportionately black.

The people in charge of these issues *do not really understand race* and are out of touch with that aspect of our society. I know that at Oklahoma most professors, our administrators, and even our regents have little contact with blacks. The people I believe who are most qualified to understand race relations and to deal with it on a human, caring level are those who deal with mixed races every day. And you know who they are? They are high school teachers and high school and college coaches.

A good point in this regard is that this is 1990 and my good friend Sylvia Lewis, a black, was the very first black ever appointed by a governor of Oklahoma to be a regent of the university . . . an institution that was established a hundred years ago.

Sometimes I also think that all that the educators, the NCAA, and the press really care about is appearances. At the 1990 annual convention of the NCAA in Dallas, Dick Schultz, executive director of the NCAA and a former coach himself, obviously recognized the problem when he said, "No one wants strong academic standards more than I do, but those standards must be fair and not limit access to certain segments of our population."

But if the actions taken by the convention and the day-to-day abuse taken by athletes from the faculty and our universities are any guide, I think Dick has a really tough job in assuring that any degree of fairness remains in the process.

If the process of creating greater restrictions and limitations continues, I believe "appearances" and graduation rates might improve, and that will certainly look better to the educators, to the media, and to a big portion of the NCAA activists in the area. But it sure as hell is going to bring about some dramatic changes that will hurt those people who can do the least for themselves.

I have seen too many kids who some damn racially biased standardized test said were too dumb to amount to anything take the opportunity of college and a burning desire to better themselves and turn it into a college degree and a secure future. This is too common, in my experience, for me to believe that the Presidents' Commission of the NCAA and the university leaders themselves really recognize the ultimate impact of the changes they have chosen to make.

But who gives a damn anyway? Maybe just a few high school teachers, me . . . and a few other coaches.

32

THE SETUP

This chapter is primarily a story that happened to one of my players in the weeks before and the days immediately after the 1988 Orange Bowl game. This story is so bizarre that I am going to make as few personal comments on it as my nature will allow. I'll just stick to the bare facts.

I have to start by introducing you to Jack Taylor. When I first met him nearly twenty years ago, he was the top investigative reporter for *The Daily Oklahoman* in Oklahoma City. Taylor's digging had much to do with the conviction of Oklahoma governor David Hall for soliciting a bribe in the early seventies.

In about 1975, Jack Taylor called and wanted to have lunch with me. I took him to the athletic dining hall on campus. I was a reader of the sports pages and didn't much follow the politics or crime stories, so I was curious what Jack Taylor might want from me. At lunch, Taylor quizzed me about gambling in college athletics. I told him the FBI came to campus and held seminars on the dangers of gambling, but we had no problem with it.

About a year later, Jack Taylor started writing some negative articles about my being a partner in the Investors Life Insurance Company in Oklahoma City. The articles dealt with campaign contributions made by one of my partners and tax writeoffs he had taken, but they proved to be of no real consequence to me, just an annoyance.

In 1976, we played California in Norman for the second game of the season. That game created another infamous "spying scandal." Lonnie Williams, who lived in Dallas, the same guy who got caught spying on Texas in earlier years, had watched California working out at Texas Stadium in Dallas and told some of our coaches what he saw. The media found out that Williams had been at the practice, so all of a sudden, we had another "spy story."

We gained about 500 yards that day but only beat California 28–17. In other words, we failed to cover the large betting spread, whatever it was. I held my regular press luncheon on the Tuesday following the game at the Holiday Inn. Frank Boggs, a nice guy who was a sportswriter for *The Daily Oklahoman,* asked me if I would visit with Jack Taylor after the luncheon.

Meanwhile, Taylor had run a series of articles that caused a lot of grief to Steve and Tinker Owens and their family and to our athletic department. Steve and Tinker had been all-Americans. Their younger brother, Jimbo, was a good player but not really good enough to receive one of our thirty scholarships. Steve was a star for the Detroit Lions at the time and worked out a deal with me that he would secretly pay Jimbo's way to school. I would sign Jimbo to a "scholarship" that actually came from Steve. This sort of thing has been done for many years. The player is proud of his "scholarship," and nobody is the wiser.

Jimbo found out about it after a couple of years, got angry, quit the team, and transferred. Boggs and Taylor went to the Owens family in Miami, Oklahoma, and wrote several articles that pitted Jimbo and his family against his older brother, me, and the University of Oklahoma. The boys' father, Peanut, was a crusty old fellow who drove an eighteen-wheeler. I'll never forget seeing Peanut in his tuxedo at "21" in New York the night Steve received his Heisman Trophy. You talk about a happy man; it was Peanut that night.

But now Peanut hated me. And I don't really know why I agreed to sit down with Jack Taylor this second time after what he had done. I guess because I sort of liked Boggs, and I was curious what Taylor might want.

We sat in the coffee shop of the Holiday Inn. Boggs and Taylor had their backs to a plate-glass window. We were drinking coffee. Taylor started critiquing the California game. He told me we had run the unbalanced line some number of times and weren't successful with it, and he wanted to know my motivation for doing that.

I could tell Taylor didn't understand what an unbalanced line is. He didn't know if he meant unbalanced with the tight end or tackle or guard. Boggs, a talented and respected sportswriter, was getting embarrassed by all this nonsense.

I stood up and Taylor stood up.

"Are you trying to say I was manipulating the score and trying to hold it under the point spread by using an unbalanced line?" I said.

"I guess you could say that," Taylor said.

Anyone who has ever punched out anyone knows that there is a split second when rationality or logic doesn't mean a thing. I reached that flashpoint. But some guardian angel stopped my trigger from going off. If I had hit him, I would have knocked him through the plate-glass window. I remember thinking it was a good thing he hadn't said this crap to Chuck Fairbanks, because Chuck would have had him lying on the sidewalk in a shower of broken glass by now. Chuck has a shorter fuse than I have.

That was the last time I ever cooperated with Jack Taylor. But he kept after me. He would phone at 2 A.M. He came to our athletic office demanding records on the tickets we gave to players (this was in the hard-ticket days). Athletic director Wade Walker and the faculty rep, Dan Gibbens, told Taylor and Boggs, "No way. Here's the door."

As he was leaving, Taylor said, "Oh, by the way, did you know you are under investigation by the NCAA?"

NCAA investigators are in the field asking questions all the time. We hadn't been notified of any investigation and would have been informed before the media if there had been one.

But the next day *The Daily Oklahoman* in World War III-type headlines said, "OKLAHOMA UNDER NCAA INVESTIGATION." You can imagine what the media did with that. Jim Delaney, now the Big-Ten commissioner, showed up on our campus working as an NCAA investigator and looked at all our records and talked to everybody.

After a week or so, Delaney told us and university president Paul Sharp that his investigation was over and there would be no official inquiry. We all thanked him, and I asked the one question I had left, "Was there really an investigation before the headlines appeared in *The Daily Oklahoman?*"

Delaney said, "No. That brought us here."

Some Sooner fans reacted by allegedly threatening to kill Taylor and bomb his house. I think somebody left a dead dog on Boggs's lawn. *Sports Illustrated* did a feature story on Boggs and Taylor, defending their media comrades. Shortly thereafter, Boggs moved to Colorado Springs.

In 1981, I had what was called an Inner Circle—people who donated $2,000 or more a year. The money that was raised—maybe $75,000 to $100,000 a year—went to pay for the TV time for my shows, which were a great recruiting tool. Nowadays, with all the cable channels, anybody can get on TV. But ten years ago, we had to buy our airtime in the Dallas and Houston markets, and if a coach didn't have $50,000 to pay for it, there were a dozen evangelist preachers waiting to take his place. This exposure was necessary for us to be able to recruit effectively in Texas.

Jack Taylor heard of the existence of this Inner Circle. He made it into a conspiracy and wrote a story with the headline "SWITZER HAS $100,000 SLUSH FUND."

"*The Daily Oklahoman* has learned through reliable sources that Coach Barry Switzer has organized an elite group of people, known only to insiders, who give money . . ." is about how his lead started on the front page.

This made a public laughingstock out of the newspaper and Jack Taylor.

At every home game, I personally paid $800 for a full-page ad in the football program that is sold at Owen Field. In this ad, I thanked all the Inner Circle members, listed their names, and explained what their money was used for, audited to the last dime.

All the TV reporters went on the air laughing and holding up the football program and telling about their reliable sources on the Inner Circle. One of them said, "Jack Taylor wouldn't have had to spend all that time investigating if he had looked at page 52 of the program."

Jack Taylor left town. I didn't hear of him again until January 5, 1988, when one of my players came to me after we returned home from the Orange Bowl and told me the incredible but true tale I am now about to relate.

This player is a big, handsome guy, a ladies' man. I will call him Big Red. Before he came to see me, Big Red and his mother had talked to "Sugar" Smith, a vice-squad detective in Oklahoma City, and then to FBI agent Phil Shockey in Norman. Well, Big Red told me that he had been walking along the campus one afternoon the previous September at the start of football season. He was single and lived in the athletic dorm. It was noon and Big Red was on his way to the chow hall.

A car pulled into the parking lot and honked at him. A girl waved and motioned for him to come over. She introduced herself as Janeeo Dior, heiress of Christian Dior. She had just moved into an apartment in Norman, and why didn't Big Red come by so she and he could get better acquainted?

They did, and he wound up staying at her apartment a lot during the fall semester. He moved in with the girl and her two children. They hired Ruthie Williams, a black lady from Oklahoma City, as a full-time housekeeper and baby-sitter.

All during the season, the girl kept asking Big Red questions about the OU football program. At first he took it that she was a fan. But he said later he began wondering why she was quizzing him all the time. Big Red and Janeeo had their ups and downs. His mother didn't like the girl, who was several years older than he was.

The worst argument between Big Red and Janeeo came when he refused to take her along on the trip to the Orange Bowl. The football team went to Miami two weeks early. Janeeo wanted desperately to go. Big Red said no. He told her to stay home.

She phoned him in Miami. She told him, "I've got a friend down there who will contact you to bring back a package for me." A few days before our game with Miami for the national championship, Big Red received a call from someone who identified herself as Janeeo's friend. She wanted to deliver a package for him to take back to Janeeo. He told her to mail the package to Janeeo. She kept insisting that he bring it home on the team plane. The more she talked, the more suspicious he became. And by the type of conversation they were having, he began to believe he was being taped.

On the phone, she finally said, "You know what's in the package, don't you?"

Big Red said, "No, and I don't care."

She said, "It's cocaine. You know it's cocaine."

Big Red said, "I don't know anything about cocaine."

She said, "You and Bosworth do cocaine together all the time, don't you?"

Big Red said, "Shit no, we've never done any cocaine in our damn lives." He hung up the phone.

The team got back into Norman on January 3. Big Red went to the apartment where he and Janeeo lived. The apartment had been cleaned out, except for a few of Big Red's things . . . and also Ruthie Williams. She had stayed there to protect Big Red's valuables and, as she also told me, to see if she could get paid for her last month's work. Big Red was glad to get rid of Janeeo, but when he opened all his monthly bills, he was shocked. He said she had charged several thousands of dollars to him.

Big Red asked Ruthie, "What the hell has been going on?"

Ruthie told him—and has since confirmed all of this for me and the Cleveland County district attorney's office—that before Big Red left for Miami, a newspaper reporter from Dallas met Janeeo in his room at the Sheraton Hotel in Norman. Ruthie went with Janeeo and was present at this meeting.

Ruthie said that the reporter told Janeeo she should move out of the apartment. The reporter had called Janeeo frequently when Big Red wasn't around, and Janeeo had placed a number of calls to the reporter. Ruthie overheard these conversations.

Ruthie also said that the reporter came by the apartment on several occasions when Big Red was away at the Orange Bowl.

Ruthie said Janeeo had been making secret tapes of conversations with black athletes, talking to them about drugs. Were they buying drugs? Were they doing drugs? In the privacy of her apartment, where the athletes thought they were chatting with the girlfriend of a teammate, they talked to her like friends—and she had the conversations bugged. Ruthie said Janeeo would give the tapes to the reporter. Ruthie said Janeeo had a lot of money on her all the time, and once she saw her with a check drawn on a Texas bank. Janeeo mentioned, too, that she had a home in Texas.

The reporter came to Norman and helped Janeeo move out of the apartment, according to Ruthie.

"Big Red, I believe they were trying to set you up," Ruthie told him.

Ruthie gave Big Red the reporter's telephone number, which Janeeo had written on a pad in the bedroom. He then looked at his December telephone bill, which was lying there with all the other bills Janeeo had left him with. And he noticed that there were fifteen or more calls made to the number Ruthie had given him. He immediately dialed the number, (214) 720–6828, and the voice answering said, "*Dallas Times Herald.*"

He was frightened enough that he went to the police, the FBI, and me. He realized what a disaster it would have been if he had brought that package home from Miami for Janeeo. He would have been busted at the airport with the entire Oklahoma football team around him. We can all speculate about what would have happened to Big Red and our program.

After Big Red finished telling me this bizarre story on January 5, 1988, in my office, I asked him to come back the next afternoon and repeat the story in detail. Big Red did come back, and he went through the whole thing again in the presence of athletic director Donnie Duncan, assistant athletic director John Underwood, faculty representative Dan Gibbens, and Norman FBI agent Phil Shockey. When he concluded his scary tale, I asked the group, "What can we do about this? Have you ever heard anything like this in your lives? Most people wouldn't believe things like this could really happen."

Then I was stunned by Phil Shockey's response, "We heard about this two weeks ago." "What?" I exclaimed. He said, "The Oklahoma Bureau of Narcotics had been tipped that an OU football player would be bringing back drugs from Miami." I couldn't wait to ask, "Did they say who had called?"

Phil replied, "It was someone who said his name was Jack Taylor."

I picked up the telephone when I got home and dialed (214) 720–6828.

The person who answered said, "This is the *Dallas Times Herald* general news line. You call here and we switch you over to whichever reporter you are looking for."

"How do I find Jack Taylor?" I said.

"Oh, his number is one digit off. If you want Jack Taylor, dial 720–6827."

I have dialed that number several times and always get a recorded voice that asks me to leave a message.

But I haven't made up my mind yet exactly what message I want to leave Jack Taylor.

PART THREE

1989

33

NIGHTMARE ON JENKINS STREET

I had hoped to get the 1989 season started off with a bang. But I didn't expect it to be the .22 caliber bang of an Iver Johnson blue-steel revolver in room 311 of Bud Wilkinson House.

It was about one-thirty in the morning on January 13, the first weekend back in school after the Christmas and semester holiday break. Players had been drifting into the dorm all evening. In room 311—these are suites with a bedroom, living room, and bath—Zarak Peters, the dorm barber, had been giving haircuts with his electric shears, listening to rap tapes, and talking to people who wandered in and out.

Zarak was 6-feet-4 and packed 265 pounds of muscle under his Spuds McKenzie T-shirt. He had been the top blue-chip defensive lineman in the state of Texas, at Willow Ridge High School in Houston. I was planning to move him to tight end in spring practice.

One of the guys waiting his turn for a haircut was Jerry Parks, a sophomore defensive back who had grown up with Peters and was his best friend. A year younger than Zarak, Jerry was also a highly recruited player, considered the top defensive back in Texas. Notre Dame wanted him badly. Big Zarak towered over little Jerry and outweighed his buddy by a hundred pounds, but there was nobody on our football team who was a fiercer hitter on the field than Jerry. He wouldn't back down to anybody.

Jerry got tired of waiting for his haircut and went out and

drank a few beers. While he was gone, a white kid named Alan Hagen, the son of a chemistry professor on campus, came into the dorm looking for Mike Gaddis. Mike's room was down the hall from Zarak's, where up to a dozen athletes were gathering. Hagen wasn't an athlete. He was a longhair. But he must not have felt intimidated by being the only white guy at the party. Because when Mike turned out not to be home, Hagen went to Zarak's room and joined right in.

Jerry returned to the dorm, a little drunk by now, and was furious to find out he hadn't moved up to first in line for a haircut. Jerry accused Zarak of stealing his favorite rap tape. Zarak told him to get his butt out of the room and shoved him into the hall.

Down in room 211 Charles Thompson was lying in bed, his leg in a cast. Jerry burst through the door and said, "Give me your car keys."

"What for?" Charles said.

"I'm gonna get my gun."

It wasn't really Jerry's gun. It belonged to Zarak Peters. They kept it in the trunk of Thompson's car. All three of them said they just liked the feeling of having a gun with them when they drove on trips back and forth to Houston.

Jerry saw the keys on the dresser and grabbed them. Being on crutches, there was nothing Thompson could do to stop him. Jerry ran down to the parking lot and found the pistol in the trunk. It had a two-inch barrel and a brown wooden grip. The pistol was so dirty that police later had to use Q-Tips to push the unused cartridges out of the cylinder.

People jumped out of the way as Jerry strode back up the stairs to room 311 with the pistol in his right hand. Five or six guys in the doorway jumped aside. In the room, the white kid, Hagen, was standing in a little dressing area out of Jerry's path but just a couple of feet from Zarak.

Jerry cocked the pistol as he entered the room. He raised it and aimed at Zarak.

"Now push me again," Jerry said.

"You don't have any bullets in that thing. Get your ass out of here," Zarak said.

"You try to make me," Jerry said.

Zarak pushed him.

The pistol fired and a round red hole appeared just above Zarak's left nipple. Zarak cried out and fell into Hagen. The hippie and the big tight end hit the floor, with the white kid underneath.

Jerry went down to the second floor and walked out onto the landing. He could hear people shouting and running toward 311. He heard the sirens coming.

Behind him, a freshman running back from Texas named Reggie Finch came out just in time to see Jerry put the pistol to his temple, cock it, and pull the trigger. Reggie ducked, expecting to see the top of Jerry's head fly apart.

But the hammer clicked. The pistol misfired.

Jerry cocked the pistol again. Reggie leaped up and stuck his hand in the pistol so that the hammer struck the webbing of Reggie's palm as Jerry pulled the trigger again. Reggie later told me in my office, "Coach, it was just like in the movie *Lethal Weapon*."

Seeming sort of bewildered, Jerry let Reggie take the pistol. They went to Charles Thompson's room. Charles told Reggie to take Jerry to Jones House, the freshman athletic dorm where Reggie lived.

It didn't take the police but a few minutes to find Jerry. Officer Kerr, a female, handcuffed him and put him in her car. Jerry said, "I shot him. I shot my best friend." He asked Officer Kerr if he could borrow her pistol to commit suicide.

I was asleep at Ann's house when the phone rang at 2 A.M. I hate 2 A.M. phone calls. You never get good news at that hour.

It was Charlie North, Zarak's tight end coach.

"We have a problem," Charles said. "Jerry Parks just shot Zarak Peters in the dorm. Tony Trousdale [the dorm mom] phoned me. Mike Jones and I are at the hospital. Zarak was lucky. The bullet hit a rib and missed his heart. The doctors are not going to cut on him to take it out. He's in stable condition. Parks is in the Cleveland County jail."

"Have you called their families?" I said.

"Mike and I already talked to them."

David Swank's assistant, Donna Murphy, was the next person to phone me. She said there would be a meeting in the interim president's office at 6:30 A.M.

I was there early. In Swank's office, OU interim police chief Neil Stone went over the official report of the shooting for Swank, Donnie Duncan, and me. When he came to the part about the white kid, Alan Hagen, being a witness, Swank wanted to know what Hagen was doing in the athletic dorm.

"He says he went to visit Mike Gaddis," Chief Stone said.

"Who is Mike Gaddis?" asked Swank.

Donnie and I glanced at one another, stunned. Mike Gaddis was only the best running back Oklahoma has had since Billy Sims. If he hadn't torn up his knee in one of those "self-tacklization" accidents in the Texas game in 1989, he would be a Heisman Trophy candidate by now. I guess I shouldn't have been so shocked that our interim president had never heard of Mike Gaddis, but I couldn't help it.

John Pierce, coach at Willow Ridge High in Missouri City, Texas, flew up to Norman to see his former players. Channel 4 television met him at the airport and wanted to know if the coach had paid his own way. They weren't there to interview him about having coached Parks and Peters for four or five years and being close to the kids. All the media wanted to know was whether OU had provided his transportation and if it was a violation of the NCAA rules (we didn't, and it wasn't).

I told Jerry's mother that he was expelled by the university but that I felt we had a moral obligation to the boy and would pay the bill for the professional counseling he needed. I hope Jerry has matured and handled his emotional problems by now and that he will finish his college football career at some other college, receive his degree, and go on to an NFL career, if that's what he wants.

As for Zarak, that big horse bounced out of the hospital and into uniform for spring practice.

I remember an early scrimmage when Zarak, at his new position of tight end, came across the middle and caught a pass. Two defensive backs flew at him and nailed him full force from either side. Zarak knocked them to the ground and took off for the end zone.

Charlie North looked over at me and said, "Zarak can really take a shot, can't he?"

We were well into recruiting season when the shooting occurred. Everywhere my coaches and I went, we were met with jokes about Oklahoma outlaws and six-guns strapped to their legs. Rival institutions beat on us unmercifully. Recruiters from other schools were warning kids they had better wear bulletproof vests if they went for an official visit to Norman.

The national media made Bud Wilkinson House sound like the OK Corral. I recently read in Brent Clark's biography of Joe Don Looney, a former OU all-American halfback, that back in 1962, Looney kept a submachine gun, a 9mm automatic, and a .357 Magnum in his room and once went out and shot a ticket booth to pieces; it was never mentioned in the press. Maybe it was because there was no one in the booth.

Despite the shooting and the NCAA probation, we were doing well recruiting. The weekend of January 21 was a visitation weekend, with recruits coming in from everywhere and being shown around the campus and the Norman area.

This happened to be the weekend that a seventeen-year-old student at a small state college in central Oklahoma (let's call her Judy, it's not her real name) decided to get a blind date with one of the football players for her friend Tammy (also not her real name). Tammy was twenty years old and a nonstudent. Both girls were white. The blind date was to be with a black athlete from OU, but Tammy didn't know which one.

The two white girls drove to Bud Wilkinson House and went to Nigel Clay's room at seven o'clock in the evening on Saturday.

After Tammy was introduced to Nigel in his room, she drove him in her car to a liquor store and they bought two bottles of booze. They returned to the dorm, mixed drinks, and served them to a bunch of athletes who were playing cards and getting in the partying mood.

Tammy told police later that she began feeling uneasy after a while because the athletes began "making passes" at her. She went to use the bathroom in the suite. When she came out, all the lights had been turned off.

Somebody grabbed her in the dark and forced her into the adjoining bedroom. She was thrown onto a bed and then fell to the floor, where she began screaming. She said someone then clamped a hand over her mouth and unzipped her dress.

Her undergarments were torn off. She managed to scream again, but the door had been blocked. She told police that the first two attempts to penetrate her failed. But the third, fourth, fifth, and sixth times she was raped.

The rapists then left her alone in the dark room. When she regained her composure, she left the dorm and returned to Oklahoma City. Tammy had been a virgin when she arrived at Bud Wilkinson House a few hours earlier.

I heard about this on Sunday morning, twenty-four hours before Tammy went to the police and filed a complaint.

I have a twenty-year-old daughter myself, and the news was horrifying. It was a terrible, brutal, stupid crime, and I wanted to find out who had done it and see that they were punished to the fullest extent of the law. If this had happened to my daughter, I think I would have found the rapists and killed them with a baseball bat.

I interviewed several of my players who I considered very responsible individuals the first thing the next morning. They had some suspicions and some names for me.

Immediately, I called Bernard Hall, Nigel Clay, and Glen Bell into my office and asked them what had happened. Their story was that there had been a lot of people in and out of the dorm, drinking and playing music, but no one had been raped. After having talked to a few other players who had been around that evening, I was personally convinced a crime had occurred.

A sophomore offensive guard, Larry Medice, a fine young man who is 6-foot-4 and weighs 290, came and told me he was in his room with his girlfriend and had heard a scream. When Larry went to investigate the scream, he saw Bernard Hall looking out of the room and a body lying on the floor, being held down. He couldn't see who was holding her down. Bernard told him it was just a misunderstanding and slammed the door. Medice returned to his own room. Later, Larry Medice became the star witness for the prosecution.

On Monday, the violated girl filed her complaint. Naturally, we had another emergency meeting in David Swank's office—Donnie Duncan, Fred Gipson, OU interim police chief Neil Stone, and me.

Chief Stone read the complaint out loud, and then he

said, "Another reported case of rape. My Lord, this is the nineteenth case of rape we've had on the campus already this year."

I said, "What?"

Stone said, "Yeah, this is the nineteenth. This includes apartments, cars, fraternity houses, general student dorms . . ."

"Why haven't we heard about them?" I said, already knowing the answer.

Swank turned to Stone and said, "Chief, there's no point in announcing a statistic like that."

Obviously, none of those other incidents involved athletes or we would have heard about them.

The national media went crazy over the rape, especially since it came so quickly after the shooting. The three TV affiliates from Oklahoma City must have spent $200,000 camping at Bud Wilkinson House with their remote trucks. Reporters were stopping kids on their way to class and interviewing them on what it was like to be on a campus where the athletes were like some serial-killer-rapist Ted Bundy lying behind every bush, as *Sports Illustrated* had tried to make it appear. It became very frustrating to the athletic department. We told the media to get their asses off our lawn.

When the rape case went to trial, Bernard Hall and Nigel Clay both got ten-year sentences. Glen Bell had been charged but was acquitted by the jury. Hall and Clay didn't appeal their sentences because their lawyer told them they might get the death penalty next time.

Bernard Hall was a tremendous athlete, an impact player from Henry Ford High in Detroit, who was influenced for OU by Billy Sims. He was a Prop 48, flunked out of school, and went to junior college, and this had been his first semester back at OU. Just a week earlier, I'd had a one-on-one talk with Bernard about keeping his conduct clean and his grades up. Bernard wasn't the smartest guy in the world, but he was 6-feet-3, weighed 240, and ran the forty in 4.5. Even if he never managed to get his degree, OU would certainly have showcased him for the pros, where he should have had a great career; he was bound to learn more of value in class than he would on the street.

Nigel Clay was from Fontana, California. We'd had a battle recruiting him away from USC and Washington. He had been the most valuable player in the California high school all-star game. He had been at Oklahoma for three years and had never caused a problem in any way. But this mistake was such that he couldn't get a second chance.

Glen Bell was from Muskogee, selected by the *Tulsa World* as the most outstanding player in the state in 1986. We had never had a problem with him before, either.

As you can imagine, with the shooting and the raping, with all the negative headlines, we in the athletic administration began taking action to try to protect our program and our school from the impact of these horrible events. Athletic director Donnie Duncan and I worked closely with the board of regents, particularly board president Ron White, and with interim president David Swank to come up with a program to address the problems and to assure the public that we were not running an outlaw program. Sure, I was embarrassed and truly shocked by it all. But I kept telling myself that most of our kids were good kids, that I hadn't failed myself, the kids, or the university.

Then the media started with the scapegoat mentality, that I was in some way personally responsible for all that had happened. While Ron White was publicly saying the truth—that is, that OU's athletic problems are still limited to a small number of players and that "It's unfortunate that so very few can make so many look so bad . . ."—we were also faced with things like an editorial in our campus newspaper, *The Oklahoma Daily*, by Ron Whitmire, that said my feeling that I was not responsible for the criminal actions of my players was, ". . . so much crap. He's responsible for bringing them here. He should take a little responsibility."

As you would expect, Whitmire's asinine comment in our campus newspaper was quickly picked up by the national press. But Whitmire's logic, which was taken as the gospel by all the fiction writers everywhere, makes me wonder who was responsible for the eighteen other rapes that took place on Oklahoma's campus that year—those not involving athletes. Is it the director of admissions, who let them into the university? Is it the interim president, David Swank? Or was it really maybe the rapists themselves?

On February 10, the very day district attorney Tully Mc-
Coy formally filed charges against the three players in the
rape case, the athletic administration appeared at a formal
meeting of the board of regents to announce what Swank
billed as *"sweeping changes* in academic standards, written codes
of conduct, and dormitory security."

It was all written down and put in a handbook. Swank
sent a letter to every OU alum saying, ". . . our main emphasis
is academics. . . . I will expect [our athletes] to follow . . . the
disciplinary rules. . . . Please remember that the University of
Oklahoma is comprised of approximately 25,000 students,
1,500 faculty, and more than 150,000 alumni . . . I pledge to
correct the problems in the Athletic Department . . ."

I agreed with everything Swank said in his letter. But you
know what? We already had all those rules he put in his handbook and bragged about in his letter. Hiring Tom Hill as assistant athletic director in charge of academics was something
new—and a very good thing, since Tom was a world-class athlete himself, an Olympic bronze medalist, with a Ph.D. from
Florida, and a very bright, "class" guy—but the rest of the
"new disciplinary code" had been in force for years.

The incidents of early 1989 had a tremendous impact in
bringing all of the possible problems to everyone's con-
sciousness, but the "new" code wasn't really new. It was just a
written codification whereby we, especially the athletes, could
see all of the rules that we could think of in one place, in one
book.

But in working up the code, we all really made the same
mistake that had been made earlier.

Nowhere in the handbook were there rules that said, "Do
not rape anybody, and do not shoot anybody, and do not sell
dope."

Donnie Duncan and I went before the regents in executive session. Regent Sam Noble questioned our drug-testing program. That's when he said, "Why, you can grab any
hundred people off the street, or out of the Noble Foundation, and you'll find more dope users than that." I wanted to
tell him, "Yeah, but if your employees knew they were going
to be tested as often as three times a week and you were going
to fire their asses if they were dirty, then you'd probably be as

clean as our football program." I didn't say it then, but I have said it since.

Ron White looked at Donnie and me and said, "We just can't have any other instances like these [the raping and shooting] happen here again." Donnie replied, "We're dealing with over three hundred people in our intercollegiate athletic programs. You can expect future occurrences. Things have happened in the past, and they're bound to happen in the future. History and statistics prove that. Hopefully, they will not be as bad as these were."

I said, "It's like Russian roulette when you're dealing with so many people."

"What else could possibly happen?" Ron White said.

How little we knew.

I went back to my office that afternoon and received another phone call from Tully McCoy, the district attorney.

I thought by this point that I was shockproof, but Tully blew my mind when he told me the FBI had a sting operation underway and they had a tape of my quarterback, Charles Thompson, selling cocaine to an undercover cop!

Tully said that Charles's buddy, Otha Armstrong, was a snitch and had set him up.

I'm not sure what I would have done if the FBI had come to me first and said, "Look, coach, we've got this sting going on and we've caught your quarterback, but we want you to keep it under your hat so you don't risk blowing our operation and maybe endangering some of our agents."

But it's irrelevant, because the FBI hadn't told me a damn thing.

All I knew was that this was a bomb that was going to explode very soon.

That same afternoon OU's legal counsel, Fred Gipson, was phoned by a judge, who told him about Thompson being caught in the sting. Donnie Duncan and David Swank also heard about it the same day from other reliable sources.

So Gipson, Duncan, and I had another meeting and reached a mutual decision that we must reveal Charles and remove him from our football program to keep him from dragging any innocent people into his web and doing more damage than he had already done. Swank agreed with us.

This was not just my decision, although I got the blame for it. The interim president, the legal counsel, the athletic director, and I agreed it was the only thing we could do.

On Sunday afternoon, I went to room 211 at Bud Wilkinson House and knocked on Charles's door. No answer. I asked other people where Charles might be, and nobody had seen him. I hammered on the door again and still no answer. I was back downstairs going to my car when Charles yelled at me from the balcony. He said he had been asleep. I shouted up at him to come to my office at nine o'clock Monday morning.

The next morning, Donnie Duncan and Fred Gipson were in the conference room across from my office when Charles showed up. I had a private talk with Charles. I told him they had him red-handed.

Charles didn't lie to me. He admitted he had been selling cocaine to make money. Charles had passed sixteen drug tests, because he was not *using* cocaine—he was *selling* it!

I told Charles he was off the team. I advised him to see an attorney. He said he didn't know one, so I contacted Buddy Pendarvis from Norman to represent him. Charles met with Pendarvis but then hired a different lawyer. I didn't care what lawyer he used.

I announced to the press that afternoon that Charles was suspended. On the advice of his attorney, Charles turned himself in to the law.

My own world was crashing down, too, but I didn't see it coming yet.

I was informed by highly placed confidential sources that the FBI was upset with me for blowing its sting. There was a big federal task force working undercover trying to bust a lot of Oklahomans, and they said I had fouled up one area of their operation. The media attacked me for exposing Charles and screwing up the government, as if it had been my decision alone.

A few days after I had dismissed Charles Thompson, FBI agents Phil Shockey and John Hershey came to my office. They wanted to know the source of my information, because they were genuinely concerned for the safety of their undercover people. I didn't want to tell them Tully's name, because

I knew it could compromise him, so I just said I would contact my source, and my source, if he wanted, would contact them.

Then, after talking with Tully by telephone, I called Phil Shockey back and told him it was Tully and that Tully had told me to tell him he would be calling. Phil is the local Norman FBI agent who I've known for years, and he had been a law-school classmate of Tully's. Those were the only conversations I ever had with the FBI about Charles Thompson.

Later, Charles pleaded guilty to dealing cocaine. The media deluge hit, and the "scapegoat mentality" immediately dominated the press—calling for my scalp for what Bernard Hall, Nigel Clay, Jerry Parks, and Charles Thompson had done. They demanded my resignation.

One thing that fascinated me about all the press and coffee-shop talk was that they all took the Charles Thompson incident as proof that either I had manipulated Charles's urine tests or that our testing program wasn't any good. The program worked for at least the sixteen weeks that Charles was on it. And it is the most comprehensive and complete testing program in college football. But what these idiots forget is that Charles did not get in trouble for using cocaine. He was not a user. He was dealing in it. He was a criminal. No program devised can test that.

In less than thirty days, our football program had been hit with the shooting, raping, and doping.

34

THE TABLE OF TRUTH

One afternoon two weeks before Charles Thompson was arrested, I received a call from Donnie Duncan. He asked me to meet him at 6:30 P.M. at my good friend Pasquale Benso's restaurant, Othello's, because he had to talk to me about Swank.

Donnie and I sat at the Table of Truth. No lies can be told at the Table of Truth in Patsy's place. After all the horrible things that had been happening, I was very curious what news Donnie had to tell me this time.

"Swank says we have to take Scott Hill off the road," Donnie said. "Scott is not allowed to go recruiting anymore."

"You've got to be kidding," I said.

"No lies at this table," Donnie said.

"Why in the hell would Swank want to impose an additional penalty on our program that is more severe than what the NCAA has already done?" I said. "The NCAA has already taken seven scholarships away from us. They've taken Mike Jones off the road, leaving us eight recruiters and me. They've banned us from bowl games and television. And now David Swank wants to give us an additional penalty that will probably cost us another five recruits? It's too close to national signing date. We'll lose every kid Scott Hill has been recruiting. Doesn't Swank understand that?"

"Sure, he understands it," Donnie said.

I went to the phone and called Swank and told him I wanted to see him the next morning.

Swank was waiting for me in his office with his reasons for removing Scott Hill from recruiting. He had two reasons. They were preposterous. First, he recited the NCAA violations in which Scott had been involved. The NCAA hadn't taken any punitive action against Scott, but Swank determined that it was best to further punish him and the program. The other reason went back to our Citrus Bowl game against Clemson in Orlando in January. The week of the game, four Clemson coaches and four Oklahoma coaches had played golf at an Orlando country club one afternoon and afterward were visiting with each other and drinking cocktails. Oklahoma and Clemson had the two biggest, heaviest tight-end coaches in the game—our Charlie North and their Wayne Bolt. Each of them weighed about 300 pounds.

During the evening, the coaches had gotten to clowning around, as boys will do. The Clemson tight-end coach was sitting in a chair. Scott Hill went over and flopped down in his lap. The chair splintered under their weight and they fell on the floor. The entire bill for damages was less than $500.

Larry Guest of the *Orlando Sentinel* had reported this as a brawl! My God, if those eight coaches had gotten into a brawl, the bill for damages would buy a new jet airplane. The press reported that Scott Hill had jumped on the chair and broken it. The press didn't say there were any Clemson coaches present. It was one of the sorriest pieces of journalism I have ever seen.

I played a hunch and asked Swank whether the regents were aware of this decision. He said no. It was solely his decision. I then said, "Well, I think that this is a matter I'm going to take up with the regents directly, because this will definitely have a negative impact on this year's recruiting." After a few minutes of this, Swank backed down and agreed that Scott could finish out the last two weeks of recruiting.

All of this, as I said earlier, had happened within a one-month period. And the only people who were having fun with it were the media.

USA Today ran a story quoting an OU engineering professor telling a meeting of the faculty senate, "The athletic program has gotten out of hand. The tail is wagging the dog. Throw the money changers out of the temple!"

The Daily Oklahoman, under the headline that read "IT'S JUST ANOTHER CHAPTER IN A LONG SORDID TALE," ran a story that said, "Evidently, for who knows how long, campus life has been nothing but an unmanned candy store for the OU players. You're all such good little boys, do anything you want, take anything you need." This article and its writer, John Rohde, are a good example of what we at Oklahoma have had to contend with over the years. When he wrote this article, Rohde was in his mid-twenties, a very young, inexperienced writer, who had been in the state of Oklahoma for a period of two years! What the hell qualified him to make that kind of a condemning judgment of me and all of my players?

About the same time, *Newsweek* ran an article under a clever headline with a double entendre: that is, "OKLAHOMA IS NOT OK—THE SOONERS GO DOWN IN HISTORY FOR THEIR OFFENSES." As you would expect, however, the article read like a rap sheet and dealt with criminal offenses rather than yardage gained.

I have always been able to deal with the pressure of winning, and winning more. I understand that. Common sense and the Football Monster tell me that 76,000 people in Owen Field expect me to win. But dealing with a lot of the "moralists" and "fiction writers" in the press, you're not dealing with common sense. You're dealing with hysteria, irrationality, prejudice, and mob psychology. And with this as the background that we were dealing with, it is easy to understand why the raping, shooting, and doping attracted the most sensational, moralistic media feeding frenzy the athletic community has ever seen.

I don't know if even the regents or the rest of the university community realize that coaches and players have more interaction with each other than any other group in the university. We understand each other. We develop a rapport with our kids. Maybe the faculty thinks we're like a lot of the history professors or the English professors, who come to class for forty-five minutes three times a week and that's the only time they see the kids. Maybe they think a coach goes in there and plunks down his notes and doesn't even call the damn roll, doesn't even know their names. He talks, closes his book, and walks out.

Well, it isn't that way. Coaches eat with the players, practice with them, go to games with them, go to class with them, talk to them, motivate them, encourage them, educate them, teach them off the field. And we don't get any hours of credit for it. We don't get recognized for it. We don't get commended for it. I know the people in my profession, and I know what kind of kids are playing this game. College football isn't in as bad a shape as many people make it out to be.

In one of our team meetings after we had gone through this raping, shooting, and doping, I told my players, "Damnit, talk to me. Tell me where I went wrong."

One kid said, "Coach, if you hadn't given Bernard a second chance, this wouldn't have happened."

Another kid stood up and said, "By God, I'm glad he gave me a second chance."

These kids knew our backs were to the wall, and they were going to live under a set of rules and restrictions that would never be allowed in the fraternity or sorority houses or in the towers. Yet our athletes were willing to be subjected to this punishment against them—and it truly came down as punitive—*even though they were all victims of the behavior of only five out of a hundred.* They were willing to accept it, because they knew our coaches and they knew my situation, and I appreciated it. I brought in Darrell Reed, J. C. Watts, and Jim Riley and other ex-players and held seminars on the role of the athlete in society. We didn't tell the papers or the TV about these things. They were among family.

Any coaches who read my book will understand what I mean. We have more influence on molding the lives of young men and women on campus than anybody else in the university, from the president to the lowest-paid guy at the physical plant. And, by and large, we do a damn good job of it.

Many of our problems as coaches are caused by people who are out of touch, who are trying to impose on us whatever image or perception they think is right. These people don't understand earrings, chains, hair length, rap music, and all that.

I deal with an eighteen-year-old product every year. The kids change style, their thinking changes, their music, their clothes, their hair, their fads. I get a year older every year, but the kid I am recruiting doesn't. He stays eighteen.

Whether Bo Schembechler or Darrell Royal or I like it or not, if we are going to chase eighteen-year-old kids for thirty years, we have to learn to adjust. I've heard a story about a recruit telling Darrell, "Get up, coach, you're sitting in my chair," and Darrell had to move. I believe that if the story is true, Darrell may have wanted to slap the shit out of him but couldn't. I've had similar things happen to me. But we must remember the credo of the recruiter: "We're the adults. He's the child. We know he's wrong. Let's teach him right—BUT YOU GOTTA SIGN HIM FIRST." And that is what a major part of coaching is all about.

Near the end of February 1989, I was supposed to go to Hawaii on a Nike trip. Ann wanted to go, and I really needed to get away for a while.

But while all my Nike family buddies were flying off to Hawaii, I was at a special seminar set up by Swank for Donnie Duncan, Dan Gibbens, and myself. These were lessons from Jim Hartz and John Meek of Washington on how we should behave with the media and what we should wear. My opinion was that Swank should issue a statement on the condition of our program and that was it. Let's not go into the national arena, where we have an adversary attacking us and we have to be on the defense. *Nightline* had called and wanted me or Donnie. That type of show doesn't give a damn about the University of Oklahoma, other than having your ass on the screen and attacking you and getting higher ratings. We all agreed we wouldn't do it.

Next thing you know, David Swank is on *Nightline* getting chopped up by Ted Koppel. It was obvious that Koppel was dumbfounded when Swank, even after having the benefit of a commercial break to compose his answer, was not able to come up with a good, "politic" answer to the question, "What kind of a won-lost record could Barry Switzer survive?" The reason Swank stammered was that there is no good, currently fashionable answer that the national public could accept. The truth is, as President Banowsky had made clear to Wade Walker and me years earlier, winning is the key to money, and money is the key to everything. Swank knew that I would survive virtually no matter what if I kept on winning championships . . . or unless something else fell in his lap to help him get rid of me.

Then I'm driving down the road listening to the radio

and all of a sudden I hear, "David Swank says Barry Switzer has one year to clean up his act or he's gone." What the hell was this? I'd just talked to David yesterday. He'd said nothing of the sort. But *The Houston Post* had sent its jet to pick up Swank in Norman and fly him to speak at the Texas Press Writers Association annual convention in Austin. This was the result.

Later I talked to Swank, and he said he was embarrassed, that he didn't mean for his speech to be interpreted that way. I went to his secretary, Lianne, and asked how long that Texas speech had been on Swank's calendar. David had accepted the speech after we had all agreed not to appear, just as he had done with *Nightline*.

One of my coaches said, "I guess Nebraska will have their jet sitting on the runway waiting to take him to Lincoln."

I said, "Yeah, and the Aggies will send a horse and wagon to haul his ass to Stillwater."

In the period of late February or March 1989, after the last of the shooting, raping, and doping, athletic director Donnie Duncan received a call from a faculty member with whom he had worked closely for a number of years on the council on athletics. Naturally, Donnie later told me of the substance of that call, since it came from a man who also had worked closely with Swank on council business. It became clear to Donnie and me that in a way, all of the tragic events of January and February 1989 were fitting neatly into David Swank's personal plans. This gentleman told Donnie it was very evident from his close dealings with Swank over an extended period of time that there were three important things on Swank's personal agenda. First, he wanted to become the full-time president of the university; then he wanted to deemphasize athletics; and he wanted to replace the head football coach of the university. He also said that in a conversation with Swank that occurred in this period of turmoil, Swank said that there would never be a better time than the present for academics to replace athletics as the focal point of the university.

Spring break finally came. At last I could relax for a few days. My daughter, Kathy, was going to take a trip with Ann and me. Some friends offered us a beautiful house down at Puerto Vallarta. I asked Kathy, "Do you want to go to Puerto

Vallarta or would you rather go skiing?" I had taken the kids skiing regularly for about fifteen years, but the last time had been a couple of years ago. Kathy chose skiing.

I called Chuck Neinas, who had a place in Beaver Creek, Colorado, and said I'd take him up on his standing offer to use his condo. Bobby Bell, my old hunting and fishing pal, came by and said, "Aw shit, coach, don't go skiing. The way your luck has been running, you'll tear your damn leg up." I told him, "Bobby, I'm a damn good skiier. I can handle any slope up there."

Ann, Kathy, and I flew to Colorado, spent the night in Breckenridge, drove to Vail, and then on to Beaver Creek the next day. We skiied the morning of March 8. Ann is a beginner and was ready to go back to the condo after lunch, so Kathy and I decided to go to the top of the mountain and really do some skiing.

We got out our trail maps and went up the mountain on a two-chair lift. We skiied down a couple of runs. On the third trip up, we were in a hurry getting off the lift and our skis got tangled and I fell over backward. The tips of my skis got caught in the chair lift and I was dragged partway down the mountain, feeling the ligaments in both knees ripping and tearing, going lukewarm, and the internal bleeding starting.

The ski patrol put me in a basket and shot me to the bottom. I was carried to Vail Hospital. The doctor who examined my knees was an OU grad. He put casts on both legs. The next day I was pushed in a wheelchair through Stapleton Airport, holding a newspaper over my face, ashamed of myself. For fifteen years, I'd been seeing injured skiiers at Stapleton, and now I was one of them.

I called Bobby Bell that night and told him, "You were wrong. I didn't tear up one leg. I tore up both of them!"

At least there was some good humor from my skiing accident.

At the Big Eight basketball tournament, people ran up to David Swank and said, "Did you hear about what happened to Switzer today?" Swank said, "No, what's happened now?" They said Switzer tore up both his knees skiing.

"Oh, thank God," exclaimed a relieved Swank. I can understand that, David, with the way my luck had been running.

At Baptist Hospital in Oklahoma City, they operated on me on March 10. The next day I was lying there in bed, thinking about all my bad luck and watching television. A national news commentator came on with a story that made me sit up.

The story said William Slater Banowsky, former president of the University of Oklahoma, had been charged by the Securities and Exchange Commission for insider trading. Banowsky had pleaded no contest and agreed to pay $750,000 in fines and penalties in order to settle charges of illegal insider trading of stock. I had a pretty good chuckle out of that. Six years before, Bill had told me I was an embarrassment to the university because of my problems with the SEC—and I was found innocent.

Kathy, of course, felt bad about my accident, but she put it into perspective for me, the way kids can do.

She said, "Just think, Dad. If we'd gone to Puerto Vallarta, you might have drowned or some shark might have eaten you."

Spring practice rolled around the next week, and I was riding in a golf cart, with both legs in a cast.

My old nemesis—the 49ers—were blasting me in the media and writing letters. J. D. Roberts and Jim Owens loudly demanded that Donnie Duncan and I be fired. By now a lot of our coaches were referring to this group of 49ers as a bunch of "fifty-year-old Prop 48s."

At our spring-practice Red and White game, the 49ers were supposed to have their fortieth-anniversary reunion. But they announced that they refused to come because of the humiliation I had caused the university. They made it sound like Bud Wilkinson was backing them. I phoned Bud, and he said, "Barry, I'm not getting involved in any of that and they'd better not even ask me. All they really told me was that there was not enough interest to do it this spring, and because of that they were planning to do it next fall."

I went on TV and said, "I'm more concerned with the 'eighty-nine team than I am the 'forty-nine team." I didn't give a damn what they thought. I knew their politics and what their motives were.

Steve Owens, Billy Sims, Steve Zabel, J. C. Watts, Darrell Reed, and many others of my former players showed up to speak on my behalf at a meeting they organized at the Marriott in Oklahoma City. They said, We are a product of his program. Don't just look at what five guys have done—look at us and see what we have accomplished. It really moved me that they would return and come to my defense against the 49ers who were raging against me. Many of the 49ers are good guys and had nothing to gain by getting me fired. It was basically that J. D. Roberts bunch, who wanted Leon Cross as athletic director.

In May, my staff and I were concerned with getting our players through finals, getting summer jobs lined up, checking eligibility, finding out who was going to summer school, who was taking correspondence courses—our regular duties. Things actually seemed to be quieting down.

I started making plans to go to the Leonard-Hearns fight in Las Vegas. The fight would be on June 12. I made reservations to go with my Texarkana friend Bob White and a bunch of other friends and associates. I was really looking forward to relaxing and having a good time.

I had no idea that the FBI was secretly interrogating Scott Hill and trying to make him implicate me in a cocaine case. I had no idea what was going on in the office of United States attorney Blair Watson, head of the drug strike-force. I had never even heard his name.

And especially I would not have guessed that in another week I would be at a big press conference at Owen Field resigning from my job as the head football coach at Oklahoma.

35

GOOD-BYE TO ALL THAT

Well, there I was in the parking lot of the Quarter Horse Inn in Stroud, Oklahoma, on June 14, 1989—glaring at my brother, Donnie, the lawyer. I didn't like what he had said any more than I had liked what Swank and Coats had said about me the previous evening.

I thanked Donnie and O. B., his partner, for coming, and started on back to Norman. My mind was racing. I've always felt that I might be paranoid, and I kept trying to remind myself of that and to convince myself that both my brother and I were making more of it than there really was. But I kept thinking.

I was in a Catch-22. The publicity from my coming out with my side of the story would doom me. Picture headlines in the newspapers: SWITZER DENIES HE GAMBLES ON OU FOOT-BALL. SWITZER DENIES DOPE TRAFFICKING. SWITZER DENIES FIXING DRUG TESTS. I thought I would have a better chance to survive a boxing match with Mike Tyson. (No one knew who Buster Douglas was at that time.) And I didn't know if I could put the university and the state I loved through that kind of additional hell.

Back in Norman, I met Donnie Duncan and Fred Gipson in the cafe at the old Ramada Inn, now Days' Inn, on Lindsey Street. Fred told me he and Swank had heard about these allegations from Blair Watson's office and that they then had gone to see Ron Hoverson, special agent in charge of the FBI in Oklahoma City at that time. Ron Hoverson told them I was not involved in any FBI investigation of any kind.

I was wondering why Swank hadn't been more emphatic

about this at the meeting last night. It would have been important for the chairman of the board of regents, Ron White, to hear that there was no FBI investigation before he went out and gave the regents an opportunity to believe the opposite by relating the crap that supposedly came from a guy named Blair Watson.

Later I asked Fred why he and Swank didn't try to go see Blair Watson, too, while they were calling on the law. He said they did, but the assistant U.S. attorney refused to talk to them.

That day in the cafe, I asked Fred to go over again exactly what I was accused of.

"You were with some people in a suite in Las Vegas five or six years ago, and cocaine was present."

"I wasn't aware of it, and that's no crime, anyway," I said. "What did Andy mean saying they have me cold?"

"He means they have you cold on wire transfer of funds across state lines for gambling."

"Who is they?"

"Blair Watson's office."

"Bullshit."

"And there's this talk of your manipulating the drug tests."

"I'm not in charge of the drug tests. Why don't you ask our trainer, Dan Pickett?"

"We're talking to Dan now."

I found out later they were giving Dan a polygraph test and he came out clean. But our drug-testing program was taken away from the athletic department and turned over to a private lab in Oklahoma City. Good for Dan. No longer does he have to watch football players pee 2,066 times in a single year, like he did in 1988.

But that day in the cafe as I listened to Fred I remembered what my brother had told me, and all of a sudden I felt mentally exhausted.

This is what it had come to, huh? I'd won more games than any Oklahoma coach will probably ever win, and now I began to realize that I would never win another.

For me the fun was gone from the game, anyhow. I was fighting for my job out of instinct, but I began to understand that there was a part of me that didn't really want the job anymore. Nineteen eighty-nine was wearing me out. Football had changed so much in the last few years that I was having a hard time pumping myself up to go recruiting, a phase of the game I had always loved and had been among the best at doing.

Or maybe football hadn't changed all that much. Maybe it was me. I was fifty-one years old and I had fed the Oklahoma Football Monster nearly half my life.

Here's a funny thing. Frank Broyles—who was my mentor—was fifty-two when he resigned at Arkansas. My angriest rival, Darrell Royal, was fifty-two when he resigned from Texas. Darrell told the newspapers that a man who becomes head coach in his early thirties (as he and Frank and I had) burns out in twenty years. There are exceptions. Woody Hayes coached at Ohio State until sixty-five and Bear Bryant at Alabama until sixty-nine. Bo Schembechler quit coaching at Michigan State in December 1988, at age sixty. Hey, Uncle Joe Pa, how are you feeling these mornings at University Park?

But Bud Wilkinson was only forty-seven when he stepped down at Oklahoma. Now I could understand why Bud Wilkinson had quit at such a young age. At the time, I had thought Bud was crazy to quit this great job. Sure, Bud had been put on probation a third time in 1960 and hadn't beaten Texas in six years. But this was the legendary Bud Wilkinson. Why would he leave?

I was just a young assistant coach at Arkansas when Bud quit. I didn't dream that the Monster he helped create had eaten him and would someday eat me, too. But now I felt I had reached a point in life where I was tired of feeding myself to the Monster.

Throughout my head-coaching career, I have worn the black hat. I have been accused of cheating, of maintaining slush funds, of spying, of ticket scalping, and even of purposely losing the Orange Bowl game and national championship in a big upset to Arkansas—maybe the most painful night of my career.

This is the sort of heat that comes with a long string of 11–1 records.

You draw attention. You make enemies. You become a wooden duck in a shooting gallery.

The worst things I was really guilty of, besides the silly spying episode, were some of the lesser of the NCAA allegations that now had us on probation, as I've explained.

In the Days' Inn cafe, I told Donnie and Fred, "It's getting close to the weekend. I don't think it's the right time to do it on a weekend. I don't want anybody to know this, but wait until Monday and I will announce my resignation."

So there I was on June 15, 1989. I was faced with the world clamoring for my head; I had the university's interim president refusing to sign the NCAA certification letter as long as I was around; I had a divided bunch of regents, some of whom were really feeling pressure from the media and were clearly against me; I was being attacked by some obscure assistant United States attorney I had never heard of and being accused of horrible, horrible things that I did not do; and I had David Swank, Ron White, and Andy Coats repeating all those lies about me to the regents. And on top of this, the Scott Hill cocaine problem was about to become public.

So after considering this incredible combination of circumstances and talking about it with Donnie Duncan in my car in front of his home until two o'clock in the morning, I realized that all choices had been taken away from me, I no longer had any free will, the people and events around me had taken away all my choices and chances for survival as head football coach. I had to resign.

Of course, it's possible that the regents might not have renewed my contract anyway. But we'll never know that, because of what all of the people mentioned and events described had done to me . . . and to all of us.

I feel that both Donnie and Fred were relieved that I had finally come to this decision. I later asked Fred to help me write my resignation speech.

I sat up with Donnie Duncan until 2 in the morning of June 16, and he told me he was going to recommend retaining the coaching staff and to name an assistant as the head coach, and he asked who I would recommend. I told him there were two guys I would recommend without any reservations— Merv Johnson and Gary Gibbs. Merv was my assistant head coach and offensive line coach and had been my close friend for thirty years. Gary was the defensive coordinator. Gary had played linebacker for some of our great teams and had coached for me fourteen years. Either man would be an excellent head coach.

I said, "I want to handle the resignation downstairs in the Big Red Room. Nobody is to know about this but you and me until we announce it at the press conference. Tell the press to show up at ten A.M. I'll meet my coaching staff at nine A.M. and give them the news first in private."

I was starting to yawn. We were both tired.

"You ought to be exhausted," Donnie said.

"Yeah, I've got to throw myself in a bed and get some rest," I said. "My kids are going to spend the weekend with me."

"Oh," Donnie said. He had known my sons, Greg and Doug, and my daughter, Kathy, since they were children and Joe Washington used to baby-sit for them and tell them nursery tales.

All three were conceived around the time of a bowl game. Greg is our 1967 Orange Bowl son. Kathy is our 1968 Astro-Bluebonnet Bowl daughter. Doug is our 1971 Sugar Bowl son. Kay was the only person in Oklahoma who was happy we were on probation in 1973 and 1974 because of this biological phenomenon.

"I'll have to tell my kids what I'm about to do," I said. "You know how emotional we Switzers are. I don't know how they'll take it."

My son Greg was a sophomore linebacker at the University of Arkansas and can play the piano right up there with the best. He arrived Friday night and brought a friend from St. Louis with him. My other son, Doug, was a sixteen-year-old junior in high school in Little Rock. He lived with his mother, Kay. My daughter, Kathy, was a sophomore at the University of Oklahoma, a Chi Omega who wanted to become a cheerleader.

My kids sensed at once that something was wrong.

I was trying not to show it, but I was acting preoccupied. I would sit in the living room and listen to Greg playing the piano I had put in my loft for him, and I knew his friend was up there with him next to the trophy case with Joe Washington's silver shoes and my twelve white footballs . . . one for each of my twelve Big Eight championships.

I didn't want to tell Greg in front of his friend. It would ruin their weekend. I wanted Doug and Kathy to enjoy visiting their daddy. I hugged and kissed them maybe even more than usual. We are a family that hugs and kisses and says "I love you," and we aren't embarrassed about it.

Kathy is very perceptive and kept wanting me to tell her what was wrong, and finally I did. I told her I was resigning. I couldn't give her any reason except that coaching wasn't fun for me anymore.

Kathy climbed into my lap and wept. One of her goals was to be a cheerleader for her daddy the coach. After a while she told me, "You know what? I'm not really an OU fan. I'm a Daddy fan." That made me feel so good that we both sat there and cried for half an hour.

On Sunday Greg's friend went back to St. Louis. Greg was upstairs playing the piano, and Doug was talking on the phone to his girlfriend. Kathy was with her boyfriend, Biff, at the Chi Omega house.

I went up to Doug and said, "When you finish your call, I want to visit with you and Greg."

Something in my voice made him hang up. I yelled for Greg to come downstairs. The three of us sat down at the game table.

I said, "Sometimes things happen in your life that you can't control but which influence major decisions you must make. I want you boys to know that I am going to resign my job tomorrow at ten o'clock. I've had good bats at Oklahoma, it's been fun, and we've all enjoyed it, and I hope you all can accept what I'm doing."

Greg and Doug weren't upset at all.

"I'm all for you in anything you want to do," Greg said. "All the brothers at Arkansas are always telling me that they think you're great. They're always telling me, 'Bring the coach over here.'"

"That's nice of you to say. But I won't coach college football anymore. There are other things I want to do with my life."

A while later, after Greg had left, Doug came over and put his arms around my neck.

"Daddy, you scared me to death," he said.

"How's that?"

"When you told me to get off the phone in that tone of voice, it scared me. Then the way you yelled up at Greg scared me."

"Why?"

"Daddy, I thought you were going to tell us you had cancer and you were dying."

Doug was grinning. He was actually happy to hear that all I was doing was resigning as head coach, because the fears in his mind had been so much worse.

If I had been having trouble with my perspective on life, Doug straightened me out in a hurry.

My ex-wife and friend, Kay, had come to Norman that weekend with Doug for reasons of her own. Kay had been my wife and my partner in the coaching business for eighteen seasons and really helped me in a lot of ways. She ought to be in on this, I thought. I called her and told her I was quitting.

I never claimed to be an all-American husband. Early in my career I was too selfish and self-centered, and when I became successful, many temptations entered my path. But I am a good father. And a good friend. Although Kay and I had been divorced for eight years, we were still close.

She came over to the house later. And that evening, all five of us—Kay, Greg, Kathy, Doug, and I—sat on the bed, laughed and cried and talked over everything we had been through together.

We remembered the time we promised to take the kids anywhere in the world they wanted to go. Rome, Paris, London—you name it and the Switzers will go take a look at it.

The kids decided they wanted to go to Midvale, Utah, to see the Barry Switzer Sewage Treatment Plant that had been named in my honor after I said that the Brigham Young University football team that had won the national championship in 1984 didn't deserve to be national champions. Those Mormons are as deathly serious about their football as any Oklahoma fanatic.

36

SEVEN MINUTES TO SAY GOOD-BYE

When I walked into the meeting with my staff at nine o'clock Monday morning, June 19, the room was alive with curiosity and anxiety.

They knew something big was about to happen, but they didn't know exactly what. Donnie Duncan had phoned Gary Gibbs in San Antonio on Saturday and told him to fly home. That set off a lot of speculation and a certain amount of fear. A major shake-up wouldn't concern just me. The lives of a dozen coaches and secretaries and their families were involved.

Amazingly enough, it had been four days since I decided to quit and the press hadn't picked up on it. Even our sports-information director, Mike Treps, didn't have a clue until Sunday night at ten, when he and assistant athletic director John Underwood were summoned to Donnie's home and told to prepare the Big Red Room under the stadium for a press conference to announce my resignation.

The president's administrative council met at 8 A.M. Monday to approve what I was about to do and to discuss my replacement as head coach, but they decided to keep their action quiet for another twenty-four hours. Monday, they said, was to be "Barry's day."

My resignation might have been the only thing we managed to keep secret in the previous sixteen years.

To those outside my family and a few in my athletic family, it wouldn't figure that I'd give up what was financially one

381

of the best coaching jobs in the country. I was officially paid $88,500 as a coach. With my four television and two radio shows that I went out and sold to a group of sponsors, and my shoe contract with Nike, I was making more than $400,000 per year that was directly connected to coaching.

I have outside business interests in oil, an insurance agency, which I call "Barry Switzer and Associates," Crown Home Entertainment Centers, and whatnot, and I could give a speech every night, now that I don't have to travel the recruiting trail. I wasn't about to go on the bum. But $400,000 a year is kind of hard for a football coach to walk away from.

Don't get the impression, though, that I was coaching for the money. Nobody coaches college football to get rich. There are plenty of good reasons to be a coach, but getting your name in the Fortune 500 is not one of them. If a college coach wins every game, he'll never have as much money as Donald Trump. I was well paid and I was not above enjoying that aspect, but I coached for the love of it, and it was the only thing I knew.

I cried when I told the staff I was quitting. I had been with these people for a long time, shared my great ups and downs with them, spent more time with them than anybody in my life. This was the hardest part of it, separating from people I really loved.

I said their jobs were safe, and I appreciated their loyalty, and either Merv or Gary would be named the new head coach tomorrow.

"There's just one favor I want to ask of you," I said. "It's very important that my kids still belong to the whole family here. They might feel like they're no longer welcome. I want you all to let them know they can come around whenever they like, especially Kathy."

They promised me they would, and they did. But the very first thing they needed to do was to get on the telephones and start calling every Oklahoma player and every recruit before the news broke.

By 10 A.M., the press conference had outgrown the Big Red Room. Donnie Duncan told me that David Swank and Ron White wanted to be part of the resignation. Newspaper, television, and radio reporters were pouring in from everywhere. The conference was rescheduled for 1:30 P.M. in the Jack Santee Lounge, the huge VIP room in the press box.

Because it was bound to be an emotional affair, some of the university officials wanted to ban live television. Speaking as legal counsel, Fred Gipson advised them to forget it—the whole world was invited to watch.

I didn't make my entrance until 2:07.

"Sorry I'm late," I told the more than two hundred who had packed into the Santee Lounge. "I'm sure nobody has left."

That drew a laugh. The TV lights were glaring and the flashbulbs popped. I was wearing a navy-blue suit, pale blue button-down shirt, and a burgundy tie—the proper outfit for looking your best on television. Three months ago, David Swank had forced Donnie Duncan and me to attend that class run by the public relations experts from Washington, D.C., who drilled us for two days on how to behave at a television interview, what to wear, and what not to say. Of course, Donnie and I were already veterans of hundreds of television interviews. Sadly for Swank, as he proved on *Nightline*, the only thing he learned in the same class was what to wear.

I had myself pretty well under control when I started my seven-minute resignation speech, but I was wiping tears out of my eyes before I finished.

"Today I am resigning as head football coach of the University of Oklahoma, effective immediately," I said. "This is the most difficult decision I ever had to make. But I have come to the conclusion that my resignation is in the best interest of the football program, the university, and Barry Switzer."

You'll have to forgive me for referring to myself in the third person, like politicians and NBA stars do. Sometimes I just can't help it.

"I deeply regret the series of events which have focused so much adverse publicity on the football program, the university, and me personally," I went on. "During this time, I have been sustained by the great support from present and former players, the university, Oklahomans, and Sooners everywhere. I thank you for your expressions of caring and support—I'll never forget that.

"You gave me the belief that I had the energy level to

carry the program through this period and lead us forward. But I have finally decided the time has come for new leadership.

"I think, as the saying goes, there has been too much water under the bridge for me to continue to be the effective leader this great football program deserves.

"I resign with great sadness but also with great appreciation for the sixteen years I have been privileged to be the head Sooner coach. And I appreciate the thoughtful concern and consideration of university officials, the board of regents, and chairman Ron White when I informed them of my decision.

"I leave with pride in our football program and pride in the won-lost record during my tenure as coach, which is the best in college football. But my greatest pride is in the young men who have come through this program and who have worked so hard to accomplish those achievements which made me proud and made you proud.

"Some received great name recognition, many didn't. But all of them made a valuable contribution to our program and I believe that our program made a valuable contribution to their lives. I thank them for their effort and their friendship, which sustains me."

I could feel my voice shaking a little now and the tears started to well up, but there were more things I had to say that I believed were important.

"In my last public appearance as head football coach, I want to make a statement and a plea on behalf of current and future athletes at universities across the country and on behalf of their coaches. If we are going to be fair to these players, we need to change some of the NCAA rules, which allow no financial help other than tuition, books, board, and room."

I knew some of the more ignorant or naive of the reporters and the Switzer haters and the big-time football haters thought I was cooking up excuses for myself. But I was speaking from the heart and telling what I believe must be done for the good of the game.

"The record should be made clear," I said. "There are a great many young men in football programs all across the country who, purely and simply, are without the means to address their basic financial needs.

"Let me state immediately that I am not blaming the NCAA for any problems in our program or for my resignation. The NCAA is an institution made up of universities and colleges including the University of Oklahoma. The universities and colleges make the rules and charge individuals with enforcing these rules. Under my leadership, our program has been found to be in violation of some of these rules.

"I am sorry this has happened. However, there are three things I want the people of Oklahoma to know and understand.

"First, Barry Switzer has never bought a player—never paid one penny for a player to come to the University of Oklahoma.

"Second, I accept full responsibility for those violations that did occur.

"Third, the University of Oklahoma football program is living up to the letter of all NCAA rules today.

"Having said this, let me say that Barry Switzer is totally frustrated working within a set of rigid rules that does not recognize the financial needs of many of our young athletes. I am not making excuses, but simply giving an explanation when I say it was difficult to turn my back on these young men when they needed help . . .

"We have created a system that does not permit me or the program to buy a pair of shoes or a decent coat for a player whose family can't afford these basic necessities. How can any coach stick to these rules when a young man's father dies many miles away and the son has no money for a plane ticket home for the funeral?"

(I read later that Dick Schultz said I didn't know the rules. The hell I didn't. That rule was softened in 1988, but I was talking about 1986, when I could have taken an NCAA shot for it.)

"How would you feel, seeing young athletes who must stay in the dormitories on the weekends because they don't have the money even to go to a movie or buy a hamburger like most other college students . . ."

(The NCAA won't allow a student-athlete to take a part-time job while enrolled in classes. I totally agree with the

NCAA on this. Playing a major sport requires more hours per week than a part-time job, anyhow.)

I said, "I want this resignation to stand for something. I want it to serve as a public commitment on my part to join with other coaches around the country who are calling for a change in the rules that will permit universities to provide players reasonable assistance, perhaps based on financial need, as proposed by Dick Schultz, executive director of the NCAA.

"The time has come to change a system where coaches must choose between abiding by certain NCAA rules or acting like caring individuals. We made these rules. We can change them.

"In closing, I would like to thank the university, my friends, and particularly my family for their support in these trying times. I received a great football program sixteen years ago. I am passing on the great football program. I urge you to support the university now more than ever, and let's keep it the winningest program in college football."

That was it. Time to get out of Dodge.

Security guys escorted me to a private elevator. Ron White was preparing to speak, and then David Swank. But I was out of there.

I spent the rest of the afternoon with Greg, Doug, and Kathy over at Ann's house, hiding out from the world. Ann is a licensed professional counselor, and I'm sure she knew the right things to say to help me from falling into a depression. This was no time to dwell on the negatives of the past. We had to focus our imagination on the positive things of the future.

True, it is quite a shock to the psyche to go from being the head coach—a job that sometimes gets you called the king of Oklahoma if you're winning—to the title of special assistant to the athletic director.

That was part of the settlement my brother, Donnie, worked out with the university. I would be given this job with duties to be assigned by the athletic director and stay on the university payroll until March 1990, when I would become eligible for retirement with full benefits, after twenty-four years as a university employee.

There were wild rumors that the university bought up my contract for a ton of money, but this is not the case. In the first place, by reason of a provision in the constitution of the state of Oklahoma, no state employee's contract can be for more than one year, not even the Oklahoma University head football coach's contract. You may have a five-year contract that is announced so the kids you are coaching and recruiting will feel confident you will be at the school as long as they are. But four years of the contract are merely a "letter of intent" that would not be legally binding on the state of Oklahoma if anybody challenged it. But nobody really wants to challenge it in court.

I returned only one call the afternoon of my resignation. It was to Rick Telander, of *Sports Illustrated*. I had always made it a point to go out of my way to be nice to certain writers, even if they were from *Sports Illustrated*, but those people had hacked me to pieces ever since they fell in love with Marcus Dupree in 1982 and blamed me for mistreating that "poor victim of society." It still makes me sick to think of how the stupidity of Marcus, his preacher agent, and *Sports Illustrated* screwed our program and also screwed Marcus.

Anyhow, I talked to Telander on the phone and answered every question he asked, and they didn't even print a story about my resignation—just a little box that said I had quit.

Then Ann and the kids and I went to dinner at Othello's, an Italian restaurant in Norman that is my favorite hangout. Pasquale Benso—we call him Patsy—owns Othello's. It was Patsy's daughter, Camille, who invented Brian Bosworth's notorious Boz haircuts. Patsy prepared us a special dinner that night, and we sat under the wicker baskets on the walls and breathed in those great Italian kitchen smells and drank a couple of bottles of wine.

It didn't affect Patsy's friendship that I had quit. "You always be da coach," he kept telling me in his true Italian accent.

I loved Patsy's sentiment, but of course I would not always be "da coach." In fact, I would never be da coach again, not in Norman or any other college town.

In the warm glow of the wine and the food and the companionship at Othello's that night, I found my mind drifting. As the Grateful Dead sang on an old record, "What a long, strange trip it's been."

From the bootlegger's boy to da coach . . .

37

THE INVESTIGATION

A few weeks after I resigned on June 19, my house was bur-
glarized and thieves made off with my twenty-five gold
championship rings, my Barry Switzer Day engraved case that
I'd been given in my hometown thirty-five years ago, my cameras, and my shotgun.

Not long afterward, Otha Armstrong III walked into one
of the three pawn shops on Main Street in Norman and sold
four Orange Bowl rings. A customer standing nearby said,
"You got any more of those rings? I'll buy 'em all from you."

"You better bring a lot of money," Otha replied.

The customer wrote down a phone number and gave it to
Armstrong. "I've got all the money in the world. You call me
at this number." Otha arranged to meet him at the Mont, a
watering hole off campus, and bring the rings. The customer
called me and the police. At 12:30 P.M., two detectives walked
into the saloon and handcuffed Otha. He was wearing one of
my rings at the time, and he had twenty others on him. The
other four, I recovered by buying them back from the customer, who had enough foresight to quickly purchase them
from the pawnshop. The pawnshop dealer knew the rings
were mine (I had visited with him earlier to warn him someone might try to sell them), but, obviously, making a profit was
more important to him than calling me or the police.

I ended up getting everything back except my engraved
case, which Otha told police he had thrown into the Canadian
River south of Norman. The shocker was that Otha ratted on
Charles Thompson as being his partner in crime. It really hurt
me to learn that Charles had done it. I remember now that

back during the time when Charles's cocaine problems were in the newspaper (but his involvement in the theft was not widely known), I got a phone call from some guy in the media who wanted to know if I thought that Charles, as my ex-quarterback, ought to be granted leniency by the courts. I said, "No comment." But as I hung up the phone, I was thinking, No matter what the bastard gets, it isn't enough.

Meanwhile, and after I had rested for several weeks, I went hard to work trying to find out the source of the allegations that:

(1) I had been in a Las Vegas hotel room with some other people who had cocaine;
(2) I had manipulated drug testing of the football program to protect players; and
(3) I had gambled on college football games (including Oklahoma's) with a bookie in Las Vegas and paid losses by interstate wire.

I had known in early June 1989 that Scott Hill's problem with the FBI was going to hit the newspapers and bring additional pressure on me and on the regents. As it turned out, the *Dallas Times Herald* did run a story about Scott on June 21, 1989, the day after it had run the story of my resignation.

But, for a few-month period back in 1985, Scott had been close to a young woman who, as it turned out, had a source of cocaine. Scott never knew the girl's source, but his association with her led to his being caught in the extensive FBI/Justice Department drug investigation that was under way in 1988 and 1989. The government believes Scott made a mistake and has filed a "distribution" charge against him for giving some cocaine to another person.

I believe Scott Hill is a young man of great talent, personality, and ability who simply made a mistake, but there is no denying that that mistake had an impact upon the events which led to my resignation.

Charles Thompson had been caught, prosecuted, and sent to prison for drug trafficking, and Scott had been caught as part of the same investigation that caught Charles. But it must be made clear that their misdeeds can hardly be compared; Charles is a criminal, and Scott is not.

Scott hired a man by the name of Stan Ward as his attorney to defend him. Stan had formerly been inside legal counsel to the University of Oklahoma. Practicing law in Norman, he was in close daily contact with officials of the university. I knew Stan very well. But I did not know the attorney he sometimes associated himself with on criminal cases, a man named Gary Gardenhire, a state senator from Norman. I figured out much later that Stan Ward and Gary Gardenhire had played a critical role in the events that forced my resignation in June 1989.

In August 1989, I went to see Ron Hoverson, special agent in charge of the FBI for the state of Oklahoma. We met in his office in Oklahoma City. I had known Ron for several years. He had come to Norman and talked to the football team about the perils of gambling, strictly as an educational and preventive measure. A number of schools have had well-publicized gambling problems lately. The center for another major university the last three years left school last November after the vice squad raided his room in the dorm, found more than two hundred betting slips, and turned him in to the university for operating a bookie shop. At Oklahoma, because of the educational program we have had in place, it would not have been possible for anything like that to have been sustained for more than a day.

In his office, Hoverson told me I was not under investigation ". . . in any area." He said my name was thrown around a lot because I was so visible and very much in the public eye, but he assured me, as a friend, "Barry, your name is not at the head of any file."

Ron also told me that he had said the very same thing to Fred Gipson and David Swank when they had come to see him! I don't guess I will ever figure out why Swank never mentioned this to the regents. I know he didn't, because regents Sylvia Lewis and Charles Sarratt told me that that bit of information had never been revealed to them until I asked them about it. As you would expect, this omission by Swank added fuel to my raging paranoia.

On September 8, 1989, my brother, Donnie, and I went to see FBI agents Phil Shockey and John Hershey at the Oklahoma City offices of the FBI. (I had my brother with me thinking that he, as a lawyer, might be able to explain any of the legal bullshit that might be said.) I wanted to see what they would tell me about the mess that had led to my resignation, and I wanted to know why this guy named Blair Watson was after me. I blew their minds when I told them about the meeting in the president's office on June 13 and the three charges against me that were being attributed to Blair Watson. I had assumed those guys would have known all about it, but these hard-nosed, experienced FBI agents were visibly shocked and disturbed.

They exchanged glances, and Phil Shockey told me, "Barry, I would be very surprised if Blair Watson would have shared any information like that with David Swank, Fred Gipson, or Andy Coats." Before Donnie and I left, Shockey and Hershey assured us that they would investigate this matter and talk with Blair Watson, David Swank, Fred Gipson, and Andy Coats. They also said they would check with the FBI office in Las Vegas to see if there was any truth to the story about the bookie having "spilled his guts" and implicated me.

I still had no answers as to how it had all gotten started.

Then on Friday, September 22, 1989, Donnie and I met again with agents Shockey and Hershey at my house. I wanted to know what they had discovered in their investigation, but they told me very little. Phil Shockey said that they had not yet had an opportunity to visit with Swank, Coats, or Gipson, but they had talked at length with assistant U.S. attorney Blair Watson. They said Watson was "totally flabbergasted" that these accusations were being laid off on him. Watson told them that he was not the source.

Agent Shockey said they had also checked the allegation about my betting on football with a bookie in Las Vegas.

Phil said, "The people who told you there is such an investigation are way out in left field."

"What are you telling me?" I said. "Are you saying these people back here don't know what the hell they're talking about?"

Phil said, "You could say that."

I had gotten some information from these agents, who I felt were being as open with me as their job allowed them to be, but I still didn't have enough. So I asked, "Would Blair Watson meet with me? He wouldn't see Swank and Gipson, so

I don't know." Hershey replied, "Yes, I'm sure that Blair would want to see you."

After agents Shockey and Hershey had left, I was convinced that my "enemies" (whoever they were) had fabricated the whole thing in a desperate effort to get rid of me, for whatever reason. I still didn't know very much, but I did know at least that I would finally get to see the mysterious Blair Watson.

I called Blair Watson's office and set up a meeting with him for October 6, 1989. My brother and I were going to go together. I was wondering what sort of a guy Blair Watson would be. I had heard someone (Fred Gipson, I believe) say that he was really "gung-ho"; that he was one of those guys who, when he was going with FBI agents on a drug raid, would check out two guns instead of one.

But I felt that before I went to see Blair Watson, I needed to see Stan Ward, the Norman attorney Scott Hill had hired. I knew from the university's inside counsel, Fred Gipson, that Ward and Gardenhire had been representing Scott and had been dealing with Blair Watson. That meant Stan fit into the puzzle somehow.

One day in late September I went by to see him. Stan had a tough time talking with me, trying not to reveal sensitive client confidences of Scott's, but it was a very informative meeting anyway. Stan told me that after Scott had been charged and the interviews started with the FBI (John Hershey and Phil Shockey), it immediately became "obvious" to Stan (and Scott) that Scott was not their prime target. Stan said he felt that they wanted to get Barry Switzer. They wanted to make a case against the man Blair Watson always referred to as "the top man." Me!

As I understand it, Stan Ward made a plea bargain with Blair Watson where it was agreed to prosecute Scott on a "distribution" charge in Houston, not Oklahoma City, under something called Rule 20. The key was that in making a plea bargain, Scott had to commit to being fully open and candid with the government and tell them everything they wanted to know about anyone.

In his conversations with the FBI, Stan said they kept pressing Scott about the time Scott and I had stopped in Las

Vegas on the way back from a recruiting trip in Los Angeles—
at the Dunes in December 1983. Again and again, Scott told
them that I had gone up to the suite, had seen the hookers
there, realized what was going on, and left. But the FBI and
Blair Watson supposedly acted like they didn't believe him.

Stan said the FBI came back a couple of times and kept
trying to "break" Scott and make him say that he had seen
Barry Switzer do drugs. He quoted Scott as telling them:

> I want to tell you guys something. Barry Switzer was
> my coach . . . more than a coach over the years. We
> were like brothers. He was like a big brother to me. I
> considered him not only to be my employer . . . but
> to be a very close personal friend and family. So what
> you are asking is some pretty heavy stuff. But I'll tell
> you again; Barry left; and then I left. I wasn't there
> (in the suite) very long. I never saw Barry Switzer use
> any kind of drugs.

They even asked him whether Barry Switzer had any "interest in drugs." And Scott told them, "Yeah, Barry had an
interest because it was something that was happening on campus . . . student-athletes had become involved with drugs. It
was something that, as a coach, Switzer had to deal with every
day."

Stan Ward had a couple of meetings with Blair Watson.
On his second one, he took Gary Gardenhire with him. When
I met with Stan Ward for the second time, in January 1990,
Gardenhire was there. Both Gary and Stan described Watson
as being very discreet, never mentioning my name, but always
referring to me as the "top man," and all of them knew who
the "top man" was. Stan again told me that it was obvious to
him that I was a "target." Significantly, Stan told me that in
one of the meetings, after Blair Watson became convinced that
I was not involved in drugs, Watson said that the "top man"
appeared to be involved in something *much worse and more embarrassing to the university than that.* When I pressed him on it,
Stan said Blair Watson had a theory that I had somehow manipulated our drug-testing program to protect certain of our
athletes.

Stan said he told Blair Watson he had a hard time believing that I could have manipulated the drug testing since he (Ward) had been legal counsel to the university when the system was first put in. It simply couldn't be manipulated the way Watson was thinking. Even if the allegations as to the drug tests had been true, and it wasn't, I cannot, even to this day, imagine why that would have been a concern of the U.S. attorney's office—since it would not have even been a crime.

With all of this background, Donnie and I went to the Federal Building in Oklahoma City on October 6. We went into the reception area, told the ladies that we were there to see Blair Watson, and waited for a couple of minutes. We were soon met by a man who introduced himself as Bob Mydans, "acting United States attorney." Then a tall, dark young man wearing glasses walked in and introduced himself as Blair Watson.

We went down a long, gray, sterile government corridor, through what appeared to be a storage room, and into someone's office, I assume Blair Watson's.

I told Mydans and Watson what had happened on June 13, that Andy Coats and David Swank had used Blair Watson's name in making the three charges against me, and I asked specifically whether Watson had told Ward I was under investigation for drugs, gambling, or anything. Watson said he had never told or meant to imply to Stan Ward that "Barry Switzer is under investigation" for anything.

He did say that he often received telephone calls from people looking for dirt on Switzer, to which his standard reply was always, "No comment." Also, he said that with Stan Ward there was "lots of dialogue," and that, "yes" the subject of Las Vegas hotels and the *possibility* of drug-testing manipulation had been discussed.

He was very forceful in insisting he had never said a word to Ward, Coats, Swank, or anyone about my involvement in gambling or wire transfers, in Las Vegas or anywhere else. In fact, he never even heard the point raised until I had mentioned it or until agents Shockey and Hershey had mentioned it to him.

Just before we left, in response to a question Donnie asked, Bob Mydans said that Andy Coats had called him sev-

eral times asking for whatever information he might be able to
give him about the football program or Barry Switzer. Mydans
wouldn't tell us what he had told Coats.

I left Blair Watson's office still somewhat confused and
still as paranoid as ever. I decided that at some point I needed
to visit again with Stan Ward, Fred Gipson, and Andy Coats. I
was sure by this time, however, that the subjects of: 1) my
being in the hotel room in Vegas when there was some dope
there; and 2) the possible manipulation of drug tests of the
athletes had traveled the loop from Blair Watson, Stan Ward,
and Gary Gardenhire to Fred Gipson and then to Swank and
Coats. I still was not sure about the source of the football gambling charge or the interstate wire transfers.

In my visits with Stan Ward and Fred Gipson, however, I
had learned that after one of his meetings with Blair Watson,
Stan had telephoned Fred and had told him of the matters
being discussed about me. Fred Gipson, naturally, relayed this
information to interim president Swank, and that eventually
led to a three-way telephone conversation among Stan Ward,
Scott Hill, and David Swank. When Stan told me about this
conversation, he said that the subjects discussed were the 1983
episode in the Dunes Hotel in Las Vegas and the possible manipulation of drug testing. *Stan did not mention that anything was
discussed with Scott and Swank about gambling on football.*

But back on June 13, 1989, Swank and Coats had insisted
that the FBI had me "cold" on gambling and interstate wire
transfers! I was determined to find out where that most damn-
ing of the accusations had come from. Swank had specifically
attributed it to Blair Watson, and Coats had said it had come
from the "office of the United States attorney."

I had not seen Scott Hill for a long time; not since he had
been forced to resign following Swank's demand that he and
Mike Jones be fired. But I ran into him on October 7, 1989,
when Oklahoma State played Oklahoma in Norman. Ironically, it was the day after I had met with Blair Watson and
Bob Mydans. Scott was living in Houston. He had put his life
in order. He was getting up at five o'clock in the morning and
lifting weights with some of his business clients. He was en-
gaged to marry a woman who had two children. He had a
good job. His case had been transferred to Houston, where he

was awaiting the judge's sentencing on the plea bargain. I wished him good luck.

I did not have a chance to talk to Scott in any detail that day. But on March 5, 1990, I had a long, private telephone conversation with him. Scott's story of the FBI interrogation of him was much like what Stan Ward had previously told me, but there was one point Scott made that Stan had not. *He said that from the very beginning, the FBI had quizzed him about any possible Las Vegas connections that I had had with gambling and bookies! It was a constant focus of their attention.*

It became clear to me then that if I had been able to talk with Scott earlier, the pieces of the puzzle might have fit together a little more quickly than they did. But at this point, I felt that I at least had some feel for how the events that had overwhelmed me had probably been created. Any Oklahoma head football coach is a high-profile figure, and with the image that has been cast upon me by some opposing coaches and the press, it is only natural that law-enforcement authorities would ask questions about me, that my name would come up, and that if my name were to come up, it would certainly be pursued to some degree. That is what comes from living in a glass house in the public eye.

I can clearly understand why Phil Shockey and John Hershey might ask Scott Hill a lot of questions about me. After all, he was one of my coaches and they were doing their jobs.

I have had the chance in recent months to visit several times with Fred Gipson about the events that led to my resignation. Fred said that he had received a telephone call on June 7 from a "source" whose name he was not free to reveal, who had told him of Scott Hill's problems and who also had said that the FBI had me "cold" on something much worse for the university than what they had Scott on. Fred didn't know at the time what to think about it other than to be worried.

Then, he said, he met with Gary Gardenhire on Thursday, June 8, and Gardenhire confirmed what was going on with Scott's case, and also said that there was an investigation into me on a "number of things." Gardenhire mentioned the Dunes Hotel incident in 1983 and that there were some other things that would prove more embarrassing to the university.

The one example he gave was Blair Watson's theory that I may have manipulated the players' drug-testing program, possibly to protect Charles Thompson and other players. But Fred said that Gardenhire did not mention anything about Las Vegas, gambling, bookies, or wire transfers.

Fred said he never heard the allegation about gambling on football games and Las Vegas bookies until the evening of June 13, the same time I heard it! He said he had been as shocked by it as I was.

Even though I was initially concerned and reluctant about it, I did decide that I had to go ahead and telephone Andy Coats. Andy said he was glad that I had called and that he had been wanting to visit with me about all that had happened. I asked him about his talks with acting U.S. attorney Mydans, and he said that during all the troubles in January and February, he had talked to Mydans several times. But each time he had asked him whether he had any information on Switzer, Mydans would say he had nothing on Switzer "in any area." Andy also said that he had never talked with Blair Watson.

Then I asked, "Andy, but where did you get that shit about the United States attorney having me 'cold' on gambling on Oklahoma and other college football games, Las Vegas bookies spilling their guts, and paying losses by wire?"

Andy replied, "Barry, an awful lot was happening very quickly, but all of that came from David Swank either on the afternoon of June thirteenth or the day before."

My brother spoke with Blair Watson by telephone on April 17, 1990, just to ask the questions one more time, just to see if he, in some fashion, had been the source of Swank's gambling accusation. Blair told Donnie that he had never met with David Swank and he has no specific recollection of ever talking with him by telephone. He qualified the last point because he remembered that he had talked to a lot of people back when he had been trying to find the source that had leaked the "sting" on Charles Thompson. Swank could have been one of the ones he talked to about that. But Blair said that he *never* reveals to outsiders anything about ongoing investigations, and he . . . "sure as hell didn't tell David Swank

anything about Switzer being tied in with any college-football gambling investigation!"

Where did you get it, David? Did the same "source" that Fred talks about as having said there were other things I was being investigated for give you that lie? Did you make it up? Or did you take the fact that the FBI asked Scott Hill *questions* about me and Las Vegas as meaning that I must have been guilty of those horrible things? Did you believe this in the same way I always felt you had believed Ivey Suber's father?

I don't know where you got your information, David, but I do know that in the early morning of June 19, 1989, you telephoned a member of the university's council on athletics to tell him of my resignation that was to take place that afternoon. That gentleman has told me and Donnie Duncan that you told him of the resignation in such a way as to lead him to believe you wanted to "take credit" for it.

David, you can have the credit if you want it. I'm sure it will make you a hero in some circles.

I still don't know what to say about Fred Gipson's "source." Maybe that unknown person is the real culprit. Fred himself has appeared to be open and honest with me, and I believe he was being dragged along in the rush of events just like I was. But I do wish he would reveal that person's identity.

I've got to believe, too, that if Scott Hill had gone to any attorney who was fully independent of the University of Oklahoma, I would still be the university's head football coach.

For reasons that I will never understand, however, Stan Ward and Gary Gardenhire somehow felt it was right for them to go to the university and reveal the *questions* that were being asked of their client by the FBI and the U.S. attorney. Frankly, I believe they should have represented their client without sticking their noses into my business and the university's business without any proof of any wrongdoing on my part!

I still don't know who created the gambling charge that broke my will to resist. It could have been the interim president, he could have been repeating something he heard from a yet unidentified source, or he could have jumped to the conclusion from the fact that the FBI's questions of Scott Hill in this regard were probably mentioned in the three-way telephone conversation he had with Scott and Stan Ward. But what I do know is that I had no chance of convincing Swank of my innocence. After all, what could a football coach do to change the mind of a university president who, in his twenty-seven years of association with the university, even as its faculty representative for athletics, had been to only one Oklahoma-Texas game! And that one was in 1989 when he was interim president and when it was at the university's expense.

As for Blair Watson, Phil Shockey, and John Hershey, as I look back on everything, I figure they were just doing their jobs. The suspicions raised by the people listening to them, however, when combined in their minds with all of the trouble that had occurred in 1989, led the listeners to believe the worst. What happened is that I was tried and convicted in their minds by rumor and suspicion made possible by the climate of general hostility created by the criminal incidents of early 1989. All of the "players" involved—Swank, Coats, Gipson, Ward, White, and Gardenhire—were obviously concerned about the university's image and didn't want anything else to come about to tarnish it even worse. But David Swank, for one, did not seem very damn concerned about how fair it all was to me.

Thinking about all the things that led me to resign, all the politics and venom and even innocent mistakes that culminated in the June 13 meeting in Swank's office, I realize I will probably never know the whole truth.

If life were like a football game, as a coach I would be able to figure out why I had lost. I would grade the film, critique the players, know analytically why we won or lost the game. The 76,000 fans in the stands would have 76,000 opinions, but the coaches would be the only ones who knew for sure why the game had turned out as it did.

But life is not like a football game, as every player has to discover for himself.

One of the greatest thrills of my life happened in Norman in August 1989, two months after my resignation.

Under the direction of my friend Lee Allen Smith, Norman was host to the United States Olympic Festival. Thousands of young men and women athletes from all over the country were there performing in track and field, swimming, basketball, and lots of other sports. In view of what Oklahoma had been going through, it was a great and proud thing to happen in the state. I was invited to participate in some of the social affairs.

The personal thrill came for me on opening night. I was invited to go to Oklahoma's Memorial Stadium—Owen Field—with many celebrities from the world of sports. It included all-American football players and Heisman Trophy winners from Oklahoma; all-American basketball players; Olympic champions in a number of sports, and a lot of others. Among the football stars were my Heisman Trophy winners Steve Owens and Billy Sims.

It was a nationally televised event, with ex-President Ronald Reagan and Bob Hope as hosts.

The stadium was packed. I would hear the 76,000 cheering and applauding as each sports celebrity was introduced by Curt Gowdy as they walked onto the field.

They saved me for last. I was standing there on the ramp thinking about what had happened to me in 1989, and wondering how I would be received by the crowd. Would they cheer me—or would they boo me? Did they think I was guilty?

I finally heard Curt Gowdy say, ". . . former Oklahoma head football coach Barry Switzer!"

As I stepped into the spotlight, I heard the steady rumble from the crowd begin, turning into a tremendous ear-shattering standing ovation. It deeply moved me with a terrific, warm excitement that made me want to laugh and cry at the same time. They were all cheering and clapping, and as I reached the field, Billy Sims let out a whoop and jumped into my arms like a kid and hugged me. The crowd went crazy with joy!

Even if my opponents wanted to do away with me, it was obvious, and gratifying, to see that the people of Oklahoma, who I love, did not feel that way.

More important than all the victories are the friendships I have formed in twenty-four years as a coach at Oklahoma, especially the coach-player relationships that grew into genuine lifelong friendships. Those are more important to me than anything except my flesh and blood family.

I was telling my brother recently that I have quit trying to figure out who to blame for planting the poisonous seeds that grew into the fatal meeting in Swank's office that June night in 1989. Maybe I make more out of it than there really was. I had a great career at Oklahoma. Nobody can go on forever doing what I was doing. Maybe it was just time for me to be moving on.

And where would that be?

People have been asking what I intend to do in the future. The fact is, I don't know. I'm not worried about the future. There are a lot of things I could do and am doing.

One thing for sure, I can go back to Arkansas. Ashley County is still dry, and I could sell whiskey. I'm still a bootlegger's boy.

INDEX

403

drug scandal and, 15–16, 26, 287,
    362–364, 368, 389, 394, 397
drug-testing program of, 22, 23, 26,
    220–221, 237, 290–295, 361–364,
    375, 389, 394, 397
false transcript affair and, 95–97, 106,
    155, 271
fans and boosters of, 246–248,
    250–254, 258, 259, 345, 399
forfeitures and probations of, 15, 25,
    97–98, 101, 106, 155, 173,
    230–231, 271
graduating students of, 51, 178, 330
history and development of, 246–260
institutional control of money by, 313,
    314
integration of, 46, 257–258, 264
"losing" seasons of, 16–17, 71,
    160–161, 173, 175, 179, 182–183
national rankings of, 105, 108, 109,
    112, 148, 151, 153, 159, 161, 193,
    199, 200, 204, 219, 242–244, 254,
    270
outlaw reputation of, 146, 153, 236,
    280, 357, 360, 366–367
playing strategy of, see Wishbone
    option; specific plays
rape incident and, 15–16, 26,
    357–362, 364
records set by, 108, 154, 155, 242–244
scholarship limits of, 151, 365
second and third team units of,
    149–150, 166, 281
shooting incident and, 15–16, 25–26,
    237–238, 353–357, 360, 364
spring training of, 166, 372
spying scandals of, 124, 342–343, 377
Switzer as assistant coach of, 67–83,
    89–94
Switzer's appointment as head coach
    of, 94–95
television coverage of, 21, 97, 105,
    152, 173, 193, 199, 213, 227–228,
    239–240, 336
tickets and passes to, 283, 300,
    310–311, 318, 344
traditional rivals of, see Nebraska,
    University of; Texas, University of
Orange Bowl, 17, 79, 90, 116, 127,
    130–133, 173, 253, 256, 301, 303
OU appearances in, 30, 71, 104,
    117–119, 131–132, 142–146, 148,
    151, 153, 158, 184, 194–196, 199,
    200, 203–204, 213, 215–216, 217,
    220–222, 223, 235, 239–240,
    254–255, 258, 273, 288, 291,
    293–294, 342, 346, 376, 378

Oregon State University, 71, 113, 148,
    160, 200
Orlando Sentinel, 366
Osborne, Roddy, 53
Osborne, Tom, 111, 129, 133, 138, 182
OSU, see Ohio State University
Othello's restaurant, 365, 387
OU, see Oklahoma, University of
Ouachita River, 34–35, 55
Oubre, Louis, 243
Outland Trophy, 80, 118, 244
Overstreet, David, 99, 107, 140, 155, 157
Owen Field, 20, 82, 110, 114, 152, 157,
    177, 199, 238, 241, 246, 266, 345,
    367, 373, 400
Owens, Jim, 249, 372
Owens, Jimbo, 343
Owens, Peanut, 343
Owens, Steve, 70–71, 89, 94, 244, 269,
    343, 372–373, 400
Owens, Tinker, 89, 103, 108, 112, 118,
    298, 343

Pace, Bill, 62
Page, Alan, 67
Parham, Duncan, 218
Parks, Jerry, 353–356, 364
Parseghian, Ara, 16, 104
Paterno, Joe, 104, 200–204, 217, 376
Paterno, Sue, 201–202, 204
Patsy's restaurant, 235, 365, 387
Patton, Sam, 38
PCP, 293
Peacock, Elvis, 107, 110, 111, 113, 115,
    124, 132
Pearl Harbor, bombing of, 35
Peete, Rodney, 226
Pendarvis, Buddy, 363
Penn Square Bank, 176–177
Pennsylvania State University, 90, 200,
    203–204, 217, 235, 273
Pepperdine College, 177
Perry, Leon, 215, 230
Peters, Tony, 103, 112
Peters, Zarak, 353–356
Pettibone, Jerry, 300
Phelps, Kelly, 164
Philadelphia, Mississippi, 161–163,
    170–171
Philadelphia Eagles, 96, 267
Philadelphia High School, 162
Phillips, Anthony, 215, 244
Phillips, Mike, 95–96
Pickett, Dan, 23, 291–294, 375
Pickett, Jeff, 196
Pierce, John, 356
Pittsburgh, University of, 21, 77, 191

Selmon, Mrs., 80
Senate, U.S., 20, 256
Sewell, Steve, Jr., 279
Sewell, Steve, Sr., 279
Sharp, Paul, 93, 120, 344–345
Shell, Art, 46
Shepard, Darrell, 155, 273
Shepard, Derrick, 136, 172, 197
Shepard, Woodie, 131
Sherrill, Jackie, 201
Shimick, Bill, 274
Shirley, Bart, 60
Shivers, Alan, 128
Shoate, Rod, 81, 109, 112, 243, 258, 270, 271
Shockey, Phil, 346, 348, 363–364, 390–392, 396, 399
shotgun houses, 24, 37, 41–42, 84
Simon, Jay, 246–247
Simpson, O. J., 34
Simpson, Travis, 196
Sims, Billy, 27, 51, 67, 99, 107, 140, 144, 161, 163, 166, 243, 244, 329–330, 359, 372–373, 400
  athletic ability of, 115, 131, 132, 148, 150–154, 273–278
Sims, Fred, 160–161, 163
Skirvin Hotel, 257–258
Smart, Mickey, 88
Smith, Boston, 252
Smith, Burt, 92
Smith, George, 282–283
Smith, Harrison, 252
Smith, Lee Allen, 133, 183–184, 399–400
Smith, "Sugar," 346
SMU, see Southern Methodist University
Sooner Schooner, 195–196
Sooners' Illustrated, 136
Southeastern Conference (SEC), 46, 137, 336
Southern California, University of (USC), 16, 77, 90, 102–103, 111–112, 150, 153, 160, 162, 214, 223, 226–227, 243
Southern Methodist University (SMU), 49, 71, 77, 92, 154, 200, 265, 271, 336
Southwest Conference (SWC), 45, 46, 48, 60, 62, 63, 71, 98, 111, 114, 143, 217, 238, 263, 266, 273, 291, 336
Spachman, Chris, 199
speed, 293
Spikes, Jack, 60
Split T formation, 54, 71
Sporting News, 242, 243
sports agents, 330

Sports Illustrated, 16, 121, 155, 161, 166–169, 171, 200, 287, 289, 298, 345, 359, 387
sportswriters, 51–53, 115–116, 150, 161, 167–168, 191, 200–201, 218, 219, 242–243, 249, 251, 285–289, 335, 343–345
Stafford, Anthony, 215, 222, 227
Stallings, Larry (Beebs), 265
Stanberry, Keith, 193, 281
Stanford University, 148, 154, 169, 192–193, 198, 262
Steinbeck, John, 35, 247
steroids, 47, 217, 220, 237, 239, 290, 291, 293–294
Stone, Neil, 356, 358–359
Straw, Carl, 227
Street, James, 72
Stroud Motor Inn, see Quarter Horse Inn
Suber, Ivey, 99–101, 106, 126, 398
Sugar Bowl, 79, 90–91, 132–133, 196, 200, 253, 378
Sukenis, Kathy, 186
Sullivan, Billy, 91
Sullivan, Glenn, 217, 218
Sullivan, Pat, 79, 90
Sun Bowl, 16, 27, 132–134, 160–161
Sun Princess, 202
Super Conference, 222–223
Supreme Court, U.S., 257
Swann, Lynn, 103
Swank, David, 15–16, 18–22, 26–29, 100, 120, 236, 330, 355–362, 365–366, 371, 374–375, 377, 382–383, 390–391, 394–399, 401
  academic career of, 18–19, 28, 225, 259, 369–370
SWC, see Southwest Conference
Sweeney, Jim, 204
Switzer, Alison (niece), 146
Switzer, Barry:
  allegations against, 21–24, 28–29, 100–101, 145–146, 304–320, 344–345, 373, 389, 391–399
  allegations answered by, 305–318, 385
  army service of, 61–62
  assistant coaching positions of, 61–66, 67–83, 89–94, 263, 269, 376
  athletic ability of, 39–40, 42–43, 48, 50
  birth of, 34
  black associates of, 38, 40, 46–47, 188–190, 296–303
  on black athletes, 46–48, 77, 95–96, 99–100, 188, 189, 296, 335–341
  business affairs of, 29, 176–177, 179, 190, 313–314, 342, 345, 372, 382